ARISTOTLE

Introductory Readings

ARISTOTLE

Introductory Readings

Translated
with Introduction, Notes, and Glossary
by

Terence Irwin and Gail Fine
Cornell University

Hackett Publishing Company, Inc.
Indianapolis / Cambridge

Printed in the United States of America

10 09 08 07 06 4 5 6 7 8 9

For further information, please address
Hackett Publishing Company, Inc.
P. O. Box 44937
Indianapolis, Indiana 46244-0937

www.hackettpublishing.com

Cover and text design by Dan Kirklin

Library of Congress Cataloging-in-Publication Data

Aristotle.
[Selections. English. 1996]
Aristotle: introductory readings
translated with introduction, notes, and glossary by
Terence Irwin and Gail Fine.
p. cm.
Includes bibliographical references.
ISBN 0-87220-340-9 (cloth)
ISBN 0-87220-339-5 (pbk.)
1. Philosophy—Early works to 1800.
I. Irwin, Terence.
II. Fine, Gail.
III. Title.
B407.A26 1996
185—dc20
96-9317
CIP

ISBN-13: 978-0-87220-340-2 (cloth)
ISBN-13: 978-0-87220-339-6 (pbk.)

CONTENTS

*Indicates a selection from a given chapter or chapters

PREFACE

This volume is extracted from *Aristotle: Selections* (Hackett, 1995). For information about the editions of the Greek text that we have used, for our decisions about textual variants in particular passages, for alternative translations, and for our policy on translation, we refer readers to *Selections*, which also contains more notes and a fuller glossary.

In preparing *Selections*, we were fortunate to receive comments and criticisms from the readers whose help we have acknowledged in the preface to that volume. In preparing this *Introductory Readings*, we are especially indebted to S. Marc Cohen, who had already been of enormous help to us as a reader for *Selections*, giving us numerous and acute comments. In thinking about how to abridge *Selections* for the present *Introductory Readings*, we have benefited from considering the table of contents in the Aristotle section of *Readings in Ancient Greek Philosophy* (ed. S. Marc Cohen, Patricia Curd, and C.D.C. Reeve [Hackett, 1995]), the section for which Cohen took primary responsibility. We are also grateful to Cohen for the considerable help he gave us in preparing the abridged notes and glossary that appear in *Readings*; that abridgment has helped us in the somewhat different abridgment we have made for the present volume.

Terence Irwin
Gail Fine

Sage School of Philosophy
Cornell University
Ithaca, New York
March 1996

ABBREVIATIONS

Works of Aristotle

The works of Aristotle are cited by abbreviations of their conventional Latin or English titles. We list both Latin and English titles below; for each treatise we translate we have used whichever title seems to be more commonly used in current English. (In many cases the English titles are mere Anglicizations rather than proper translations.) In cases where no English title is in common use, a rough translation has been placed in square brackets.

APo	Analytica Posteriora	Posterior Analytics
APr	Analytica Priora	Prior Analytics
Catg.	Categoriae	Categories
DA	De Anima	On the Soul
DC	De Caelo	On the Heavens
DI	De Interpretatione	On Interpretation
EE	Ethica Eudemia	Eudemian Ethics
EN	Ethica Nicomachea	Nicomachean Ethics
GA	De Generatione Animalium	Generation of Animals
GC	De Generatione et Corruptione	Generation and Corruption
HA	Historia Animalium	History of Animals
IA	De Incessu Animalium	Progression of Animals
MA	De Motu Animalium	Movement of Animals
Met.	Metaphysica	Metaphysics
Metr.	Meteorologica	Meteorology
MM	Magna Moralia	[Great Ethics]
PA	De Partibus Animalium	Parts of Animals
Phys.	Physica	Physics
PN	Parva Naturalia	[Short Natural Treatises]
Poet.	De Arte Poetica	Poetics
Pol.	Politica	Politics
Rhet.	Rhetorica	Rhetoric
Top.	Topica	Topics

'ROT' refers to The Revised Oxford Translation (see Further Reading).

ABBREVIATIONS

Subscripts

English	*Greek*	*Glossary entry*
$being_o$	*ousia*	SUBSTANCE #1
$essence_o$	*ousia*	SUBSTANCE #2
$form_l$	*logos*	REASON #5
$form_m$	*morphē*	FORM #5
$know_e$	*epistasthai*	KNOW #1
$know_g$	*gignōskein*	KNOW #1
$know_o$	*eidenai*	KNOW #1

INTRODUCTION

1. Aristotle's Life

Aristotle was born in Stagira in Macedon (now part of northern Greece) in 384 B.C. In his lifetime the kingdom of Macedon, first under Philip and then under his son Alexander ('the Great'), conquered the Greek cities in Europe and Asia, and then went on to conquer the Persian Empire. Though Aristotle spent much of his adult life in Athens, he was not an Athenian citizen.

Aristotle was the son of Nicomachus, a doctor who had been attached to the Macedonian court. In 367 Aristotle came to Athens, and was a member of PLATO's[1] Academy until the death of Plato in 347. In these twenty years Plato wrote his later dialogues, in which he reconsidered many of the doctrines of his earlier dialogues and pursued new lines of thought. The exploratory and critical outlook of the Academy probably encouraged Aristotle's own philosophical growth.

After leaving Athens in 347, Aristotle spent thirteen years in Asia Minor, in the islands of the eastern Aegean, and in Macedon. Some of the observations used in Aristotle's biological works seem to be drawn from the eastern Aegean, and so it is reasonable to suppose that he pursued his biological research during his years away from Athens.

Aristotle returned to Athens in 334, and founded his own school, the Lyceum. We do not know how formally the Lyceum was organized, but by the end of Aristotle's life it had become a well-established school for lectures and research. In 323 Alexander died; in the resulting outbreak of anti-Macedonian feeling in Athens Aristotle left for Chalcis, on the island of Euboea, where he died in 322. His student Theophrastus succeeded him as head of the Lyceum.

2. Aristotle's works

The nearly complete modern English translation of Aristotle (in ROT) fills about 2450 pages. Many of his works, however, have been lost, and those that survive complete are quite different in

1. Words in CAPITALS refer to entries in the Glossary. For abbreviations see the List of Abbreviations.

character from many of the lost works.[2] Among the lost works are dialogues, probably similar in character to some of Plato's dialogues, and other treatises designed for publication. Only fragments of these works survive.

The Aristotelian Corpus, as we have it, largely consists of works that appear to be closely related to Aristotle's lectures. We cannot tell how many of his treatises Aristotle regarded as 'finished'. It is most unlikely that he intended to publish anything like our present *Metaphysics*, or even intended a course of lectures to proceed in anything like the order of the present treatise. (Parts of Book i are almost repeated in Book xiii. Book xi summarizes parts of Book iv. The authenticity of Book xi is suspected, and Book ii is probably not by Aristotle at all.) These facts about the Corpus suggest that we ought not to treat Aristotle's treatises as finished literary works that the author intended to publish at a particular time.

3. The order of Aristotle's works

We have printed Aristotle's works in the order in which they appear in the Greek manuscripts. This order goes back to the Aristotelian commentators (from the first to the sixth centuries A.D.); it reflects their view not about the order in which the works were written, but about the order in which they should be studied.

Speculations about the order of the works are rather controversial, but some possible indications may be these:

1. It is easier to understand the relation of the doctrine of SUBSTANCE in the *Catg*. to the doctrine and argument of *Met*. vii if we suppose that the treatment in the *Catg*. is earlier.
2. None of the works in the Organon (see Part 4) mentions matter. This may be because (i) Aristotle had not yet thought of it, or because (ii) he regarded it as irrelevant to the topics considered in the Organon. The first explanation is probably (though by no means indisputably) preferable; if it is correct, the works in the Organon precede the works on natural philosophy.
3. Facts about place names (see Part 1 above) suggest that some of the research resulting in some of the biological works belongs to the period that Aristotle spent away from Athens. If this is

2. Ancient lists of titles of Aristotle's works are printed in ROT p. 2386.

right, then it is reasonable to suppose that some of the biological works may not be the latest works in the Corpus.

4. The contents of Aristotle's works

In the standard arrangement, the treatises are grouped as follows:[3]

1. *Catg., DI, APr, APo, Top.* These are traditionally known as the 'Organon' (i.e., 'instrument') because they deal with LOGIC (in Aristotle's broad sense), which is an instrument of philosophical thinking, not a discipline with its own specific subject matter. Aristotle himself seems to think of the *Analytics* and *Topics* as part of a single inquiry (see *Top.* 184b1).
2. *Phys., DC, GC, Metr., DA, PN, HA, PA, MA, IA, GA.* These belong to natural philosophy, dealing with different aspects of NATURE.
3. *Met.* This deals with 'first PHILOSOPHY'.
4. *EN, MM, EE, Pol.* These belong to 'practical' philosophy, which deals with ACTION rather than PRODUCTION.
5. *Rhet., Poet.* These deal with PRODUCTION rather than ACTION.[4]

A brief outline of a few of the main themes of different works in the Corpus may help to give the reader some idea of what to expect.

Top. i gives a brief account of DIALECTIC, which supplies the method of argument most commonly used in Aristotle's philosophical works. Dialectical method is derived from the Socratic conversations presented in Plato's dialogues, but Aristotle practises it without the dialogue form. Dialectic begins from COMMON BELIEFS, assumptions widely shared by 'the many and the wise'; it studies, and seeks to solve, the puzzles arising from these beliefs. The common beliefs that Aristotle considers include the views of his predecessors (discussed most elaborately in *Met.* i; cf. *DA* i,

3. This list excludes (a) works generally agreed to be spurious that have been included in the Aristotelian Corpus; (b) the lost works; (c) the *Constitution of Athens* (probably not by Aristotle himself), which was discovered after the standard arrangement of Aristotle's works was established. All of (a) and (c), and some surviving fragments, or supposed fragments, of (b), are included in ROT.

4. For Aristotle's own division of disciplines see *PA* 640a1, *Met.* 982b11, 993b20, vi 1.

Pol. ii). He argues that the discussion of difficulties emerging from their views helps us to find better solutions to the problems that they raise.

The *Physics* is a dialectical examination of nature, *phusis*, the subject of Presocratic inquiries. Like the NATURALISTS, Aristotle wants to find the laws and regularities that make natural change intelligible; he argues that to find the right laws, we must recognize both MATTER and FORM as CAUSES. He examines Presocratic views in *Met.* i; in *Phys.* ii and *PA* i, he presents his account of causes, and his reasons for recognizing form as a cause. Aristotle argues that the ESSENCE of artifacts is their form, not simply their matter. A hammer, for instance, is not simply a lump of wood and metal, but an instrument for driving nails into wood; the function of driving nails into wood is the form that the matter acquires by being made into a hammer. In Aristotle's view, something similar holds (though with important qualifications) for natural organisms; he argues that a plant or animal is not simply a collection of flesh, bone, and tissue, but a whole organized for a particular set of functions, and these functions are to be identified with the form.

These claims about form and matter are the basis for Aristotle's most elaborate account of SUBSTANCE, presented in *Met.* vii–ix. Substance is introduced in the *Categories* without reference to form and matter; Aristotle identifies a particular man or particular dog, as opposed to their color, size, or shape, as substances. In the *Phys.* and *GC*, he connects his claims about substance with his views on form and matter. In the *Met.* he argues that questions about substance are among the basic questions of first philosophy, and he re-examines them at length in Book vii. He argues that substance is form; he supports and clarifies his argument by explaining the relation between matter and form by reference to POTENTIALITY and ACTUALITY (Book ix). This account of ordinary perceptible, material substances is used in Book xii to develop an account of immaterial divine substance.

Aristotle's views on substance are also applied to questions about the relation of SOUL and body. Though his treatise 'On the Soul' (*De Anima*) is placed (quite reasonably) among the works on nature, the assumptions that he relies on are best understood in the light of *Met* vii–ix. In Aristotle's view, disputes about soul and body are simply a special case of the more general disputes about form and matter; the different views of the Presocratics and of Plato need a dialectical examination. Aristotle argues that soul is substance because it is the form of a natural body, and that the body is the matter informed by the soul.

The aspects of Aristotle's philosophy mentioned so far belong mostly to metaphysics (in the modern sense of the term) and to philosophy of mind. Aristotle has no treatise devoted to epistemology; but parts of several treatises discuss questions about the nature and acquisition of KNOWLEDGE, and the relation between knowledge and PERCEPTION. In *DA* ii–iii Aristotle discusses the different senses, APPEARANCE, and UNDERSTANDING and their contributions to knowledge. In the *APo* he describes the logical and epistemological structure of a completed science (as opposed to the process of empirical inquiry that leads to scientific knowledge). In *Met.* i–iv he examines the sort of knowledge that is possible for ultimate principles that cannot be defended by appeal to more ultimate principles. Aristotle's claims about the nature of knowledge also have metaphysical implications, which he examines in *Met.* vii and xiii 4 (see UNIVERSAL).

Aristotle's ethical works begin from common beliefs about morality and the puzzles that they generate. Aristotle begins with different people's conceptions of the human good, identified with HAPPINESS. He seeks to resolve puzzles by defending his own account of the nature of happiness, referring to the human FUNCTION. Here he seems to appeal to his own account of the soul to explain some of his ethical principles. Most of the rest of the *Ethics* examines the different VIRTUES and the actions that result from them; these actions, in Aristotle's view, are the ones that achieve the human good.

The *Ethics* leads directly into the *Politics*; indeed, the two treatises are parts of a single inquiry that belongs to political science. The *Pol.* begins with Aristotle's claims about the connection between human nature and the human good. A human being, he claims, is a political animal insofar as human capacities and aims are completely fulfillled only in a COMMUNITY; the individual's happiness must involve the good of fellow-members of a community. In the light of these claims Aristotle examines the successes and failures of actual CITIES in promoting the human good, and considers the proper design of a city that would actually realize the good of its citizens. In the *Poet.* he considers some of the moral issues that are raised by tragedies, and the emotions that are aroused by the presentation of these issues in dramatic form.

These are only a few of the main themes and issues discussed in the selections translated in this volume. Readers should be able to form some idea of the extent of Aristotle's philosophical interests and of the arguments and discussions that assure him of a place in the first rank of philosophers.

This volume does not, however, reflect the proportions of different parts of the Aristotelian Corpus. It does not include, for instance, the *Prior Analytics*, Aristotle's enormously influential treatise on formal logic. Nor does it reflect the important fact that a large proportion of the Corpus is devoted to the presentation and interpretation of detailed collections of empirical data. The biological treatises take up roughly a quarter of the entire Corpus, and large sections of the *Metr*. and the *Pol*. contain detailed empirical argument in their respective areas.

5. This edition

This translation tries to reproduce the details, not merely the general drift, of Aristotle's sentences and arguments, insofar as this can be done in reasonably natural English. It does not reproduce the grammatical or syntactical structure of the Greek. Still, we use more connectives ('for', 'but', 'however', and so on) than are usual in contemporary English, and some of the sentences are more complex than a contemporary English sentence would normally be; in such cases we thought that a slight sacrifice of English idiom or custom was justified by increased clarity in conveying Aristotle's argument.

We have used bracketed supplements in cases where it seemed reasonable to point out to the reader that no precise equivalent for the bracketed words appears in the Greek text. In some cases, for instance, Aristotle's sentence has no expressed subject, because he means the subject to be understood from the context; since it is not always clear what subject is to be understood, brackets indicate the translators' decision about how to resolve the ambiguity. In other cases the supplements are intended to clarify. In some cases where the same English term is used to translate more than one Greek term and it seems important to know what the Greek term is, we have resorted to subscripts (explained in the glossary and listed in the list of abbreviations).

The notes to the translation contain some very selective comments on some passages that seem both difficult and important.

The glossary indicates the correspondence between Greek terms and their English renderings, explains some of Aristotle's terms, and sketches some of the philosophical doctrines that they convey. A word in capital letters in the notes directs the reader to the relevant entry in the glossary. One way to understand Aristotle better is to look up the passages cited in the entries in the glossary, and to examine them in their context. The references are not entirely confined to passages included in this volume, but they are certainly not exhaustive.

The translation follows the division into books that is found in all editions of Aristotle. The division into books goes back to antiquity. The length of a book was determined by the requirements of ancient book production, and hence the divisions between books do not always correspond to natural divisions in the subject matter. The capitulation found in modern editions, and in our translation, has no ancient authority. The marginal numbering is derived from Bekker's edition.[5] The italicized headings are ours; they have no authority in the manuscripts. Asterisks in the translation indicate omissions. Aristotle's works are cited throughout by the abbreviated titles given in the list of abbreviations.

5. '1094a10', for instance, refers to line 10 of the left-hand column of page 1094 of Bekker's edition. Since Bekker's pagination is continuous, a Bekker page and line uniquely identify a particular passage. These Bekker pages and lines are standardly used to give precise references to passages in Aristotle; we have used them ourselves in the notes and glossary. Since they refer to pages and lines of the *Greek* text, they correspond only roughly to an English translation.

CATEGORIES

[*PRELIMINARY EXPLANATIONS*]

1

If things have only a name in common, and the account of the essence$_o$ corresponding to the name is different, they are called homonymous. Both a man and a painted animal, for instance, are animals homonymously; for these have only a name in common and the account (corresponding to the name) of the essence$_o$ is different. For if one says what being an animal is for each of them, one will give a different account in each case.

If things have both the name in common and the same account (corresponding to the name) of the essence$_o$, they are called synonymous. Both a man and an ox, for instance, are animals <synonymously>, since each is called animal by a common name, and the account of the essence$_o$ is the same. For if one gives an account of each, saying what being an animal is for each of them, one will give the same account.

If things are called what they are by having a name that is derived from something else, but with a different inflection, they are called paronymous; for example, the grammarian is so called from grammar, and the brave person from bravery.

2

Among things said, some involve combination, while others are without combination. Things involving combination are, for instance, man runs, man wins; things without combination are, for instance, man, ox, run, wins.

Among beings[1] some are said of a subject but are not in any subject; man, for instance, is said of a subject, an individual man, but is not in any subject. Some are in a subject but are not said of any subject. (By 'in a subject' I mean what belongs in something, not as a part, and cannot exist separately from what it is in.) For example, an individual <instance of> grammatical knowledge is

1. **beings** (*onta*): Or 'things that there are' or 'existing things'.

in a subject, the soul, but is not said of any subject; and an individual <instance of> white is in a subject, the body (for all color is in body), but is not said of any subject. Some things are both said 1b of a subject and in a subject; knowledge, for instance, is in a subject, the soul, and is said of a subject, grammatical knowledge. Some things are neither in a subject nor said of a subject. This is true, for instance, of an individual man or horse; for nothing of this sort is either in a subject or said of a subject.

Things that are individual and numerically one are, without exception, not said of any subject. But nothing prevents some of them from being in a subject; for an individual <instance of> grammatical knowledge is one of the things in a subject.

3

Whenever one thing is predicated of another as of a subject, everything said of what is predicated is also said of the subject. Man, for instance, is predicated of an individual man, and animal of man; and so animal will also be predicated of an individual man, since an individual man is both a man and an animal.

Genera which are different and not subordinate to one another have differentiae that are different in species—for instance, the differentiae of animal and of knowledge. For footed, winged, aquatic, and biped are differentiae of animal, but none of them is a differentia of knowledge; for one sort of knowledge is not differentiated from another by being biped. But if one genus is subordinate to another, nothing prevents them from having the same differentiae; for the higher genera are predicated of those below them, so that the subject will also have all the differentiae of the thing predicated.

4

Of things said without combination, each signifies either substance or quantity or quality or relative or where or when or being in a position or having or acting on or being affected. To describe these in outline, here are some examples:

Substance:	man, horse
Quantity:	two feet long, three feet long
Quality:	white, grammatical

Relative:	double, half, larger
Where:	in the Lyceum, in the marketplace 2a
When:	yesterday, last year
Being in a position:	is lying, is sitting
Having:	has shoes on, has armor on
Acting on:	cutting, burning
Being affected:	being cut, being burned

None of the things just mentioned is said all by itself in any affirmation; an affirmation results from the combination of these things with one another. For every affirmation seems to be either true or false, whereas nothing said without combination—for instance, man, white, runs, wins—is either true or false.

[*SUBSTANCE*]

5

What is called substance most fully, primarily, and most of all, is what is neither said of any subject nor in any subject—for instance, an individual man or horse. The species in which the things primarily called substances belong are called secondary substances, and so are their genera. An individual man, for instance, belongs in the species man, and animal is the genus of the species; these things, then (for instance, man and animal), are called secondary substances.

It is evident from what has been said that if something is said of a subject, then both its name and its account must be predicated of the subject. For instance, man is said of a subject, an individual man, and the name is predicated (since you will predicate man of an individual man); moreover, the account of man will also be predicated of an individual man (since an individual man is also a man). And so both the name and the account will be predicated of the subject.

On the other hand, if something is in a subject, in most cases neither its name nor its account is predicated of the subject. In some cases the name may well be predicated of the subject, but the account still cannot be predicated. White, for instance, is in a subject, body, and is predicated of the subject (for body is said to be white); but the account of white is never predicated of body.

All other things are either said of the primary substances as subjects or in them as subjects. This is evident if we examine particular cases. Animal, for instance, is predicated of man, and so also of an individual man; for if it is not predicated of any 2b individual man, neither is it predicated of man at all. Again, color is in body, and so also in an individual body; for if it is not in any of the particular bodies, neither is it in body at all.

Hence all the other things are either said of the primary substances as subjects or in them as subjects. If, then, the primary substances did not exist, neither could any of the other things exist. For all the other things are either said of these as subjects or are in these as subjects, so that if the primary substances did not exist, neither could any of the other things exist.

Among secondary substances, the species is more a substance than the genus, since it is nearer to the primary substance; for if someone says what the primary substance is, it will be more informative and more appropriate if he mentions the species than if he mentions the genus. It will be more informative, for instance, to say that an individual man is a man than to say that he is an animal, since man is more distinctive of an individual man, while animal is more common; and it will be more informative to say that an individual tree is a tree than that it is a plant.

Further, the primary substances are subjects for all the other things, and all the other things are predicated of them or are in them; this is why they, most of all, are called substances. But as the primary substances are related to other things, so also is the species related to the genus; for the species is a subject for the genus, since the genera are predicated of the species, whereas the species are not reciprocally predicated of the genera. And so for this reason too the species is more a substance than the genus.

Among species that are not themselves genera, however, one is no more a substance than another; for it is no more appropriate to say that an individual man is a man than it is to say that an individual horse is a horse. And, similarly, among primary substances one is no more a substance than another; for an individual man is no more a substance than an individual ox is.

It is not surprising that, after the primary substances, only their species and genera are said to be secondary substances; for they are the only things predicated that reveal the primary substance. For if one says what an individual man is, it will be appropriate to mention the species or the genus, though it will be more informative to mention man than animal. But it would be inappropriate to mention anything else—for instance, white or runs or any other such thing. It is not surprising, then, that species and genera are the only other things said to be substances.

Further, it is because the primary substances are subjects for everything else that they are said to be substances most fully. But as the primary substances are related to everything else, so also the species and genera of primary substances are related to all the other <species and genera>; for all the others are predicated of them. For you will call an individual man grammatical, and so you will call both man and animal grammatical; and the same is true in the other cases.

A feature common to every substance is not being in a subject; for a primary substance is neither said of nor in a subject. In the same way, it is evident that secondary substances are not in a subject either; for man is said of a subject—an individual man—but is not in a subject, since man is not in an individual man. Similarly, animal is said of a subject—an individual man—but animal is not in an individual man.

Further, while things in a subject may sometimes have their name predicated of the subject, their account can never be predicated of it. Secondary substances, on the other hand, have both their account and their name predicated of the subject; for you will predicate both the account of man and the account of animal of an individual man. Hence no substance is in a subject.

This, however, is not distinctive of substance. The differentia is not in a subject either; for footed and biped are said of a subject—man—but are not in a subject, since neither footed nor biped is in man. Again, the account of the differentia is predicated of whatever subject the differentia is said of; for instance, if footed is said of man, the account of footed will also be predicated of man, since man is footed.

We need not be worried that we will ever be compelled to say that the parts of substances, being in a subject (the whole substance), are not substances. For when we spoke of things in a subject, we did not mean things belonging in something as parts.

It is a feature of substances and differentiae that everything called from them is so called synonymously; for all the predications from these are predicated of either the individuals or the species. (For there is no predication from a primary substance—since it is not said of any subject—and among secondary substances the species is predicated of an individual, and the genus 3b is predicated both of the species and of an individual. Similarly, differentiae are also predicated both of the species and of the individuals.) Now the primary substances receive the account both of the species and of the genera, and the species receives the account of the genus; for whatever is said of what is predicated will also be said of the subject. Similarly, both the species and the individuals receive the account of the differentiae; and we saw that synonymous things are those that both have the name in common and also have the same account. Hence everything called from substances and differentiae is so called synonymously.

Every substance seems to signify a this. In the case of primary substances, it is indisputably true that each of them signifies a this; for what is revealed is an individual and is numerically one. In the case of secondary substances, it appears from the character of the name, whenever one speaks of man or animal, that they also signify a this. But this is not true. Rather, each signifies a sort of thing;[2] for the subject is not one, as the primary substance is, but man and animal are said of many things. On the other hand, it does not unqualifiedly signify a sort of thing, as white does. For white signifies nothing other than a sort of thing, whereas the species and the genus demarcate a sort of substance; for they signify a substance of a certain sort. One demarcates more with the genus than with the species; for in speaking of animal one encompasses more than in speaking of man.

It is also a feature of substances that nothing is contrary to them. For what could be contrary to a primary substance? Nothing is contrary, for instance, to an individual man; nor is anything contrary to man or animal. This is not distinctive of substance, however, but is also true of many other things—of quantity, for instance, since nothing is contrary to two feet long, nor to ten, nor to anything else of this kind. One might say that many is contrary to few, or large to small; but no definite quantity is contrary to any other.

Substance does not seem to admit of more or less. By this I do not mean that one substance is no more a substance than another; for we have said that one type of substance is more a substance

2. **a sort of thing**: *poion ti*. In the rest of this paragraph (and elsewhere; see QUALITY) Aristotle uses *poion* to refer both to secondary substance and to the category of quality.

than another. Rather, I mean that no substance is said to be more or less what it is. For example, if this substance is a man, it will not be more or less a man either than itself or than another. For one man is no more a man than another, in the way that one white thing is whiter than another, or one beautiful thing is more beautiful than another. In some cases a thing is called more or less something than itself—for example, the body which is white is said to be more white now than it was before, and the body which is hot is said to be more or less hot <than it was>. But substance is not spoken of in this way; for a man is not said to be more a man now than before, nor is this said of any other substance. Thus substance does not admit of more or less.

It seems most distinctive of substance that numerically one and the same thing is able to receive contraries. In no other case could one cite something numerically one that is able to receive contraries. For example, the color that is numerically one and the same will not be pale and dark, nor will the action that is numerically one and the same be bad and good, and the same is true of anything else that is not a substance. But a substance that is numerically one and the same is able to receive contraries. An individual man, for instance, being one and the same, becomes at one time pale, at another time dark, and hot and cold, and bad and good; nothing of this sort appears in any other case.

Someone might object, however, that statements and beliefs are like this, since the same statement seems to be both true and false. If, for instance, the statement that someone is seated is true, when he has stood up this same statement will be false. The same is true of belief; for if someone were to believe truly that someone is seated, he will believe falsely if he has the same belief about the same person when he has stood up.

But even if one were to accept this, the way in which these receive contraries is still different. For in the case of substances, a thing is able to receive contraries by itself changing; for it changed when it became cold from hot (since it altered), or dark from pale, or good from bad, and similarly in the other cases it is able to receive contraries by itself changing. But statements and beliefs themselves remain completely unchanged in every way; it is because the object <they are about> changes that the contrary comes to be about them. For the statement that someone is seated remains the same, but it comes to be true at one time, false at another time, when the object has changed. The same is true of belief. Hence at least the way in which substance is able to receive contraries—by a change in itself—is distinctive of it, if indeed one were to accept it as true that beliefs and statements are also able to receive contraries.

In fact, however, this is not true. For a statement and a belief are said to be able to receive contraries not because they themselves receive something, but because something else has been affected. For it is because the object is or is not some way that the statement is said to be true or false, not because the statement itself is able to receive contraries; for, without exception, no statement or belief is changed by anything. And so, since nothing comes to be in them, they are not able to receive contraries. But substance is said to be able to receive contraries, because it receives them itself. For it receives sickness and health, or paleness and darkness; and because it itself receives each thing of this sort, it is said to be able to receive contraries.

Hence it is distinctive of substance that numerically one and the same thing is able to receive contraries. So much, then, about substance.

* * * * * * *

DE INTERPRETATIONE

[*LANGUAGE, THOUGHT, AND REALITY*][1]

1

We must first establish what names and verbs are, then what 16a
negations, affirmations, statements, and sentences are.

Spoken sounds are symbols of affections in the soul, and written marks are symbols of spoken sounds; and just as written marks are not the same for everyone, neither are spoken sounds. But the primary things that these signify (the affections in the soul) are the same for everyone, and what these affections are likenesses of (actual things) are also the same for everyone. We have discussed these questions in *On the Soul*; they belong to another inquiry.

Some thoughts in the soul are neither true nor false, while others must be one or the other; the same is true of spoken sounds. For falsity and truth involve combination and division. Names and verbs by themselves, when nothing is added (for instance, 'man' and 'pale') are like thoughts without combination and separation, since they are not yet either true or false. A sign of this is the fact that 'goatstag' signifies something but is not yet true or false unless 'is' or 'is not' is added, either without qualification or with reference to time.

2

A name is a spoken sound that is significant by convention, without time, of which no part is significant in separation. For in 'Grancourt', the 'court' does not signify anything in itself, as it does in the phrase 'a grand court'. But complex names are not the same as simple ones; for in simple names the part is not at all significant, whereas in complex names the part has some force but does not signify anything in separation—for instance, 'fact' in 'artifact'. I say 'by convention' because nothing is a name by nature; something is a name only if it becomes a symbol. For even

1. 'Interpretation' (*hermēneia*) is used for the linguistic means of expressing or SIGNIFYING something.

inarticulate noises—of beasts, for example—reveal something, but they are not names.

'Not-man' is not a name, nor is any established name rightly applied to it, since neither is it a sentence or a negation. Let us call it an indefinite name.

16b 'Philo's', 'to-Philo', and the like are not names but inflections of names. The same account applies to them as to names, except that a name with 'is' or 'was' or 'will be' added is always true or false, whereas an inflection with them added is neither true nor false. For example, in 'Philo's is' or 'Philo's is not' nothing is yet either true or false.

3

A verb is <a spoken sound> of which no part signifies separately, and which additionally signifies time; it is a sign of things said of something else. By 'additionally signifies time', I mean that, for instance, 'recovery' is a name but 'recovers' is a verb; for it additionally signifies something's holding now. And it is always a sign of something's holding, that is to say, of something's holding of a subject.

I do not call 'does not recover' and 'does not ail' verbs; for, although they additionally signify time and always hold of something, there is a difference for which there is no established name. Let us call them indefinite verbs, since they hold of anything whether it is or is not.

Similarly, 'recovered' and 'will-recover' are not verbs, but inflections of verbs. They differ from verbs because verbs additionally signify the present time, whereas inflections of verbs signify times outside the present.

A verb said just by itself is a name and signifies something, since the speaker fixes his thought and the hearer pauses; but it does not yet signify whether something is or is not. For 'being' or 'not being' is not a sign of an object (not even if you say 'what is' without addition); for by itself it is nothing, but it additionally signifies some combination, which cannot be thought of without the components.

4

A sentence is a significant spoken sound, of which some part is significant in separation as an expression, not as an affirmation.

I mean that 'animal', for instance, signifies something, but not that it is or is not (but if something is added, there will be an affirmation or negation), whereas the single syllables of 'animal' signify nothing. Nor is the 'ice' in 'mice' significant; here it is only a spoken sound. In the case of double names, as was said, a part signifies, but not by itself.

Every sentence is significant, not because it is a <naturally 17a
suitable> instrument but, as we said, by convention. But not every sentence is a statement; only those sentences that are true or false are statements. Not every sentence is true or false; a prayer, for instance, is a sentence but it is neither true nor false. Let us set aside these other cases, since inquiry into them is more appropriate for rhetoric or poetics; our present study concerns affirmations.

* * * * * * *

[*ARGUMENTS FOR AND AGAINST FATALISM*]

9

In the case of what is and what has been, then, it is necessary 18a28
that the affirmation or negation be true or false. And in the case of universal statements about universals, it is always <necessary> for one to be true and the other false; and the same is true in the case of particulars, as we have said. But in the case of universals not spoken of universally, this is not necessary; we have also discussed this.[2] But in the case of particulars that are going to be, it is not the same.

2. Aristotle explained this in 17b29ff.: 'Of contradictory universal statements about a universal, one or the other must be true or false; similarly if they are about particulars—for instance, "Socrates is pale" and "Socrates is not pale". But if they are about universals, but are not universal <statements>, it is not always the case that one is true, the other false. For it is true to say at the same time that a man is pale and that a man is not pale, and that a man is handsome and that a man is not handsome; for if ugly, then not handsome. And if something is becoming F, it is also not F. This might seem strange at first sight, since "A man is not pale" might appear to signify at the same time that no man is pale; but it does not signify the same, nor does it necessarily hold at the same time.'

For if every affirmation or negation is true or false, then it is also necessary that everything either is the case or is not the case. And so if someone says that something will be and another denies the same thing, clearly it is necessary for one of them to speak truly, if every affirmation is true or false. For both will be not be the case at the same time in such cases.

18b For if it is true to say that something is pale or not pale, it is necessary for it to be pale or not pale; and if it is pale or not pale, it was true to affirm or deny this. And if it is not the case, one speaks falsely; and if one speaks falsely, it is not the case. Hence it is necessary for the affirmation or the negation to be true or false.[3]

Therefore nothing either is or happens by chance or as chance has it; nor will it be nor not be <thus>. Rather, everything <happens> from necessity and not as chance has it, since either the affirmer or the denier speaks truly. For otherwise, it might equally well happen or not happen; for what happens as chance has it neither is nor will be any more this way than that.

Further, if something is pale now, it was true to say previously that it would be pale, so that it was always true to say of any thing that has happened that it would be. But if it was always true to say that it was or would be, it could not not be, or not be going to be. But if something cannot not happen, it is impossible for it not to happen; and what cannot not happen necessarily happens. Everything, then, that will be will be necessarily. Therefore, nothing will be as chance has it or by chance; for if it is by chance it is not from necessity.

But it is not possible to say that neither is true—that, for example, it neither will be nor will not be. For, first, <if this is possible,

3. **Hence it is . . . to be true or false**: This paragraph might be taken in two ways: (1) Aristotle means that it is necessary that (if p is true, then the state of affairs described by p obtains); he does not mean that if p is true, then the state of affairs described by p is necessary. The necessity governs the conditional, not its consequent. In the next paragraph (which seems to argue fallaciously from the necessity of the conditional to the necessity of the consequent) Aristotle articulates the fatalist's argument, which he goes on to reject. (2) In this paragraph Aristotle himself argues that if p is true, then the state of affairs described by p is necessary; he ascribes necessity to the consequent, as well as to the whole conditional. In that case the next paragraph expresses his own view.

then> though the affirmation is false, the negation is not true; and though the negation is false, it turns out <on this view> that the affirmation is not true.

Moreover, if it is true to say that it is pale and dark, both must be the case; and if <both> will be the case tomorrow, <both> must be the case tomorrow. But if it neither will nor will not be tomorrow, even so, the sea battle, for instance, will not happen as chance has it; for in this case, the sea battle would have to neither happen nor not happen.

These and others like them are the absurd consequences if in every affirmation and negation (either about universals spoken of universally or about particulars) it is necessary that one of the opposites be true and the other false, and nothing happens as chance has it, but all things are and happen from necessity. Hence there would be no need to deliberate or to take trouble, thinking that if we do this, that will be, and if we do not, it will not be; for it might well be that ten thousand years ago one person said that this would be and another denied it, so that whichever it was true to affirm at that time will be so from necessity.

Nor does it make a difference whether or not anyone made the contradictory statements; for clearly things are thus even if someone did not affirm it and another deny it. For it is not because of the affirming or denying that it will be or will not be the case, nor is this any more so for ten thousand years ago than for any other time.

Hence if in the whole of time things were such that one or the other statement was true, it was necessary for this to happen, and each thing that happened was always such as to happen from necessity. For if someone has said truly that something will happen, it cannot not happen; and it was always true to say of something that has happened that it would be.

But surely this is impossible. For we see that both deliberation and action originate things that will be; and, in general, we see in things that are not always in actuality that there is the possibility both of being and of not being; in these cases both being and not being, and hence both happening and not happening, are possible.

We find that this is clearly true of many things. It is possible, for instance, for this cloak to be cut up, though <in fact> it will not be cut up but will wear out first instead. Similarly, its not being cut up is also possible; for its wearing out first would not have been the case unless its not being cut up were possible.

Hence the same is true for other things that happen, since this sort of possibility is ascribed to many of them.

Evidently, then, not everything is or happens from necessity. Rather, some things happen as chance has it, and the affirmation is no more true than the negation. In other cases, one alternative <happens> more than the other and happens usually, but it is still possible for the other to happen and for the first not to happen.

It is necessary for what is, whenever it is, to be, and for what is not, whenever it is not, not to be. But not everything that is necessarily is; and not everything that is not necessarily is not. For everything's being from necessity when it is is not the same as everything's being from necessity without qualification; and the same is true of what is not.[4]

The same argument also applies to contradictories. It is necessary for everything either to be or not to be, and indeed to be going to be or not be going to be. But one cannot divide <the contradictories> and say that one or the other is necessary. I mean that, for instance, it is necessary for there to be or not to be a sea battle tomorrow, but it is not necessary for a sea battle to happen tomorrow, nor is it <necessary> for one not to happen. It is necessary, however, for it either to happen or not to happen.

And so, since the truth of statements corresponds to how things are, it is clear that, for however many things are as chance has it and are such as to admit contraries, it is necessary for the same to be true of the contradictories. This is just what happens with things that neither always are nor always are not. For in these cases it is necessary for one of the contradictories to be true and the other false. It is not, however, <necessary> for this or that one <more than the other one to be true or false>. Rather, <it is true or false> as chance has it; or <in the case of things that

4. **It is necessary . . . true of what is not**: This paragraph might be understood in two ways: (1) Aristotle uncovers the fatalist's fallacy, by distinguishing necessity WITHOUT QUALIFICATION from conditional necessity. It is true to say that necessarily (when x is, x is); but we cannot validly infer from this that when x is, x necessarily is. Certainly x is conditionally necessary, in that, necessarily (when x is, x is); but x is not necessary without qualification, i.e., necessary on its own. (2) Aristotle affirms that when x is (i.e., is present), then x necessarily is. He affirms the necessity of the present and past, in contrast to the non-necessity of the future.

happen usually> one is more true than the other, but not thereby true or false <without qualification>.

Clearly, then, it is not necessary that of every affirmation and 19b
negation of opposites, one is true and one false. For what holds for things that are <always> does not also hold for things that are not <always> but are capable of being and of not being; in these cases it is as we have said.

* * * * * * *

POSTERIOR ANALYTICS[1]

Book I

[*KNOWING AND LEARNING*]

1

71a All teaching and all intellectual learning result from previous knowledge$_{g}$. This is clear if we examine all the cases; for this is how the mathematical sciences and all crafts arise. This is also true of both deductive and inductive arguments, since they both succeed in teaching because they rely on what is previously known: deductive arguments begin with premisses we are assumed to comprehend, and inductive arguments prove the universal by relying on the fact that the particular is already clear. Rhetorical arguments also persuade in the same way, since they rely either on examples (and hence on induction) or on argumentations (and hence on deduction).

Previous knowledge is needed in two ways. In some cases we must presuppose that something is (for example, that it is true that everything is either asserted or denied truly <of a given subject>). In other cases we must comprehend what the thing spoken of is (for example, that a triangle signifies this); and in other cases we must do both (for example, we must both comprehend what a unit signifies and presuppose that there is such a thing). For something different is needed to make each of these things clear to us.

We may also come to know that q by having previously known that p and acquiring knowledge of q at the same time <as we acquire knowledge of r>. This is how, for instance, we acquire knowledge of the cases that fall under the universal of which we possess knowledge; for we previously knew$_{o}$ that, say, every triangle has angles equal to two right angles, but we come to know$_{g}$ that this figure in the semicircle is a triangle at the same

1. On the title see LOGICAL. In this work Aristotle argues that genuine scientific KNOWLEDGE must be displayed in the demonstrative structure of a science.

time as we perform the induction <showing that this figure has two right angles>. For in some cases we learn in this way (rather than coming to know the last term through the middle); this is true when we reach particulars, i.e., things not said of any subject.

Before we perform the induction or the deduction, we should presumably be said to know$_e$ in one way but not in another. For if we did not know$_o$ without qualification whether <a given triangle> is, how could we know without qualification that it has two right angles? But clearly we know$_e$ it insofar as we know it universally, but we do not know it without qualification. Otherwise we will face the puzzle in the *Meno*, since we will turn out to learn either nothing or else nothing but what we <already> know$_o$.[2]

For we should not agree with some people's attempted solution to this puzzle. Do you or do you not know that every pair is even? When you say you do, they produce a pair that you did not think existed and hence did not think was even. They solve this puzzle by saying that one does not know that every pair is even, but rather one knows that what one knows to be a pair is even. In fact, however, <contrary to this solution,> one knows 71b
that of which one has grasped and still possesses the demonstration, and the demonstration one has grasped is not about whatever one knows to be a triangle or a number, but about every number or triangle without qualification; for <in a demonstration> a premiss is not taken to say that what you know to be a triangle or rectangle is so and so, but, on the contrary, it is taken to apply to every case.

But, I think, it is quite possible for us to know$_e$ in one way what we are learning, while being ignorant of it in another way. For what is absurd is not that we <already> know$_o$ in some way the very thing we are learning; the absurdity arises only if we already know it to the precise extent and in the precise way in which we are learning it.

2. **Otherwise we . . . <already> know$_0$:** Plato presents the puzzle (*Meno* 80a–d) as follows: (1) For any item x, either one knows x or one does not know x. (2) If one knows x, one cannot inquire into x. (3) If one does not know x, one cannot inquire into x. (4) Therefore, whether one knows or does not know x, one cannot inquire into x. Aristotle here rejects (2); he probably also rejects (3).

[*KNOWLEDGE AND DEMONSTRATION*]

2

We think we know$_e$ a thing without qualification, and not in the sophistic, coincidental way,[3] whenever we think we know$_g$ the explanation because of which the thing is <so>, know that it is the explanation of that thing, and know that it does not admit of being otherwise. Clearly, then, knowing$_e$ is something of this sort; for both those who lack knowledge and those who have it think they are in this condition, but those who have the knowledge are really in it. So whatever is known without qualification cannot be otherwise.

We shall say later whether there is also some other way of knowing$_e$; but we certainly say that we know through demonstration. By 'demonstration' I mean a deduction expressing knowledge; by 'expressing knowledge' I mean that having the deduction constitutes having knowledge.

If, then, knowing is the sort of thing we assumed it is, demonstrative knowledge must also be derived from things that are true, primary, immediate, better known$_g$ than, prior to, and explanatory of the conclusion; for this will also ensure that the principles are proper to what is being proved. For these conditions are not necessary for a deduction, but they are necessary for a demonstration, since without them a deduction will not produce knowledge$_e$.

<The conclusions> must be true, then, because we cannot know what is not <true> (for example, that the diagonal is commensurate). They must be derived from <premisses> that are primary and indemonstrable, because we will have no knowledge unless we have a demonstration of these <premisses>; for to have non-coincidental knowledge of something demonstrable is to have a demonstration of it.

They must be explanatory, better known$_g$, and prior. They must be explanatory, because we know$_e$ something whenever we know$_o$ its explanation. They must be prior if they are indeed explanatory.

3. **sophistic, coincidental way**: Someone may prove separately that all scalene triangles, all isosceles triangles, and all equilateral triangles have two right angles; but these proofs do not result in knowledge$_e$ that all triangles (i.e., all triangles insofar as they are triangles) have two right angles.

And they must be previously known$_g$ not only in the sense that we comprehend them, but also in the sense that we know$_o$ that they are <true>. Things are prior and better known$_g$ in two ways; for what is prior by nature is not the same as what is prior to us, 72a
nor is what is better known <by nature> the same as what is better known to us. By 'what is prior and better known to us' I mean what is closer to perception, and by 'what is prior and better known without qualification' I mean what is further from perception. What is most universal is furthest from perception, and particulars are closest to it; particular and universal are opposite to each other.

Derivation from primary things is derivation from proper principles. (I mean the same by 'primary things' as I mean by 'principles'.) A principle of demonstration is an immediate premiss, and a premiss is immediate if no others are prior to it. A premiss is one or the other part of a contradiction, and it says one thing of one thing. It is dialectical if it takes either part indifferently, demonstrative if it determinately takes one part because it is true. A contradiction is an opposition which, in itself, has nothing in the middle. The part of the contradiction that asserts something of something is an affirmation, and the part that denies something of something is a denial.

By 'thesis' I mean an immediate principle of deduction that cannot be proved, but is not needed if one is to learn anything at all. By 'axiom' I mean a principle one needs in order to learn anything at all; for there are some things of this sort, and we usually apply the name especially to these.

If a thesis asserts one or the other part of a contradiction—for example, that something is or that something is not—it is an assumption; otherwise it is a definition. For a definition is a thesis (since the arithmetician, for example, lays it down that a unit is what is indivisible in quantity), but it is not an assumption (since what it is to be a unit and that a unit is are not the same).

Since our conviction and knowledge$_o$ about a thing must be based on our having the sort of deduction we call a demonstration, and since we have this sort of deduction when its premisses obtain, not only must we have previous knowledge$_g$ about all or some of the primary things, but we must also know them better. For if x makes y F, x is more F than y; if, for instance, we love y because of x, x is loved more than y. Hence if the primary things produce knowledge$_o$ and conviction, we must have more knowledge and conviction about them, since they also produce it about subordinate things.

Now if we know q, we cannot have greater conviction about p than about q unless we either know p or are in some condition better than knowledge about p. This will result, however, unless previous knowledge <of the principles> is the basis of conviction produced by demonstration; for we must have greater conviction about all or some of the principles than about the conclusion.

If we are to have knowledge$_e$ through demonstration, then not only must we know$_g$ the principles better and have greater
72b conviction about them than about what is proved, but we must also not find anything more convincing or better known that is opposed to the principles and allows us to deduce a mistaken conclusion contrary <to the correct one>. For no one who has knowledge$_e$ without qualification can be persuaded out of it.

3

Some people think that because <knowledge through demonstration> requires knowledge$_e$ of the primary things, there is no knowledge; others think that there is knowledge, and that everything <knowable> is demonstrable. Neither of these views is either true or necessary.

The first party—those who assume that there is no knowledge at all—claim that we face an infinite regress. They assume that we cannot know$_e$ posterior things because of prior things, if there are no primary things. Their assumption is correct, since it is impossible to go through an infinite series. If, on the other hand, the regress stops, and there are principles, these are, in their view, unknowable$_g$, since these principles cannot be demonstrated, and, in these people's view, demonstration is the only way of knowing$_e$. But if we cannot know$_o$ the primary things, then neither can we know$_e$ without qualification or fully the things derived from them; we can know them only conditionally, on the assumption that we can know the primary things.

The other party agree that knowledge results only from demonstration, but they claim that it is possible to demonstrate everything, since they take circular and reciprocal demonstration to be possible.

We reply that not all knowledge$_e$ is demonstrative, and in fact knowledge of the immediate premisses is indemonstrable. Indeed, it is evident that this must be so; for if we must know the prior things (i.e., those from which the demonstration is derived), and if eventually the regress stops, these immediate premisses must be indemonstrable. Besides this, we also say that there is not only knowledge$_e$ but also some origin of knowledge$_e$, which gives us knowledge$_g$ of the definitions.

Unqualified demonstration clearly cannot be circular, if it must be derived from what is prior and better known$_g$. For the same things cannot be both prior and posterior to the same things at the same time, except in different ways (so that, for example, some things are prior relative to us, and others are prior without qualification—this is the way induction makes something known$_g$.) If this is so, our definition of unqualified knowledge$_o$ will be faulty, and there will be two sorts of knowledge$_o$; or <rather> perhaps the second sort of demonstration is not unqualified demonstration, since it is derived from what is <merely> better known$_g$ to us.

Those who allow circular demonstration must concede not only the previous point, but also that they are simply saying that something is if it is. On these terms it is easy to prove anything. This is clear if we consider three terms—for it does not matter whether we say the demonstration turns back through many or few terms, or through few or two. For suppose that if A is, necessarily B is, and that if B is, necessarily C is; it follows that if A is, C will be. Suppose, then, that if A is, then B necessarily is, and if B is, A is (since this is what circular argument is), and let A be C. In that case, to say that if B is, A is is to say that <if B is,> C is; this <is to say> that if A is, C is. But since C is the same as A, it follows that those who allow circular demonstration simply say that if A is, then A is. On these terms it is easy to prove anything.

But not even this is possible, except for things that are reciprocally predicated, such as distinctive properties. If, then, one thing is laid down, we have proved that it is never necessary for anything else to be the case. (By 'one thing' I mean that neither one term nor one thesis is enough; two theses are the fewest <needed for a demonstration>, since they are also the fewest needed for a deduction.) If, then, A follows from B and C, and these follow from each other and from A, then in this way it is possible to prove all the postulates from each other in the first figure, as we proved in the discussion of deduction. We also proved that in the other figures, the result is either no deduction or none relevant to the things assumed. But it is not at all possible to give a circular proof of things that are not reciprocally predicated. And so, since there are few things that are reciprocally predicated in demonstrations, it is clearly empty and impossible to say that demonstration is reciprocal and that for this reason everything is demonstrable.

4

Since what is known$_e$ without qualification cannot be otherwise, what is known by demonstrative knowledge will be necessary. Demonstrative knowledge is what we have by having a demonstration; hence a demonstration is a deduction from things that are necessary. We must, then, find from what and from what sorts of things demonstrations are derived. Let us first determine what we mean by '<belonging> in every case', 'in its own right', and 'universal'.

By '<belonging> in every case' I mean what belongs not <merely> in some cases, or at some times, as opposed to others. If, for example, animal belongs to every man, it follows that if it is true to say that this is a man, it is also true to say that he is an animal, and that if he is a man now, he is also an animal now. The same applies if it is true to say that there is a point in every line. A sign of this is the fact that when we are asked whether something belongs in every case, we advance objections by asking whether it fails to belong either in some cases or at some times.

A belongs to B in its own right in the following cases:

(a) A belongs to B in what B is, as, for example, line belongs to triangle, and point to line; for here the essence$_o$ of B is composed of A, and A is present in the account that says what B is.

(b) A belongs to B, and B itself is present in the account revealing what A is. In this way straight and curved, for instance, belong to line, while odd and even, prime and compound, equilateral and oblong, belong in this way to number. In all these cases either line or number is present in the account saying what <straight or odd, for example,> is. Similarly in other cases, this is what I mean by saying that A belongs to B in its own right. What belongs in neither of these ways I call coincidental—as, for instance, musical or pale belongs to animal.

(c) A is not said of something else B that is the subject of A.

A walker or a pale thing, for example, is a walker or a pale thing by being something else; but a substance—i.e., whatever signifies a this—is not what it is by being something else. I say, then, that what is not said of a subject is <a thing> in its own right, whereas what is said of a subject is a coincident.

(d) Moreover, in another way, if A belongs to B because of B itself, then A belongs to B in its own right; if A belongs to B, but not because of B itself, then A is coincidental to B. If, for example, lightning flashed while you were walking, that was coincidental; for the lightning was not caused by your walking but, as we say, was a coincidence. If, however, A belongs to B because of B itself, then it belongs to B in its own right. If, for example, an animal was killed in being sacrificed, the killing belongs to the sacrificing in its own right, since the animal was killed because it was sacrificed, and it was not a coincidence that the animal was killed in being sacrificed.

Hence in the case of unqualified objects of knowledge$_e$, whenever A is said to belong to B in its own right, either because B is present in A and A is predicated of B, or because A is present in B, then A belongs to B because of B itself and necessarily. <It belongs necessarily> either because it is impossible for A not to belong to B or because it is impossible for neither A nor its opposite (for example, straight and crooked, or odd and even) to belong to B (for example, a line or a number). For a contrary is either a privation or a contradiction in the same genus; even, for example, is what is not odd among numbers, insofar as this follows. Hence, if it is necessary either to affirm or to deny, then what belongs to a subject in its own right necessarily belongs to that subject.

Let this, then, be our definition of what belongs in every case and of what belongs to something in its own right.

By 'universal' I mean what belongs to its subject in every case and in its own right, and insofar as it is itself. It is evident, then, that what is universal belongs to things necessarily. What belongs to the subject in its own right is the same as what belongs to it insofar as it is itself. A point and straightness, for instance, belong to a line in its own right, since they belong to a line insofar as it is a line. Similarly, two right angles belong to a triangle insofar as it is a triangle, since a triangle is equal in its own right to two right angles.

A universal belongs <to a species> whenever it is proved of

an instance that is random and primary. Having two right angles, for instance, is not universal to figure; for though you may prove that some figure has two right angles, you cannot prove it of any random figure, nor do you use any random figure in proving it, since a quadrilateral is a figure but does not have angles equal to two right angles. Again, a random isosceles triangle has angles equal to two right angles, but it is not the primary case, since the triangle is prior. If, then, a random triangle is the primary case that is proved to have two right angles, or whatever it is, then
74a that property belongs universally to this case primarily, and the demonstration holds universally of this case in its own right. It holds of the other cases in a way, but not in their own right; it does not even hold universally of the isosceles triangle, but more widely.

* * * * * * *

Book II

* * * * * * *

[*DEMONSTRATION AND DEFINITION*]

8

93a3 Knowing what a thing is is the same as knowing the explanation of whether it is. The argument for this is that there is some explanation <of whether a thing is> and this is either the same <as what the thing is> or something else, and if it is something else, then it is either demonstrable or indemonstrable. If, then, it is something else and is demonstrable, the explanation must be a middle term, and must be proved in the first figure, since what is being proved is universal and affirmative.

One type of proof, then, would be the one examined just now—proving what something is through something else. For in proofs of what a thing is it is necessary for the middle term to be what <the thing> is, and in proofs of distinctive properties it is necessary for the middle term to be a distinctive property. Hence in one case you will, and in another case you will not, prove the essence of the same object. Now this type of proof, as has been said before, is not a demonstration, but a logical deduction of what something is.

Let us say, then, starting again from the beginning, how a demonstration is possible. In some cases we seek the reason for something when we have already grasped the fact, and in other cases they both become clear at the same time; but it is never possible to come to know$_g$ the reason before the fact. It is clear, then, that in the same way we cannot come to know the essence of a thing without knowing that the thing is; for it is impossible to know$_o$ what a thing is if we do not know whether the thing is.

Our grasp of whether a thing is is in some cases <merely> coincidental, while in other cases we grasp whether a thing is by grasping some aspect of the thing itself. We may grasp, for instance, whether thunder is, by grasping that it is some sort of noise in the clouds; whether an eclipse is, by grasping that it is some sort of deprivation of light; whether a man is, by grasping that he is some sort of animal; and whether a soul is, by grasping that it initiates its own motion.

In cases where we know$_o$ <only> coincidentally that a thing is, we necessarily have no grasp of what the thing is, since we do not even know that the thing is; to investigate what a thing is when we have not grasped that the thing is is to investigate nothing. But in the cases where we do grasp some <aspect of the thing itself>, it is easier <to investigate what the thing is>. And so we acquire knowledge of what the thing is to the extent that we know that the thing is.

As a case where we grasp some aspect of what a thing is, let us take first of all the following: Let A be an eclipse, C the moon, and B blocking by the earth. Then to investigate whether it is eclipsed or not is to investigate whether B is or not. This question is just the same as the question whether there is an account of <A>; and if there is an account of <A>, we also say that <A> is. Or perhaps we ask which of two contradictories—for example, the triangle's having or not having two right angles—satisfies the account.

When we find <the account>, we know$_o$ both the fact and the reason at the same time, if <we reach the fact> through immediate <premisses>; if <the premisses are not immediate>, then we

know the fact, but not the reason. For instance, let C be the moon, A an eclipse, and B the inability to cast a shadow at the full moon when there is nothing apparent between us and it. Suppose, then,
93b that B (inability to cast a shadow when there is nothing between us and it) belongs to C, and that A (being eclipsed) belongs to B. In that case it is clear that the moon has been eclipsed, but it is not thereby clear why it has been eclipsed; we know$_{o}$ that there is an eclipse, but we do not know what it is.

If it is clear that A belongs to C, then <to investigate> why it belongs is to investigate what B is—whether it is the blocking <by the earth> or the rotation of the moon or its extinguishing. And this is the account of one extreme term—in this case the account of A, since an eclipse is a blocking by the earth.

<Or take another example:> What is thunder? Extinguishing of fire in a cloud. Why does it thunder? Because the fire is extinguished in the cloud. Let C be a cloud, A thunder, B extinguishing of fire. Then B belongs to C, a cloud (since the fire is extinguished in it), and A, the noise, belongs to B; and in fact B is the account of A, the first extreme term. And if there is a further middle term <explaining> B, this will be found from the remaining accounts <of A>.

We have said, then, how one grasps the what-it-is, and how it comes to be known$_{g}$. And so it turns out that though the what-it-is is neither deduced nor demonstrated, still it is made clear through deduction and demonstration. Hence, in the case where the explanation of a thing is something other than the thing, a demonstration is required for knowledge$_{g}$ of what the thing is, even though there is no demonstration of what the thing is, as we also said in setting out the puzzles.

9

Some things have something else as their explanation, while other things do not; and so it is clear that in some cases the what-it-is is immediate and a principle. In these cases we must assume (or make evident in some other way) both that it is and what it is—as the students of arithmetic do, since they assume both what the unit is and that it is. In the other cases—those that have a middle term, and where something else is the explanation of their essence$_{o}$—it is possible, as we said, to make clear what something is through demonstration, even though the what-it-is is not demonstrated.

10

Since a definition is said to be an account of the what-it-is, it is evident that one type will be an account of what a name or some other name-like account signifies[1]—for example, what triangle signifies. When we have grasped that <a thing> is <this>, we investigate why it is; but it is difficult to grasp in this way <why a thing is>, given that we do not know$_0$ that the thing is. The reason for this difficulty has been mentioned before: <if we know only what a thing's name signifies>, we do not even know whether or not the thing is, unless <we know this> coincidentally. (An account is unified in either of two ways—either by connection, like the *Iliad*, or by revealing one <property> of one <subject> noncoincidentally.)

This, then, is one definition of definition; another sort of definition is an account revealing why something is.[2] Hence the first type of definition signifies but does not prove, whereas the second type will clearly be a sort of demonstration of what something is, but differently arranged—for saying why it thunders is different from saying what thunder is. We will answer the first question by saying 'Because fire is extinguished in the clouds'. And what is thunder? A noise of fire being extinguished in the clouds. These are two different statements, then, of the same account; the first is a continuous demonstration, the second a definition. Moreover, a definition of thunder is noise in the clouds, which is the conclusion of a demonstration of what it is. In contrast to this, the definition of something immediate is an indemonstrable positing of what it is.

One sort of definition, then, is an indemonstrable account of the what-it-is; a second is a deduction of the what-it-is, differing in arrangement from a demonstration; and a third is the conclusion of a demonstration of the what-it-is.

What we have said, then, has made it evident, first, in what

1. **an account of . . . account signifies**: This is often (though not by Aristotle) called a 'nominal definition'.

2. **another sort . . . something is**: This is often (though not by Aristotle) called a 'real' definition.

way the what-it-is is demonstrable and in what way it is not, and what things are demonstrable and what things are not; secondly, in how many ways a definition is spoken of, in what way it proves the what-it-is and in what way it does not, and what things have definitions and what things do not; and, thirdly, how definition is related to demonstration, and in what way there can be both definition and demonstration of the same thing and in what way there cannot.

* * * * * * *

[*THE ULTIMATE PRINCIPLES OF DEMONSTRATION*]

19

It is evident, then, what deduction and demonstration are and how they come about; the same holds for demonstrative knowledge$_{e}$, since it is the same <as demonstration>. But how do we come to know$_{g}$ principles, and what state knows$_{g}$ them? This will be clear from the following argument, if we first state the puzzles.

We said before that we cannot know$_{e}$ through demonstration without knowing$_{g}$ the first, immediate principles. But one might be puzzled about whether knowledge$_{g}$ of the immediate principles is or is not the same <as knowledge of truths derived from them>; whether there is knowledge$_{e}$ of each, or knowledge of one but something else of the other; and whether the states are acquired rather than <innately> present or are <innately> present in us without our noticing them.[3]

It would be absurd if we had the principles <innately>; for then we would possess knowledge$_{g}$ that is more exact than demonstration, but without noticing it. If, on the other hand, we acquire the principles and do not previously possess them, how could we know$_{g}$ and learn them from no prior knowledge? That is impossible, as we also said in the case of demonstration. Evidently, then, we can neither possess the principles <innately> nor acquire them if we are ignorant and possess no state <of knowledge>. Hence we must have some <suitable> potentiality,

3. **and not <innately> . . . noticing them**: Cf. Plato, *Meno* 81a–86c.

but not one that is at a level of exactness superior to that of the knowledge we acquire.

All animals evidently have <such a potentiality>, since they have the innate discriminative potentiality called perception. Some animals that have perception (though not all of them) also retain <in memory> what they perceive; those that do not retain it have no knowledge$_g$ outside perception (either none at all or none about what is not retained), but those that do retain it keep what they have perceived in their souls even after they have perceived. When this has happened many times a <further> difference arises: in some, but not all, cases, a rational account[4] arises from the retention of perceptions.

From perception, then, as we say, memory arises, and from repeated memory of the same thing experience arises; for a number of memories make up one experience. From experience, or <rather> from the whole universal that has settled in the soul—the one apart from the many, whatever is present as one and the same in all of them—arises a principle of craft (if it is about what comes to be) or of science (if it is about what is).

Hence the relevant states are not <innate> in us in any determinate character and do not arise from states that have a better grasp on knowledge$_g$; rather, they arise from perception. It is like what happens in a battle when there is a retreat: first one soldier makes a stand, then a second, then another, until they reach a starting point. The soul's nature gives it a potentiality to be affected in this way.

Let us state again, then, what we stated, but not perspicuously, before. When one of the undifferentiated things makes a stand, that is the first universal in the soul; for though one perceives the particular, perception is of the universal—of man, for instance, not of Callias the man. Again, in these <universals something else> makes a stand, until what has no parts and is universal makes a stand—first, for example, a certain sort of animal makes a stand, until animal does, and in this <universal> something else makes a stand in the same way. Clearly, then, we must

4. **rational account**: Aristotle may mean to explain (1) the acquisition of universal concepts (e.g., the concept of horse) from perception (e.g., of particular horses); or (2) the acquisition of knowledge of universal truths (e.g., that horses have four legs) from perception (e.g., that this horse has four legs, that horse . . . etc.) or (3) both (1) and (2).

come to know$_g$ the first things by induction; for that is also how perception produces the universal in us.

Among our intellectual states that grasp the truth, some—knowledge$_e$ and understanding[5]—are always true, whereas others—for example, belief and reasoning—admit of being false; and understanding is the only sort of state that is more exact than knowledge$_e$. Since the principles of demonstration are better known$_g$ <than the conclusions derived from them>, and since all knowledge$_e$ requires an account, it follows that we can have no knowledge$_e$ of the principles. Since only understanding can be truer than knowledge$_e$, we must have understanding of the principles.

The same conclusion follows from the further point that since the principle of a demonstration is not a demonstration, the principle of knowledge$_e$ is not knowledge$_e$. If, then, the only sort of state apart from knowledge$_e$ that is <always> true is understanding, understanding must be the principle of knowledge$_e$. The principle, then, will grasp the principle, and, similarly, all knowledge$_e$ will grasp its object.

5. **understanding**: This is the sort of cognitive grasp that was demanded in i 3, to avoid a circle or infinite regress of justification.

TOPICS[1]

Book I

[*THE THEORY AND PRACTICE OF DIALECTIC*]

1

The purpose of our discussion is to discover a line of inquiry that will allow us to reason deductively from common beliefs on any problem proposed to us, and to give an account ourselves without saying anything contradictory. First, then, we must say what a deduction is and what different types of it there are, so that we can grasp what dialectical deduction is—for this is what we are looking for in our proposed discussion.

A deduction, then, is an argument in which, if p and q are assumed, then something else r, different from p and q, follows necessarily through p and q. It is a demonstration whenever the deduction proceeds from true and primary premisses or our knowledge$_g$ of the premisses is originally derived from primary and true premisses. A dialectical deduction is the one that proceeds from common beliefs.

The premisses that are true and primary are those that produce conviction not through other things, but through themselves. For in the principles of knowledge$_e$ we must not search further for the reason why; rather, each of the principles must be credible itself in its own right.

The common beliefs are the things believed by everyone or by most people or by the wise (and among the wise by all or by most or by those most known and commonly recognized). A contentious deduction is one proceeding from apparent common beliefs that are not really common beliefs, or one apparently proceeding from real or apparent common beliefs. <We speak of 'apparent' common beliefs,> because not everything that appears

1. The *Topics* is about *topoi*, 'places' (hence 'commonplaces'). 'Places' probably refers to a technique for remembering a list of items by correlating them with a previously learned grid or list of places. Hence the dialectical 'places' are common forms of argument to be remembered for use in dialectical discussions.

to be a common belief really is one; for none of the things called common beliefs has the appearance entirely on the surface. On this point they differ from what happens in the case of the principles of contentious arguments. For in the latter case the nature of the falsity is especially clear straightaway to those with even a little ability to trace consequences. The first kind of deduction that we have called contentious, then, should indeed count as a genuine deduction, whereas the other kind is a contentious deduction, but not a genuine deduction, since it appears to make a deduction, but does not actually do so.

Further, apart from all the types of deduction just mentioned, there are fallacious arguments that start from premisses that are proper to a given science, as happens in the case of geometry and cognate sciences. For this type of argument would seem to be different from the types of deduction previously mentioned; for someone who draws the wrong diagram deduces a conclusion neither from true and primary premisses nor from common beliefs. He does not fall into either class, since he does not accept what is believed by all, or by most people, or by the wise (either all or most or the most commonly recognized of these), but produces his deduction by accepting things that are proper to the science but are not true. For example, he produces his fallacious argument either by describing the semicircles wrongly or by drawing lines wrongly.

These, then, are, in outline, the types of deduction. In general, both in all the cases we have discussed and in all those to be discussed later, this degree of determinateness is to be taken as adequate. For <in undertaking this discussion> the account we decide to give on any subject is not an exact account, but enough for us to describe it in outline. We assume that the ability to recognize these things in some way is entirely adequate for the proposed line of inquiry.

2

Our next task is to say what areas, and how many, there are in which our discussion is useful. It is useful, then, for three purposes—for training, for encounters, and for the philosophical sciences.

Its usefulness for training is immediately evident; for if we have a line of inquiry, we will more easily be able to take on a

question proposed to us. It is useful for encounters, because once we have catalogued the beliefs of the many, our approach to them will begin from their own views, not from other people's, and we will redirect them whenever they appear to us to be wrong. It is useful for the philosophical sciences, because the ability to survey the puzzles on each side of a question makes it easier to notice what is true and false. Moreover it is useful for finding the primary things in each science. For from the principles proper to the science proposed for discussion nothing can be derived about the principles themselves, since the principles are primary among all <the truths contained in the science>; instead they 101b
must be discussed through the common beliefs in a given area. This is distinctive of dialectic, or more proper to it than to anything else; for since it cross-examines, it provides a way toward the principles of all lines of inquiry.

* * * * * * *

5

We must say, then, what a definition, a distinctive property, a 101b37
genus, and a coincident are.

A definition is an account that signifies the essence. One provides either an account to replace a name or an account to replace 102a
an account—for it is also possible to define some of the things signified by an account. Those who merely provide a name, whatever it is, clearly do not provide the definition of the thing, since every definition is an account. Still, this sort of thing—for example, 'the fine is the fitting'—should also be counted as definitory. In the same way one should also count as definitory a question such as 'Are perception and knowledge$_e$ the same or different?'; for most of the discussion about definition is occupied with whether things are the same or different. Speaking without qualification, we may count as definitory everything that falls under the same line of inquiry that includes definition.

It is clear immediately that all the things just mentioned meet this condition. For if we are able to argue dialectically that things are the same and that they are different, we will in the same way be well supplied to take on definitions; for once we have shown that two things are not the same, we will have undermined the

<attempted> definition. The converse of this point, however, does not hold; for showing that two things are the same is not enough to establish a definition, whereas showing that two things are not the same is enough to destroy a definition.

A distinctive property is one that does not reveal what the subject is, though it belongs only to that subject and is reciprocally predicated of it. It is distinctive of man, for instance, to be receptive of grammatical knowledge; for if someone is a man, he is receptive of grammatical knowledge, and if someone is receptive of grammatical knowledge, he is a man. For no one counts as a distinctive property what admits of belonging to something else—for instance, no one counts being asleep as a distinctive property of a man, even if at some time it happens to belong only to him. If, then, something of this sort were to be called a distinctive property, it would be called distinctive not without qualification, but at a time, or in relation to something; being on the right, for instance, is distinctive of something at a particular time, while being a biped is distinctive of one thing in relation to another—of man, for instance, in relation to horse and dog. It is clear that nothing that admits of belonging to something else is reciprocally predicated of its subject; it is not necessary, for instance, that what is asleep is a man.

A genus is what is essentially predicated of a plurality of things differing in species. Let us count as essentially predicated whatever it is appropriate to mention if we are asked what a given thing is; when we are asked what man is, for instance, it is appropriate to say that it is an animal. It is also relevant to the genus to say whether two things are in the same genus, or each is in a different genus, since this also falls under the same line of inquiry as the genus. If, for instance, we argue dialectically that animal is the genus of man, and also of ox, we will have argued that they are in the same genus; and if we prove that something is the genus of one thing but not of another, we will have argued that these two things are not in the same genus.

A coincident is what though it is none of these things—neither a definition nor a distinctive property nor a genus—belongs to the subject. Again, it is whatever admits both of belonging and of not belonging to one and the same subject. Being seated, for instance, admits both of belonging and of not belonging to one and the same subject, and so does being pale, since the same subject may easily be pale at one time and not pale at another.

The second of these two definitions of coincident is better. For if the first is stated, we will not understand it unless we first know what a definition, a distinctive property, and a genus are; the second, however, is sufficient in its own right for our knowing$_{g}$ what is meant.

Let us also add to the <class of> coincidents the comparisons between things whose descriptions are derived in some way from the coincident. These include, for instance, the question whether the fine or the advantageous is more choiceworthy, or whether the life of virtue or the life of gratification is pleasanter, and any other questions similar to these. For in all such cases the question proves to be about whether the thing predicated is more <properly> a coincident of the one subject or of the other.

It is immediately clear that a coincident may easily be distinctive of a subject at a particular time and in relation to a particular thing. Whenever, for instance, someone is the only one seated, being seated, which is a coincident, is distinctive at that time; and when he is not the only one seated, being seated is distinctive of him in relation to those not seated. Hence a coincident may easily turn out to be distinctive in relation to a particular thing and at a particular time, but it is not a distinctive property without qualification.

* * * * * * *

PHYSICS[1]

Book I

[*THE METHOD OF INQUIRY*]

1

In every line of inquiry into something that has principles or causes or elements, we achieve knowledge$_o$—that is, scientific knowledge$_e$—by knowing$_g$ them; for we think we know$_g$ a thing when we know its primary causes and primary principles, all the way to its elements. Clearly, then, it is also true in the science of nature that our first task is to determine the principles.

The natural path is to start from what is better known$_g$ and more perspicuous to us, and to advance to what is more perspicuous and better known by nature; for what is better known to us is not the same as what is better known without qualification. We must advance in this way, then, from what is less perspicuous by nature but more perspicuous to us, to what is more perspicuous and better known by nature.

The things that, most of all, are initially clear and perspicuous to us are inarticulate wholes; later, as we articulate them, the elements and principles come to be known$_g$ from them. We must, then, advance from universals to particulars;[2] for the whole is better known in perception, and the universal is a sort of whole, since it includes many things as parts. The same is true, in a way, of names in relation to their accounts. For a name—for instance, 'circle'—signifies a sort of whole and signifies indefinitely, whereas the definition <of a circle> articulates it by stating the particular <properties>. Again, children begin by calling all men 'father' and all women 'mother'; only later do they distinguish different men and different women.

1. The treatise on NATURE.

2. **from universals to particulars**: This is how we clarify very general principles that we do not fully understand at the start. Contrast *APo* 72a4 (which describes INDUCTION).

* * * * * * *

[*THE GENERAL PRINCIPLES OF COMING TO BE*]

7

Let us, then, give our own account of coming to be, in the following way. And first let us deal with all of coming to be; for the natural procedure is to speak first about what is common to every case, and then to study what is special to each case.

When we say that something comes to be one thing from being another and different thing, we are speaking about either simple or compound things. What I mean is this: It is possible that a man comes to be musical, that the not-musical thing comes to be musical, and that the not-musical man comes to be a musical man. By 'simple thing coming to be <F>' I mean the man and the not-musical thing; and by 'simple thing that comes into being'[3] I mean the musical thing. By 'compound' I mean both the thing that comes into being and what comes to be that thing, whenever we say that the not-musical man comes to be a musical man.

In one type of case we say not only that something comes to be F, but also that it comes to be F *from* being G; for instance, <the man not only comes to be musical, but also comes to be> musical from being not-musical. But we do not say this for all <properties>; for <the man> did not come to be musical from being a man, but rather the man came to be musical.

When something comes to be F (in the sense in which we say a simple thing comes to be <something>), in some cases it remains when it comes to be F, and in other cases it does not remain. The man, for instance, remains a man and is still a man when he comes to be musical, whereas the not-musical or unmusical thing, either simple or compound, does not remain.

Now that we have made these distinctions, here is something we can grasp from every case of coming to be, if we look at them all in the way described. In every case there must be some subject that comes to be <something>; even if it is one in number, it is

3. **thing that comes into being'**: This refers to the product of the coming to be—in this case, to the musical thing that comes into being as a result of the man becoming musical.

not one in form, since being a man is not the same as being an unmusical thing. (By 'in form' I mean the same as 'in account'.) One thing <that comes to be> remains, and one does not remain. The thing that is not opposite remains, since the man remains; but the not-musical thing, or the unmusical thing, does not remain. Nor does the thing compounded from both (for instance, the unmusical man) remain.

We say that something comes to be F from being G, but not that the G comes to be F, more often in cases where G does not remain; for instance, we say that <a man> comes to be musical from being unmusical, but not that <the unmusical comes to be musical> from a man. Still, sometimes we speak in the same way in cases where G remains; we say, for instance, that a statue comes to be from bronze, but not that the bronze comes to be a statue. If, however, something comes to be F from being G, where G is opposite to F and G does not remain, we speak in both ways, saying both that something comes to be F from being G and that the G comes to be F; for it is true both that the man comes to be musical from being unmusical and that the unmusical one comes to be musical. That is why we also say the same about the compound: we say both that the musical man comes to be musical from being an unmusical man and that the unmusical man comes to be musical.

Things are said to come to be in many ways, and some things are said not to come to be, but to come to be something; only substances are said to come to be without qualification. In the other cases it is evident that there must be some subject that comes to be <something>; for in fact, when <something> comes to be of some quantity or quality, or relative to another, or somewhere, something is the subject <underlying the change>, because
190b a substance is the only thing that is never said of any other subject, whereas everything else is said of a substance.[4]

However, substances—the things that are without qualification—also come to be from some subject. This will become evident if we examine it. For in every case there is something that is a

4. **said of a substance**: In *Catg.* 1a21 'said of a subject' is confined to the predication of essential properties. Here it also includes nonessential properties (and so includes the cases where the *Catg.* speaks of 'being in a subject').

subject from which the thing that comes to be comes to be, as plants and animals come to be from seed.

Some of the things that come to be without qualification do so by change of figure (for instance, a statue); some by addition (for instance, growing things); some by subtraction (for instance, Hermes from the stone); some by composition (for instance, a house); some by alteration (for instance, things changing in accordance with their matter). It is evident that everything that comes to be in this way comes to be from a subject.

And so it is clear from what has been said that, in every case, what comes to be is composite: there is something that comes into being and something that comes to be this. And this latter thing is of two sorts: either the subject or the opposite. I mean, for instance, that the unmusical is opposite, and the man is subject; and that the lack of figure, shape, and order is the opposite, and the bronze, stone, or gold is the subject.

Suppose, then, that there are indeed causes and principles of natural things, from which they primarily are and have come to be—not come to be coincidentally, but come to be what each thing is called in accordance with its essence$_0$. It evidently follows that everything comes to be from the subject and the shape. For in a way the musical man is composed from man and musical, since you will analyze him into their accounts. It is clear, then, that whatever comes to be does so from these things.

The subject is one in number but two in form. Man, gold, and matter in general is countable, since it is a this more <than the privation is>, and what comes to be comes to be from it not coincidentally. The privation—the contrariety—is a coincident. The form is one—for instance, structure, musicality, or anything else predicated in this way.

Hence we should say that in one way there are two principles, and that in another way there are three. In one way they are contraries—if, for instance, one were to speak of the musical and the unmusical, or the hot and the cold, or the ordered and the disordered. But in another way they are not contraries, since contraries cannot be affected by each other. This <puzzle about how becoming is possible> is also solved by the fact that the subject is something different, since it is not a contrary.

Hence, in a way the principles are no more numerous than the contraries, but, one might say, they are two in number. On the other hand, because they differ in being, they are not 191a two in every way, but three; for being man is different from being unmusical, and being shapeless is different from being bronze.

We have said, then, how many principles are relevant to the coming to be of natural things, and we have described the different ways they should be counted. And it is clear that some subject must underlie the contraries, and that there must be two contraries. In another way, however, there need not be two; for just one of the contraries is enough, by its absence or presence, to produce the thing.

The nature that is subject is knowable$_e$ by analogy. For as bronze is to a statue, or wood is to a bed, or as the shapeless before it acquires a shape is to anything else that has a shape, so the nature that is subject is to a substance, a this, and a being.

This, then, is one principle; it is not one or a being in the way a this is. Another principle is the one specified by the account, and a third is the contrary of this, the privation. The way in which these are two, and the way in which they are more than two, has been stated above.

First, then, it was said that only the contraries were principles. Later we added that something further is needed as subject and that there must be three principles. And from what we have said now it is evident how the contraries differ, how the principles are related to one another, and what the subject is. It is not yet clear, however, whether the form or the subject is substance. Still, it is clear that there are three principles, and in what way there are three, and what sorts of things they are. This, then, should allow us to observe how many principles there are, and what they are.

8

This is also the only solution to the puzzle raised by the earlier philosophers, as we shall now explain. Those who were the first to search for the truth philosophically and for the nature of beings were diverted and, so to speak, pushed off the track by inexperience. They say that nothing that is either comes to be or perishes. For, they say, what comes to be must come to be either from what is or from what is not, and coming to be is impossible in both cases; for what is cannot come to be (since it already is), while nothing can come to be from what is not (since there must be some subject). And then, having reached this result, they make things worse by going on to say that there is no plurality, but only being itself.

They accepted this belief for the reason mentioned. We reply as follows: The claim that something comes to be from what is or from what is not, or that what is or what is not acts on something or is acted on or comes to be anything whatever, is in one way no different from the claim that, for instance, a doctor acts on 191b something or is acted on, or is or comes to be something from being a doctor. We say this about a doctor in two ways; and so, clearly, we also speak in two ways when we say that something is or comes to be something from what is, and that what is is acting on something or being acted on.

Now a doctor builds a house, not insofar as he is a doctor, but insofar as he is a housebuilder; and he becomes pale, not insofar as he is a doctor, but insofar as he is dark. But he practices medicine, or loses his medical knowledge, insofar as he is a doctor. We speak in the fullest sense of a doctor acting on something or being acted on, or coming to be something, from being a doctor, if it is insofar as he is a doctor that he is acted on in this way or produces these things or comes to be these things. So it is also clear that coming to be from what is not signifies this: coming to be from it insofar as it is not.

The early philosophers failed to draw this distinction and gave up the question. This ignorance led them into more serious ignorance—so serious that they thought nothing else <besides what already is> either is or comes to be, and so they did away with all coming to be.

We agree with them in saying that nothing comes to be without qualification from what is not, but we say that things come to be in a way—for instance, coincidentally—from what is not. For something comes to be from the privation, which in itself is not and which does not belong to the thing <when it has come to be>. But this causes surprise, and it seems impossible that something should come to be in this way from what is not.

Similarly, there is no coming to be, except coincidentally, from what is, or of what is. But coincidentally what is also comes to be, in the same way as if animal came to be from animal and a certain animal from a certain animal. Suppose, for instance, that a dog came to be from a horse.[5] For the dog would come to be not only from a certain animal, but also from animal, though not insofar as it is animal (for that is already present). But if a certain <sort of> animal is to come to be, not coincidentally, it will not be from animal; and if a certain thing that is <is to come to be>, it will not be from what is, nor from what is not. For we have said what 'from what is not' signifies—i.e., insofar as it is not. Further, we are not doing away with <the principle that> everything is or is not.[6]

This is one way <of solving this puzzle>. Another is <to note> that the same things can be spoken of in accordance with potentiality and actuality; this is discussed more exactly elsewhere.

And so, as we have said, we have solved the puzzles that compelled people to do away with some of the things we have mentioned. For this is why earlier thinkers were also diverted from the road leading them to <an understanding of> coming to be, perishing, and change in general. For if they had seen this nature <of the subject>, that would have cured all their ignorance.

* * * * * * *

Book II

[*NATURE AS MATTER AND AS FORM*]

1

192b8 Some existing things are natural, while others are due to other causes. Those that are natural are animals and their parts, plants, and the simple bodies, such as earth, fire, air and water;

5. **Suppose . . . from a horse**: Aristotle appears to be considering an imaginary case of a horse turning into a dog. The horse is the subject of the coming to be, not because it is a horse or an animal, but because (we imagine) it provides matter suitable for the coming to be of a dog.

6. **Further . . . is not**: The statue, e.g., comes to be from the bronze, which is (i.e., exists), but also is not (is not statue-shaped, when it still has the privation), and comes to be coincidentally from the privation (since the bronze is coincidentally shapeless before it is shaped).

for we say that these things and things of this sort are natural. All these things evidently differ from those that are not naturally constituted, since each of them has within itself a principle of motion and stability in place, in growth and decay, or in alteration.

In contrast to these, a bed, a cloak, or any other <artifact>—insofar as it is described as such, <i.e., as a bed, a cloak, or whatever>, and to the extent that it is a product of a craft—has no innate impulse to change; but insofar as it is coincidentally made of stone or earth or a mixture of these, it has an innate impulse to change, and just to that extent. This is because a nature is a type of principle and cause of motion and stability within those things to which it primarily belongs in their own right and not coincidentally. (By 'not coincidentally' I mean, for instance, the following: Someone who is a doctor might cause himself to be healthy, but it is not insofar as he is being healed that he has the medical science; on the contrary, it is coincidental that the same person is a doctor and is being healed, and that is why the two characteristics are sometimes separated from each other.)[1]

The same is true of everything else that is produced, since no such thing has within itself the principle of its own production. In some things (for instance, a house or any other product of handicraft) the principle comes from outside, and it is within other things. In other things (those that might turn out to be coincidental causes for themselves) the principle is within them, but not in their own right.

A nature, then, is what we have said; and the things that have a nature are those that have this sort of principle. All these things are substances; for <a substance> is a sort of subject, and a nature is invariably in a subject. The things that are in accordance with nature include both these and whatever belongs to them in their own right, as travelling upward belongs to fire—for this neither is nor has a nature, but is natural and in accordance with nature. We have said, then, what nature is, and what is natural and in accordance with nature.

To attempt to prove that there is such a thing as nature would

1. **(By 'not coincidentally' . . . from each other.)**: If there were some explanatory connection between S's needing to be cured and S's being a doctor (as there is, e.g., between a plant's need for water and its having roots), then being a doctor would be noncoincidentally connected with S's needing to be cured.

be ridiculous; for it is evident that there are many things of the sort we have described. To prove what is evident from what is not evident betrays an inability to discriminate what is known[g] because of itself from what is not. (It is clearly possible to suffer from this inability: someone blind from birth might still make deductions about colors.) And so such people are bound to argue about <mere> names and to understand nothing.

Some people think that the nature and substance of a natural thing is the primary constituent present in it, having no order in its own right, so that the nature of a bed, for instance, <would be> the wood, and the nature of a statue <would be> the bronze. A sign of this, according to Antiphon, is the fact that, if you were to bury a bed and the rotting residue were to become able to sprout, the result would be wood, not a bed. He thinks that this is because the conventional arrangement, i.e., the craft <making the wood into a bed>, is a <mere> coincident of the wood, whereas the substance is what remains continuously while it is affected in these ways. And if each of these things is related to something else in the same way (bronze and gold, for instance, to water; bones and wood to earth; and so on with anything else), that thing is their nature and substance.[2]

This is why some people say that fire or earth or air or water is the nature of the things that exist; some say it is some of these, others say it is all of them. For whenever any of these people supposed one, or more than one, of these things to be <the primary constituent>, he takes this or these to be all the substance there is, and he takes everything else to be attributes, states, and conditions of these things; and each of these is held to be everlasting, since they do not change from themselves, but the other things come to be and are destroyed an unlimited number of times.

This, then, is one way we speak of a nature: as the primary matter that is a subject for each thing that has within itself a principle of motion and change.

In another way the nature is the shape, i.e., the form in accordance with the account. For just as we speak of craftsmanship in what is in accordance with craft and is crafted, so also we speak of nature in what is in accordance with nature and is natural. But if something were only potentially a bed and still lacked the form

2. **substance**: Aristotle might be thinking of substance as basic subject, or of substance as essence, or (most probably) of both.

of a bed, we would not yet speak of craftsmanship or of a product in accordance with craft; nor would we say the corresponding thing about anything that is constituted naturally. For what is only potentially flesh or bone does not have its nature, and is not naturally flesh or bone, until it acquires the form in accordance with the account by which we define flesh or bone and say what it is. In another way, then, the nature is the shape and form of things that have within themselves a principle of motion; this form is not separable except in account. (What is composed of form and matter—for instance, a man—is not a nature, but is natural.)

Indeed, the form is the nature more than the matter is. For something is called <flesh, bone, and so on> when it is actually so, more than when it is only potentially so. Further, a man comes to be from a man, but not a bed from a bed. In fact that is why some say that the nature of the bed is not the shape but the wood, because if it were to sprout the result would be wood, not a bed. If this shows that the wood is the nature, then the shape is also the nature, since a man comes to be from a man. Further, nature, as applied to coming to be, is really a road toward nature; it is not like medical treatment, which is a road not toward medical science, but toward health. For medical treatment necessarily proceeds *from* medical science, not *toward* medical science. But nature <as coming to be> is not related to nature in this way; rather, what is growing, insofar as it is growing, proceeds from something toward something <else>. What is it, then, that grows? Not what it is growing from, but what it is growing into.[3] Therefore, the shape is the nature.

Shape and nature are spoken of in two ways; for the privation is also form in a way. We must consider later whether or not there is a privation and a contrary in unqualified coming to be.

2

Since we have distinguished the different ways we speak of nature, we should next consider how the mathematician differs from the student of nature; for natural bodies certainly have sur-

3. **What is it . . . growing into**: The process of growth is described with reference to the goal rather than to the beginning. We say 'the tree (= the goal) is growing', when the sapling is getting bigger.

faces, solids, lengths, and points, which are what the mathematician studies. We should also consider whether astronomy is different from or a part of the study of nature; for it would be absurd if a student of nature ought to know what the sun or moon is but need not know any of their coincidents in their own right—especially since it is evident that students of nature also discuss the shape of the sun and moon, and specifically whether or not the earth and the world are spherical.

These things are certainly the concern of both the mathematician and the student of nature. But the mathematician is not concerned with them insofar as each is the limit of a natural body, and he does not study the coincidents of a natural body insofar as they belong to a natural body. That is why he also separates these coincidents; for they are separable in thought from motion, and his separating them makes no difference and results in no falsehood.

Those who say there are Ideas do not notice that they do this too; for they separate natural objects, though these are less separable than mathematical objects. This would be clear if one tried to state the formulae of both natural and mathematical objects—of the things themselves and of their coincidents. For odd and even, straight and curved, and also number, line, and point do not involve motion, whereas flesh, bones, and man do—we speak of them as we speak of the snub nose, not as we speak of the curved.

This is also clear from the parts of mathematics that are more related to the study of nature—for instance, optics, harmonics, and astronomy. These are in a way the reverse of geometry; for geometry investigates natural lines, but not insofar as they are natural, whereas optics investigates mathematical lines, but insofar as they are natural, not insofar as they are mathematical.

Since we speak of nature in two ways—both as form and as matter—we should study it as though we were investigating what snubness is, and so we should study natural objects neither independently of their matter nor <simply> insofar as they have matter. For indeed, since there are these two types of nature, there might be a puzzle about which one the student of nature should study. Perhaps the compound of the two? If so, then also each of them. Then is it the same or a different discipline that knows$_g$ each one of them?

If we judge by the early thinkers, the student of nature would seem to study <only> matter, since Empedocles and Democritus touched only slightly on form and essence. Craft, however, imitates nature, and the same science knows$_o$ both the form and the matter up to a point. The doctor, for instance, knows health, and also the bile and phlegm in which health <is realized>; similarly, the housebuilder knows both the form of the house and that its matter is bricks and wood; and the same is true in the other cases. The science of nature, therefore, must also know$_g$ both types of nature.

Moreover the same discipline studies both what something is for—i.e., the end—and whatever is for the end. Nature is an end and what something is for; for whenever a continuous motion has some end this sort of terminus is also what the motion is for. That is why it was ludicrous for the poet to say 'He has reached the end he was born for'; it was ludicrous because by 'end' we mean not every terminus but only the best one.

For crafts produce their matter (some by producing it without qualification, others by making it suitable for their work); and we use all <matter> as being for our sake, since we are also an end in a way. (For what something is for is of two sorts,[4] as we said in *On Philosophy*.)

There are two crafts that control the matter and involve knowledge$_g$: the craft that uses <the matter> and the craft that directs this productive craft. Hence the using craft also directs in a way, but with the difference that the directing craft knows the form, whereas the productive craft knows the matter. For instance, the pilot knows what sort of form the rudder has, and he prescribes <how to produce it>, whereas the boatbuilder knows what sort of wood and what sorts of motions are needed to make it. With products of a craft, then, we produce the matter for the sake of the product; with natural things, the matter is already present.

Further, matter is relative; for there is one <sort of> matter for one form, and another for another.

How much, then, must the student of nature know$_o$ about form and what-it-is? Perhaps as much as the doctor knows about sinews, or the smith about bronze—enough to know what something is for. And he must confine himself to things that are separable in form but are in matter—for a man is born from a man and the sun. But it is a task for first philosophy to determine what is separable and what the separable is like.

4. **two sorts**: See *DA* 415b2. *On Philosophy* is a work of Aristotle's that survives only in fragments.

[*CAUSE AND CHANCE*]

3

Now that we have determined these points, we should consider how many and what sorts of causes there are. For our inquiry aims at knowledge$_{o}$; and we think we know something only when we find the reason why it is so, i.e., when we find its primary cause. Clearly, then, we must also find the reason why in the case of coming to be, perishing, and every sort of natural change, so that when we know their principles we can try to refer whatever we are searching for to these principles.

In one way, then, that from which, as a <constituent> present in it, a thing comes to be is said to be that thing's cause—for instance, the bronze and silver, and their genera, are causes of the statue and the bowl.

In another way, the form—i.e., the pattern—is a cause. The form is the account (and the genera of the account) of the essence (for instance, the cause of an octave is the ratio[5] two to one, and in general number), and the parts that are in the account.

Further, the source of the primary principle of change or stability is a cause. For instance, the adviser is a cause <of the action>, and a father is a cause of his child; and in general the producer is a cause of the product, and the initiator of the change is a cause of what is changed.

Further, something's end—i.e., what it is for—is its cause, as health is of walking. For why does he walk? We say, 'To be healthy'; and in saying this we think we have provided the cause. The same is true of all the intermediate steps that are for the end, where something else has initiated the motion, as, for example, slimming, purging, drugs, or instruments are for health; all of these are for the end, though they differ in that some are activities, while others are instruments.

We may take these, then, to be the ways we speak of causes.

Since causes are spoken of in many ways, there are many noncoincidental causes of the same thing. Both the sculpting craft and the bronze, for instance, are causes of the statue, not insofar as it is something else, but insofar as it is a statue. But they are not causes in the same way: the bronze is a cause as matter, the sculpting craft as the source of the motion. Some things are causes

5. **account . . . ratio**: Both terms render *logos*. See REASON.

of each other: hard work, for instance, is the cause of fitness, and fitness of hard work. But they are not causes in the same way: fitness is what the hard work is for, whereas hard work is the principle of motion. Further, the same thing is the cause of contraries; for sometimes if a thing's presence causes F, that thing is also, by its absence, taken to cause the contrary of F, so that, for instance, if a pilot's presence would have caused the safety of a ship, we take his absence to have caused the shipwreck.

All the causes just mentioned are of four especially evident types: (1) Letters are the cause of syllables, matter of artifacts, fire and such things of bodies, parts of the whole, and the assumptions of the conclusion, as that out of which. In each of these cases one thing—for instance, the parts—is cause as subject, while (2) the other thing—the whole, the composition, and the form—is cause as essence. (3) The seed, the doctor, the adviser and, in general, the producer, are all sources of the principle of change or stability. (4) In other cases, one thing is a cause of other things by being the end and the good. For what the other things are for is taken to be the best and their end—it does not matter <for present purposes> whether we call it the good or the apparent good.[6] These, then, are the number of kinds of causes there are.

Although there are many types of causes, they are fewer when they are arranged under heads. For causes are spoken of in many ways, and even among causes of the same type, some are prior and others posterior. For example, the cause of health is a doctor and <speaking more generally> a craftsman, and the cause of an octave is the double and <speaking more generally> number; in every case the inclusive causes are posterior to the particular.

Further, some things and their genera are coincidental causes. Polycleitus and the sculptor, for instance, are causes of the statue in different ways, because being Polycleitus is coincidental to the sculptor. What includes the coincident is also a cause—if, for example, the man or, quite generally, the animal is a cause of the statue. Some coincidental causes are more remote or more 195b
proximate than others; if, for instance, the pale man or the musician were said to be the cause of the statue <it would be a more remote cause than Polycleitus is>.

We may speak of any <moving> cause, whether proper or

6. **the good or the apparent good**: For the difference see *DA* 433a28, *EN* 1113a22–4.

coincidental, either as having a potentiality or as actualizing it; for instance, we may say either that the housebuilder, or that the housebuilder actually building, is causing the house to be built.

Similar things may also be said about the things of which the causes are causes. For example, we may speak of the cause of this statue, or of a statue, or of an image in general; or of this bronze, or of bronze, or of matter in general. The same is true of coincidents. We may speak in this same way of combinations—of Polycleitus the sculptor, for instance, instead of Polycleitus or a sculptor.

Still, all these ways amount to six, each spoken of in two ways. For there is (1) the particular and (2) the genus, and (3) the coincident and (4) the genus of the coincident; and these may be spoken of either (5) in combination or (6) simply. Each of these may be either active or potential. The difference is the following. Active and particular causes exist and cease to exist simultaneously with the things they cause, so that, for instance, this one practising medicine exists simultaneously with this one being made healthy, and in the same way this one housebuilding exists simultaneously with this thing being built into a house. But this is not true of every cause that is potential; for the house and the housebuilder do not perish simultaneously.

Here as elsewhere, we must always seek the most precise cause. A man, for example, is building because he is a builder, and he is a builder insofar as he has the building craft; his building craft, then, is the prior cause, and the same is true in all cases. Further, we must seek genera as causes of genera, and particulars as causes of particulars; a sculptor, for instance, is the cause of a statue, but this sculptor of this statue. And we must seek a potentiality as the cause of a potential effect, and something actualizing a potentiality as the cause of an actual effect.

This, then, is an adequate determination of the number of causes, and of the ways in which they are causes.

4

Luck and chance are also said to be causes, and many things are said to be and to come to be because of them. We must, then, investigate how luck and chance are included in the causes we have mentioned, whether luck is or is not the same as chance, and, in general, what they are.

Some people even wonder whether luck and chance exist. For 196a they say that nothing results from luck; rather, everything that is said to result from chance or luck has some definite cause. If, for instance, as a result of luck someone comes to the marketplace and finds the person he wanted to meet but did not expect,[7] they say the cause is his wanting to go to market. Similarly, for every other supposed result of luck, they say it is possible to find some cause other than luck. For if there were such a thing as luck, it would appear truly strange and puzzling that none of the early philosophers who discussed the causes of coming to be and perishing ever determined anything about luck; in fact it would seem that they also thought that nothing results from luck. But this too is surprising; for surely many things come to be and exist as a result of luck and chance. Though people know perfectly well that everything that comes to be can be referred to some cause, as the old argument doing away with luck says, everyone nonetheless says that some of these things result from luck and that others do not.

That is why the early philosophers should have mentioned luck in some way or other. But they certainly did not think luck was among the causes they recognized—for instance, love or strife or mind or fire or anything else of that sort. In either case, then, it is strange, whether they supposed there was no such thing as luck, or supposed there was such a thing but omitted to discuss it. It is especially strange considering that they sometimes appeal to luck. Empedocles, for example, appeals to luck when he says that air is separated out on top, not always but as luck has it; at least, he says in his cosmogony that 'it happened to run that way at that time, but often otherwise'. And he says that most of the parts of animals result from luck.

Other people make chance the cause of our heaven and of all worlds. For they say that the vortex, and the motion that dispersed and established everything in its present order, resulted from chance. And this is certainly quite amazing. For animals and plants, they say, neither are nor come to be from luck, but rather nature or mind or something of that sort is the cause, since it is not just any old thing that comes to be from a given type of seed, but an olive-tree comes from one type, and a man from another; and yet they

7. **as a result of luck . . . did not expect**: The lucky thing is the conjunction of the two events (the creditor's being there and the debtor's being there).

say that the heaven and the most divine of visible things result from chance and have no cause of the sort that animals and plants have.

If this is so, it deserves attention, and something might well have been said about it. For in addition to the other strange aspects of what they say, it is even stranger to say all this when they see that nothing in the heaven results from chance, whereas many things happen as a result of luck to things whose existence is not itself a result of luck. Surely the contrary would have been likely.

Other people suppose that luck is a cause, but they take it to be divine and superhuman, and therefore obscure to the human mind.

And so we must consider chance and luck, and determine what each is, and whether they are the same or different, and see how they fit into the causes we have distinguished.

5

First, then, we see that some things always, others usually, come about in the same way. Evidently luck and the result of luck are not said to be the cause of either of these things—either of what is of necessity and always or of what is usually. But since apart from these there is a third sort of event which everyone says results from luck, it is evident that there is such a thing as luck and chance; for we know that this third sort of event results from luck and that the results of luck are of this sort.

Further, some events are for something and others are not. Among the former, some are in accordance with a decision while others are not, but both sorts are for something. And so it is clear that even among events that are neither necessary nor usual there are some that admit of being for something. (Events that are for something include both the actions that result from thought and also the results of nature.) This, then, is the sort of event that we regard as a result of luck, whenever an event of that sort comes about coincidentally.[8] For just as some things are something in their own right, and others are something coincidentally, so also it is possible for a cause to be of either sort. For example, the

8. **This, then . . . coincidentally**: An event type (e.g., meeting in the marketplace, which has many tokens) has a final cause when it is characteristically and USUALLY true that its tokens (e.g., these people meeting in the marketplace on this occasion) have a final cause. Lucky events are those tokens that lack the final cause that is characteristic of the type.

cause of a house is, in its own right, the housebuilder, but coincidentally the pale or musical thing. Hence the cause in its own right is determinate, but the coincidental cause is indeterminate, since one thing might have an unlimited number of coincidents.

As has been said, then, whenever this <coincidental causation> occurs among events of the sort that are for something the events <that have these coincidental causes> are said to result from chance and luck. The difference between chance and luck will be determined later; we may take it as evident for the moment that both are found among events of the sort that are for something.

For instance, A would have come when B was collecting subscriptions, in order to recover the debt from B, if A had known <B would be there>.[9] In fact, however, A did not come in order to do this; it was a coincidence that A came <when B happened to be there>, and so met B in order to collect the debt—given that A neither usually nor of necessity frequents the place <for 197a
that purpose>. The end—collecting the debt—is not a cause <of A's action> in A, but it is the sort of thing that one decides to do and that results from thought. And in this case A's coming is said to result from luck; but if A always or usually frequented the place because he had decided to and for the purpose of collecting the debt, then <A's being there when B was there> would not result from luck.

Clearly, then, luck is a coincidental cause found among events of the sort that are for something, and specifically among those of the sort that are in accordance with a decision. Hence thought (since decision requires thought) and luck concern the same things.

Now the causes whose results might be matters of luck are bound to be indeterminate. That is why luck also seems to be something indeterminate and obscure to human beings, and why, in one way, it might seem that nothing results from luck. For, as we might reasonably expect, all these claims are correct. For in one way things do result from luck, since they are coincidental results and luck is a coincidental cause. But luck is not the unqualified <and hence non-coincidental> cause of anything. The

9. **For instance . . . would be there>**: A wants to collect a debt from B; one day A comes to the marketplace for some other reason (e.g., wanting to sell his olives) and meets B who happens to be there at the same time collecting dues for a club of which B is the treasurer.

<unqualified> cause of a house, for instance, is a housebuilder, and the coincidental cause a flute-player; and the man's coming and collecting the debt, without having come to collect it, has an indefinite number of coincidental causes—he might have come because he wished to see someone, or was going to court or to the theater.

It is also correct to say that luck is contrary to reason. For rational judgment tells us what is always or usually the case, whereas luck is found in events that happen neither always nor usually. And so, since causes of this sort are indeterminate, luck is also indeterminate.

Still, in some cases one might be puzzled about whether just any old thing might be a cause of a lucky outcome. Surely the wind or the sun's warmth, but not someone's haircut, might be the cause of his health; for some coincidental causes are closer than others to what they cause.

Luck is called good when something good results, bad when something bad results; it is called good and bad fortune when the results are large. That is why someone who just misses great evil or good as well <as someone who has it> is fortunate or unfortunate; for we think of him as already having <the great evil or good>, since the near miss seems to us to be no distance. Further, it is reasonable that good fortune is unstable; for luck is unstable, since no result of luck can be either always or usually the case.

As we have said, then, both luck and chance are coincidental causes, found in events of the sort that are neither without exception nor usual, and specifically in events of this sort that might be for something.

6

Chance is not the same as luck, since it extends more widely; for results of luck also result from chance, but not all results of chance result from luck. For luck and its results are found in things that are capable of being fortunate and in general capable of action, and that is why luck must concern what is achievable by action. A sign of this is the fact that good fortune seems to be the same or nearly the same as being happy, and being happy is a sort of action, since it is doing well in action. Hence what cannot act cannot do anything by luck either. Hence neither inanimate things nor beasts nor children do anything by luck, because they are incapable of decision. Nor do they have good or bad fortune, except by a <mere> similarity—as Protarchus said that the stones from which altars are made are fortunate, because they are honored, while their fellows are trodden underfoot. Still, even these things are affected by the results of luck in a way, whenever an agent affects them by some lucky action; but otherwise they are not.

Chance, on the other hand, applies both to animals other than man and to many inanimate things. We say, for instance, that the horse came by chance, since it was saved because it came but did not come in order to be saved. And the tripod fell by chance, because it did not fall in order to be sat on, although it was left standing in order to be sat on.

Hence it is evident that among types of events that are for something (speaking without qualification), we say that a particular event of such a type results from chance if it has an external cause and the actual result is not what it is for: and we say that it results from luck if it results from chance and is an event of the sort that is decided on by an agent who is capable of decision. A sign of this is the fact that we say an event is pointless if it <is of the sort that> is for some result but <in this case> that result is not what it is for. If, for instance, walking is for evacuating the bowels, but when he walked on this occasion it was not <for that reason>, then we say that he walked pointlessly and that his walking is pointless. We assume that an event is pointless if it is naturally for something else, but does not succeed in <being for> what it is naturally for. For if someone said that his washing himself was pointless because the sun was not eclipsed, he would be ridiculous, since washing is not for producing eclipses. So also, then, an event happens by chance (as the name suggests) whenever it is pointless.[10] For the stone did not fall in order to hit someone; it fell by chance, because it might have fallen because someone threw it to hit someone.

The separation of chance from luck is sharpest in natural events. For if an event is contrary to nature, we regard it as a result of chance, not of luck. But even this is different from <other cases

10. **by chance,** *automaton* . . . **pointless,** *matēn.* Aristotle appeals to supposed etymology.

of chance; the other cases> have an external cause, but <events contrary to nature> have an internal cause.

We have said, then, what chance and luck are and how they differ. Each of them falls under the sort of cause that is the source of the principle of motion. For in every case they are either among natural causes or among those resulting from thought, and the number of these is indeterminate.

Chance and luck are causes of events <of the sort> that mind or nature might have caused, in cases where <particular> events <of this sort> have some coincidental cause. Now nothing coincidental is prior to anything that is in its own right; hence clearly no coincidental cause is prior to something that is a cause in its own right. Chance and luck are therefore posterior to mind and nature. And so however true it might be that chance is the cause of the heavens, still it is necessary for mind and nature to be prior causes of this universe and of many other things.

7

It is clear, then, that there are causes, and that there are as many different types as we say there are; for the reason why something is so includes all these different types <of causes>. For we refer the ultimate reason why (1) in the case of unmoved things, to the what-it-is (for instance, in mathematics; for there we refer ultimately to the definition of straight or commensurate or something else), or (2) to what first initiated the motion (for instance, why did they go to war?—because the other side raided them), or (3) to what it is for (for instance, in order to set themselves up as rulers), or (4) in the case of things that come to be, to the matter.

It is evident, then, that these are the causes and that this is their number. Since there are four of them, the student of nature ought to know$_o$ them all; and in order to give the sort of reason that is appropriate for the study of nature, he must trace it back to all the causes—to the matter, the form, what initiated the motion, and what something is for. The last three often amount to one; for what something is and what it is for are one, and the first source of the motion is the same in species as these, since a man generates a man; and the same is true generally of things that initiate motion by being in motion.

Things that initiate motion without being in motion are outside the scope of the study of nature. For although they initiate motion, they do not do so by having motion or a principle of motion within themselves, but they are unmoved. Hence there are three inquiries: one about what is unmoved, one about what is in motion but imperishable, and one about what is perishable.

And so the reason why is given by referring to the matter, to the what-it-is, and to what first initiated the motion. For in cases of coming to be, this is the normal way of examining the causes—by asking what comes to be after what, and what first acted or was acted on, and so on in order in every case.

Two sorts of principles initiate motion naturally. One of these principles is not itself natural, since it has no principle of motion within itself; this is true of whatever initiates motion without itself being in motion—for instance, what is entirely without motion (i.e., the first of all beings) and also the what-it-is (i.e., the form), since this is the end and what something is for. And so, since natural processes are for something, this cause too must be known$_{o}$.

The reason why should be stated in all these ways. For instance, (1) this necessarily results from that (either without exception or usually); (2) if this is to be (as the conclusion from the premisses); (3) that this is the essence; and (4) because it is better thus—not unqualifiedly better, but better in relation to the essence$_{o}$ of a given thing.

[*FINAL CAUSES AND NECESSITY IN NATURE*]

8

We must first say why nature is among the causes that are for something, and then how necessity applies to natural things. For everyone refers things to necessity, saying that since the hot, the cold, and each element have a certain nature, certain other things are and come to be of necessity. For if they mention any cause other than necessity (as one thinker mentions love or strife, and another mentions mind), they just touch on it, then let it go.

A puzzle now arises: why not suppose that nature acts not for something or because it is better, but of necessity? Zeus's rain does not fall in order to make the grain grow, but of necessity. For it is necessary that what has been drawn up is cooled, and that what has been cooled and become water comes down, and it is coincidental that this makes the grain grow. Similarly, if someone's grain is spoiled on the threshing floor, it does not rain in order to spoil the grain, and the spoilage is coincidental.

Why not suppose, then, that the same is true of the parts of natural organisms? On this view, it is of necessity that, for example, the front teeth grow sharp and well adapted for biting, and the back ones broad and useful for chewing food; this <useful> result was coincidental, not what they were for. The same will be true of all the other parts that seem to be for something. On this view, then, whenever all the parts came about coincidentally as though they were for something, these animals survived, since their constitution, though coming about by chance, made them suitable <for survival>. Other animals, however, were differently constituted and so were destroyed; indeed they are still being destroyed, as Empedocles says of the man-headed calves.

This argument, then, and others like it, might puzzle someone. In fact, however, it is impossible for things to be like this. For these <teeth and other parts> and all natural things come to be as they do either always or usually, whereas no result of luck or chance comes to be either always or usually. (For we do not regard frequent winter rain or a summer heat wave, but only summer rain or a winter heat wave, as a result of luck or coincidence.) If, then, these[11] seem either to be coincidental results or to be for something, and they cannot be coincidental or chance results, they are for something. Now surely all such things are natural, as even those making these claims <about necessity> would agree. We find, then, among things that come to be and are by nature, things that are for something.

Further, whenever <some sequence of actions> has an end, the whole sequence of earlier and later actions is directed toward the end. Surely what is true of action is also true of nature, and what is true of nature is true of each action, if nothing prevents it. Now actions are for something; therefore, natural sequences are for something. For example, if a house came to be naturally, it would come to be just as it actually does by craft, and if natural things came to be not only naturally but also by craft, they would come to be just as they do naturally; one thing, then, is what the

11. **If, then, these**: 'These' might refer (a) to all natural things including, e.g., the winter rain mentioned in the previous sentence, or, more probably, (b) to the 'these' mentioned in 198b34, which were teeth and other parts of organisms.

other is for. In general, craft either completes the work that nature is unable to complete or imitates nature. If, then, the products of a craft are for something, clearly the products of nature are also for something; for there is the same relation of later stages to earlier in productions of a craft and in productions of nature.

This is most evident in the case of animals other than man, since they use neither craft nor inquiry nor deliberation in producing things—indeed this is why some people are puzzled about whether spiders, ants, and other such things operate by understanding or in some other way. If we advance little by little along the same lines, it is evident that even in plants things come to be that promote the end—leaves, for instance, grow for the protection of the fruit. If, then, a swallow makes its nest and a spider its web both naturally and for some end, and if plants grow leaves for the sake of the fruit, and send roots down rather than up for the sake of nourishment, it evidently follows that this sort of cause is among things that come to be and are by nature. And since nature is of two sorts, nature as matter and nature as form, and the form is the end, and since everything else is for the end, the form must be what things are for.

Errors occur even in productions of craft; grammarians, for instance, have written incorrectly, and doctors have given the wrong medicine. Clearly, then, errors are also possible in productions of nature. 199b

In some productions by crafts, the correct action is for something, and in cases of error the attempt is for something but misses the mark. The same will be true, then, of natural things; freaks will be errors, missing what they are for. Hence in the original formations of things, a defective principle would also have brought the <man-headed> calves into being, if they were unable to reach any definite term and end—just as, in the actual state of things, <freaks> come to be when the seed is defective. Further, it is necessary for the seed to come into being first, and not the animal straightaway; in fact the 'all-natured first' was seed.

Further, in plants as well as in animals things happen for something, though in a less articulate way. Then what about plants? Did olive-headed vines keep coming into being, as he says <man-headed> calves did? Surely not—that is absurd—but surely they would have to have come into being, if the animals did.

Further, <on Empedocles' view> coming to be would also have

to be merely a matter of chance among seeds. But whoever says this does away entirely with nature and natural things. For things are natural when they are moved continuously from some principle in themselves and so arrive at some end. From each principle comes, not the same thing in each case, but not just any old thing either; in every case it proceeds to the same <end>, if nothing prevents it.

Now certainly both the end that a process is for and the process that is for this end might also result from luck. We say, for instance, that a friend in a foreign country came by luck and paid the ransom and then went away, when he did the action as though he had come in order to do it, though in fact that was not what he came to do. This end is achieved coincidentally, since (as we said before) luck is one of the coincidental causes. But whenever the end results always or usually, it is neither coincidental nor a result of luck. And in natural things that is how it is in every case, unless something prevents it.

Besides, it is strange for people to think there is no end unless they see an agent initiating the motion by deliberation. Even crafts do not deliberate. Moreover, if the shipbuilding craft were in the wood, it would produce a ship in the same way that nature would. And so if what something is for is present in craft, it is also present in nature. This is clearest when a doctor applies medical treatment to himself—that is what nature is like.

It is evident, then, that nature is a cause, and in fact the sort of cause that is for something.

9

Is the necessity present <in nature only> conditional, or is it also unqualified?

The sort of necessity that is ascribed nowadays to things that come to be is the sort there would be if someone supposed that a wall came into being of necessity. On this view, heavy things naturally move downward, and light things upward, and that is why the stones and the foundations are below, while the earth is above because of its lightness, and the wooden logs are on the very top because they are lightest of all.

Nonetheless, though the wall certainly requires these things, it did not come to be because of them (except insofar as they are its material cause), but in order to give shelter and protection.

The same is true in all other cases that are for something: although they require things that have a necessary nature, they do not come to be because of these things (except insofar as they are the material cause), but for some end. For instance, why does a saw have such and such features? In order to perform this function, and for this end. But this end cannot come to be unless the saw is made of iron; and so it is necessary for it to be made of iron if there is to be a saw performing its function. What is necessary, then, is conditional, but not <necessary> as an end; for necessity is in the matter, whereas the end is in the form$_{l}$.

Necessity is found both in mathematics and in things that come to be naturally, and to some extent the two cases are similar. For instance, since the straight is what it is, it is necessary for a triangle to have angles equal to two right angles. It is not because the triangle has angles equal to two right angles that the straight is what it is; but if the triangle does not have angles equal to two right angles, the straight will not be what it is either.

The reverse is true in the case of things that come to be for an end: if the end is or will be, then the previous things are or will be too. Just as, in the mathematical case, if the conclusion <about the triangle> is false, the principle <about the straight> will not be true either, so also in nature if the <materials> do not exist, the end that the process is for will not come about either. For the end is also a principle; it is a principle not of the action, but of the reasoning. (In the mathematical case <also> the principle is the principle of the reasoning, since in this case there is no action.)

And so, if there is to be a house, it is necessary for these things to come to be or to be present; and in general, the matter that is for something must exist (for example, bricks and stones if there is to be a house). The end, however, does not exist because of these things, except insofar as they are the material cause, nor will it come about because of them; still, in general, the end (the house or the saw) requires them (the stones or the iron). Similarly, in the mathematical case the principles require the triangle to have two right angles.

Evidently, then, necessity in natural things belongs to the material cause and to the motions of matter. The student of nature should mention both causes, but more especially what something is for, since this is the cause of the matter, whereas the matter is not the cause of the end. The end is what something is for, and the principle comes from the definition and the form$_{l}$.

200b The same is true in productions of craft. For instance, since a house is this sort of thing, these things must come to be and be present of necessity; and since health is this, these things must come to be and be present of necessity. In the same way, if a man is this, these things must come to be and be present of necessity; and if these, then these.

But presumably necessity is present in the form$_{l}$ as well <as in the matter>. Suppose, for instance, that we define the function of sawing as a certain sort of cutting; this sort of cutting requires a saw with teeth of a certain sort, and these require a saw made of iron.[12] For the form$_{l}$, as well as the matter, has parts in it as matter of the form$_{l}$.

Book VI

* * * * * * *

[*ZENO'S PARADOXES*]

9

239b5 Zeno argues fallaciously. If, he says, in every case a thing is at rest when it occupies a space equal <to itself>, and in every case what is travelling is in the now, then it follows that the travelling arrow is not in motion. This is false; for time is not composed of indivisible nows,[1] any more than any other magnitude is.

Zeno has four arguments about motion, and they cause trouble to someone trying to solve them.

According to the first argument, nothing is in motion, because the travelling object must first reach the halfway mark before it reaches the end. We have examined this argument in our previous discussion.

12. **this sort of cutting requires . . . and these require . . . iron**: These two requirements express unqualified necessity (it is necessary, irrespective of any end, that only teeth of a certain kind will cut). See *PA* 642a31–b4.

1. **For time . . . indivisible nows**: Aristotle accepts (1) In any now the arrow travels no distance. But he rejects the inference to (2) In the smallest part of the time during which it is travelling, the arrow travels no distance. For he denies that the now is a part of time.

The second argument is the one called the Achilles. According to this, the slowest runner will never be caught, while it is running, by the fastest; for the pursuer must first reach the place where the leader has left, so that the slower must always be some distance ahead.

This argument is the same as the bisection, except that it differs insofar as it divides, instead of bisecting, whatever magnitude you care to take. The conclusion that the slower runner is not overtaken results from the argument by the same method as in the bisection. For in both arguments the result is failure to arrive at the end because the magnitude is divided in some way. But in the Achilles it is added that even the fastest runner (this is the dramatic element added) will not reach the end in its pursuit of the slowest.

And so the solution must be the same <as that of the bisection>. To claim that the leader is not overtaken is false. Certainly it is not overtaken while it is in the lead, but it is overtaken nonetheless, if you grant that it is possible to traverse a finite distance.

These, then, are the first two arguments. The third is the one we have mentioned, that the arrow is at rest while it travels. This conclusion results from supposing that time is composed of nows; for if this is not conceded, the deduction will not go through.

In the fourth argument, blocks of equal size are moving past each other in a stadium, from opposite ends, one lot beginning from the starting line of the stadium, the other lot from the far end, moving at equal speed. The conclusion, according to Zeno, is that half the time is equal to double the time.

The error in this argument is the assumption that equal magnitudes moving at equal speeds, one past a moving object, the other past a stationary object, travel by in an equal time. This assumption is false.

Suppose, for instance, that AA are the stationary equal blocks; that BB are the blocks, equal in number and size to AA, beginning from the middle; and that CC are the ones, equal in number and size to the preceding, and travelling at equal speed to BB, beginning from the end. The result, then, is that <as the Bs and Cs> move past each other, the first B reaches the last <C>, and the first C <reaches the last B>. But a further result is that the <first> C has passed all the Bs, while the <first> B has passed half <the As>; hence the time taken <by the first B> must be half <the time taken by the first C>, since each takes an equal <time>

to pass each block. Further, at this same time the first B will have passed all the Cs; for the first C and the first B will reach the opposite extremes of the stadium at the same time, because both take equal time to pass the As.

This, then, is the argument. The false move in it is the one we have mentioned.

* * * * * * *

Book VIII

* * * * * * *

[*MOTION AND THE UNMOVED MOVER*]

5

256a4 <Everything that is moved is moved by something.> This is true in two ways. For either (1) B initiates motion in A not because of B itself, but because of something else C that initiates motion in B, or (2) B initiates motion in A because of B itself. In the second case this is true either (2a) because B is the first thing immediately preceding A, or (2b) because B initiates the motion in A through a number of intermediaries. For instance, <in case (2b)> the stick initiates motion in the stone, and the stick is moved by the agency of the hand, which is moved by the agency of the man; he <is set in motion, but> not by being moved by the agency of some further thing. We say that both the last and the first mover[1] initiate motion, but the first mover does so to a higher degree. For the first mover initiates motion in the last mover, but the last does not initiate motion in the first. Moreover, without the first mover the last mover will not initiate motion, but the first will initiate it without the last; the stick, for instance, will not move <the stone> unless the man moves <the stick>.

1. **mover**: i.e., the initiator of motion. In this example the first mover is the man, and the last mover is the stick.

It is necessary, then, for whatever is moved to be moved by the agency of some mover, either by the agency of a mover that is in turn moved by the agency of something else moving it or by the agency of a mover that is not moved by the agency of something else moving it. And if it is moved by the agency of something else moving it, there must be some first mover that is not moved by the agency of something else; and if this is the character of the first mover, it is not necessary for there to be another mover. For it is impossible to have an infinite series of movers each of which initiates motion and is moved by the agency of something else; for there is no first term in an infinite series.

If, then, everything that is moved is moved by the agency of something, and if the first mover is moved, but not by the agency of something else, then it necessarily follows that it is moved by its own agency.

Moreover, it is also possible to carry out the same argument in the following way. Every mover moves something and moves it by means of something; for it moves something either by means of itself or by means of something else. The man, for instance, initiates motion either himself or by means of the stick; again, either the wind itself knocked the thing over, or the stone pushed by the wind knocked it over. But if C moves A by means of B, then B cannot move A unless there is something else that initiates motion by means of itself. But if C initiates motion by means of itself, there need not be anything else B by means of which C initiates motion. And if there is something else B by means of which C initiates motion, then there is something that initiates motion not by means of something <else>, but by means of itself—otherwise there will be an infinite regress.

If, then, something initiates motion by being moved, we must come to a stop, and not go on to infinity. For if the stick initiates motion by being moved by the hand, the hand moves the stick, and if something else initiates motion by means of the hand, then there is something else that moves the hand. And so, in each case when one thing moves another by means of something, there must be something prior that initiates motion in itself by means of itself. If, then, this is moved, but what moves it is not something else, it must initiate motion in itself.

And so this argument also shows that either what is moved

is moved immediately by what initiates motion in itself or eventually we come to a mover of this sort.

* * * * * * *

6

258b10 Since motion must be everlasting and must never fail, there must be some everlasting first mover, one or more than one. The question whether each of the unmoved movers[2] is everlasting is irrelevant to this argument; but it will be clear in the following way that there must be something that is itself unmoved and outside all change, either unqualified or coincidental, but initiates motion in something else.

Let us suppose, then, if you like, that in the case of some things it is possible for them to be at one time and not to be at another without any coming to be or perishing—for if something has no parts, but it is at one time and is not at another time, perhaps it is necessary for it to be at one time and not to be at another without changing. Let us also suppose that, among the principles that are unmoved but initiate motion, it is possible for some to be at one time and not to be at another time.

Still, this is not possible for every principle of that sort; for it is clear that there is something that causes the self-movers to be at one time and not to be at another time. For every self-mover necessarily has some magnitude, if nothing that lacks parts is moved; but from what we have said it is not necessary for every mover to have magnitude. Hence the cause explaining why some things come to be and other things perish, and in a continuous sequence, cannot be any of the things that are unmoved but do not always exist; nor can some things be the cause of some <parts of the sequence> and other things the cause of other <parts>; for neither any one of them nor all of them together is the cause explaining why the sequence is everlasting and continuous. For the sequence is everlasting and necessary, whereas all these movers are infinitely many and they do not all exist at the same time.

259a It is clear, then, that however many unmoved movers and self-

2. **unmoved movers**: i.e., SOULS.

movers perish and are succeeded by others, so that one unmoved mover moves one thing and another moves another, still there is something that embraces them all and is apart from each of them, which is the cause explaining why some exist and some do not exist, and why the change is continuous. This is the cause of motion in these <other movers>, and these are the cause of motion in the other things.

If, then, motion is everlasting, the first mover is also everlasting, if there is just one; and if there are more than one, there are more than one everlasting movers. But we must suppose there is one rather than many, and a finite rather than an infinite number. For in every case where the results <of either assumption> are the same, we should assume a finite number <of causes>; for among natural things what is finite and better must exist rather <than its opposite> if this is possible. And one mover is sufficient; it will be first and everlasting among the unmoved things, and the principle of motion for the other things.

* * * * * * *

[*FURTHER DISCUSSION OF ZENO ON BISECTION*]

8

If we divide a continuous length into two halves, we treat the 263a23
single point as two, since it makes a beginning <of one half> and an end <of the other>. And that is what we do by counting, as well as by dividing into halves. But if this is the way we divide, then neither a line nor a motion will be continuous; for a continuous motion is of something continuous, and in something continuous infinitely many halves are indeed present—but potentially present, not actually present. If we produce them in actuality, we do not produce a continuous motion but bring it to a halt. This evidently results in the case of counting the halves; for one necessarily counts just one point as two, since it will be the end of one 263b
half and the beginning of the other, if we count not the one continuous line, but the two halves.

And so, in reply to someone asking the question whether it is possible to traverse infinitely many things in time or in length, we say that in one way it is possible, and in another way it is not. For if the infinitely many things are in actuality, it is not possible to traverse them, but if they are in potentiality, it is possible. For someone in continuous motion has traversed infinitely many things coincidentally, but not without qualification; for the line is coincidentally infinitely many halves, but its essence$_o$ and being are different from this.

* * * * * * *

GENERATION AND CORRUPTION[1]

Book I

[*DIFFERENT TYPES OF CHANGE*]

* * * * * * *

4

Let us now describe the difference between coming to be and alteration, since we say that these changes are different from each other.

A subject is different from an attribute that is by its nature said of the subject, and each of these may change. Alteration occurs whenever the subject, being perceptible, remains but changes in its attributes, these being either contraries or intermediates. A body, for instance, is at one time healthy and at another time sick, still remaining the same <body>; and the bronze is at one time round and at another time angular, still remaining the same <bronze>.

But whenever the whole <subject> changes and something perceptible does not remain as the same subject (as, for instance, blood comes to be from the whole seed, or air from <the whole of the> water, or water from the whole of the air), then this is a case of the coming to be of one thing, <for instance, the blood>, and the perishing of the other, <for instance, the seed>. This is so especially if the change is from something imperceptible to something perceptible (perceptible by touch, or by all the senses)—whenever, for instance, water comes to be, or perishes into air (since air is fairly imperceptible).

In such cases <of unqualified coming to be>, sometimes the same attribute (which is one of a pair of contraries) that belongs to the thing that has perished remains in the thing that has come to be, when water, for instance, comes to be from air, if both are transparent or cold. But in these cases the thing resulting from the change

1. This is an Anglicization of the Latin translation of the Greek title, which means 'On (unqualified) COMING TO BE and perishing'.

must not itself be an attribute of this <attribute that remains>—if it were, the change would be an alteration. Suppose that a musical man, for instance, perished, and an unmusical man came to be, and the man remains as the same thing. If, then, musicality and unmusicality were not attributes of the man in their own right, it would have been a coming to be of the unmusical and a perishing of the musical. In fact, however, each of these is an attribute of the thing that remains; that is why they are attributes of the man, and it is <only> a coming to be or perishing of the musical or unmusical man. That is why such cases count as alterations.

A change between contrary quantities, then, is growth or decay; between contrary places it is locomotion; and between contrary
320a attributes and qualities it is alteration. But when nothing remains that has <the contrary resulting from the change> as its attribute or as any sort of coincident, the change is a coming to be, and <its contrary> is a perishing.

Matter is most of all and most fully the subject that admits the <unqualified> coming to be and perishing <of another thing>; but the subject for the other types of change is also matter in a way, since every subject admits <its proper> contraries.

Let this, then, be our account of whether or not there is coming to be and in what way there is, and of alteration.

* * * * * * *

[GROWTH]

5

321a29 One might also be puzzled about what grows. Is it the thing to which something is added? If, for instance, someone grows in his shin, is it the shin, rather than the food by which it grows, that is bigger? Why, then, have both not grown, since what has grown and that by which it grows have both increased—just as, when you mix wine with water, each component alike is increased?

Perhaps the reason is that the substance of the leg, not of the food, remains. For in the other case also we refer to the mixture
321b by its dominant component—as wine, for instance, since the mixture as a whole performs the function of wine, not of water. The same is true of alteration; if <the subject> continues to be flesh, i.e., to be what it is, and it now possesses some intrinsic attribute

that it did not previously possess, then this subject has been altered, and that by which it has been altered has sometimes itself been affected, sometimes not. But what initiates the alteration, i.e., the principle of the motion, is in <the subject> that grows or is altered; for what initiates the motion is in <one or the other of> these. For though sometimes the body that enters as well as the body that feeds on it may become greater (if, for instance, after entering, it becomes wind, still, once it has been affected this way, it has perished, and what initiates the motion is not in this.

Since we have examined the puzzle adequately, we must also try to find a solution of it. We must retain the beliefs that something grows when it remains and has something added, and decays when <it remains and> has something removed; that every perceptible particle has become bigger or smaller; that the body contains no void; that no two magnitudes are in the same place; and that nothing grows by <the addition of> something incorporeal.

To grasp the cause <of growth> we must draw some distinctions. First, a nonuniform part grows by the growth of uniform parts, since it is composed of them. Second, flesh and bone and each of these <uniform> parts, like the other things that have form in matter, have two aspects, since both matter and form are called flesh or bone. It is possible, then, for something, insofar as it is form, to grow in every part by the addition of something; but insofar as it is matter, this is not possible. For we must take it to be similar to measuring water with the same measure, where what comes to be is always one thing after another. Similarly, when the matter of flesh grows, not every single part of it receives addition, but rather one <part> flows out and another is added; every part of the shape and the form, however, receives addition.

It is clearer in the case of the nonuniform parts—for instance, a hand—that the growth is proportional <in every part>. For here it is clearer than it is in the case of flesh and the <other> uniform parts that the matter is different from the form; and that is why a dead body would more readily seem to have flesh and bone than to have a hand or an arm.

In a way, then, every <part> of the flesh has grown, and in a way it has not; for insofar as it is form, every part has received addition, but insofar as it is matter, it has not. But the whole has

322a become bigger by the addition of something (i.e., food) that is contrary and by <the added matter> changing into the same form—as if, for instance, wet were added to dry and after having been added, it changed and became dry. For in a way like grows by like, and in a way unlike by unlike.

* * * * * * *

322a28 The form, as a sort of channel, is a kind of potentiality in the matter. If, then, matter is added that is potentially a channel and that also has quantity potentially, then these channels will get bigger. But if it is no longer able to do this—just as more and more water mixed in wine eventually makes the wine watery and turns it to water—then it will make the quantity decay; but the form still remains.

* * * * * * *

Book II

[*MATTER AND CHANGE*]

* * * * * * *

2

329b7 Since we are seeking the principles of perceptible body, that is to say, of tangible body, and since what is tangible is what is perceived by the sense of touch, it is evident that not all contrary properties, but only contrary tangible properties, constitute forms and principles of bodies; for <primary bodies> are distinguished not only by having contrary properties but specifically by having contrary tangible properties. That is why neither paleness and darkness nor sweetness and bitterness nor, equally, any of the other pairs of perceptible contraries constitute any element. Admittedly, since sight is prior to touch, the <visible> subject is also prior; but it is not an attribute of tangible body insofar as it is tangible, but insofar as it is something else that may indeed be naturally prior.

Among the tangible properties themselves, we must first distinguish the primary differentiae and pairs of contraries. The pairs of contraries corresponding to touch are these: hot and cold, dry and wet, heavy and light, hard and soft, sticky and brittle, rough and smooth, coarse and fine. Among these, heavy and light neither act nor are affected; for these are not called what they are called by acting on or by being affected by anything else, whereas the elements must be capable of mutual action and affection, since they combine and change into each other.

Hot and cold, dry and wet, however, are so called insofar as they either act or are affected. Hot is what holds together things of the same kind; for dispersal, which is said to be the action of fire, is really holding together things of the same kind, since the result of the dispersal is the removal of the foreign things. Cold is what brings and holds together both things of the same kind and things of different kinds. Wet is what is not confined by any limit of its own, but is easily confined within <another> limit. Dry is what is easily confined within its own limit, but is hard to confine within <another> limit.

* * * * * * *

3

Fire, earth, and the other things we have mentioned[1] are not simple, 330b22
but mixed. The simple bodies are similar to these, but they are not the same. If, for instance, there is a simple body that is similar to fire, it is fiery but not fire, and the one similar to air is airy, and so on. Fire is a predominance of heat, just as ice is a predominance of cold; for freezing and boiling are types of predominance—of cold and heat, respectively. If, then, ice is the freezing of what is wet and cold, fire is the boiling of what is dry and hot—that is why nothing comes to be from ice or from fire.

* * * * * * *

4

We have previously determined that the simple bodies come to be 331a7
from one another. Moreover, perception makes this evident; for if they did not, there would be no alteration, since alteration involves the attributes of tangible things. We must, then, describe the way they change into each other, and consider whether each of them can come to be from every other one, or only some can, and others cannot.

1. **Fire . . . mentioned**: i.e., the recognized 'four elements'.

It is evident that all of them naturally change into each other; for coming to be begins from one contrary and ends in the other, and each element has some quality contrary to a quality of each of the others, since their differentiae are contraries. For some <elements>—fire and water—have both properties contrary <to each other> (since fire is dry and hot, and water is wet and cold), while others—air and water—have only one property contrary <to that of the other element>, (since air is wet and hot, and water is wet and cold).

In general, therefore, it is evident that each <element> naturally comes to be from each of the others. It is easy to see how this is so when we come to particular cases; for each will come from each, but the process will be quicker or slower, and harder or easier. For if bodies have corresponding qualities, change from one to the other is quick; otherwise it is slow, since one quality changes more easily than many. Air, for instance, will come from fire when just one quality changes; for fire is hot and dry, and air hot and wet, so that if the dry is overcome by the wet, air will result. Again, water will result from air if the hot is overcome by the cold; for air is hot and wet, and water is cold and wet, so that if the hot changes, water will result.

* * * * * * *

5

332a3 But let us also consider the following points about <the elements>. If fire, earth, and so on are, as some people think, the matter of natural bodies, there must be either one or two or more than two of them. Now they cannot all be one—for instance, they cannot all be air or all water or all fire or all earth—since change is into contraries. For if they are all air, then, since this will remain, there will be alteration, not coming to be; and besides, it does not seem to happen in such a way that water would at the same time be air or any other <element>. There will therefore be some contrariety and differentia of which <water will have one member> and some <element> will have the other member, as fire, for instance, has heat. Nor again is fire hot air; for in that case <the change from air to fire> would be an alteration, but this is not what it appears to be. Moreover, if air came from fire, it would come from hot changing into its contrary, so that this contrary would be present in air, and air would be something cold. Hence fire cannot be hot air, since that would make the same thing both hot and cold.

Both <air and fire>, then, must be some other thing that is the same for both, i.e., some other matter common to them.[2] The same argument applies to all the elements, showing that there is no one of them from which everything comes.

Nor again is there anything else apart from these—something intermediate, for instance, between air and water (coarser than air, but finer than water) or between fire and air (coarser than fire but finer than air). For this intermediate element will be air and fire (respectively) when a contrariety is added to it; but since one of a pair of contraries is a privation, the intermediate element cannot exist alone at any time (as some people say the indefinite and all-inclusive does). It is therefore one or another of the elements, or nothing.

If, then, nothing (or nothing perceptible at least) is prior to these elements, they will be everything. They must, then, either always remain without changing into each other, or else change into each other; if they change, then either all of them do, or else some do and some do not, as Plato wrote in the *Timaeus*.[3] We have shown previously that they must change into each other, and that one does not come to be from another equally quickly in each case, because those that have a corresponding property come to be more quickly from each other, and those that have none come to be more slowly.

If, then, the elements change within just one pair of contraries, there must be two of them; for the matter, being imperceptible and inseparable, is intermediate between them. But since we see that 332b
there are more than two elements, there must also be at least two pairs of contraries; and if there are two <pairs of contraries>, there must be, as in fact there appear to be, four elements, not three. For that is the number of combinations <of qualities>; though there are six <describable combinations>, two of them cannot occur because they are contrary to one another.

* * * * * * *

2. **matter common to them**: often taken to refer to 'prime matter'; see MATTER #3.

3. **in the *Timaeus***: See 54b–d.

DE ANIMA

Book I

* * * * * * *

[INTRODUCTION TO THE STUDY OF THE SOUL]

1

402a We suppose that knowing$_o$ is fine and honorable, and that one type of knowing is finer and more honorable than another either because it is more exact or because it is concerned with better and more wonderful things. On both grounds, we might reasonably place inquiry into the soul in the first rank. Moreover, knowledge$_g$ of it seems to make an important contribution to <knowledge of> the truth as a whole, and especially to the <knowledge of> nature, since the soul is a sort of principle of animals.[1] We seek to study and know the nature and essence$_o$ of the soul, and then all of its coincidents; some of these seem to be distinctive attributes of the soul, while others also seem to belong to animals because they have souls.

And yet it is altogether in every way a most difficult task to reach any conviction about the soul. For, as in many other areas of study, we are seeking the essence$_o$ and the what-it-is; and so someone might perhaps think some single line of inquiry is appropriate for every case where we want to know the substance—just as demonstration suits all coincidents that are distinctive of a given subject. On this view, then, we should seek this single line of inquiry. If, however, no single line of inquiry is suitable for the what-it-is, our task turns out to be still more difficult, since in that case we must discover how to study each area. But even if it is evident whether demonstration or division or some further line of inquiry is the right one, the question of where to begin our investigation causes

1. **principle of animals**: This COMMON BELIEF mentions only animal souls. Later Aristotle assumes that plants have souls too. See 413a25.

many puzzles and confusions; for different things—for instance, numbers and surfaces—have different principles.

First of all, presumably, we must determine the soul's genus and what it is. Is it, in other words, a this and a substance, or a quality, or a quantity, or something in one of the other predications that we have distinguished? Further, is it something potential or is it more of an actuality? That makes quite a bit of difference. We should also examine whether it is divisible into parts or has no parts. Do all souls belong to the same species or not? If not, do they differ in species, or in genus? As things are, those who discuss and investigate the soul would seem to examine only the human soul. Nor should we forget to ask whether there is just one account of the soul, as there is of animal, or a different account for each type of soul—for instance, of horse, dog, man, god—so that the universal animal either is nothing or else is posterior to these.[2] The same will apply to any other common thing predicated.

Further, if there are not many types of soul, but <one type of soul with many> parts, must we begin by investigating the whole soul, or by investigating the parts? It is also difficult to determine which parts differ in nature from each other and whether we should begin by investigating the parts or their functions. Should we, for instance, begin with understanding, perceiving, and so on, or with the part that understands and the part that perceives? And if we should begin with the functions, we might be puzzled anew about whether we should investigate the corresponding objects before the functions—the object of perception, for instance, before perceiving, and the object of understanding before understanding.

It would indeed seem useful to know$_{g}$ the what-it-is, in order to study the causes of the coincidents of substances. In mathematics, for instance, it is useful to know what straight and curved are or what a line and a surface are, in order to notice how many right angles the angles of a triangle are equal to. Conversely, however, the <knowledge of the> coincidents is also very important for knowing$_{o}$ the what-it-is. For we can state the essence$_{o}$ best once we can describe how all or most

2. **so that . . . to these:** This is a consequence of the second alternative (that there is a different account for each type of soul), and hence it is not Aristotle's own view.

of the coincidents appear to be; for since the what-it-is is the principle of all demonstration, a definition will clearly be dialectical and empty unless it results in knowledge$_g$, or at least in ready conjecture, about the coincidents.

A further puzzle arises about whether all the affections of the soul also belong to what has the soul or there is also some affection that is distinctive of the soul itself. We must find the answer, but it is not easy.

In most cases (for instance, being angry or confident, having an appetite, or perceiving in general), it appears that without the body the soul neither is affected nor acts. Understanding, more than the other affections, would seem to be distinctive <of the soul>; but if it is also some sort of appearance or requires appearance, then understanding also requires a body. And so if some function or affection of the soul is distinctive of it, then the soul would be separable; but if not, then it would not be separable. Similarly, the straight, insofar as it is straight, has many coincidents—for instance, that it touches a bronze sphere at a point—but if it is separated, it will not touch the sphere in this way; for it is inseparable, given that in every case it requires some body.

In fact, all the affections of the soul—emotion, gentleness, fear, pity, confidence, and, further, joy, loving, and hating—would seem to require a body, since whenever we have them the body is affected in some way. An indication of this is the fact that sometimes, though something severe and obvious affects us, we are not provoked or frightened; and sometimes we are moved by something small and faint, if the body is swelling and in the condition that accompanies anger. It is still more evident that sometimes, though nothing frightening is happening, people are affected just as a frightened person is.

If this is so, then clearly affections are forms$_l$ that involve matter. Hence the formulae will be, for instance: 'Being angry is a certain motion of this sort of body or part or potentiality by this agency for this end'. Hence study of the soul—either every sort or this sort[3]—turns out to be a task for the student of nature.

3. **this sort**: i.e., the sort that requires a body. On the role of the student of nature cf. *Phys*. 194a15, *PA* 641a29.

The student of nature and the dialectician would give different definitions of each of these affections—of anger, for instance. The dialectician would define it as a desire to inflict pain in return for pain, or something of that sort, whereas the student of nature would define it as a boiling of the blood and of the hot <element> around the heart. The student of nature describes the matter, whereas the dialectician describes the form and the account: for desire, for instance, is the form$_1$ of the thing, but its existence requires this sort of matter. Similarly, the account of a house is of this sort—that it is a shelter preventing destruction by wind, rain, or heat; someone else will say that it is stones, bricks, and timber; and someone else will say that it is the form in these <stones, for instance,> for the sake of this end. Who, then, is the <real> student of nature—the one who is concerned with the matter but is ignorant of the account, or the one who is concerned only with the account? Or is the <real> student of nature more properly the one who mentions both form and matter? If so, then what is each of the first two?

Perhaps in fact no one is concerned with the inseparable affections of matter but not concerned with them insofar as they are separable. Rather, the student of nature is concerned with all the actions and affections of this sort of body[4] and this sort of matter; what is not of this sort concerns someone else, perhaps a craftsman (for instance, a carpenter or a doctor). Inseparable affections, insofar as they are not affections of this sort of body but <are considered> by abstraction, concern the mathematician; insofar as they are separated, they concern first philosophy.

We should return to where our discussion began. We were saying, then, that the affections of the soul (for instance, emotion and fear) are, insofar as they are affections of the soul, inseparable (unlike surface and line) from the natural matter of animals.

* * * * * * *

4. **this sort of body**: a natural body, in contrast to the artifacts that are mentioned next.

Book II

[*DEFINITION OF THE SOUL*]

1

412a3 So much for the views on the soul that our predecessors have handed down. Let us now return and make a new start, trying to determine what the soul is and what account of it best applies to all souls in common.

We say, then, that one kind of being is substance. One sort of substance is matter, which is not a this in its own right; another sort is shape or form, which makes <matter> a this; and the third sort is the compound of matter and form. Matter is potentiality, and form is actuality; actuality is either, for instance, <the state of> knowing or <the activity of> attending <to what one knows>.

What seem to be substances most of all are bodies, and especially natural bodies, since these are the sources of the others.[1] Some natural bodies are alive and some are not—by 'life' I mean self-nourishment, growth, and decay.[2]

It follows that every living natural body is a substance and, <more precisely,> substance as compound. But since every such body is also this sort of body—i.e., the sort that is alive—the soul cannot be a body, since the body <is substance> as subject and matter and is not said of a subject. The soul, then, must be substance as the form of a natural body that is potentially alive. Now, substance is actuality; hence the soul will be the actuality of this specific sort of body.

Actuality is spoken of in two ways—one corresponding to <the state of> knowing$_e$ and the other to attending to <what one knows>. Evidently, then, the soul is the same sort of actuality that knowing is. For both being asleep and being awake require the presence of the soul; being awake corresponds to attending and being asleep to the state of inactive knowing. Moreover, in the same subject the state of knowing precedes the activity. Hence

1. **sources of the others**: since artifacts are made from natural bodies. Cf. *Phys*. 192b19.

2. **self- . . . decay**: 'Self-' governs 'growth' and 'decay' as well as 'nourishment', since in living creatures these all have an internal *archē*.

the soul is the first actuality[3] of a natural body that is potentially alive.

The sort of natural body that is potentially alive[4] is an organic 412b
one. The parts of plants are also organs, though altogether simple ones; the leaf, for instance, is a shelter for the shell, and the shell for the fruit, and similarly the roots correspond to a mouth, since both draw in food. And so, if we must give an account common to every sort of soul, we will say that the soul is the first actuality of a natural organic body.

Hence we need not ask whether the soul and body are one, any more than we need to ask this about the wax and the seal or, in general, about the matter and the thing of which it is the matter. For while one and being are spoken of in several ways, the actuality <and what it actualizes> are fully one.

We have said in general, then, that the soul is substance that corresponds to the account; and this <sort of substance> is the essence of this sort of body. Suppose some instrument—an axe, for instance—were a natural body; then being an axe would be its substance, and its soul would also be this <i.e., being an axe>; and if this substance were separated from it, it would no longer be an axe, except homonymously. In fact, however, it is an axe;[5] for the soul is not the essence and form$_1$ of this sort of body but of the specific sort of natural body that has in itself a principle of motion and rest.

We must also study this point by applying it to the parts <of living things>. If the eye, for instance, were an animal, sight would be its soul. For sight is the eye's substance that corresponds to the account, while the eye is the matter of sight; if an eye loses its sight, it is no longer an eye, except homonymously, as a stone eye or a painted eye is. We must apply this point about the part to the whole living body; for what holds for the relation of part <of the faculty of perception> to part <of the body> holds equally for the relation of the whole <faculty of> perception to the whole perceptive body, insofar as it is perceptive. The sort of body that

3. **first actuality**: Aristotle applies this term to the state exemplified by having knowledge, contrasted with attending to what one knows.

4. **The sort . . . alive**: Only bodies that are actually alive have the relevant potentiality for being alive. Cf. 412b25, *Met*. 1048b37–1049a18.

5. **it is an axe**: Since it is an artifact, it has no soul.

is potentially alive is not the one that has lost its soul but the one that has it; and the seed or the fruit is potentially this sort of body.

Being awake, then, is a <second> actuality, corresponding to cutting or seeing. The soul is <a first> actuality, corresponding to <the faculty of> sight and to the potentiality of the instrument <to cut>; and the body is potentially this. And as an eye is the pupil plus sight, so an animal is soul plus body.

It is clear, then, that the soul is not separable from the body. At least, some parts of it are not, if it is divisible into parts; for the actuality of some <parts of the soul> is <the actuality> of the parts <of the body> themselves. Still, some <parts of the soul> might well not be actualities of any body and might therefore be separable. Moreover, it is still unclear whether the soul is the actuality of the body in the way a sailor is of a ship.[6]

Let this, then, be our outline definition and sketch of the soul.

2

Since what is perspicuous and better known$_{g}$ from the point of view of reason emerges from what is less perspicuous but more evident, we must start again and apply this approach to the soul. For the defining account must not confine itself, as most definitions do, to showing the fact; it must also include and indicate its cause. The accounts that are customarily stated in formulae are like conclusions, so that if we ask, for instance, what squaring is, we are told that it is making an equilateral rectangle equal to an oblong rectangle. This sort of formula is an account of the conclusion, whereas the one that defines squaring as the finding of the mean states the cause of the fact.

To begin our examination, then, we say that living is what distinguishes things with souls from things without souls. Living is spoken of in several ways—for instance, understanding, perception, locomotion and rest, and also the motion involved in nourishment, and decay and growth. And so whatever has even one of these is said to be alive.

6. **sailor . . . ship**: Perhaps Aristotle means: just as a sailor ceases to be a sailor when he leaves the ship, so also the intellectual part of the soul survives the body, but is no longer a soul or part of a soul. See 413b24, 415a11, 430a22.

This is why all plants as well <as animals> seem to be alive, since they evidently have an internal potentiality and principle through which they both grow and decay in contrary directions. For they grow up and down and in all directions alike, not just up rather than down; they are continually nourished, and they stay alive as long as they can absorb nourishment. This <sort of life> can be separated from the others, but in mortal things the others cannot be separated from it. This is evident in the case of plants, since they have no other potentiality of the soul.

This principle, then, is what makes something alive. What makes something an animal is primarily perception; for whatever has perception, even without motion or locomotion, is said to be an animal, not simply to be alive. Touch is the primary type of perception belonging to all animals, and it can be separated from the other senses, just as the nutritive <potentiality> can be separated from touch and the other senses.

The part of the soul that belongs to plants as well as to animals is called nutritive; and all animals evidently have the sense of touch. Later we will state the explanation of each of these facts. For now let us confine ourselves to saying that the soul is the principle of the <potentialities> we have mentioned—for nutrition, perception, understanding, and motion—and is defined by them.

Is each of these a soul or a part of a soul? And if a part, is it the sort that is separable only in account, or is it also separable in place? In some cases the answer is easily seen, but some parts raise a puzzle. For some plants are evidently still alive when they are cut <from one plant> and are separated from each other; for, we assume, the soul in each plant is actually one but potentially more than one. And we see that the same is also true of other differentiae of the soul. <This is clear> in the case of insects that are cut in two. For each part has both perception and locomotion; if it has perception, then it also has appearance and desire. For if it has perception, then it has pain and pleasure, and if it has these, then it necessarily also has appetite.

So far, however, nothing is evident about understanding and the potentiality for theoretical study. It would seem to be a different kind of soul, and to be the only part that admits of being separated, just as the everlasting <admits of being separated> from the perishable.

It evidently follows, however, that the other parts of the soul are not separable, as some say they are. But they evidently differ in account; for perceiving is different from believing, and hence being the perceptive part is different from being the believing part, and so on for each of the other parts mentioned.

Further, animals are differentiated by the fact that some of them have all of these parts, some have some of them, and some have only one; we should investigate the reason for this later. Practically the same is true of the senses: some animals have all of them, some have some of them, and some have only the most necessary one, touch.

When we say we live and perceive by something, we speak in two ways, just as we do when we say we know$_e$ by something. For we say we know either by knowledge or by the soul, since we say we know by each of these; and similarly, we are healthy in one way by health, in another way by some part or the whole of the body. In these cases, knowledge or health is a sort of shape and form, i.e., an account[7] and a sort of actuality of what is receptive of knowledge or health; for the actuality of the agent seems to occur in the thing that is acted on and suitably disposed.

Now the soul is that by which we primarily live, perceive, and think, and so it will be an account and a form, not matter and subject. For substance, as we said, is spoken of in three ways, as form, matter, and the compound of both; of these, matter is potentiality, form actuality. Since, therefore, the compound of body and soul is ensouled, body is not the actuality of soul, but the soul is the actuality of some sort of body.

This vindicates the view of those who think that the soul is not a body but requires a body; for it is not a body, but it belongs to a body, and for that reason it is present in a body, and in this sort of body. Our predecessors were wrong, then, in trying to fit the soul into a body without further determining the proper sort of body, even though it appears that not just any old thing receives any old thing. Our view, however, is quite reasonable, since a thing's actuality naturally comes to be in what has the potentiality for it, i.e., in the proper matter.

It is evident from this, then, that the soul is a certain sort of actuality and form$_l$ of what has the potentiality to be of this sort.

7. **account**: *logos*. The *logos* actually seems to be what the account is an account of. See REASON #5.

3

As we said, some things have all the potentialities of the soul that were previously mentioned, while other things have some of these potentialities, and others have only one. The potentialities we mentioned were those for nutrition, perception, desire, locomotion, and understanding. Plants have only the nutritive part. Other things have the nutritive part and also the perceptive part, and if they have the perceptive part, they also have the desiring part. For desire includes appetite, emotion, and wish; but all animals have at least the sense of touch, and whatever has any perception has pleasure and pain and finds things pleasant or painful. Whatever finds things pleasant and painful also has appetite, since appetite is desire for what is pleasant.

Further, animals have the perception of nourishment; for touch is perception of nourishment, since all living things are nourished by things that are dry and wet and hot and cold, and touch is the perception of these. Animals are nourished by other objects of perception only coincidentally, since neither sound nor color nor smell contributes anything to nourishment, and flavor is an object of touch. Now, hunger and thirst are appetites for the dry and hot, and the wet and cold, respectively, while flavor is a sort of pleasant relish belonging to these.

We must make these points clear later on. For now let us confine ourselves to saying that living things that have touch also have desire. Whether they all have appearance is not clear, and must be considered later.

Besides these parts, some things have the locomotive part. Others—human beings, for instance, and any thinking being that is different from, or superior to, a human being—also have the thinking part and understanding.

Clearly, then, soul will have one single account in the same way that figure has; for just as figure is nothing apart from the triangle and the figures that follow in order, so equally the soul is nothing apart from those <potentialities> we have mentioned. Still, in the case of figures we can find a common account that fits all of them and is distinctive of none; the same is true for the souls we have mentioned. It is ridiculous, then, in these and other such cases, to seek a common account that is not distinctive of any being and does not fit the proper and indivisible species, if we neglect this <distinctive> account. Hence[8] we must ask what the soul of each particular <kind of thing>—for instance, a plant, a human being, or a beast—is.

What is true of the soul is similar to what is true of figure; for in both cases the earlier is invariably present potentially in its successor—for instance, the triangle in the square, and the nutritive in the perceptive. We must consider why they are in this order. For the perceptive part requires the nutritive, but in plants the nutritive is separated from the perceptive. Again, each of the other senses requires touch, whereas touch is found without the other senses, since many animals lack sight, hearing, and smell. Among things that perceive, some but not all have the locomotive part. Finally and most rarely, some have reasoning and thinking. For perishable things that have reasoning also have all the other parts of the soul; but not all of those that have each of the other parts also have reasoning—on the contrary, some animals lack appearance, while some live by appearance alone. Theoretical intellect requires a different account.

Clearly, then, the account of each of these parts of the soul is also the most proper account of <each type of> soul.

[*NUTRITION*]

4

If we are to examine these <parts of the soul>, we must find what each of them is and then investigate the next questions and those that follow. And if we ought to say what, for instance, the understanding or the perceptive or the nutritive part is, we should first say what it is to understand or perceive, since actualities and actions are prior in account to potentialities. If this is so, and if in addition the objects corresponding to the actualities are prior to them and so must be studied first, then we must, for the same reason, begin by determining the objects corresponding to nutrition, sense, and understanding. And so we should first discuss nourishment and generation; for the nutritive soul belongs to other living things as well as <to plants>, and it is the first and most widely shared potentiality of the soul, the one that makes all living things alive.

8. **Hence . . . beast is**: 414b32–3 have been transposed to 414b28.

Its functions are generation and the use of nourishment. For the most natural of all functions for a living thing, if it is complete and not defective and does not come to be by chance, is to produce another thing of the same sort as itself (an animal, if it is an animal, and a plant, if it is a plant), in order to share as far as it can in the everlasting and divine. For this is the end they all strive 415b for, and for its sake they do every action that accords with nature. (What something is for is of two types—the goal and the beneficiary.)[9] These living things cannot share in the everlasting and divine by continuously existing, since no perishable thing can remain numerically one and the same; hence they share in it as far as they can, to different degrees, and what remains is not the <parent> itself, but something else of the same sort as <the parent>—something that is specifically, not numerically, one with <the parent>.

The soul is the cause and principle of the living body. Now, causes are spoken of in many ways, and the soul is a cause in three of the ways distinguished—as the source of motion, as what something is for, and as the substance of ensouled bodies.

It is clearly the cause as substance; for a thing's substance is the cause of its being, and the being of living things is their living, the cause and principle of which is soul. Moreover, the actuality is the form$_1$ of what is potentially.

The soul is evidently also a cause by being what something is for. For just as productive thought aims at something, so does nature, and what it aims at is its end. In living things the natural end is the soul; for all natural bodies, of plants no less than of animals, are organs of the soul, since they are for the sake of the soul. (The end for the sake of which is of two types, either the goal or the beneficiary.)

Moreover, the soul is also the source of locomotion, though not all living things have this potentiality. Alteration and growth also depend on the soul; for perception seems to be some kind of alteration, and nothing that lacks a soul perceives. The same applies to growth and decay; for nothing either decays or grows naturally without being nourished, and nothing that has no share of life is nourished.

Empedocles is wrong when he adds that plants grow by putting

9. **the goal and the beneficiary**: Here Aristotle is concerned with the goal, and in 415b20–1 below with the beneficiary.

416a down roots because earth naturally moves downward, and that plants grow by extending upward because fire naturally moves upward. His conception of up and down is wrong. For up and down are not the same for each particular <sort of> thing as they are for the universe as a whole; in fact, if we ought to call organs the same or different in accordance with their functions, a plant's roots correspond to an animal's head. Besides, what is it that holds the fire and earth together when they are moving in contrary directions? For they will be torn apart unless something prevents it; whatever prevents it will be the soul, the cause of growing and being nourished.

Some think the nature of fire is the unqualified cause of nourishment and growth, since it is the only body that is evidently nourished and grows, and hence one might suppose that it also performs this function in both plants and animals. In fact, however, fire is a sort of joint cause, but not the unqualified cause; it is the soul, rather than fire, that is the unqualified cause. For while fire grows without limit, as long as there is fuel, the size and growth of everything naturally constituted has a limit and form$_1$, which are characteristic of soul, not of fire—i.e., of the form$_1$ rather than of the matter.

Since one and the same potentiality of the soul is both nutritive and generative, we must first determine the facts about nutrition; for this is the function that distinguishes the nutritive potentiality from others.

Contrary seems to nourish contrary, not in every case, but only when they not only come to be but also grow from each other; for many things come to be from each other (healthy from sick, for instance) without gaining any quantity. And not even those contraries that grow seem to nourish each other in the same way; water, for instance, nourishes fire, but fire does not nourish water. It seems to be true, then, of the simple bodies more than of other things, that one thing nourishes and the other is nourished.

A puzzle arises: while some say that like nourishes like, just as (they say) like grows by like, others, as we have said, hold the opposite view, that contrary nourishes contrary; for, they say, like is unaffected by like, but nourishment changes and is digested, and everything changes into its opposite or into the intermediate. Moreover, nourishment is affected by the thing nourished, whereas the thing nourished is unaffected by the nourishment—just as the matter is affected by the carpenter, who is unaffected by it and merely changes from inactivity to activity.

It matters for this question whether nourishment is the first or last thing added.[10] Perhaps it is both, if undigested nourishment is added first, and digested nourishment last. If so, then it would be possible to speak of nourishment in both ways; for insofar as nourishment is undigested, contrary nourishes contrary, and insofar as it has been digested, like nourishes like. Evidently, then, each view is in a way both correct and incorrect.

Since nothing is nourished except what has a share of life, the ensouled body, insofar as it is ensouled, is what is nourished. Nourishment, therefore, is also relative, not coincidentally, to an ensouled thing. However, nourishing something is not the same as making it grow; for an ensouled thing is caused to grow insofar as it has some quantity, but it is nourished insofar as it is a this and a substance. For it preserves its substance and exists as long as it is nourished; and what it generates is not itself, but something else of the same sort—for its own substance already exists, and a thing does not generate, but preserves, itself.

Hence this sort of principle in the soul is a potentiality of the sort that preserves the ensouled thing, insofar as it is ensouled, and nourishment equips it for its actuality; and so if it has been deprived of nourishment it cannot exist. Further,[11] since a thing's end rightly determines what we should call it, and in this case the end is the generation of another thing of the same sort, this first soul will be the generative soul, generating another thing of the same sort.

We must distinguish three things—what is nourished, what it is nourished by, and what nourishes. What nourishes is this first soul, what is nourished is the ensouled body, and what it is nourished by is the nourishment. What the soul nourishes by is of two types—just as what we steer by is both the hand and the rudder: the first both initiates motion and undergoes it, and the second simply undergoes it. Since all nourishment must be digestible and the hot element produces digestion, every ensouled thing contains heat.

10. **last thing added**: To the organism that is nourished.

11. **Further, since . . . same sort**: 416b23–5 are transposed to 416b20.

This, then, is an outline of what nutrition is; we should describe it more clearly later in the discussions proper to it.

[*PERCEPTION*]

5

Now that we have determined this, let us discuss perception in general. Perception occurs in being moved and affected, as we have said, since it seems to be a type of alteration.[12] Some also say that like is affected by like; we have said in our general discussion of acting and being affected how this is or is not possible.

A puzzle arises about why we do not perceive the senses themselves, and about why they do not produce perception without external objects, despite the presence of fire, earth, and the other elements, whose intrinsic or coincidental properties are the things that are perceived. Clearly, then, the perceptive part is <what it is> by merely potential, not actual, <perceiving>, and so it does not perceive <without an external object>—just as what is combustible is not burned all by itself without something to burn it, since otherwise it would burn itself with no need of actual fire.

We speak of perceiving in two ways; for we say that something sees or hears both in the case of something that has the potentiality for seeing or hearing, even though it is asleep at the time, and in the case of something that is actually seeing or hearing at the time. It follows that perception is also spoken of in two ways, as potential and as actual, and in the same way both what is potentially perceived and what is actually perceived are called objects of perception.

First, then, let us speak as though the actuality were the same as being affected and moved—for motion is in fact a sort of actuality, though an incomplete one, as we have said elsewhere. Now, everything is affected and moved by an agent that has the relevant property in actuality, so that in a way like is affected by like, and in a way unlike by unlike—for what is being affected

12. **a type of alteration:** Aristotle gradually modifies this claim. See 417b2–16.

is unlike the agent, but when it has been affected it is like the agent.

We must also distinguish types of potentiality and actuality, since just now we were speaking of them without qualification. One way in which someone might know$_e$ is the way we have in mind in saying that a man knows because man is a kind of thing that knows and has knowledge; another way is the way we have in mind in saying that someone who has grammatical knowledge knows. These knowers have different sorts of potentiality—the first has a potentiality because he has the right sort of genus and matter, whereas the second has a potentiality because he has the potentiality to attend to something when he wishes, if nothing external prevents it.[13] A third sort <of knower> is someone who is attending to something at the time, actualizing his knowledge and fully knowing (for instance) this A. In the first and second case we pass from potentially to actually knowing; but in the first case we do so by being altered through learning, and by frequent changes from the contrary state, while in the second case—where we pass from having arithmetical or grammatical knowledge without actualizing it, to actualizing it—we do so in another way.

Further, there is not just one way of being affected. On the contrary, one way of being affected is a destruction of contrary by contrary, while the other way is more properly preservation, not destruction, of a potential F by an actual F, when the potential F is <not contrary, but> like the actual F, in the way that a potentiality is like its actuality. For the second case—where the possessor of knowledge comes to attend to what he knows—either is not a case of alteration at all (since the addition leads to <the knowledge> itself and to the actuality) or is a different kind of alteration. That is why we should not say that the intelligent subject is altered in exercising his intelligence, just as we should not say that the builder is altered in <actually> building.

First, then, when an understanding and intelligent subject is led from potentiality to actuality, we should not call this teaching but give it some other name. Again, if a subject with potential knowledge learns and acquires knowledge from a

13. **the potentiality . . . prevents it**: The second type of potentiality seems to be the 'first actuality' of 412a10, 22.

teacher with actual knowledge, then we should say either, as we said, that this is not a case of being affected, or that there are two ways of being altered, one of which is a change into a condition of deprivation, and the other of which is a change into possession of a state and into <the fulfilllment of the subject's> nature.

In the perceiver, the first change[14] is produced by its parent; and at birth it possesses perception corresponding to <the second type of> knowledge. We speak of actual perceiving in a way that corresponds to attending, except that the visible, audible, and other perceptible objects that produce the actuality are external. This is because actual perception is of particulars, while knowledge$_e$ is of universals, which are, in a way, in the soul itself; hence it is up to us to think whenever we want to, but it is not up to us to perceive whenever we want to, since perception requires the presence of its object. The same is true for the types of knowledge$_e$ that are about perceptible things, and for the same reason—namely that perceptible things are particulars and external.

There may be an opportunity to explain these points more perspicuously another time, but for the moment let us be content with the distinctions we have made. There are different types of potentiality: One is what is meant in saying that a child is potentially a general. A second is what is meant in attributing the potentiality to someone of the right age, and <this second type> applies to the perceptive part. Since the difference between these cases has no name, though our distinctions have shown that they are different, and in what ways, we have to use 'being affected' and 'being altered' as though they were the strictly correct names.

The perceiver is potentially what the perceptible object actually is already, as we have said. When it is being affected, then, it is unlike the object; but when it has been affected it has been made like the object and has acquired its quality.

6

We should first discuss the objects of perception, taking each sense in turn. An object of perception is spoken of in three ways:

14. **first change**: This change results in the genus and matter that are suitable for perception (as opposed to the genus and matter of, say, a plant).

two types are perceived intrinsically, and one coincidentally. One type of intrinsic object is proper to each sense; the other type is common to all the senses.

By 'proper object' I mean the one that cannot be perceived by another sense and about which we cannot be deceived. Sight, for instance, is of color; hearing of sound; taste of flavor; and touch has a number of different objects. At any rate, each sense discriminates among its proper objects, and a sense is not deceived about whether, for instance, something is a color or a sound, but it can be deceived about whether or where the colored or sounding thing is. These objects, then, are said to be proper to each sense.

Motion, rest, number, shape, and size are the common objects, since they are not proper to any one sense, but are common to them all—a certain sort of motion, for instance, is perceptible by both touch and sight.

Something is said to be coincidentally perceptible if, for instance, the pale <thing> is the son of Diares. For we perceive the son of Diares coincidentally, since he coincides with the pale thing we perceive, and hence we are not affected at all by the perceptible object insofar as it is <the son of Diares>.[15]

Among the intrinsic objects of perception, the proper objects are most properly perceptible, and the essence of each sense is by nature relative to these.

* * * * * * *

11

The objects of touch are the differentiae of body insofar as it *423b27*
is body, i.e., those that distinguish the elements—hot, cold, dry, and wet; we have discussed these earlier in what we said about the elements. Their tactile sense organ, the primary seat of the sense called touch, is the part that has these qualities
potentially. For perceiving is a way of being affected; hence *424a*
the agent causes the thing that is affected, which potentially has the quality that the agent has, to have that quality actually.

15. **insofar . . . Diares>**: We are not aware of it as the son of Diares, but only insofar as it is an object of sight.

Hence we do not perceive anything that is as dry or wet, or hard or soft, <as the organ>, but only the excesses in either direction, because the sense is a sort of intermediate condition between the contraries in objects of perception. And that is why a sense discriminates among its objects; for what is intermediate discriminates, since in relation to each extreme it becomes the other extreme. And just as what is going to perceive both pale and dark must be actually neither pale nor dark but potentially both, and similarly in the other cases, so also in the case of touch, <what is going to perceive the contraries> must be neither hot nor cold.

Further, just as we found that sight in a way perceives both the visible and the invisible, and similarly the other senses perceive the opposites, so also touch perceives the tangible and the intangible. What is intangible is either something that either has altogether very few of the differentiating properties of tangibles—air, for instance—or has an excess of tangible qualities—for instance, things that destroy <the sense>.

We have spoken in outline, then, of the senses, one by one.

12

A general point to be grasped is that each sense receives the perceptible forms without the matter.[16] Wax, for instance, receives the design on a signet ring without the iron or gold; it acquires the design in the gold or bronze, but not insofar as the design is gold or bronze. Similarly, each sense is affected by the thing that has color or flavor or sound, but not insofar as it is said to be that thing <for instance, a horse>, but insofar as it has a given quality <for instance, color> and in accordance with the form$_1$ <of the sense>.

The primary sense organ is the seat of this sort of potentiality. Hence the organ and the potentiality are one, but their being is different. For though <the sense organ> that perceives is of

16. **perceptible forms without the matter**: A 'perceptible' form is not the form that makes a particular man a man, but the form that makes him perceptible. On the 'form in the soul' without matter see *Met.* 1032b1.

some magnitude, being perceptive is not, and <so> the sense is not something with magnitude but is a <specific sort of> form$_{l}$ and potentiality of the organ.

It is also evident from this why excesses in objects of perception destroy the sense organs. For if the motion is too strong for the sense organ, then the form$_{l}$, i.e., the sense, is destroyed, just as the harmony and tension are destroyed if the strings of an instrument are struck heavily.

This also makes it evident why plants do not perceive, even though they have one part of soul, and are affected in some ways by objects of touch, since they are chilled and heated. The reason is that they lack a <suitable> intermediate condition and a principle suitable for receiving the form of perceptible things; instead, they are affected <by the form> with the matter.

A puzzle arises about whether something that cannot smell can be at all affected by odor, or something that cannot see can be affected by color, and so on for the other cases. If the object of smell is odor, then anything produced by odor must be <the act of> smelling; hence nothing that is incapable of smelling anything can be affected by odor (the same applies to the other cases), and any such thing must be affected insofar as it is a perceiver. A further argument makes the same conclusion clear. For a body is affected neither by light and darkness nor by sound nor by odor, but only by their subject, as, for instance, the air that comes with the thunder splits the log.

On the other hand, tangible <qualities> and flavors affect bodies; otherwise, what would affect and alter soulless things? Then will the other objects of perception also affect bodies? Perhaps not every body is liable to be affected by odor and sound, and those that are affected are indefinite and impermanent—air, for instance, since it acquires an odor as though affected in some way.

Then what is there to smelling, apart from being affected? Perhaps smelling is <not only being affected, but> also perceiving, while air that is affected <by odor>, by contrast, soon becomes an object of perception <not a perceiver>.

* * * * * * *

Book III

* * * * * * *

[*APPEARANCE*]

3

If appearance is that in virtue of which some object appears to us, in contrast to what is so called metaphorically, then is it one of those potentialities or states in virtue of which we discriminate and attain truth or falsity? These are perception, belief, knowledge$_e$, and understanding.

It is clear as follows that appearance is not the same as perception. For perception is either a potentiality, such as sight, or an actuality, such as seeing; but we have appearances when we have neither of these—in dreams, for instance. Moreover, perception is present in every <animal>, but appearance is not. If they were the same in actuality, then it would be possible for all beasts to have appearance, whereas in fact it does not seem possible <for all>; ants or bees, for instance, and grubs <do not have it>. Further, perceptions are always true, whereas most appearances are false. Again, whenever we are actually perceiving accurately, we do not say that this appears to us <to be> a man; we are more inclined to say <that something appears to be so> in cases where we do not see clearly whether something is true or false. Further, as we were saying before, sights appear to us even when we have our eyes closed.

The remaining question is whether appearance is belief; for belief may also be either true or false. Belief, however, implies conviction—since one cannot believe things if one does not find them convincing—whereas no beasts have conviction, though many have appearance. Further, belief implies conviction, conviction implies being persuaded, and persuasion implies reason, whereas no beasts have reason, though some have appearance.

It is evident, then, that appearance is neither belief that involves perception, nor belief that is produced through perception, nor a combination of belief and perception. This is so both for the reasons given and also because <on this view> belief will not be about anything other than the thing, if there is one, that is the object of perception.

I mean, for instance, that the combination of a belief about the pale and a perception of the pale will turn out to be appearance; for surely it will not be the combination of a belief about the good and a perception of the pale—for appearance will be having a belief noncoincidentally about the very thing one perceives. In fact, however, we sometimes have false appearances about the same things at the same time as we have a true supposition about them, as when, for instance, the sun appears a foot across, even though we are convinced that it is bigger than the inhabited world.

It turns out, then, <on the view being considered> that either we have lost the true belief we had, even though the thing still exists and we have neither forgotten our belief nor been persuaded to change it, or else, if we still have the true belief, the same belief must at the same time be both true and false. But in fact it could have become false only if the thing changed without our noticing it. It follows, then, that appearance cannot be any of these things, nor a product of them.

It is possible, however, when one thing has been set in motion, for a second thing to be set in motion by the first. Moreover, appearance seems to be a sort of motion, to involve perception, to be present in things that have perception, and to be about the objects of perception. Now, it is also possible for motion to result from actual perception, and this motion must be similar to the perception.

Hence this motion cannot occur without perception or in things that do not have perception. Things that have appearance act and are affected in many ways in accordance with it, and it can be either true or false.

* * * * * * *

[*UNDERSTANDING*]

4

Now we must consider the part by which the soul has knowledge$_{g}$ and intelligence, and ask whether it is separable, or it is not separable in magnitude but only in account; and what its differentia is, and how understanding comes about.

Now, if understanding is like perceiving, it consists either in being affected by the object of intellect or in something else of the same sort. Hence the intellect must be unaffected, but receptive of the form; it must have the quality <of the object> potentially, not actually; and it must be related to its object as the perceiving part is related to the objects of perception.

Hence the intellect, since it understands all things,[1] must be unmixed, in order, as Anaxagoras says, to 'master' them (i.e., to know$_g$ them); for the intrusion of any foreign thing would hinder and obstruct it. And so it has no nature except this—that it is potential. Hence the part of the soul called intellect (by which I mean that by which the soul thinks and supposes) is not actually, before it understands, any of the things there are. It is also unreasonable, then, for intellect to be mixed with the body, since it would then acquire some quality (for instance, hot or cold) or even, like the perceiving part, have some organ, whereas in fact it has none.

And so those who say that the soul is a place of forms are right, except that it is the intellectual soul, not the whole soul, which is—potentially, not actually—the forms.

The condition of the sense organ and of the faculty of perception makes it evident that the perceiving part and the intellectual
429b part are unaffected in different ways. For after a sense perceives something very perceptible, it cannot perceive; after hearing very loud sounds, for instance, it cannot hear sound, and after seeing vivid colors or smelling strong odors, it cannot see or smell. But whenever intellect understands something that is very intelligible, it understands more, not less, about inferior objects;[2] for intellect is separable, whereas the perceiving part requires a body.

When the intellect becomes each thing <that it understands>, as it does when someone is said to have actual knowledge$_e$ (this comes about whenever someone is able to actualize his knowledge through himself), even then it is still potential in a way, though not in the same way as before it learned or discovered; and then it is capable of understanding itself.

Magnitude is different from being magnitude and water from being water; and the same applies in many other cases too, though not in all, since in some cases the thing is the same as its being. It

1. **understands all things**: i.e., is capable of understanding all kinds of things (it is not restricted to knowledge of birds as opposed to numbers).

2. **For after a sense . . . inferior objects**: We do not, for instance, find it more difficult to measure a room after thinking about complex geometry.

follows that to discriminate being flesh we use something different, or something in a different state, from what we use in discriminating flesh; for flesh requires matter, and, like the snub, it is this <form> in this <matter>. Hence to discriminate the hot and the cold and the things of which flesh is some sort of form$_l$, we use the perceptive part; but to discriminate being flesh, we use something else that is either separable <from body> or related to it as a formerly bent line is related to the straight line it has become.

Further, if we turn to things whose being depends on abstraction, the straight is similar to the snub, since it requires something continuous. But if being straight is different from the straight, then so is the essence of straight (duality, let us say) different from the straight, and therefore to discriminate it we use something different, or something in a different state. In general, then, the <separability> of intellect corresponds to the way in which objects are separable from matter.

A puzzle arises. If intellect is simple and unaffected, having, as Anaxagoras says, nothing in common with anything, then how can it understand, if understanding consists in being affected? For it seems that two things must have something in common if one is to affect the other. Again, is intellect itself an object of intellect? For if nothing other <than itself> makes it an object of intellect, and if all objects of intellect are one in species, then the other objects of intellect will also be intellect; alternatively, it will need something mixed into it, to make it an object of intellect in the same way as the other objects of intellect are.

On the other hand, our previous discussion of ways of being affected because of something in common has shown that the intellect is in a way potentially the objects of intellect, but before it understands them, it is none of them actually. Its potentiality is that of a writing tablet with nothing actually written on it—which is also true of intellect.

Further, intellect itself is an object of intellect in the same way as its objects are. For in the case of things without matter, the understanding part and its object are one, since actual knowledge$_e$ and its object are the same. (We should investigate why it is not <engaged in the activity of> understanding all the time.) In things that have matter, each object of intellect is potentially present; hence intellect will not be in them (since it is a potentiality for being such things without their matter), but it will be an object of intellect.

5

In the whole of nature each kind of thing has something as its matter, which is potentially all the things in the kind, and something else as the cause and producer, which produces them all—for instance, the craft in relation to its matter. These differences, then, must also be found in the soul. One sort of intellect corresponds to matter, by becoming all things. Another sort corresponds to the producer by producing all things in the way that a state,[3] such as light, produces things—for in a way light makes potential colors into actual colors. This second sort of intellect is separable, unaffected, and unmixed, since its essence$_{o}$ is actuality.

For in every case the producer is more valuable than the thing affected, and the principle is more valuable than the matter. Actual knowledge$_{e}$ is the same as its object; potential knowledge is temporally prior in an individual <knower>, but in general it is not even temporally prior. But <productive intellect> does not understand at one time and not at another.

Only when it has been separated is it precisely what it is, all by itself. And this alone is immortal and everlasting. But <when it is separated> we do not remember, because this <productive intellect> is unaffected, whereas the intellect that is affected is perishable. And without this <productive intellect> nothing understands.

* * * * * * *

[*DESIRE AND ACTION*]

10

433a9 There are apparently two parts that move us—both intellect and desire, if we take appearance to be a kind of understanding. For many people follow their appearances against their knowledge$_{e}$, and the other animals have appearance but lack understanding

2. **a state**: A state, *hexis*, is contrasted with some process of change. Light makes things visible simply by shining on them, not by undergoing any change in the course of shining on them. Aristotle may suggest that productive intellect is more like a permanent feature of intellect than like a potentiality that is activated at one time and not at another.

and reasoning. Both intellect and desire, then, move us from place to place. This is the intellect that reasons for some goal and is concerned with action; its <concern with an> end distinguishes it from theoretical intellect. All desire also aims at some goal; for the object of desire is the starting point of intellect concerned with action, and the last stage <of our reasoning> is the starting point of action.

Hence it is reasonable to regard these two things—desire, and thought concerned with action—as the movers. For the object of desire moves us, and thought moves us because its starting point is the object of desire. Moreover, whenever appearance moves us, it requires desire.

And so there is one mover, the desiring part. For if there were two—intellect and desire—they would move us insofar as they had a common form. In fact, however, intellect evidently does not move anything without desire,[4] since wish is desire, and any motion in accordance with reasoning is in accordance with wish; desire, on the other hand, also moves us against reasoning, since appetite is a kind of desire. Now, intellect is always correct, but desire and appearance may be either correct or incorrect. Hence in every case the mover is the object of desire, but the object of desire is either the good or the apparent good[5]—not every sort of good, but the good that is achievable in action. What is achievable in action admits of being otherwise.

Evidently, then, the potentiality of the soul that moves us is the one called desire. People who divide the soul into parts—if they divide it into separate parts corresponding to the different potentialities—will find very many of them—the nutritive, perceptive, intellectual, and deliberative parts, and, moreover, the desiring part; for the difference between these parts is greater than the one between the appetitive and emotional parts.

Desires that are contrary to each other arise, however, when reason and appetite are contrary, which happens in subjects that perceive time. For intellect urges us to draw back because of what is to come, while appetite <urges us on> because of what is present; for the pleasant thing that is present appears both unqual-

4. **moves nothing without desire**: On the roles of thought and desire see *EN* 1139a35.

5. **the good or the apparent good**: Cf. *EN* iii 4.

ifiedly pleasant and unqualifiedly good, because we do not see what is to come.

Hence the mover is one in species—the desiring part, insofar as it is desiring. Indeed, the first mover of all is the object of desire, since it moves us without being moved, by being present to understanding or appearance. But the movers are numerically more than one.

We must distinguish three things—the mover, its instrument, and the subject moved. There are two types of movers: the unmoved mover[6] and the moved mover. The unmoved mover is the good achievable in action, and the moved mover is the desiring part; for the thing that is moved is moved insofar as it desires, and desire, insofar as it is actual, is a sort of motion. The thing moved is the animal. When we reach the instrument by which desire moves, we reach something bodily, and so we should study it when we study the functions common to soul and body.

To summarize for the present: What moves something as an instrument is found where the same thing is both the starting point and the last stage. In the hinge-joint, for instance, the convex is last, and hence at rest, while the concave is the starting point, and hence is moved. These are different in account, though they are spatially inseparable. For since everything is moved by pushing and pulling, something must remain at rest, as in a circle, and the motion must originate from this.

In general, then, as we have said, an animal moves itself insofar as it has desire. For desire needs appearance; and appearance is either rational appearance or the perceptual appearance that other animals share <with human beings>.

11

434a We should also consider what moves incomplete animals, whose only form of perception is touch. Can they have appearance and appetite, or not? For they evidently have pleasure and pain; if they have these, they must have appetite. But how could they have appearance? Well, perhaps, just as they are moved indeterminately, so also they have appearance and appetite, but have them indeterminately.

Now, the other animals as well <as human beings> also have

6. **unmoved mover**: See *Phys.* viii 5.

perceptual appearance, as we have said, but <only> reasoning animals have deliberative appearance. For when we come to the question whether one is to do this or that, we come to a task for reasoning. And <in this case> one must measure by one <standard>, since one pursues the greater <good>. And so one is able to make one object of appearance out of many. And this is why <nonrational animals> do not seem to have belief; it is because they lack the <appearance> resulting from reasoning.

That is why desire lacks the deliberative part. And sometimes one desire overcomes and moves another, while sometimes the second overcomes and moves the first, like one sphere moving another, whenever incontinence[7] occurs. By nature the <desire> that is superior is dominant in every case and moves <the agent>, and so it turns out that three motions are initiated <in the agent>. The part that has knowledge$_e$ stays at rest and is not moved.

One sort of supposition and statement is universal, while another is about what is particular; for the first says that this sort of agent ought to do this sort of thing, and the second says that this is this sort of thing and I am this sort of agent. Hence the second belief, not the universal belief, initiates motion; or <rather> both initiate motion, but the first does so by being more at rest, in contrast to the second.

* * * * * * *

7. **incontinence**: Cf. *EN* i 13, vii 3.

PARTS OF ANIMALS[1]

Book I

[*INTRODUCTION TO THE STUDY OF NATURE*]

1

639a In every sort of study and line of inquiry, more humble and more honorable alike, there appear to be two sorts of competence. One of these is rightly called scientific knowledge$_e$ of the subject, and the other is a certain type of education; for it is characteristic of an educated person to be able to reach a judgment based on a sound estimate of when people expound their conclusions in the right or wrong way. For this is in fact what we take to be characteristic of a generally educated person, and this is the sort of ability that we identify with being educated. We expect one and the same individual with this general education to be able to judge in practically all subjects; but if someone <is educated in some narrower area>, we take him to have this ability <only> for some determinate area—for it is possible for someone to have the ability of an educated person about a restricted area.

Clearly, then, in inquiry into nature as elsewhere, there must be standards of this sort that we can refer to in deciding whether to accept the way in which a conclusion is proved, apart from whether or not the conclusion is true.

Should we, for instance, consider each single substance[2]—the nature of man, for instance, or ox or any other <species>, taking them one at a time—and determine what belongs to it in its own right? Or should we begin with the coincidents that belong to them all insofar as they have some common property? For often the same properties—for instance, sleep, breathing, growth, shrinkage, death, and all the other attributes and conditions of this sort—belong to many different kinds of things.

1. The actual study of the parts of animals begins in Book ii. The chapters translated from Book i are a general discussion of the methods and value of biological studies.

2. **substance**: i.e., secondary SUBSTANCE (see *Catg*. 2a14).

For, as things are, the right way to discuss these questions is unclear and indeterminate. Evidently, if we discuss them one species at a time, we will repeat ourselves on many topics. For in fact each of the properties mentioned actually belongs to horses, dogs, and human beings; and so, if we describe the coincidents one species at a time, we will be compelled to describe the same things many times over—in the case of each property that belongs to specifically different animals but is not itself different in each species. Presumably, though, there are also properties that have the same predicate but differ specifically in the different species. 639b The mobility of animals, for instance, is apparently not specifically one, since flying, swimming, walking, and creeping differ from one another.

Hence we should consider the right way to examine such questions: Should we begin by studying a whole genus in common before going on to study the special properties of the different species? Or should we study the particular species one at a time? For, as things are, this has not been determined.

Another question that has not been determined is this: Should the student of nature follow the procedure of the mathematician who proves truths about astronomy? If he does, he will first study the appearances about animals and about the parts of each type of animal, and then go on to state the reason why and the causes. Or should he follow some other procedure?

Further, we see that natural coming to be has more than one cause—for instance, both the cause that is for something and the cause that is the source of the principle of motion. We must, then, also determine which is primary and which is secondary among these.

The primary cause is apparently the one that we say is for something. For this is the form$_{\text{l}}$,[3] and the form$_{\text{l}}$ is the principle, both in the products of craft and equally in naturally constituted things. For the doctor or the builder begins by focussing, by thought or perception, on the definition of health or a house, and goes on to supply the forms$_{\text{l}}$ and the causes of each thing he produces, explaining why it should be produced in this way. And, moreover, what something is for—i.e, the fine result—is

3. **form$_{\text{l}}$**: What the craftsman has in his soul is the 'FORM without the matter' of the product he means to produce.

more fully present in the products of nature than in the products of craft.

Further, what is of necessity is not present in the same way in everything that is in accordance with nature. Practically all <students of nature>, however, try to refer their accounts back to what is of necessity, without having distinguished the different ways necessity is spoken of.

Unqualified necessity belongs to everlasting things, whereas conditional necessity belongs to everything that comes to be, just as it belongs to the products of crafts—to a house, for instance, and to anything else of that sort. In such cases it is necessary for the right sort of matter to be present if there is to be a house or some other end; first this must come to be and be moved, then this, and so on in order in the same way, until it reaches the end
640a for which a thing comes to be and is.[4] And the same is true of what comes to be by nature.

The appropriate type of demonstration and necessity, however, is not the same in the study of nature as it is in the theoretical sciences; we have discussed this in another work. For in the latter case the principle we begin from is what something is, but in the former case it is what will be. For since F (for instance, health or a man) is of this sort, it is necessary for G to be or to come to be, whereas it is not true that since G is or has come to be, F is or will be of necessity. Nor can you combine the necessity of such demonstration forever, so as to say that since one thing is, another thing is. In another work we have discussed both these questions, and also the sorts of things that are necessary, and in what cases necessities are reciprocal, and why.

We must also consider whether we should follow the procedure of our predecessors, by studying how a thing naturally comes to be rather than how it is. For it matters quite a bit which procedure we follow.

Now, it would seem that in the case of coming to be we should begin from how things are; for, just as we said before, we must begin with the appearances about a given kind of thing and then go on to state their causes. For in the case of building also, this comes about because the form of a house is of this sort, whereas it is not true that a house is of this sort because this is how it

4. **In such cases . . . and is**: Cf. *Phys.* 200a5–15.

comes to be; for coming to be is for the sake of being$_o$, not for the sake of coming to be.

That is why Empedocles was wrong to say that many things belong to animals because they came about coincidentally in the course of the animals' coming to be. He says, for instance, that the backbone has vertebrae because of the coincidence that the foetus got twisted and the backbone was broken. He did not know, first, that the seed resulting in the animal must already have the right potentiality, and, secondly, that the producer is prior in time as well as in account—for a human being generates a human being, so that the character of the parent explains the way in which the offspring comes to be.

The same point applies to the <natural> things that seem to come to be by chance, as it also does in the case of things produced by craft.[5] For some things—for instance, health—are the same when they come to be by chance as when they come to be from craft. In those cases, then, where the producer comes first (in statue making, for instance), the product does not come to be by chance. The craft is the account (without the matter) of the product; and the same is true for things resulting from luck, since how they come to be corresponds to the character of the craft.

Hence the best thing to say is that since being a human being is this, this is why he has these parts, since it is impossible for him to be without these parts. If we cannot say this, we must come as close as we can, and say either that it was quite impossible any other way or that it is done well this way. And these <means to the end> follow: since this is the character of the product, it is necessary for the coming to be to have this character and to happen in this way—that is why first this part comes to be, and then this part. And the same is true equally in the case of everything that is naturally constituted.

The early philosophers,[6] the first to study nature, investigated the material principle and cause, to see what it is and of what sort, how the whole universe comes to be from it, and what initiates the motion. <In their view>, strife, for instance, or love, or mind, or chance initiates the motion, and the matter that is the subject necessarily has a certain sort of nature; fire, for instance,

5. **The same point . . . craft.**: On chance see LUCK. Cf. *Met*. 1034b4.

6. **The early philosophers**: the NATURALISTS discussed in *Met*. i 3.

has a hot and light nature, earth a cold and heavy nature. This, indeed, is their account of how the world order comes into being.

They give the same sort of account of how animals and plants come into being. On their account, for example, the flowing of water in the body results in the coming to be of the stomach and of every receptacle for food and waste, and the flow of air results in the breaking open of the nostrils. Air and water are the matter of <living> bodies, since all <these philosophers> constitute nature from <elementary> bodies of this sort.

If, however, human beings and animals and their parts are natural, then we should discuss flesh, bone, blood, and all the uniform parts, and equally all the nonuniform parts, for instance, face, hand, and foot; and we should ask what gives each of them its character, and what potentiality is involved.

For it is not enough to say what constituents each of these parts is made of—of fire or earth, for instance. If we were speaking of a bed or any other <artifact>, we would try to distinguish its form rather than its matter (for instance, bronze or wood), or at any rate <the relevant matter> would be the matter of the compound. For a bed is this form in this matter, or this matter of this sort. And so we ought to speak of the thing's <formal> figure[7] and the sort of character it has as well <as of its matter>, since the nature corresponding to the form_{m} is more important than the material nature.

If, then, an animal and its parts have their being by having their <visible> figure and color, what Democritus says will turn out to be right, since this is what he seems to suppose. At any rate he says it is clear to everyone what the human form_{m} is, on the assumption that a human being is known_{g} by his <visible> figure and his color. <This is false>, however, <since> a dead human being has the same <visible> shape and figure that the living human being has, but still it is not a human being. Further, it is impossible for something <with the right visible figure and color> to be a hand, if it is not in the right condition—if, for instance, it is a bronze or wooden hand; in that case it can be a hand only homonymously, just as the doctor <painted in a picture is a doctor only homonymously>. For it will lack the potentiality to perform the function of a hand, just as the painted doctor or

7. **figure**: From here to 641a20, the supplements indicate Aristotle's different uses of 'FIGURE'.

stone flute lacks the potentiality to perform the function of a doctor or flute. Similarly, none of the parts of a dead human being is any longer the relevant sort of part—an eye or a hand, for instance.

Hence Democritus' claim lacks the appropriate qualifications; it is no better than a carpenter claiming that a wooden hand is a hand. For such a claim is typical of the naturalists' account of the coming to be and the causes of something's <formal> figure. For suppose we ask, 'What potentialities produced this?' Presumably the carpenter will mention an axe or an auger, whereas the naturalist will mention air and earth. The carpenter, however, gives the better answer.[8] For he will not suppose that it is enough to say that when his tool struck the wood, this part became hollow and this part plane. He will also mention the cause that explains why and for what end he struck this sort of blow—that is to say, in order to produce this or that sort of shape.

It is clear, then, that the natural philosophers are wrong, and that we must say that an animal has the <formal> character we have described. We must say, both about the animal itself and about each of its parts, what it is and what sort of thing it is, just as we also speak of the form of the bed.

Now, this form is either the soul or a part of the soul, or requires the soul. At any rate, when the soul has left, the animal no longer exists, and none of its parts remains the same, except in <visible> figure, like the things in stories that are turned to stone. If this is so, it is the task of the student of nature[9] to discuss and to know$_o$ about the soul—if not about all soul, then about the soul insofar as it makes the animal the sort of thing it is. He should know what the soul is, or what the relevant part of it is, and he should know about the coincidents that belong to it insofar as it has this sort of substance.

This is especially important because nature is, and is spoken of, in two ways, as matter and as substance. Now, substance is both the cause initiating motion and the end; and the soul, all or part of it, is both sorts of cause of the animal. Hence, for this reason also, the student of nature should discuss the soul more than the matter, to the extent that the <animal's> matter is its

8. **better answer**: Cf. *Phys.* 199b34–200a7.
9. **student of nature**: On this task cf. *DA* 404a24–b19.

nature because of the soul, rather than the other way round—for the wood is a bed or a tripod because it is one potentially.

Reflection on what we have said might raise a puzzle about whether the study of nature should consider all soul, or only some. If it considers all soul, then there will be no branch of 641b philosophy apart from the science of nature. For since understanding grasps the objects of understanding, the study of nature will be knowledge$_g$ of everything. For if two correlatives fall under the same study, as perception and its object do, and if understanding and its object are correlatives, then the same study will be concerned both with understanding and with its object.

Perhaps, however, not all soul, and not every part of soul, is a principle of motion. Rather, perhaps the principle of growth is the same part as in plants, the principle of alteration is the perceiving part, and the principle of local motion is some other part[10] distinct from understanding, since local motion is found in other animals as well as in human beings, but understanding is not found in any of them. It is clear, then, that we should not discuss all soul; for it is not all soul, but only one or more parts of it, that is nature.

Further, it is impossible for natural science to study any product of abstraction, because nature produces everything for something. For it is apparent that, just as craft is present in artifacts, so also in natural things themselves there is another cause and principle of this sort, which we get, as we get the hot and the cold, from the whole universe. Hence it is more plausible to suppose that the heaven has come to be by such a cause (if indeed it has come to be at all) and remains in being because of it, than to suppose this about mortal animals. For what is ordered and determinate is far more apparent in the heavens than in us, whereas variations from one time to another and matters of chance are more apparent in mortal things.

Some other people, however, hold that whereas every animal comes to be and remains in being by nature, the heaven was constituted as it is from luck and chance. They say this even though nothing at all resulting from luck and disorder is apparent in the heaven.[11]

10. **some other part**: Presumably the desiring part. For this division of parts of the soul cf. *DA* 413b11–414a3.
11. **They say . . . heaven**: Cf. *Phys*. 196a24–b5.

Again, whenever some end is apparent toward which a motion progresses if nothing impedes, we say that the motion is for the end. Hence it is evident that there is something of this sort, which we call nature. For not just any old thing comes to be from a given type of seed, but this sort of thing from this sort of seed; nor does any old body produce any old seed. Hence the <body> that the seed comes from is the principle that produces the seed that comes from it. For this happens naturally—at any rate, the body grows naturally from the seed.

But prior still is what it is the seed of. For the seed is a case of becoming, and the end is being$_{o}$. And what produces the seed is prior both to the seed and to what comes from the seed. For it is a seed in two ways—as the seed produced by something and as the seed of something.[12] For in fact it is the seed of what produced it (for instance, a horse), and also the seed of what comes to be from it (for instance, a mule), but it is not the seed of both in the same way; it is the seed of each in the way just described. Moreover, the seed is potentially <the organism>, and we know how potentiality is related to actuality.

There are, then, two causes—what something is for and what is of necessity (since many things come to be because it is necessary <for them to come to be>). And presumably a puzzle might arise about the sort of necessity that is meant by those who speak of what is of necessity; for neither of the two types defined in our treatises on philosophy can apply to this case.

There is a third type, however, in things that come to be. For we speak of food as necessary in neither of these two ways, but because an organism cannot exist without it. This, one might say, is conditional necessity. For instance, since an axe is needed for splitting wood, it is necessary for it to be hard; and in that case it is necessary for it to be made of iron.[13] In the same way, the body is also an instrument, since each of its parts, and the whole likewise, is for something; it is necessary, then, for it to be of this sort and to be composed of things of this sort, if what it is for is to result.

It is clear, then, that there are two types of cause and that in what we say we must either find both of them or, alternatively,

12. **For it is . . . seed of something**: For these two ways cf. *Met*. 1072b30–1073a3.
13. **since an axe . . . of iron**: Cf. *Phys*. 200a11–15.

try to make it clear, at any rate, that we cannot find both. It is also clear that people who do not do this might be said to tell us nothing about nature; for nature is a principle more than matter is.

Sometimes, indeed, Empedocles is led by the truth itself, and stumbles on the right sort of cause, and is compelled to say that the form$_l$ is a thing's substance and nature. When, for instance, he expounds what bone is, he does not say that it is one, two, three, or all of its elements, but that it is the form$_l$ of their mixture. It is clear, then, that flesh and every other part of that sort have this character.

The reason our predecessors did not discover this character is that they did not grasp the essence or the practice of defining substance. Democritus was the first to make some contact with them, but that was all he did—and not because he supposed it to be necessary for the study of nature, but because the facts themselves carried him away <from his own views>. In the time of Socrates, this <concern with essence and definition> grew, but investigation into nature stopped, and philosophers turned away to studying the virtue that is relevant to the conduct of life, and to political study.

Our proof should be on these lines—that respiration, for instance, is for this, but this comes about because of these things of necessity. Necessity sometimes signifies that if that end is to result, it is necessary for these things to be; and sometimes that they are so by nature. <In the second case> it is necessary, for instance, for the hot to go out and to come back in when it meets
642b resistance, and for the air to flow in. This is all necessary; and when the hot that is inside resists as cooling goes on, the air outside enters or leaves.

This, then, is the procedure of our line of inquiry, and these are the sorts of things whose causes we must find.

* * * * * * *

5

644b Among the substances constituted by nature, some, we say, neither come to be nor perish for all time, and others share in coming to be and perishing. It turns out that we have fewer ways of studying the first type of substances, honorable and divine though they are; for very few things indeed are apparent in perception to give us a basis for inquiry into what we would like to know about these things. We are better supplied, however, with opportunities for knowledge$_g$ about perishable plants and animals, since we live among them. For someone willing to undertake the appropriate labor can discover many of the facts about each kind of plant and animal.

Each of the two types of substance has some appeal. For even though we have little contact with the divine substances, still their honorable nature makes it pleasanter to know them than to know all the things around us—just as a chance glimpse of some small part of someone we love is pleasanter than an exact view of many other great things. On the other hand, since we can know$_e$ better and know more about the substances around us, the knowledge of them has some superiority. Further, the fact that they are closer to us and more akin to our nature compensates to some degree for <the superior attraction of> philosophy about divine things.

We have finished our discussion of divine things, saying what appears to us. The remaining task, then, is to speak of animal nature, whether more or less honorable, leaving nothing out, as far as possible. For even though some of the animals we study are unattractive to perception, still the nature that has produced them provides amazing pleasures for those who are capable of knowing$_g$ the causes and are naturally philosophers. For in studying representations of them, we also delight in studying the painter's or sculptor's craft that has produced them; how absurd it would be, then, not to like studying those naturally constituted things themselves, provided, of course, that we are able to notice the causes.

That is why we must avoid childish complaints about examining the less honorable animals; for in all natural things there is something admirable. The story goes that when some strangers wanted to see Heracleitus, they stopped on their way in, since they saw him warming himself at the oven; but he kept urging them, 'Come in, and don't worry; for there are gods here also.' In the same way, then, we must go forward without embarrassment with our search into each type of animal, assuming that there is something natural and fine in each of them.

For <processes> that are for something and are not a matter of luck are most characteristic of the products of nature; and the end for which these things are constituted or have come to be counts as something admirable. And anyone who regards the study of other animals as dishonorable ought to take the same view about himself; for one is bound to feel great distaste at the constituents of the human species—blood, flesh, bones, veins, and parts of that sort.

Similarly, when someone is discussing some part or equipment, we should not suppose that he is drawing attention <simply> to the matter, or that he is concerned with it for its own sake; he is concerned with the form$_{m}$ as a whole. In the case of a house, for instance, <we are concerned with the form>, not with the bricks, mud, and wood. So also, in studying nature we are concerned with the composite structure and with the substance as a whole, not with the things that are never found in separation from their substance.

* * * * * * *

METAPHYSICS[1]

Book I

[*THE SCIENCE OF FIRST CAUSES*]

1

All human beings by nature desire to know$_{o}$. A sign of this is our liking for the senses; for even apart from their usefulness we like them for themselves—especially the sense of sight, since we choose seeing above practically all the others, not only as an aid to action, but also when we have no intention of acting. The reason is that sight, more than any of the other senses, gives us knowledge$_{g}$ of things and clarifies many differences among them.

Animals possess sense-perception by nature at birth. In some but not all of these, perception results in memory, making them more intelligent and better at learning than those that cannot remember. Some animals that cannot hear sounds (for instance, bees and similar kinds of animal) are intelligent but do not learn; those that both perceive sounds and have memory also learn.

Nonhuman animals live by appearances and memories but have little share in experience, whereas human beings also live by craft and reasoning. In human beings experience results from memory, since many memories of the same thing result in the potentiality for a single experience.[2] Experience seems to be quite like science and craft, and indeed human beings attain science and craft through experience; for, as Polus correctly says, experience has produced craft, but inexperience only luck.

A craft arises when many thoughts that arise from experience result in one universal view about similar things. For the view that in this illness this treatment benefited Callias, Socrates, and others, in many particular cases, is characteristic of experience, but the view that it benefited everyone of a certain sort (marked out by a single kind) suffering from a certain disease (for instance, phlegmatic or bilious people when burning with fever) is characteristic of craft.

1. On this title see PHILOSOPHY.

2. **experience**: See *APo* 100a3–6.

For practical purposes, experience seems no worse than craft; indeed we even see that experienced people are actually more successful than those who have a rational account but lack experience. The reason is that experience is knowledge$_g$ of particulars, whereas craft is knowledge of universals. Moreover, each action and event concerns a particular; in medical treatment, for instance, we do not heal man (except coincidentally) but Callias or Socrates or some other individual who is coincidentally a man.[3] If, then, someone has a rational account but lacks experience, and knows$_g$ the universal but not the particular falling under it, he will often give the wrong treatment, since treatment is applied to the particular.

Nonetheless, we attribute knowing$_o$ and comprehending to craft more than to experience, and we suppose that craftsmen are wiser than experienced people, on the assumption that in every case knowledge$_o$, rather than experience, implies wisdom. This is because craftsmen know$_o$ the cause, but <merely> experienced people do not; for experienced people know$_o$ the fact that something is so but not the reason why it is so,[4] whereas craftsmen know$_g$ the reason why, i.e., the cause.

That is why we believe that the master craftsmen[5] in a given 981b craft are more honorable, know$_o$ more, and are wiser than the manual craftsmen, because they know$_o$ the causes of what is produced. The manual craftsmen, we think, are like inanimate things that produce without knowing$_o$ what they produce, in the way that, for instance, fire burns; the latter produce their products by a natural tendency, while the manual craftsmen produce theirs because of habit. We assume, then, that some craftsmen are wiser than others not because they are better in practice, but because they have a rational account and know$_g$ the causes.

And in general, a sign that distinguishes those who know$_o$ from those who do not is their ability to teach. Hence we think craft, rather than experience, is knowledge$_e$, since craftsmen can teach, while merely experienced people cannot.

Further, we do not think any of the senses is wisdom, even

3. **coincidentally a man**: i.e., coincidentally from the point of view of healing. Aristotle does not mean that being a man is a COINCIDENTAL property of Socrates.

4. **that . . . is so**: Cf. *APo* 93a16, *EN* 1095b6.

5. **master craftsmen**: Cf. *Phys.* 194a33–b7.

though they are the most authoritative ways of knowing$_g$ particulars. They do not tell us why anything is so; for instance, they do not tell us why fire is hot, but only that it is hot.

It is not surprising, then, that in the earliest times anyone who discovered any craft that went beyond the perceptions common to all was admired not only because he discovered something useful, but also for being a wise person, superior to others. Later on, as more crafts were discovered—some related to necessities, others to [leisuretime] pursuits—those who discovered these latter crafts were in every case taken to be wiser than the others, because their sciences did not aim at practical utility. Hence, finally, after all these crafts had been established, the sciences that aim neither at pleasure nor at necessities were discovered, initially in the places where people had leisure. This is why mathematical crafts arose first in Egypt; for there the priestly class were allowed to be at leisure.

The difference between craft and science and other similar sorts of things has been discussed in the *Ethics*.[6] The point of our present discussion is to show that in everyone's view any discipline deserving the name of wisdom must describe the first causes, i.e., the principles. And so, as we said earlier, the experienced person seems to be wiser than those who have just any old perception; the craftsman seems to be wiser than those with nothing more than experience; the master craftsman wiser than the manual craftsman; and the purely theoretical sciences wiser than the productive sciences. It is clear, then, that wisdom is knowledge$_e$ of certain sorts of principles and causes.

2

Since this is the science we are seeking, we should consider what sorts of causes and principles wisdom is the science of. Perhaps this will become clearer if we consider our views about the wise person. First, we suppose that he has knowledge$_e$ about all things as far as possible, without, however, having it about each particular <kind of thing>. Next, the one who is capable of knowing$_g$ difficult things, i.e., things not easily known by human beings, is the wise person; for sense-perception is common to everyone, and that is why it is easy and not characteristic of wisdom. Further,

6. **the *Ethics***: See *EN* vi 2.

someone is wiser in a given science if he is more exact, and a better teacher of the causes. Again, if one of two sciences is choiceworthy for itself—<purely> for the sake of knowing$_o$ it—and the other is choiceworthy <only> for the sake of its results, the first has a better claim to be wisdom than the second. Moreover, the superior science has a better claim than the subordinate science; for the wise person must give orders, not take them, and those who are less wise must follow his orders, not he theirs. These, then, are our views about wisdom and wise people.

Of these features, we suppose that knowledge$_e$ about everything necessarily belongs to the one who has the best claim to universal science; for he in a way knows$_o$ everything that is a subject for a science. These most universal things are also just about the most difficult for human beings to know$_g$, since they are furthest from perceptions.[7] Further, the most exact sciences are those that, more than the others, study the first things; for the sciences that are derived from fewer principles (for instance, arithmetic) are more exact than those (for instance, geometry) that require further principles. Moreover, the science that studies the causes is more of a teacher, since teachers are those who state something's causes. Besides, knowledge$_o$ and science for their own sake are most characteristic of the science of the most appropriate object of knowledge$_e$. For one who chooses knowledge$_e$ for its own sake will choose above all the science that is a science to the highest degree. This science is the science of the most appropriate objects of knowledge$_e$; these objects are the first things, i.e., the causes, since we know$_g$ the subordinate things because of these and from these, not the other way round. Further, the most superior science—the one that is superior to any subordinate science—is the one that knows$_g$ the end for which a given thing should be done; this end is something's good, and in general the end is what is best in every sort of nature.

From everything that has been said, then, we find that the name under discussion, <i.e., 'wisdom'>, applies to the same science; for we find that wisdom must study the first principles and causes, and the good, the end, is one of the causes.

The fact that this science is not productive is also clear from those who first engaged in philosophy. For human beings originally began philosophy, as they do now, because of wonder, at

7. **furthest from perceptions**: Cf. *APo* 72a1–5.

first because they wondered at the strange things in front of them, and later because, advancing little by little, they found greater things puzzling—what happens to the moon, the sun and the stars, how the universe comes to be. Someone who wonders and is puzzled thinks he is ignorant (this is why the myth lover is also a philosopher in a way, since myth is composed of wonders); since, then, they engaged in philosophy to escape ignorance, they were evidently pursuing scientific knowledge for the sake of knowing$_{o}$, not for any further use.

What actually happened is evidence for this view. For it was only when practically everything required for necessities and for ease and <leisuretime> pursuits was supplied that they began to seek this sort of understanding; clearly, then, we do not seek it for some further use. Just as we describe a free person as one who exists for his own sake and not for someone else's, so we also describe this as the only free science, since it is the only one that exists for its own sake.

Hence the possession of this science might justifiably be thought to be beyond human capacity. For in many ways human nature is in slavery, so that, as Simonides says, 'the god alone would have this privilege', and it is unfitting for human beings to transgress their own level in their search for the science. If there actually is something in what the poets say, and the divine nature is spiteful, divine spite would be likely in this case, and all those who go too far would suffer misfortunes. The divine nature, however, cannot be spiteful: as the proverb says, 'Poets tell many lies'.

Nor ought we to take any science to be more honorable than this one, since the most divine science is also the most honorable, and this science that we are describing is the most divine. It alone is most divine in two ways: for the divine science <may be understood> as (i) the one that a god more than anyone else would be expected to have, or as (ii) the science of divine things. Only this science <of first causes> satisfies both conditions <for being divine>. For (i) the god seems to be among the causes of all things, and to be some sort of principle, and (ii) this is the sort of science that the god, alone or more than anyone else, would be expected to have. Hence all the other sciences are more necessary than this one, but none is better.

However, the possession of this science must in a way leave us in a condition contrary to the one we were in when we began our search. For, as we said, everyone begins from wonder that something is the way it is, as they wonder at toys that move spontaneously, or the turnings of the sun, or the incommensurability of the diagonal (for people who have not yet studied the cause are filled with wonder that there is something that is not measured by the smallest length). But we must end up in the contrary and (according to the proverb) the better state, the one that people achieve by learning <the cause> in these other cases as well—for nothing would be more amazing to a geometer than if the diagonal turned out to be commensurable.

We have described, then, the nature of the science we are seeking, and the goal that our search and our whole line of inquiry must reach.

[*SURVEY OF PREVIOUS PHILOSOPHERS: THE PRESOCRATICS*]

3

It is evident, then, that we must acquire knowledge$_e$ of the original causes, since we say we know$_o$ a thing whenever we think we know$_g$ its primary cause. Causes are spoken of in four ways. One of these, we say, is the being$_o$ and essence; for the reason why is traced back ultimately to the account, and the primary reason why is the cause and principle. Another is the matter and subject. A third is the source of the principle of motion. The fourth is what something is for, i.e., the good—the opposite to the third cause, since it is the end of all coming to be and motion.

We have studied these causes adequately in our work on nature.[8] Still, let us also enlist those who previously took up the investigation of beings and pursued philosophical study about the truth; for it is clear that they also mention causes and principles of some sort. A discussion of their views, then, will advance our present line of inquiry; for either we shall find some other kind of cause or we shall be more convinced about those we have just mentioned.

Most of the first philosophers, then, thought that the only principles of all things were material. For, they say, there is some <subject> that all beings come from, the first thing they come to be

8. **on nature**: See *Phys.* ii 3.

from and the last thing they perish into, the substance remaining throughout but changing in respect of its attributes. This, they say, is the element and the principle of beings. And for this reason they think that nothing either comes to be or is destroyed, on the assumption that this nature <that is the subject> persists in every change, just as we say that Socrates does not come to be without qualification when he comes to be good or musical, and that he is not destroyed when he loses these states (because the subject, Socrates himself, remains)—so also they say that nothing else either comes to be or perishes without qualification (for there must be some nature, either one or more than one, that persists while everything else comes to be from it).[9]

But they do not all agree about the number or type of this material principle. Thales, the originator of this sort of philosophy, says it is water (that is why he also declared that the earth rests on water). Presumably he reached this view from seeing that what nourishes all things is wet and that the hot itself comes from the wet and is kept alive by it (and what all things come to be from is their principle). He also reached this view because he thought that the seeds of all things have a wet nature (and water is the principle of the nature of wet things).

Some people think that even those who first gave accounts of the gods in very ancient times, long before the present, accepted this view about nature. For the ancients made Oceanus and Tethys the parents of coming to be and described the oath of the gods as water, which they called Styx; for what is oldest is most honored, and what is most honored is the oath. It is perhaps unclear whether this belief about nature is in fact old or even ancient, but at any rate this is what Thales is said to have declared about the first cause. (No one would think of including Hippon among these philosophers, given the triviality of his thought.)

Anaximenes and Diogenes take air to be both prior to water and also the primary principle of all the simple bodies, while Hippasus of Metapontium and Heracleitus of Ephesus say this about fire. Empedocles takes the four bodies to be principles, adding earth as a fourth to the ones mentioned. These, he says, always remain, and do not come to be, except insofar as they

9. **(for there must . . . come to be from it)**: This parenthesis and the two in the next paragraph are Aristotle's explanatory comments, not attributed to the monists.

come to be more or fewer, being combined into one and dispersed from one into many.

Anaxagoras of Clazomenae, who was older than Empedocles but wrote later, says that the principles are unlimited; for he says that practically all the uniform things (for instance, water or fire) come to be and are destroyed only[10] in the ways we have mentioned, by being combined and dispersed; they do not come to be or get destroyed in any other way, but always remain.

If one went by these views, one might suppose that the material cause is the only sort of cause. But as people thus advanced, reality itself showed them the way and compelled them to search. For however true it might be that all coming to be and perishing is from one (or more than one) thing, still, *why* does this happen, and what is the cause? For certainly the subject does not produce change in itself. I mean, for instance, neither the wood nor the bronze causes itself to change, nor does the wood itself produce a bed, or the bronze a statue, but something else causes the change. And to search for this is (in our view) to search for the second principle—the source of the principle of motion.

Those who were the very first to undertake this line of inquiry into nature, who said that the subject is one, were quite satisfied with this. But at least some[11] of those who said that the subject is one, as though defeated by this search <for an explanation of change>, said that the one, i.e., nature as a whole, is immobile, not only as regards coming to be and perishing (that was an old belief agreed on by all), but also as regards every other sort of change. This view is distinctive of them.

Of those who said that the universe is one element, none managed to notice this <second> cause, unless Parmenides did; he noticed it only insofar as he posited not only one cause, but also in a way two causes. Indeed those who recognize more than one element—for instance, hot and cold, or fire and earth—make it easier to state <the cause that initiates motion>, since they regard fire as having a nature that initiates motion, and water, earth, and other such things as having natures contrary to this.

After these sorts of principles were proposed by these people, other people found them inadequate to generate the nature of

10. **uniform things**: See PART.

11. **some**: the Eleatics, especially PARMENIDES in his 'Way of Truth'.

beings; once again, as we said, it was as though the truth itself compelled them, and so they began to search for the next sort of principle.[12] For presumably it is unlikely that fire or earth or anything else of that sort would cause some things to be in a good and fine state and would cause other things to come to be in that state, and unlikely that people would think so; still, it was unsatisfactory to entrust so great a result to chance and luck. And so when one of them said that mind is present (in nature just as in animals) as the cause of the world order and of all its arrangement, he seemed like a sober person, and his predecessors seemed like babblers in comparison. We know that Anaxagoras evidently made a start on giving such accounts, but an earlier statement of them is ascribed to Hermotimus of Clazomenae. Those who held this view posited a principle of beings that is at once both the cause of things' turning out well and the sort of cause that is the source of motion for beings.

4

One might suspect that the first to search for this sort of cause was Hesiod and anyone else who counted desire or appetite among beings as a principle, as Parmenides, for instance, also did. For he too, in describing the coming to be of the whole universe, says: 'Desire was the first of all the gods she devised'.[13] And Hesiod says: 'Before everything else that came to be, there was chaos, and then the broad-fronted earth, and desire, preeminent among all the immortals.'[14] He assumes that there must be some cause among beings to initiate motion in things and to bring them together. Let us leave it till later to determine which of these people was the first <to discover this sort of cause>.

Moreover, the contraries of good things (i.e., disorder and ugliness no less than order and beauty) were also apparent in nature, and bad things were apparently more numerous than good things, and base things more numerous than beautiful things. For this rea-

12. **the next sort of principle**: the moving cause.

13. **'Desire was . . . devised'**: From Parmenides' 'Way of Opinion'. The subject of 'she' is probably Aphrodite, the goddess of sexual desire and love.

14. **'Before . . . immortals'**: Hesiod.

son someone else introduced love and strife so that each of them would be the cause of one of these two sorts of things. For if we follow Empedocles' argument, and do not confine ourselves to his mumbling way of expressing it, but attend to what he has in mind, we will find that love is the cause of good things, and strife of bad. And so, if one were to claim that in a way Empedocles said—indeed was the first to say—that the good and the bad are principles, one would perhaps be right, if the cause of all goods is the good itself.

These people, then, as we say, evidently made this much progress in fastening on two of the four causes that we distinguished in our work on nature—the matter and the principle of motion. But they did so dimly and not at all perspicuously. They were like unskilled boxers in fights, who, in the course of moving around, often land good punches, but are not guided by knowledge$_e$; in the same way these thinkers would seem not to know$_o$ what they are saying, since they evidently make practically no use of these causes, except to a slight degree.

Anaxagoras, for instance, uses mind as an artificial contrivance for the production of the universe; it is when he is puzzled about the cause of something's being necessarily as it is that he drags in mind, but in other cases he recognizes anything but mind as the cause of things that come to be. Empedocles, admittedly, uses these causes more than Anaxagoras does, but he too still makes insufficient use of them, and he does not succeed in using them consistently. At any rate, he often makes love draw things apart, and strife draw them together. For whenever strife scatters the universe into its elements, all the fire is gathered into one, and so is each of the other elements; and whenever love brings things back together again into one, the parts from each element are necessarily scattered again.

Empedocles, then, went beyond his predecessors. He was the first to distinguish this cause and to introduce it; he did not take the principle of motion to be one, but assumed different and contrary principles. Moreover, he was the first to say that there are four material elements. In fact, though, he does not use all four, but treats them as two, treating fire in its own right as one nature, and its opposites—earth, air, and water—as together constituting another; this may be gathered from studying his poems. As we say, then, this is how many principles he recognized, and this is what he said about them.

Leucippus and his colleague Democritus, on the other hand,

say that the elements are the full and the empty, and that, of these, the full and solid is what is, and the empty is what is not. That is why they also say that what is is no more of a being than what is not, because body is no more of a being than the empty is. They take these to be the material causes of beings.

Those who take the substance that is the subject to be one explain how everything else comes to be by referring to the ways in which the subject is affected, taking the rare and the dense to be the principle of the ways it is affected. In the same way, Leucippus and Democritus take the differentiae[15] to be the causes of the other things. They say, however, that there are three of these differentiae—shape, order, and position. For they say that what is is differentiated only by <what they call> 'rhythm', 'touching', and 'turning'. Of these rhythm is shape, touching is order, and turning is position; for A differs from N in shape, AN from NA in order, and Z from N in position. Like the other <naturalists>, however, they were too lazy to take up the question about motion and to ask from what source and in what way it arises in beings.

This, then, would seem to be the extent, as we say, of the earlier thinkers' search for these two causes.

* * * * * * *

[*CRITICISMS OF PLATO*]

6

Plato's work came after the philosophical views we have mentioned;[16] 987a29 it agreed with them in most ways, but it also had distinctive features setting it apart from the philosophy of the Italians. For in his youth Plato first became familiar with Cratylus and with the Heracleitean beliefs that all perceptible things are always flowing and that there is no knowledge$_e$ of them; he held these views later too. Socrates, on the other hand, was concerned with 987b ethics and not at all with nature as a whole; he was seeking

15. **differentiae**: of the atoms, the solid bodies referred to in general terms as 'the full'.

16. **views we have mentioned**: Aristotle has been discussing the Eleatics and Pythagoreans, whom he calls the 'Italians'.

the universal in ethics and was the first to turn his thought to definitions. Plato agreed with Socrates, but because of his Heracleitean views he took these definitions to apply not to perceptible things but to other things; for, he thought, the common formula could not be of any of the perceptible things, since they are always changing. Beings of this sort <that definitions are of>, then, he called Ideas, and he said that perceptible things are apart from these, and are all called after them, since the things with the same names as the Forms are what they are by participation in them.

In speaking of 'participation' he changed only the name; for the Pythagoreans say that things are what they are by imitating numbers, and Plato (changing the name) said they are what they are by participating <in Forms>. But they left it to others to investigate what it is to participate in or to imitate Forms.

Further, he says that, apart from perceptible things and Forms, there are also mathematical objects in between. These differ from perceptible things in being everlasting and immobile; they differ from Forms in that there are many of the same kind, whereas there is only one Form for each kind of thing.

Since the Forms are the causes of other things, he thought that their elements are the elements of all beings. The great and the small, then, as matter, and the one, as substance, are principles; for Forms come from these, by participating in the one. And yet he said, agreeing with the Pythagoreans, that the one is substance, and that it is not said to be one by being something else. He also agreed with them in saying that numbers are the causes of the being$_{o}$ of other things; but in positing a duality instead of treating the indefinite as one, and in taking the great and small to constitute the indefinite, he held a distinctive view of his own. Moreover, in his view numbers exist apart from perceptible things; whereas the Pythagoreans take the objects themselves to be numbers, and do not place mathematical objects between perceptible things and Forms.

His claim that the one and numbers exist apart from the other objects (in contrast to the Pythagorean view) and his introduction of the Forms were the result of his investigation of arguments; for none of his predecessors engaged in dialectic. He made the other nature <besides the One> a duality because he thought that numbers (except the primes) could be neatly produced from the duality, as though from something malleable.

What actually happens, though, is the contrary of this, and it is implausible to think it would happen in the way they <the Platonists> say. For in their view many things are made out of the matter, but the Form generates only once; in fact, however, only one table is apparently made out of one <bit of> matter, whereas the agent who applies the form, though he is one, makes many tables. Similarly, in the case of male and female, the female is impregnated from one copulation, whereas the male impregnates many females. And yet these things[17] are imitations of those principles <that they believe in>.

This, then, was what Plato determined about the questions we are investigating. It is evident from what has been said that he used only two causes, the cause involving the what-it-is and the material cause; for the Forms are causes of the what-it-is of other things, and the one is the cause of the what-it-is of Forms. The nature of the matter that is the subject for the Forms (in the case of perceptible things) and for the one (in the case of Forms) is also evident: it is the duality, the great and the small. Further, he has assigned the cause of good and bad to the elements, one to each, as we say some earlier philosophers, such as Empedocles and Anaxagoras, also sought to do.

* * * * * * *

9

As for those who posited Ideas, the first objection is that in seeking 990a34
to grasp the causes of the beings in this world, they introduced 990b
different things, equal in number to them. It is as though someone wanted to count things and thought he could not do it if there were fewer of them, but could do it if he added more. For the Forms they resorted to in their search for the causes of things in this world are practically equal in number to—or at any rate are no fewer than—the things in this world. For take each <kind of> thing that has a one over many, both substances and nonsubstances, both things in this world and everlasting things; in

17. **these things**: matter and form.

each case there is some <one over many> that has the same name[18] <as the many>.

Further, none of the proofs we[19] offer to show that there are Forms appears to succeed; for some of them are invalid, while some also yield Forms of things that we think have no Forms. For the arguments from the sciences yield Forms of all the things of which there are sciences; the one over many yields Forms even of negations; and the argument from thinking about something that has perished yields Forms of things that perish, since there is an appearance of these. Further, among the more accurate arguments, some produce Ideas of relatives, whereas we deny that these are a kind of things that are in their own right; others introduce the Third Man.

* * * * * * *

Book IV

[*THE SCIENCE OF BEING*]

1

1003a21 There is a science that studies being insofar as it is being,[1] and also the properties of being in its own right. It is not the same as any of the so-called special sciences. For none of them considers being quite generally, insofar as it is being; rather, each of them cuts off some part of being and studies the relevant coincident of that part, as, for instance, the mathematical sciences do.

Since we are seeking the principles, i.e., the highest causes,

18. **same name**: Platonic Forms are (in Aristotle's view) similar to the corresponding sensible things (so that the Form of just, e.g., is simply another just thing, and the Form of man is simply another man; cf. *EN* 1096a34–b5).

19. **we**: Aristotle thinks of himself as one of the Platonic school, though he does not endorse their position.

1. **insofar as**: Aristotle refers to ordinary beings, studied with reference to the properties that belong to them INSOFAR AS they are beings. Cf. 1004b5–17.

clearly they must be the causes of the nature of some subject as it is in its own right. If, then, those who were seeking the elements of beings were also seeking these highest principles, the elements must also be the elements of being not coincidentally, but insofar as it is being. That is why we also ought to find the first causes of being insofar as it is being.

2

Being is spoken of in many ways, but always with reference to one thing—i.e., to some one nature—and not homonymously. Everything healthy, for instance, is spoken of with reference to health—one thing because it preserves health, another because it produces health, another because it indicates health, another because it can receive health. Similarly, the medical is spoken of with reference to medical science; for one thing is called medical because it has the medical science, another because it is naturally suited to medical science, another because it is the function of medical science, and we shall find other things spoken of in ways similar to these.

Similarly, then, being is spoken of in many ways, but in all cases it is spoken of with reference to one principle. For some things are called beings because they are substances, others because they are attributes of substance, others because they are a road to substance, or because they are perishings or privations or qualities of substance, or productive or generative of substance or of things spoken of with reference to it, or because they are negations of one of these or of substance. This is why we also say that not being is—i.e., is not being.

A single science studies all healthy things, and the same applies in the other cases. For it is not only things that are spoken of in accordance with one <common property> that are studied by a single science; the same is true of things that are spoken of with reference to one nature, since these things are also, in a way, spoken of in accordance with one <common property>. Clearly, then, it is also the task of a single science to study beings insofar as they are beings.

In every case the dominant concern of a science is with its primary object, the one on which the others depend and because of which they are spoken of as they are. If, then, this primary object is substance, the philosopher must grasp the principles and causes of substances.[2]

1004a2 There are as many parts of philosophy as there are <types of> substances, and so there must be a first philosophy, and a second philosophy following it; for being is divided immediately into genera, which is why the sciences will also conform to these. For the philosopher is spoken of in the same way as the mathematician is; for mathematical science also has parts, and in mathematics there is a first and a second science and others succeeding in order.

1003b19 For every single genus there is a single <sort of> perception and a single science; there is, for instance, a single grammatical science, and it studies all the <types of> sounds. Hence it is also the task of a science that is one in genus to study all the species of being insofar as it is being; it is the task of the species of that science to study the species <of being>.

Being and unity are the same and a single nature, since they imply each other, as principle and cause do, though they are not one and the same in the sense of being revealed by the same account (though indeed it does not matter if we take them to have the same account; that would be even more suitable for our purpose). For one man is the same as a man, and moreover a man who is is the same as a man, and 'he is a man and a man who is' reveals nothing different by the repetition in what is said, since clearly a man and a man who is are separated neither in coming to be nor in perishing. The same also applies to unity. It is evident, then, that in these cases the addition <of 'one'> reveals the same thing <as 'is' reveals>, and that unity is nothing different from being. Moreover, the substance of a thing is noncoincidentally one thing; and similarly it is essentially some being.

It follows that there are as many species of being as of unity. Hence it is a task for a science that is the same in genus to study the what-it-is about these species—for instance, about same,
1004a similar and other such things. Practically all the contraries are referred to this principle; our study of these in the Selection of Contraries will suffice.

It is the task of one science to study opposites, and plurality is the opposite of unity. It is also the task of one science to study

2. The next paragraph consists of 1004a2–9 transposed to an apparently more suitable place.

negation and privation, since in both cases we study the one thing of which it is the negation or the privation. For either we say without qualification that something does not belong to the subject, or we say that it does not belong to some genus of the subject. In the latter case a differentia is added apart from what is in the negation—for the negation is the absence of that property, but the privation also involves some nature that is the subject of which the privation is said.

And so it is also the task of the science we have mentioned to know about the contraries of the things we have mentioned—different, unlike, unequal, and everything else that is spoken of either with respect to these or with respect to plurality and unity. Contrariety is also one of these; for it is a type of difference, and difference is a type of otherness. And so, since unity is spoken of in many ways, these will also be spoken of in many ways; but still it is the task of a single science to know them all. For the mere fact that things are spoken of in many ways does not imply that they cannot be studied by one and the same science; different sciences are required only if it is true both that the things have no one <common property> and that their accounts are not referred to one thing.

Since in each case everything is referred to the primary thing (for instance, everything that is called one is referred to the primary unity), this is also what we ought to say about same, different, and contraries. And so we should first distinguish how many ways each thing is spoken of, and then show how each of the things we have distinguished is spoken of with reference to the primary thing in each predication; for some things will be spoken of as they are because they have that primary thing, others because they produce it, others in other such ways.

Evidently, then, it is the task of a single science to take account both of these things and of substance (this was one of the questions that raised puzzles), and it is the philosopher's task to be able to study all <these> things. For if this is not his task, who will consider whether Socrates is the same as seated Socrates,[3] or whether one thing has <just> one contrary, or what contrariety is, or how many ways it is spoken of? And the same is true for other questions of that sort.

We have found, then, that these are attributes of unity insofar

3. **whether . . . seated Socrates**: Cf. *Met*. 1032a8n.

as it is unity, and of being insofar as it is being; each is an attribute of unity and being in their own right, not insofar as they are numbers or lines or fire.[4] Hence it is clearly the task of that science <of being> to know both what being and unity are, and also their coincidents. The mistake of those who currently consider these questions is not that they fail to practice philosophy but that, although substance is prior, they comprehend nothing about it.

There are attributes distinctive of number insofar as it is number (for instance, oddness and evenness, commensurability and inequality, being more and being less), and these belong to numbers both in their own right and in relation to one another. Likewise there are other attributes distinctive of the solid, both moved and unmoved, and <of the moved>, both weightless and having weight. In the same way, then, there are also some attributes distinctive of being insofar as it is being, and it is the philosopher's task to investigate the truth about these.

Here is a sign <to show that it is his task>. Dialecticians and sophists assume the same guise as the philosopher. For sophistic has the appearance of wisdom, though nothing more, and dialecticians practice dialectic about all things; being is common to all things, and clearly they practice dialectic about all things because all things are proper to philosophy. For sophistic and dialectic treat the same genus as philosophy, but philosophy differs from dialectic in the type of power it has, and it differs from sophistic in its decision about how to live. Dialectic tests in the area where philosophy achieves knowledge, while sophistic has the appearance <of knowledge>, but not the reality.

* * * * * * *

3

1005a19 We ought to say whether it is the task of one and the same science or of different sciences to study both the axioms (as they are called in mathematics) and substance. Evidently it is also the task of one and the same science—the philosopher's—to examine

4. **of one and being . . . or fire**: The beings that we discuss may in fact be mathematical or physical objects, but this is irrelevant, since we consider beings INSOFAR AS they are beings.

these, since these belong to all beings and are not distinctive of one genus in separation from the others.

Every scientist uses the axioms because they belong to being insofar as it is being, and each genus is a being. But each uses them to the extent he needs them, and that is however far the genus about which he presents his demonstrations extends. Clearly, then, the axioms belong to all things insofar as they are beings (for this is what all things have in common); and so it is also the task of the one who knows being insofar as it is being to study the axioms.

This is why none of those who investigate a special area—for instance, a geometer or an arithmetician— undertakes to say anything about whether or not the axioms are true. The ones who did so were some of the students of nature; and it is not surprising that they did this, since they were the only ones who thought they were examining the whole of nature and examining being. In fact, however, there is someone still higher than the student of nature, since nature is only one kind of being; and so investigating these axioms will also be a task of this universal scientist, the one who studies primary substance. The study of nature is also a type 1005b
of wisdom, but not the primary type.

Now, some of those who argue about when a conclusion should properly be accepted as true object that one should not accept <principles that have not been demonstrated>. They do this because they lack education in analytics;[5] for someone who comes <to the science of being> must already know$_e$ about analytics and not ask about it when he studies <the science of being>.

Clearly, then, study of the principles of deductions is also a task for the philosopher—i.e., for the one who studies the nature of all substance. Whoever has the best claim to knowledge$_g$ of a given genus ought to be able to state the firmest principles of his subject matter; hence whoever has the best claim to knowledge of beings insofar as they are beings should be able to state the firmest principles of all things. This person is the philosopher.

The firmest principle of all is one about which it is impossible to be mistaken. For this sort of principle must be known$_g$ best (for what we make mistakes about is invariably what we do not

5. **Now some . . . in analytics**: Education in the nature of DEDUCTION and DEMONSTRATION, as set out in Aristotle's *Analytics*, shows why there is no demonstration of first principles.

know), and it cannot be an assumption. For a principle that we must already possess in order to understand anything at all about beings is not an assumption;[6] and what we must know in order to know anything at all is a principle we must already possess. Clearly, then, this sort of principle is the firmest of all.

Let us next say what this principle is: that it is impossible for the same thing both to belong and not to belong at the same time to the same thing and in the same respect (and let us assume we have drawn all the further distinctions that might be drawn to meet logical complaints). This, then, is the firmest principle of all, since it has the distinguishing feature previously mentioned.

For it is impossible for anyone to suppose that the same thing is and is not, though some people take Heracleitus to say this; for what one says need not be what one supposes to be true. For it is impossible for contraries to belong at the same time to the same thing (and let us assume that the customary further distinctions are added to this statement). But what is contrary to a belief is the belief in its contradictory. Hence evidently it is impossible for the same person at the same time to suppose that the same thing is and is not, since someone who makes this mistake would have contrary beliefs at the same time. This is why all those who demonstrate refer back to this belief as ultimate; for this is by nature the principle of all the other axioms as well.

[*DEFENCE OF THE PRINCIPLE OF NONCONTRADICTION*]

4

There are some people, however, who, as we said, themselves affirm not only that it is possible for the same thing to be and not to be but also that they believe this; many students of nature also make use of this claim. But we have just now found that it is impossible for the same thing to be and not to be at the same time, and through this we showed that this is the firmest principle of all.

Now, some people actually demand that we demonstrate even this, but their demand is the result of lack of education; for we

6. **For a . . . an assumption**: An ASSUMPTION is a PRINCIPLE of a special science, not of all knowledge.

lack education if we do not know$_{g}$ what we should and should not seek to have demonstrated. For in general it is impossible to demonstrate everything, since there would be an infinite regress, and so even then there would be no demonstration; and if there are some things of which we must not seek a demonstration, these people could not say what principle is more appropriately left without demonstration than this one <the Principle of Noncontradiction>.

Still, even about this <denial of the Principle of Noncontradiction> it is possible to demonstrate by refutation that it is impossible,[7] if only the disputant speaks of something.[8] If he speaks of nothing, it is ridiculous for us to seek to engage in rational discourse with someone who does not engage in rational discourse about anything, insofar as he does not engage in it;[9] for insofar as he does not engage in any rational discourse, he is like a plant. It should be noticed, though, that demonstration by refutation is different from demonstration. For in attempting to demonstrate <the Principle of Noncontradiction>, someone might seem to beg the question; but if the respondent is responsible <for speaking of something>, it will be a refutation, not a demonstration.

Now the starting point for all such things is not the demand that the respondent speak of something either as being or as not being (for someone might perhaps suppose that this would be begging the question), but the demand that he signify something[10] both to himself and to another. For he must do this if he speaks of something; for otherwise he does not engage in any rational discourse either with himself or with another. And if he grants this, there will be a demonstration <by refutation>, since something will be definite as soon as he grants this. In allowing this

7. **Still, even . . . impossible**: A 'demonstration by refutation' is not a normal demonstration, since it does not argue from a prior and better-known principle (cf. *APo* 71b21).

8. **speaks of something**: Or 'SAYS something'.

9. **insofar . . . in it**: If I do not concede that I am speaking of something, you cannot treat the sounds I utter as constituting rational discourse, and so you have no reason to believe that any sounds I might utter when you ask me questions are intended to answer your questions.

10. **signify something**: This might mean (a) 'man' SIGNIFIES man, i.e., rational animal (a nonlinguistic item), or (b) 'man' signifies 'rational animal' (the sense of the word).

it is he, not the demonstrator, who is responsible <for something's being definite>; for in rejecting rational discourse, he allows it. Moreover, in conceding this he has conceded that something is true apart from demonstration, so that not everything will be F and not F.

First of all, clearly this much is true, that the name signifies being or not being this, so that not everything will be F and not F.

Further, if 'man' signifies one thing, let this be biped animal. By 'signifying one thing' I mean that if a man is this, then if anything is a man, its being a man is this. If someone says that
1006b 'man' signifies more than one thing, that makes no difference, provided that he says it signifies a definite number of things; for if he says that, a different name can be assigned to each account. Suppose, for instance, he says that 'man' signifies many things, not just one, and that biped animal is the account of one of the things signified, but there are also several other accounts, though a definite number of them. His saying this makes no difference, since a different name can be assigned to correspond to each account. If, however, a different name is not assigned, and he says the name signifies an indeterminate number of things, then evidently there will be no rational discourse. For to signify no one thing is to signify nothing, and if names do not signify, then rational discussion with one another, and indeed even with oneself, is destroyed (for we cannot think without thinking of one thing, and if we can think, then one name can be assigned to this one thing we are thinking of).

Suppose, then, that, as we said at the beginning, the name signifies something and some one thing; it follows that being a man cannot signify essentially not being man, if 'man' not only signifies about one thing but also signifies one thing. For we do not suppose that signifying one thing is merely signifying about one thing; if it were merely that, then 'musical thing', 'pale thing', and 'man' would also signify one thing, and so <being musical, being pale, and being a man> would all be one, since they would be synonymous.[11]

11. **For we do not . . . synonymous**: If we did not distinguish signifying one thing from signifying about one thing, then 'musical', 'pale', and 'man' would also signify one and the same thing, and hence would be SYNONYMOUS.

Further, it will not be possible for the same thing to be and not to be, except by homonymy of the sort that would arise if, for instance, others called not a man the one whom we call a man. The puzzle, however, is not about whether the same thing at the same time can both be and not be a man in name, but about whether this is possible in actual fact.

Now, if 'man' and 'not man' do not signify something different, then plainly neither does not being a man signify something different from what being a man signifies, and so being a man will be not being a man, since they will be one thing. For being one signifies being as cloak and cape are, i.e., having one account; and if <man and not man> are one, then being a man and not being a man will signify one thing. It has been shown, however, that they signify different things. Necessarily, therefore, if it is true to say of something that it is a man, it is a biped animal, since this, we saw, is what 'man' signifies. And if this is necessary, then it is not possible for the same thing in that case not to be a biped animal; for 'necessary for it to be' signifies precisely that it is impossible for it not to be. Hence it cannot be at the same time true to say that the same thing is a man and is not a man.

The same also applies to not being a man. For being a man and not being a man signify something different, if being a pale thing and being a man are different; for not being a man is much more opposed <than being pale is to being a man>, and therefore it signifies something different. If the respondent also says that 'pale' signifies the same one thing <that 'man' signifies>, we will tell him again, as we did before, that this will make all things, not merely opposites, one. And if this is not possible,[12] then the conclusion that was drawn earlier still follows, as long as he answers the question he is being asked.

If we ask him the question without qualification, but he adds the negations, then he is not answering the question he is being asked. For although it is quite possible for the same thing to be a man and pale and a thousand other things, still the question was whether it is true to say that this is a man or not; and so he

12. **And . . . possible**: If 'all things were one' (i.e., everything signified the same), then 'x is F and not F' would be equivalent to 'x is F and F', and so would not violate Noncontradiction. The opponent, however, must take 'x is F and not F' to violate Noncontradiction, since otherwise he cannot state his thesis.

should answer with what signifies one thing, not adding that this thing is also pale and large. For it is impossible to list the coincidents, since they are indeterminate; and so he should list either all or none of them. Similarly, then, even if the same thing is a thousand times a man and not a man, still the question was whether it is a man, and the answer should not add that it is also at the same time not a man. He should not add this unless he should also add the other coincidents, all the things it is or is not; but if he adds these, he is not engaged in rational discussion.

And in general our opponents do away with substance and essence; for they must say that everything is coincidental and that there is no such thing as being essentially a man or being essentially an animal. For if there is such a thing as being essentially a man, it will not be being not a man or not being a man; but these are the negations of being a man. For, as we saw, one thing is signified, and this is the substance of something. Now, to signify a thing's substance is to signify that being that thing is nothing other <than its substance>; but if the thing's being essentially a man is being essentially not a man or essentially not being a man, then being that thing will be something other <than its substance>. Hence they must say that nothing has the sort of account <that signifies substance>, but everything is coincidental. For precisely this is the difference between substance and coincident; for pale is a coincident of a man because, though a man is pale, he is not essentially pale.[13]

If everything is spoken of coincidentally, nothing will be the primary subject of which <something is predicated>, since in every case the coincident signifies a predication of some subject. 1007b Hence the predication must go on with no determinate limit; but this is impossible, since no more than two things are combined <in a predication>. For no coincident is a coincident of a coincident, except insofar as both are coincidents of the same <subject> (for instance, the pale is musical and the musical pale because both are coincidents of the man); but what makes Socrates musical is not this, that both <Socrates and the musical> are coincidents of something else. Hence some things are called coincidents in this way, and others in the other way.

13. **for pale . . . essentially pale**: Since the opponents believe that for any subject x, each of x's properties can be denied of x, they must believe that all of x's properties are COINCIDENTAL.

And so things that are called coincidents in the way in which the pale is a coincident of Socrates cannot form an indeterminate upward series (so that, for instance, something else would be a coincident of the pale that is a coincident of Socrates); for these together do not amount to one thing. Nor yet can something else—the musical, for instance—be a coincident of the pale, since it is no more a coincident of the pale than the pale is of it. Moreover, we have distinguished the things that are coincidents in this way from those that are coincidents in the way in which the musical is a coincident of Socrates, and we have found that the coincident is a coincident of the coincident in the first case, but not in the second.

Hence not everything is spoken of by coincidence. In this way too, then, there is something signifying substance. And if this is so, it is shown that contradictories cannot be predicated at the same time.

Moreover, if all contradictories are true of the same thing at the same time, then clearly all things will be one. For the same thing will be a warship, a wall, and a man, if it is possible both to affirm and to deny anything of everything—as those who state the argument of Protagoras must say. For if a man seems to someone not to be a warship, then clearly he is not a warship; then he is also a warship, if the contradictory is true; and so the result is that, as Anaxagoras said, all things are together, so that no one thing truly belongs <to anything>. Hence they would seem to be speaking of the indefinite, and though they think they are speaking of what is, they are really speaking of what is not; for the indefinite is what potentially is but actually is not.

Further, they must affirm or deny every property of every subject; for it is absurd if it is true to say <as our opponents claim> that F is not F, but not true to say that F is not G, even though G does not belong to F. If, for instance, it is true to say that a man is not a man, then clearly he is also either a warship or not a warship; and so if the affirmation <of warship> is true, the negation must also be true. If, alternatively, the affirmation <of warship> does not belong, at least its negation must belong more than the negation of man does; if, then, the negation of man belongs, so does the negation of warship, and if this belongs, so does the affirmation.

These are the results, then, for those who give this argument.

It also results that it is not necessary either to affirm or to deny. For if it is true that he is a man and not a man, then clearly he will also be neither a man nor not a man. For each of the affirmations has a negation; and if one of the affirmations has two components, it will be opposed by one negation <that also has two components>.

Moreover, either this <rejection of the Principle of Noncontradiction> holds for everything (so that everything is also pale and not pale, and being and not being, and similarly for the other affirmations and negations), or it does not hold for everything, but holds for some affirmations and negations and not for others. If it does not hold for all of them, then the exceptions will be agreed on. But if it holds for all, then once again either the negation is true of everything of which the affirmation is true and the affirmation is true of everything of which the negation is true, or else the negation is true of everything of which the affirmation is true but the affirmation is not true of everything of which the negation is true.

If this last claim is true, then something will be fixed as not being, and this will be a firm belief; and if not being is something firm and known$_g$, the opposed affirmation will be still better known. But if it is also true to affirm whatever it is true to deny, then necessarily either it is true to divide and say, for instance, that it is pale and again that it is not pale, or it is not.

If it is not true to divide and say it, then he is not really *saying*[14] these things, and nothing has any being—and how could things that are not utter sounds or walk? And all things will be one, as we also said before, and the same thing will be man, god, warship, and stone, and the contradictories of these; for if they are true of each thing in the same way, there will be no difference between one thing and another, since, if there were any difference, this fact would be true and would be distinctive of the thing it belonged to.

Similarly, if it is possible to divide and speak truly, we reach the result we mentioned. Moreover, it follows that everyone speaks truly and everyone speaks falsely, and that he agrees

14. **not saying**: If the opponent utters (1) 'x is F and not F' but is not willing to divide (1) into (2) 'x is F' and (3) 'x is not F', then he cannot be taken to be asserting a conjunction, and so he cannot after all be asserting (1); he will merely be uttering the sounds.

that he himself speaks falsely. And at the same time it is evident that if we attempt to examine what he says, there is nothing to examine; for he speaks of nothing, because he speaks neither thus nor not thus, but both thus and not thus, and then again he denies both, saying that it is neither thus nor not thus—for if he did not deny both, something would thereby be definite.

Further, if the negation is false whenever the affirmation is true, and the affirmation is false whenever the negation is true, then it will not be possible both to affirm and to deny the same thing truly. But presumably he might say that this was the very point proposed for discussion at the beginning.

Further, is someone speaking falsely if he supposes that something is some way or that it is not, and speaking truly if he supposes both? If he speaks truly in the second case, then what is being said in the statement that such is the nature of beings? If he does not speak truly, but speaks more truly than the one who supposes the other thing, then beings will be some way, and this will be true and not also not true at the same time. And if all alike speak both falsely and truly, then anyone of whom this is true cannot utter or say anything; for at the same time he says this and not this. But if he supposes nothing, but thinks this no more than he does not think this, how is his state any different from a plant's?

From this it is especially evident that no one at all, including those giving this argument, is in this condition. For why, when he thinks he ought to walk toward Megara, does he walk toward it, instead of staying where he is? And why does he not get up in the morning and walk straight into a wall or a pit, whichever it happens to be? Why does he instead evidently take care to avoid it, on the assumption that he does not think falling in is both good and not good? Clearly, then, he supposes one thing is better and the other is not better. If so, he must also suppose that one thing is a man and another is not a man, and that one thing is sweet and another is not sweet. For if he thinks it is better to drink water and see a man, and then he seeks them, he does not seek and suppose all things indiscriminately, which he would have to do if the same thing were alike both a man and not a man. But in fact, as was said, everyone evidently takes care to avoid some things and not others.

It would seem, then, that everyone supposes that things are some way without qualification; even if they do not suppose this about everything, they at least suppose it about the better and the worse. And if this supposition counts as belief rather than knowledge$_e$, one should pay all the more attention to truth, just as one should pay more attention to health when one is sick than when one is healthy; for indeed someone who has a belief is not in a healthy condition in relation to the truth, compared to someone with knowledge.

Further, however true it might be that everything is thus and not thus, nonetheless the more and less is in the nature of beings. For we would not say that two and three are even to the same degree, or that the one who thinks four are five is mistaken to the same degree as someone who thinks four are a thousand. If they are not mistaken to the same degree, then clearly one of them is less mistaken, so that he speaks more truly. Now if what is more F is nearer to being F, then there will be some truth to which the more true is nearer; and even if there is not, still at least in this case something is firmer and has more of the character of the truth. In that case, we are rid of the extreme argument that prevents us from having anything definite in thought.

[*PHILOSOPHY AS KNOWLEDGE OF OBJECTIVE REALITY*]

5

The argument of Protagoras[15] arises from the same belief <that leads to the denial of the Principle of Noncontradiction>, and each view must be true or false if the other is. For if everything that seems and appears is true, everything must at the same time be true and false. For many people suppose things contrary to other people and think those who do not believe what they believe have false beliefs; hence the same things must both be and not be. And if this is so, then whatever seems must be true. For those who believe falsely and those who believe truly believe opposite things; and so, if beings are <opposite ways at the same time>, everyone will have true beliefs. Clearly, then, both arguments are based on the same line of thought.

15. **The argument of Protagoras**: Cf. Plato, *Theaetetus* 152a.

But not everyone who holds these views requires the same treatment; rather, some need persuasion, while others need force. For those who supposed this because they were puzzled are easily cured of their ignorance; for our approach to them should focus on their line of thought, not on the argument <they actually give>. But those who state it for the sake of argument must be cured by refutation of their argument in their utterance and in their words.

Those who are really puzzled have reached their belief from perceptible things. They have reached their belief that contradictory and contrary belong <to the same subject> at the same time, because they see that contraries come to be from the same thing, and they infer that since what is not cannot come to be, the thing from which the contraries came was previously both contraries alike. This is the point of Anaxagoras' statement that everything is mixed in everything and of what Democritus says—for he says that the empty and the full belong to every part alike, and that one of these is being and one is not being.

Our reply to those who suppose as they do on this basis is that in a way what they say is correct, but in a way they are mistaken. For in fact being is spoken of in two ways, so that in one way it is possible, and in another way it is not possible, for something to come to be from what is not.[16] Similarly, it is possible for the same thing at the same time both to be and not to be, but not in the same respect; for it is possible for the same thing at the same time to have contrary properties potentially, but not to have them actually. Further, we will demand that they recognize the existence of another sort of substance, to which neither motion nor perishing nor coming to be belongs at all.

Similarly, some people have been led to believe in the truth of appearances because of perceptible things. In their view, one ought not to judge the truth of something by the large or small number <of people who believe it>.[17] But the same thing seems sweet to some who taste it, bitter to others, so that if all were sick or all insane except for two or three healthy or sane people, these two or three, not the majority, would seem to be sick or insane. Further, many of the other animals have appearances contrary to ours about the same things, and even for each one of us in relation

16. **in one way . . . what is not**: See *Phys*. 187a27, 191a23–b4.

17. **the truth . . . believe it>**: Cf. Plato, *Theaetetus* 152bc, 154a, 158a–e.

to himself things do not always seem the same as far as perception goes. It is unclear, then, which appearances are true or false; for one lot are no more true than another lot, but all are true or false alike. This is why Democritus says that either nothing is true or, at any rate, what is true is unclear to us.

In general, the reason they say that what appears in perception must be true is that they suppose both that perception is understanding and that it is <simply> alteration.[18] For this is how Empedocles, Democritus, and all the others (we may say) have been trapped by such beliefs. Empedocles, for instance, says that when one's state changes, one's understanding also changes: 'For man's cunning increases in relation to what is present'. And elsewhere he says: 'To the extent that their nature was altered, to that extent understanding presented altered things to them.' Parmenides, in the same way, affirms: 'Whatever the state of the mixture of their much-bent limbs, so is the state of mind present to men. For the nature of the limbs, in each and every man, is precisely what understands; what predominates is thought.' A saying of Anaxagoras to some of his companions is also recorded, that 'beings will be for them such as they suppose them to be'. People say that even Homer evidently had this belief, because he says that Hector was knocked out of his wits by a blow and lay 'with his understanding knowing other things'; they take him to mean that even those with deranged understanding have understanding, though not about the same things. It is clear, then, that if both <the normal and the deranged states have> understanding, then beings are also at the same time both thus and not thus.

This result, indeed, is the hardest to accept. For if those who more than anyone else have seen such truth as it is possible to see—those who more than anyone else search for it and love it—if they believe and affirm such views about truth, how can we expect beginners in philosophy not to lose heart? The search for truth would be a wild goose chase.

They reached this view because they were investigating the truth about beings and supposed that the only beings were perceptible things; in these, however, there is much of the nature of the indeterminate, i.e., of the sort of being we have described. Hence it is not surprising that they say what they say, but what

18. **alteration**: i.e., merely a bodily process. Cf. *DA* 416b32–417a20, 424b3–18.

they say is not true. (This is a more appropriate comment than Epicharmus' comment on Xenophanes.)

Further, since they saw that all of this nature around us is in motion and that nothing true can be said about what is changing, they said it is impossible to say anything true about what undergoes every sort of change in every respect. From this view there blossomed the most extreme of the views we have mentioned, that of the self-styled Heracleitizers. This was the sort of view held by Cratylus, who ended up thinking he must say nothing, and only moved his finger.[19] He criticized Heracleitus for saying one could not step into the same river twice; for Cratylus thought one could not do it even once.

We also reply to this argument as follows. Though they do have some argument for their view that what is changing, when it is changing, is not, still this is at any rate disputable. For what is losing something has some of what is being lost, and some of what is coming to be must already be. And in general, if something is perishing, there must be something that it is; and if something is coming to be, there must be something from which it comes to be and something that generates it, and this does not go on without limit.

But let us leave these arguments aside and insist that a change in <a subject's> quantity is not the same as a change in the sort of thing <the subject is>. Hence, even if we concede that something is unstable in quantity, still we know$_{g}$ each thing by its form.[20]

Further, those who suppose <that everything changes> should also be criticized for something else. The things that they saw <constantly changing> are a minority even of perceptible things, but they declared that the same <constant change> was true of the whole universe. In fact it is only the area of the perceptible universe around us that is in constant destruction and generation, and this is an insignificant part of the whole universe. And so it would be more just to acquit this part <of the world from constant change> because of the other part than to condemn the other part <for constant change> because of these things. Again, clearly we shall also

19. **moved his finger**: to point at things, since he did not think they were stable enough to apply any words to them.

20. **we know . . . form**: Hence a subject cannot always be changing in respect of the sort of thing it is. Aristotle identifies FORM (or species: *eidos*), with the sort of thing (*poion*) a subject is. See QUALITY, *Catg*. 3b13–23, 4a10–21; Plato, *Theaetetus* 182cd.

say in response to these people what we said before; for they should be shown and persuaded that there is some unmoved nature.

In any case, to say that things simultaneously are and are not is to imply that they are at rest rather than that they are moving; for there is nothing for anything to change into, since everything
1010b belongs to everything.

As for the truth, we say that not everything that appears is true. First, even if perception, at least of its proper objects,[21] is not false, still, appearance is not the same as perception.

Further, one may justifiably be surprised if they are puzzled by such questions as these: 'Are magnitudes and colors such as they appear to be to observers from a distance or such as they appear to be to observers close at hand? Are they such as they appear to be to healthy people or such as they appear to be to sick people? Are things heavier if they appear so to feeble people or if they appear so to vigorous people? Are things true if they appear so to people asleep or if they appear so to people awake?' For it is evident that at any rate they do not really think <the appearances of the dreamer are true>—certainly no one who is in Libya and one night supposes <in a dream> that he is in Athens goes off toward the Odeion.[22]

Further, as for the future, as Plato[23] says, the belief of a doctor and of an ignorant person surely are not equally authoritative about, for instance, whether someone is or is not going to be healthy.

Further, among perceptions themselves, a sense's perception of the object of another sense is less authoritative than its perception of its own proper object, and its perception of a neighboring object is less authoritative than the perception of its own object. In the case of color it is sight, not taste, that is authoritative, and in the case of flavor it is taste, not sight; and none of these senses ever says that the same thing at the same time is both thus and not thus. And even when different times are involved, there is no dispute about the <perceptible> attribute but only about that <subject> of which the attribute is a coincident. I mean, for instance, that the same wine might seem sweet at one time but

21. **proper objects**: See *DA* 418a7–16, 428b17–20.

22. **goes off toward the Odeion**: sc. when he wakes up. The Odeion is a building in Athens.

23. **Plato**: See *Theaetetus* 178bc.

not at another, if it or the body <of the perceiver> had changed; but what sweetness is, whenever it is present, has never yet changed—one always has the truth about it, and whatever is to be sweet is necessarily of this sort.

And yet this is eliminated by all these arguments: just as nothing has a substance, so also nothing is of necessity. For what is necessary cannot be both one way and another, and so if something is thus of necessity, it will not be both thus and not thus.

And in general, if there are only perceptible things, nothing would exist unless animate things existed, since without them there would be no perception. Now presumably it is true that <without animate things> there would be neither perceptible things nor perceivings, since this is a way in which a perceiver is affected; but there must be subjects that cause perception and that exist whether or not they are perceived. For perception is certainly not of itself; on the contrary, there is also something else apart from the perception, which is necessarily prior to perception. For what initiates a motion is naturally prior to what is moved, *1011a* and this is just as true even if what initiates the motion and what is moved are spoken of in relation to each other.[24]

* * * * * * *

Book V[1]

* * * * * * *

[*BEING*]

7

Being is spoken of both coincidentally and in its own right. It is *1017a7* spoken of coincidentally when we say, for instance, that the just one is musical, the man is musical, and the musician is a man; this

24. **For what initiates . . . to each other**: Cf. *DA* 425a15–26.

1. The book from which these two chapters are excerpted discusses important philosophical terms that are 'said in many ways' (see HOMONYMY).

is just like saying that a musician builds, because being musical is coincidental to the builder, or being a builder to the musician—for the F being G signifies G being coincidental to the F.[2] That is how it is in the cases mentioned, whenever we say that the man is musical, or that the musician is a man, or that the pale one is musical, or that the musician is pale. <In the third case> it is because both are coincidental to the same thing; <in the first case> it is because <the coincident—musical, for instance—> is coincidental to the thing that is <for instance, the man. In the second case> the musical <thing> is a man because the musical is coincidental to the man—this is the way in which the not-pale is said to be, because it is coincidental to something that is.

The things that are said to be coincidentally, then, are so called either because each of two things belongs to the same thing that is, or because the first belongs to the second, a thing that is, or because the second is predicated of the first, the first belongs to the second, and the second is a thing that is.

The things that are said to be in their own right are all those that are signified by the types of predication; for they are said to be in as many ways as there are ways of signifying being. Among things predicated, some signify what-it-is, some quality, some quantity, some relative, some acting, some being acted on, some where, some when; and so being signifies the same as each of these. For there is no difference between 'a man is flourishing' and 'a man flourishes', or between 'a man is walking (or cutting)' and 'a man walks (or cuts)', and the same is true in the other cases.

Further, being and 'is' signify that something is true; and not being signifies that something is not true but false, in affirmation and negation alike. For example, that Socrates is musical signifies that this is true, and that Socrates is not-pale signifies that this is true, while that a diagonal is not commensurable signifies that this is false.[3]

1017b Being and what is also signify that some of the things mentioned are potentially, others actually. We say, for instance, that something *is* a thing that sees, both if it potentially sees and if it actually sees. Similarly, we say that something knows$_e$ both if it

2. **for F . . . coincidental to G**: See 1007b2–16.

3. **and that Socrates . . . this is false**: The first 'not' is attached to 'pale' and the second to 'is'.

is capable of exercising its knowledge and if it is exercising it; we say that something rests both if it is at rest at the time and if it is capable of being at rest.

The same is true of substances. We say that Hermes *is* in the stone, and the half-line <in the line, because they are in it potentially> and that what is unripe is grain <because it is grain potentially>.[4] We must determine elsewhere[5] the conditions in which something has or does not yet have a potentiality.

[*SUBSTANCE*]

8

The things called substances are, first, the simple bodies (earth, fire, water, and everything like that) and in general bodies and the things composed from them (animals and divine things and their parts). All these things are said to be substances because they are not said of a subject, but the other things are said of them.

In another way, that which, by being present in things that are not said of a subject, is the cause of their being—for instance, the soul for an animal—is called substance.

Further, the parts present in such things, defining them and signifying a this, the things with whose destruction the whole is destroyed, are called substances; for instance, the body is destroyed with the destruction of the plane (as some people say), and the plane with the destruction of the line. And in general it seems to some people that number is this sort of thing, since if it is destroyed nothing exists, and it defines all things.

Further, the essence, whose account is a definition, is also said to be the substance of a thing.

It turns out, then, that substance is spoken of in two ways.[6] It is both the ultimate subject, which is no longer said of anything else, and whatever, being a this,[7] is also separable—this is true of the shape, i.e., the form, of a thing.

* * * * * * *

4. **We say that . . . potentially>**: Cf. *Met*. 1048a32–5.
5. **elsewhere**: *Met*. 1048b37–1049a17.
6. **two ways**: Cf. 1028b32–6, 1038b1–8, 1042a25–31, 1049a27–36.
7. **a this**: Cf. 1028a12, 1029a27–8, 1039a1.

Book VII

* * * * * * *

[*THE STUDY OF SUBSTANCE*]

1

Being is spoken of in many ways, which we distinguished previously in the work on how many ways things are spoken of. For one <type of being> signifies what-it-is and a this; another signifies quality, or quantity, or any of the other things predicated in this way. But while being is spoken of in this many ways, it is evident that among these the primary being is the what-it-is, which signifies substance. For whenever we say what quality this has, we call it good or bad, not six feet long or a man, whereas whenever we say what it is, we call it a man or a god, not pale or hot or six feet long; and the other things are called beings by belonging to this type of being—some as quantities, some as qualities, some as affections, some in some other such way.

That is why someone might actually be puzzled about whether walking, flourishing, or sitting signifies a being; for none of these is in its own right nor is any of them capable of being separated from substance, but it is more true that the walking or sitting or flourishing thing is a being (if indeed it is a being). This latter type of thing is apparently more of a being because it has some definite subject—the substance and the particular—which is discerned in such a predication; for this subject is implied in speaking of the good or sitting thing. Clearly, then, it is because of substance that each of those other things is also a being, so that what is in the primary way—what is not something,[1] but is without qualification a being—is substance.

Now the primary is so spoken of in many ways, but still, substance is primary in every way: in nature, in account, and in knowledge$_{g}$.[2] For none of the other things predicated is separable,

1. **what is not something**: i.e., (probably) what is not something *else*, as the sitting thing is something else, e.g., a man.

2. **in nature . . . knowledge$_{g}$**: Alternative text: 'in account, in knowledge, and in time'. See PRIOR.

but only substance. Substance is also primary in account, since its account is necessarily present in the account of each thing. Moreover, we think we know a thing most of all whenever we know what, for instance, man or fire is, rather than when we know its quality or quantity or place; for indeed we know each of these only when we know *what* the quantity or the quality *is*.

Indeed, the old question—always pursued from long ago till now, and always raising puzzles—'What is being?' is just the question 'What is substance?' For it is substance that some say is one and others say is more than one, some saying that it is limited in number, others that it is unlimited. And so we too must make it our main, our primary, indeed (we may say) our only, task to study what it is that is in this way.

2

The most evident examples of substances seem to be bodies. That is why we say that animals and plants and their parts are substances, and also natural bodies, such as fire, water, earth, and all such things, and whatever is either a part of these or composed of all or some of them—for instance, the universe and its parts, the stars, moon, and sun. But we ought to consider: Are these the only substances there are, or are there also others? Or are only some of these things substances, or some of these and also some other things? Or are none of these things substances, but only some other things?

Some people think that the limits of a body—for instance, a surface, a line, a point, and a unit—are substances, and are so to a higher degree than a body and a solid. Further, some think there are no substances apart from perceptible things, while to others it seems that there are also everlasting substances, which are more numerous and are beings to a higher degree. Plato, for example, thinks that Forms and mathematicals are two <types of> substances, and that the substance of perceptible bodies is a third <type>. Speusippus posits even more substances, beginning with the one, and posits a principle for each <type of> substance—one for numbers, another for magnitudes, and then another for soul; and in this way he multiplies the <types of> substances. Some say that Forms and numbers have the same nature, and that everything else comes after them—lines, planes, and everything else, extending to the substance of the universe and to perceptible things.

We must consider, then, which of these views are correct or incorrect; what substances there are; whether or not there are any substances apart from perceptible substances, and in what way these perceptible substances are <substances>; and whether or not there is any separable substance apart from perceptible ones, and, if there is, why there is, and in what way it is <substance>. But before doing this, we must first sketch what substance is.

[*SUBSTANCE AS SUBJECT*]

3

Substance is spoken of, if not in several ways, at any rate in four main cases. For the essence, the universal and the genus seem to be the substance of a given thing, and the fourth of these cases is the subject.

Now, the subject is that of which the other things are said, but which is not itself in turn said of any other thing; hence we must first determine what it is, since the primary subject seems to be substance most of all.

What is spoken of in this way <as the primary subject> is in one way the matter, in another way the form$_{m}$, and in a third way the thing composed of these. (By the matter I mean, for example, the bronze; by the form$_{m}$ I mean the figure and character; and by the thing composed of them I mean the statue, i.e., the compound.) And so if the form is prior to the matter, and more of a being, it will also, by the same argument, be prior to the thing composed of both.

We have now said in outline, then, what substance is: it is what is not said of a subject but has the other things said of it.

However, we must not confine ourselves to this answer. For it is inadequate: for, first, it is itself unclear; and further, the matter turns out to be substance.[3] For if the matter is not substance, it is hard to see what other substance there is; for when all the other

3. **turns out to be substance**: This might be (i) an identity statement ('matter = substance'), or (ii) a predication ('matter is a substance').

things are removed, nothing <but the matter> evidently remains.[4] For the other things are affections, products, and potentialities of bodies; and length, breadth, and depth[5] are kinds of quantities but not substances (for quantity is not substance), but the primary <subject> to which these belong is more of a substance than they are. But when length, breadth, and depth are abstracted, we see that nothing is left, except whatever is determined by these. And so, if we examine it in this way, the matter necessarily appears as the only substance.

By matter I mean what is spoken of in its own right neither as being something, nor as having some quantity, nor as having any of the other things by which being is determined. For there is something of which each of these is predicated, something whose being is different from that of each of the things predicated; for the other things are predicated of the substance, and the substance is predicated of the matter. And so the last thing is in its own right neither something nor of some quantity nor any other <of the things mentioned>; nor is it <in its own right> the negations of these, since what we have said implies that the negations as well <as the positive properties> belong to it <only> coincidentally.

And so, if we study it from this point of view, the result is that the matter is substance;[6] but that is impossible. For being separable and being a this seem to belong to substance most of all; that is why the form and the <compound> of both <matter and form> would seem to be substance more than the matter is.

And so the substance composed of both—I mean composed of the matter and the form$_m$—should be set aside, since it is posterior to the other two, and clear. The matter is also evident in a way. We must, then, consider the third type of substance, since it is the most puzzling.

Since some of the perceptible substances are agreed to be sub- 1029b
stances, we should begin our search with these.

4. **nothing . . . evidently remains:** This might mean (a) 'It is not evident that anything <but the matter> remains'; or (b) 'It is evident that nothing <but the matter> remains'.

5. **length, breadth, and depth**: the essential properties of bodies.

6. **the matter is substance**: Probably (in the light of 'appears as the only substance' in a19) this is intended to be an identity statement.

[SUBSTANCE AS ESSENCE]

4

Since we began by distinguishing the things by which we define substance and since essence seems to be one of these, we ought to study it. For it is useful to advance toward what is better known, since this is how anyone succeeds in learning, by advancing through what is less well known$_g$ by nature to what is better known. In questions about action, our task is to advance from what is good to ourselves, and so to make what is good without reservation good to ourselves; in the same way, then, we should advance from what is better known to ourselves, and so make what is well known by nature well known to ourselves. Admittedly, what is well known and known first to any given type of person is often only slightly known and has little or no hold on being; still, we must begin from what is poorly known but known by us and try to come to know what is known without reservation, by advancing, as has been said, through the very things that are known to us.

First let us make some logical remarks about it. The essence of a thing is what the thing is said to be in its own right. For being you is not the same as being a musician, since you are not a musician in your own right; hence your essence is what you are in your own right.

Nor indeed is your essence all of what you are in your own right. For a thing's essence is not what belongs to it in its own right in the way that pale belongs in its own right to a surface; for being a surface is not the same as being pale. But neither is a thing's essence the same as the combination of the thing and what belongs in its own right to it—for instance, being a pale surface, since here surface is added. It follows that the account of a thing's essence is the account that describes but does not mention the thing; and so if being a pale surface is the same as being a smooth surface, being pale and being smooth are one and the same.

There are composites <not only among substances but> also in the other predications, since each of these (for instance, quality, quantity, when, where, and motion) has a subject; hence we should ask whether there is an account of the essence of each of these composites, and whether an essence belongs to them—to a pale man, for instance—as well as to substances. Let us, then, call this composite 'cloak'. What is being a cloak?

One might object, however, that a cloak is not spoken of in its own right either. <We reply:> There are two ways in which we speak of what is not in its own right: one way is from addition, the other is not. In the first case, something is said <not to be in its own right> because the thing to be defined is added to something else—if, for instance, one gave the account of pale man as a definition of pale. In the second case, something is said not to be in its own right because something else is added to it—if, for instance, 'cloak' signified a pale man, but one were to define cloak as pale. A pale man, then, is pale, but is not what being pale is.

But is being a cloak an essence at all? Perhaps not. For an essence is what something essentially is, but whenever one thing is said of another, the composite of the two is not essentially a this; the pale man, for instance, is not essentially a this, since only a substance is a this. Hence the things that have an essence are those whose account is a definition. But the mere fact that a name and an account signify the same thing does not imply that the account is a definition. If it did, then all accounts would be formulae (since for every account, we can find a name that signifies the same), so that even the *Iliad* would be a definition.[7] Rather, an account is a definition <only> if it is of some primary thing; primary things are those that are spoken of in a way that does not consist in one thing's being said of another. Hence essence will belong only to species of a genus and to nothing else,[8] since <only> these seem to be spoken of in a way that does not consist in one thing's participating in another, or in one thing's being an attribute or coincident of another. Admittedly, everything else <besides members of a species>, if it has a name, will also have an account saying what it signifies (i.e., that this belongs to this) or, instead of an unqualified account, a more exact one; but nothing else will have a definition or essence.

7. **so that . . . definition**: We could say that the whole poem is the definition corresponding to the name 'Iliad'. Cf. 1045a12, *APo* 93b35.

8. **Hence essence . . . to nothing else**: Two possible interpretations: (1) Essences are found only within species and genera (of substances), i.e., only members of these substantial species and genera have essences. (2) Species and genera (as opposed to individual members of them) are the only things that have essences.

Perhaps, however, definitions, like what-it-is, are spoken of in several ways. For in fact what-it-is in one way signifies substance and a this, and in another way signifies each of the things predicated—quantity, quality, and all the rest. For just as being belongs to them all—not in the same way, but to substance primarily and to the other things derivatively—so also the what-it-is belongs without qualification to substance and derivatively to the other things. For we might ask what a quality is, so that quality is also a what-it-is, though not without qualification; just as some people say, speaking logically, that not-being is (not that it is without qualification, but that it is not-being), so also we say what a quality is.

We must certainly consider what ought to be said about a particular question, but we must consider no less how things really are. That is why, in this case, since what is said is evident <we must consider how things are>. We find that essence, like what-it-is, belongs primarily and without qualification to substance, and derivatively to the other things, where it will be the essence of quality or quantity, not the essence without qualification. For we must say that these <nonsubstances> are beings either homonymously or by addition and subtraction, as we say that what is not known is known <not to be known>. The right answer is that they are beings neither homonymously nor in the same way. What is medical, for instance, is spoken of with reference to one and the same thing, not by being one and the same thing, but not homonymously either—for a body, a procedure, and an instrument are called medical neither homonymously nor by having one <nature>, but with reference to one thing. The same applies to beings.

It does not matter which alternative we accept: in either case substances evidently have a definition and essence of the primary type, i.e., a definition and essence without qualification. Certainly other beings also have definitions and essences, but not primarily. For if we accept this view of definition, not every name that signifies the same as an account will necessarily have a definition corresponding to it; rather, in order to be a definition, the account must be of the right type, namely an account of something that is one—and something that is one not merely by continuity (like the *Iliad*, or like things that are tied together) but that is one in one of the ways in which one is spoken of. Now, one is spoken of in the same ways as being, and one type of being signifies a this, another quantity, another quality. That is why there will also be an account and a definition of the pale man, but not in the way that there is of pale and of the substance.

* * * * * * *

6

We should investigate whether a thing is the same as or different from its essence. For this is useful for our investigation of substance; for a thing seems to be nothing other than its own substance, and something's substance is said to be its essence.

In the case of things spoken of coincidentally, a thing might seem to be different from its essence; a pale man, for instance, is different from being a pale man. For if it is the same, then being a man is the same as being a pale man; for, they say, a man is the same as a pale man, so that being a pale man is the same as being a man.

Perhaps, however, it is not necessary for things to be the same if one is a coincident of the other, since the extreme terms are not the same in the same way. But presumably it might seem to follow that the extremes, the coincidental things, turn out to be the same—for instance, being pale and being musical. In fact, however, it seems not to follow.[9]

But is it necessary for things spoken of in their own right to be the same as their essences? For instance, what about substances of the sort some say Ideas are, ones that have no other substances or natures prior to them? If the good itself <the Idea> is different from the essence of good, and the animal itself from the essence of animal, and the being itself from the essence of being, then there will be further substances, natures, and Ideas apart from those mentioned, and these will be prior substances and substances to a higher degree, if essence is substance.

If, then, <the Ideas and the essences> are severed from each

9. **But presumably . . . seems not to follow**: The conclusion (that coincidental things such as pale man are not the same as their essences) follows only if we assume—falsely, in Aristotle's view—that pale man and musical man are the same as man. In 1032a22, Aristotle offers what he takes to be a sound argument for the conclusion.

other, it follows that <the Ideas> will not be known$_e$ and that <the essences> will not be beings. (By 'severed' I mean that the essence of good does not belong to the good itself, and being good does not belong to the essence of good.) For we know$_e$ a thing whenever we know$_g$ its essence. Further, what applies to good applies equally to the other essences, so that if the essence of good is not good, then neither will the essence of being be, nor the essence of one be one. But since all essences alike either are or are not, it follows that, if not even the essence of being is a being, none of the other essences is a being either. Moreover, if the essence of good does not belong to a given thing, that thing is not good.

The good, then, is necessarily one with the essence of good, and the fine with the essence of fine. The same applies to all the primary things, those spoken of in their own right, not insofar as they belong to something else. For if this is true <i.e., that something is a primary being>, it already implies <that the primary being is identical to its essence>, even if it is not a Form—though presumably <the conclusion> is all the more <necessary> if the thing is a Form.

Further, if the Ideas are what some people say they are, then clearly the subject will not be substance. For Ideas must be substances, but not by <being predicated> of a subject, since <if they were predicated of a subject>, they would exist <only> by being participated in.

From these arguments, then, we find that a thing itself and its essence are noncoincidentally one and the same, and that knowing$_e$ a thing is knowing$_e$ its essence; and so even isolating the Forms shows that a thing and its essence must be some one thing.

But because what is spoken of coincidentally—for instance, the musical or the pale—signifies two things, it is not true to say that it is the same as its essence. For the pale signifies both the subject of which pale is a coincident and the coincident;[10] and so in a way it is the same as its essence, and in a way it is not the

10. **the pale . . . itself>**: We can use 'the pale' (neuter article + adjective) to refer (i) to the man who is pale (i.e., to the pale thing) or (ii) to his quality (i.e., his paleness). On this double use of the neuter adjective see *Phys*. 188a36, 189b35, *Met*. 1028a24.

same—for <the pale> is not the same as man or as pale man, but it is the same as the attribute.

We can also see that it is absurd <for something not to be the same as its essence>, if we give a name to each essence; for apart from that essence there will be another essence as well— for instance, another essence will be the essence of the essence of horse. But why not let some things be essences at once, going no further, since essence is substance? Moreover, not only is <a thing> one <with its essence>, but their account is also the same; for one and being one are noncoincidentally one. Moreover, if there is another essence, the essences will go on to infinity; for one thing will be the essence of the one, and another will be the one, so that the same argument will also apply in their case.

Clearly, then, in the case of the primary things, those spoken of in their own right, a thing and its essence are one and the same. And it is evident that the sophistical refutations aimed against this position are all resolved in the same way as is the puzzle of whether Socrates and being Socrates are the same; for there is no difference in the premisses from which one would ask the questions or in the premisses from which one would find a solution.

We have said, then, in what way something's essence is the same as the thing, and in what way it is not.

* * * * * * *

[*FORM, ESSENCE, AND DEFINITION*]

10

A definition is an account, and every account has parts; and a part of the account corresponds to a part of the thing defined in the way in which the whole account corresponds to the whole thing defined. Hence a puzzle arises about whether or not the account of the parts must be present in the account of the whole. For in some cases the accounts of the parts evidently are present and in some cases they evidently are not; the account of a circle, for instance, does not include that of the segments, but the account of a syllable includes that of the letters, even though the circle is divided into its segments just as the syllable is divided into its letters.

Moreover, if a part is prior to a whole, and an acute angle is part of a right angle, and a finger of an animal, then an acute angle would be prior to a right angle, and a finger to a man. In fact, however, the whole seems to be prior, since the account of the part refers to the whole, and the whole is prior by being independent.

Alternatively, perhaps a part is spoken of in many ways, and a quantitative measure is only one type of part; leaving this type aside, we should examine the parts that compose substance.

1035a If, then, there is matter, form, and the compound of these, and matter, form, and the compound of them are all substance, then it follows that in one way matter is also called a part of something, but in another way it is not, and in this second way only the components of the account[11] of the form are parts. For example, flesh is not a part of concavity (since it is the matter in which concavity comes to be), but it is a part of snubness. Again, bronze is a part of the compound statue, but not a part of the statue spoken of as form. For it is the form of the statue—i.e., the statue insofar as it has form—and never the material aspect in its own right, that should be spoken of as the statue.

This is why the account of a circle does not include that of the segments, whereas the account of a syllable does include that of the letters; for the letters are not matter, but parts of the account of the form, while the segments are parts as matter in which the form comes to be. Still, the segments are nearer to the form than bronze is to the circle in the cases where circularity comes to be in bronze.

In a way, however, not every sort of letters—for instance, those in wax or those in air—will be included in the account of the syllable; for these also <like the bronze in the circle> are a part of the syllable as its perceptible matter. For if a line is divided and perishes into halves, or a man into bones, sinews, and bits of flesh, it does not follow that these compose the whole as parts of the substance, but only that they compose it as its matter. They are parts of the compound, but when we come to the form, which is what the account is of, they are not parts of it; that is why they are not included in accounts either.

11. **account**: See REASON #5.

Hence the account of some things will include that of these material parts, but the account of other things, if it is not of something combined with matter, must not include it. For this reason, the principles composing a given thing are, in some but not all cases, the material parts into which it perishes.

If, then, something—for instance, the snub or the bronze circle—is form and matter combined, then it perishes into these <material parts>, and matter is a part of it. But if something is without matter, not combined with it, so that its account is only of the form, then it does not perish—either not at all, or at least not in this way. Hence these <material parts> are parts and principles of things combined with matter, but neither parts nor principles of the form.

That is why the clay statue perishes into clay, the ball into bronze, and Callias into flesh and bones. Moreover, the circle perishes into its segments, because one type of circle is combined with matter; for the circle spoken of without qualification and the particular circle are called circles homonymously, because the particular[12] has no distinctive name.

We have now given the true answer, but let us take up the question again, and state the answer more perspicuously. Parts of the account— i.e., the things into which the account is divided—are, either all or some of them, prior to the whole. The account of the right angle, by contrast, does not include that of the acute angle, but, on the contrary, that of the acute angle includes that of the right angle; for we use the right angle in defining the acute, which is <defined as> less than a right angle. This is also the relation of the circle to a semicircle, since the semicircle is defined by the circle. Similarly, a finger is defined by reference to the whole, since this sort of part of a man is a finger.

And so all the material parts—i.e., those into which the whole is divided as its matter—are posterior to it, but the parts that are parts of the account and of the substance corresponding to the account are, either all or some of them, prior to the whole.

Now, an animal's soul—the substance of what is ensouled—is the substance corresponding to the account; it is the form and essence of the right sort of body. At any rate, a proper definition

12. **the particular**: the material particular ring. Since the Greek '*kuklos*' is used both for 'circle' and for 'ring', Aristotle remarks that it is homonymous.

of each part requires reference to its function, and this function requires perception. Hence the parts of the soul, either all or some of them, are prior to the compound animal, and the same is true in the case of the particular.

The body and its parts are posterior to this substance <i.e., the soul>, and its parts are the matter into which the compound, but not this substance, is divided. In a way they are prior to the compound, but in a way they are not, since they cannot exist when they are separated; for a finger is not an animal's finger in all conditions—on the contrary, a dead finger is only homonymously a finger. Some of them are simultaneous,[13] if they are the controlling parts, those on which the account and the substance primarily depend—the heart or the brain, for instance (for it does not matter which of the two it is).

Now, man or horse or anything else that applies in this way to particulars, but universally, is not a substance, but a sort of compound of this account and this matter as universal. When we come to particulars, Socrates is composed of ultimate matter, and the same is true in the other cases.

A part may be either of the form (by 'form' I mean the essence), or of the compound of the form and the matter, or of the matter itself. But only parts of the form are parts of the account, and the account is of the universal; for being circle is the same as circle, and being soul is the same as soul. But a compound such as this particular circle, either perceptible (for instance, bronze or wooden) or intelligible (for instance, a mathematical object), has no definition, but we know$_g$ it with the help of understanding or perception. When it has departed from actual understanding or perception, it is unclear whether or not it exists; but still, we always speak of it and know it by means of the universal account, whereas the matter is unknowable in its own right.

One sort of matter is perceptible, another intelligible. Examples of perceptible matter are, for instance, bronze and wood, and all matter that is capable of motion; intelligible matter is the matter present in perceptible things (as, for instance, mathematical objects are present in them), but not insofar as they are perceptible.

We have now stated the facts about whole and part and about prior and posterior. If someone asks whether the right angle, or

13. **simultaneous**: i.e., neither prior nor posterior to the compound of soul and body.

circle, or animal is prior to the parts composing it, i.e., the parts into which it is divided, or whether, alternatively, the parts are prior to the whole, we must answer that neither is true without qualification.

For suppose first that the soul is the animal, or rather the ensouled thing, or that a thing's soul is the thing itself, that being circle is the circle, and that being right angle, i.e., the essence$_0$ of the right angle, is the right angle. In that case, we should say that <the particular compound>—both the bronze right angle including <perceptible> matter and the right angle in particular lines—is posterior to the things in the account and to one sort of right angle,[14] and that the right angle without matter is posterior to the things in its account, but prior to the parts in the particular. We should <add these conditions and> not give an unqualified answer. Suppose, alternatively, that the soul is not the animal but different from it. In this case too we should say that some things are <prior> and some are not, as we have said.

11

Not surprisingly, a further puzzle arises: What sorts of parts are parts of the form, and what sorts are parts of the combined thing, not of the form? If this is not clear, we cannot define anything; for definition is of the universal and of the form. If, then, it is not evident which sorts of parts count as matter and which do not, it will not be evident what an account is either.

In cases where something evidently occurs in different kinds of things, as a circle, for instance, is found in bronze, stone, and wood, it seems clear that the bronze or stone (for instance) is not part of the substance of a circle, because a circle is <also found> separated from it. Even if it is not seen to be separated, the case may still be similar to those just mentioned. This would be true *1036b* if, for example, all the circles that were seen were bronze; for it would still be true that the bronze is not part of the form <of circle>, even though it is hard to remove the bronze in thought. Now the form of man, for instance, always appears in flesh and bones, and in parts of this sort. Does it follow that these are also parts of the form and the account? Perhaps not; perhaps they are only matter, and we are incapable of separating them from the

14. **one sort of right angle**: i.e., the form.

form because it does not also occur in other <sorts of material parts>.

Since this sort of thing seems to be possible, but it is unclear when <it is possible>, some people are puzzled even when they come to a circle or a triangle. They suppose that it is not suitably defined by lines and by the continuous, and that we speak of these in the same way as we were speaking of the flesh and bones of a man, or the bronze or stone of a statue.[15] Hence they reduce everything to numbers, and say that the account of the line is the account of the two.

Those who talk about the Ideas also <offer accounts.> Some of them say that the dyad is line-itself; others say that it is the form of line since, they say, in some cases—for instance, dyad and the form of dyad—the form is the same as the thing whose form it is, but in the case of the line it is not. The result is that there is one form for many things whose form appears different (this was also the result of the Pythagorean view); and then it is possible to make this form the one form of all things, and to make nothing else a form. On this argument, however, all things will be one.

We have said, then, that questions about definitions raise a puzzle, and why they raise it. That is why this reduction of everything <to numbers and Forms> and the abstracting of matter goes too far;[16] for presumably some things are <essentially> this form in this matter, or these material parts with this form.[17] And Socrates the Younger was wrong in his habitual comparison of an animal <and its parts with circle and bronze>. For his comparison leads us away from the truth; it makes us suppose that a man can exist without his parts, as a circle can exist without bronze. But in fact the two cases are not similar; for an animal is a perceiver,[18] and cannot be defined without reference to motion, and

15. **They suppose . . . of a statue**: They suppose that lines are simply the matter of a triangle, as bronze is the matter of a statue, and so they infer that the definition of triangle does not mention lines.

16. **That is why**: The puzzles about definition show that the process of ABSTRACTION can be taken too far. Hence they show that the error involved in the reduction to Forms and numbers is the error of excessive abstraction.

17. **this form . . . this form**: Cf. *PA* 640b27.

18. **perceiver**: Alternative text: 'perceptible'.

therefore to parts in the right condition. For a hand is not a part of a man in just any condition, but only when it is capable of fulfilling its function, and hence only when it is ensouled—when it is not ensouled, it is not a part <of a man>.

But in the case of mathematical objects, why are accounts <of parts>—for instance, of semicircles—not parts of accounts <of wholes>—for instance, of circles? For these are not perceptible. But perhaps this makes no difference; for some non-perceptible things have matter too, and in fact everything that is not an essence and form itself in its own right, but a this, has some sort of matter. Hence these semicircles will not be parts of the universal circle, but they will be parts of particular circles, as we said before; for one sort of matter is perceptible, one sort intelligible.

It is also clear that the soul is the primary substance, the body is matter, and man or animal is composed of the two as universal. As for Socrates or Coriscus, if <Socrates'> soul[19] is also Socrates, he is spoken of in two ways; for some speak of him as soul, some as the compound. But if he is without qualification this soul and this body, then what was said about the universal also applies to the particular.

We must postpone an investigation of whether there is another sort of matter apart from the matter of these <perceptible> substances, and whether we must search for some other sort of substance—for instance, numbers or something of the sort. For we also have this in view in trying to determine <the answers to questions> about perceptible substances as well <as non-perceptible substances>, since in a way the study of nature, i.e., second philosophy, has the task of studying perceptible substances.[20] For the student of nature must know not only about matter but also, and even more, about the substance corresponding to the account.

We must also postpone an investigation of the way in which the things in the account are parts of the definition, and of why the definition is one account. For it is clear that the thing defined is one. But what makes it one, given that it has parts?

We have said generally, then, about all cases, what the essence is; in what way it is itself in its own right; why in some cases the

19. **<Socrates'> soul**: Probably (not certainly) Aristotle is thinking of a particular soul.

20. **For we have . . . substances**: Aristotle anticipates the argument of Bks xii–xiv. See PHILOSOPHY.

account of the essence includes the parts of the thing defined and in some cases it does not; and that in the account of substance the parts that are matter will not be present, because they are parts of the compound substance, not of the substance corresponding to the account.

The compound substance has an account in one way, but in another way it has none. Taken together with matter, it has no account, since that is indefinable;[21] but it has an account corresponding to the primary substance, so that the account of man, for instance, is the account of soul. For <the primary> substance is the form present in the thing, and the compound substance is spoken of as composed of the form and the matter. Concavity, for instance, <is a form of this sort>; for snub nose and snubness are composed of concavity and nose (for nose will be present twice in these). And the compound substance (for instance snub nose or Callias) will also have matter in it.

1037b We have also said that in some cases, as in the case of primary substances, a thing and its essence are the same; curvature, for instance, is the same as being curvature, if curvature is primary. (By 'primary substance' I mean the substance that is so called not because x is in y and y is the subject of x by being the matter of x.) But if a thing is <a substance> by being matter or by being combined with matter, it is not the same as its essence. Nor, however, are they one <only> coincidentally, as Socrates and the musical are; for these are the same <only> coincidentally.

* * * * * * *

[*SUBSTANCE, FORM, AND UNIVERSAL*]

13

1038b Since we are investigating substance, let us return to it again. Just as the subject and the essence are said to be substance, so too is the universal. We have discussed the first two of these, namely essence and subject; we have seen that something is a subject in

21. **that is indefinable**: This might refer either to matter or to the compound.

one of two ways, either by being a this (as an animal is the subject for its attributes) or as matter is the subject for the actuality. But some also think that the universal is a cause and principle more than anything else is; that is why we should also discuss the universal.

For it would seem impossible for anything spoken of universally to be substance. For, first, the substance of a thing is the substance that is distinctive of it, which does not belong to anything else, whereas the universal is common; for what is called universal is what naturally belongs to more than one thing. Then which thing's substance will the universal be?[22] For it must be the substance either of all or of none of them. It cannot be the substance of all; but if it is the substance of one of them, then the others will be this one too, since things that have one substance also have one essence and are themselves one.[23]

Further, what is called substance is what is not said of a subject, whereas every universal is said of a subject.

Now, suppose someone says: 'Admittedly, a universal cannot belong to something as its essence. Still, it is present in the essence, as animal is present in man and horse.' Surely it is clear that it will be some account of <the essence it is present in>.[24] It does not matter even if it is not an account of everything in the substance; for this <universal> will still be the substance of something, as man is of the man in which it is present. And so the result will be the same once again; for <the universal>—for instance, animal—will be the substance of whatever it is present in by being its distinctive property.

Further, it is both impossible and absurd for a this and substance, if it is composite, to be composed not from substances

22. **which thing's . . . be?**: The universal F belongs to particular Fs. If it is their substance, it must be the substance of one, or of some, or of all of them.

23. **since things . . . are themselves one**: If, then, the universal is the substance of all its instances, all its instances will be one (given the principle stated in 1038b10–12). Hence the universal must be the substance of none of its instances. Alternative rendering: 'since things that have one substance and [or 'i.e.'] one essence are themselves one'.

24. **it will be . . . present in>**: Alternatively: 'there is some account of <the universal>'.

and not from a this, but from a sort of thing;[25] for it will follow that a nonsubstance, a sort of thing, will be prior to substance, to a this. But that is impossible; for attributes cannot be prior to substance, either in account or in time or in knowledge—for if they were, they would also be separable.

Moreover, a substance will be present in <the substance> Socrates, so that <the universal> will be the substance of two things.

In general, if a man[26] and things spoken of in this way are substances, it follows that nothing in their account is the substance of any of them or exists separately from them or in anything else. I mean, for instance, that there is no animal, or anything else mentioned in the accounts, apart from the particular animals.

If we study them in this way, then, it is evident that nothing that belongs universally is a substance and that what is predicated in common signifies this sort of thing,[27] not a this. If it is a this, then many <difficulties> result, including the Third Man.

Further, our conclusion can also be made clear from the following points. Substance cannot be composed of substances that are actually present in it; for things that are actually two in this way are never actually one, but if they are potentially two they are <actually> one. A double line, for instance, is composed of halves that are <only> potentially two things; for the actuality separates them. And so if substance is one, it will not be composed of substances that are actually present in it. Democritus is right about actuality, when he says that one cannot come to be from two, or two from one; he says this because he regards the indivisible magnitudes as the substances. Clearly, then, the same will apply in the case of number if, as some say, number is a combination of units; for either the pair is not one or else a unit is not actually in it.

This conclusion, however, raises a puzzle. For if no substance can be composed of universals (because a universal signifies this sort of thing, not a this) and if no substance can be composed of substances actually present in it, then it follows that every substance will be incomposite, so that none will have any account.

25. **sort of thing**: *poion*. Or 'such'. See 1039a2n, QUALITY.

26. **a man**: i.e., a particular man. Alternatively, 'man', i.e. the species.

27. **this sort of thing**: See QUALITY.

And yet, it seems to everyone, and we have said much earlier,[28] that substances alone, or most of all, have formulae, whereas now they too turn out not to have them. And so either nothing will have a definition or else in a way things will have definitions, and in a way they will not. What this means will be clearer from what follows.

* * * * * * *

15

We have found that the compound and the form$_{l}$ are different sorts of substance; I mean that the first sort of substance is substance by being the form$_{l}$ combined with matter, and the second sort is the form$_{l}$ without qualification. Now, all the substances spoken of as compounds perish, since all of them also come to be; but the form$_{l}$ does not perish in such a way that it is ever <in the process of> perishing, since neither is it ever <in the process of> coming to be. For it is the essence of this house, not the essence of house, that is <in the process of> coming to be, whereas forms$_{l}$ are and are not without <any process of> coming to be and perishing, since we have shown that no one generates or produces them.

For this reason there is neither definition nor demonstration about particular perceptible substances, because they have matter whose nature admits of both being and not being; that is why all <perceptible> particulars are perishable.

Now, demonstrations and definitions that express knowledge$_{e}$ are of necessary things. And just as knowledge cannot be knowledge at one time and ignorance at another, but what admits of such variation is belief, so also neither demonstration nor definition admits of such variation; belief is what is concerned with what admits of being otherwise. It clearly follows that there will be neither definition nor demonstration of these <particular perceptible things>. For whenever perishing things pass from perception, they are unclear to those with knowledge, and though the accounts still remain in the souls of those with knowledge, there

28. **much earlier**: 1030a2–27.

will be neither definition nor demonstration <about perceptible things>. That is why, whenever anyone who looks for a formula is defining a particular, he ought to realize that the definition can in every case be undermined, since particulars cannot be defined.

Nor, indeed, can Ideas be defined. For Ideas are particulars, they say, and separable. But accounts must be composed of names, and the definer will not make a <new> name (since it would be unknown); yet each of the established names is common to all <the particulars of a given kind>, and so they must also belong to something else <as well as to a given particular>. If, for instance, someone defines you, he will say you are a thin or pale animal, or something else that belongs to something else as well as to you.

Someone might say: 'Even though each name <in the definition> belongs separately to many things, still it is possible that all together belong only to this.' We should answer, first, that biped animal, for instance, belongs both to animal and to biped—indeed, this must be so with everlasting things, since they are prior to and parts of the composite thing. Moreover, they are also separable if man is separable; for either none of the three is separable or both animal and biped are. And so if none of them is separable, the genus will not exist apart from the species; but if the genus is separable, so is the differentia. Moreover, <animal and biped> are prior in being <to biped animal>, and therefore they are not destroyed when it is.

Further, if Ideas are composed of Ideas (for the things they are composed of are less composite), then the components of the Idea—for instance, animal and biped—will also have to be predicated of many things. If they are not, how will they be known? For there will be an Idea which cannot be predicated of more than one thing. But that does not seem to be so; on the contrary, every Idea can, it seems, be participated in.

As has been said, then, we fail to notice that everlasting things <that are particulars> are indefinable. This is especially true in the case of those that are unique—for instance, the sun and the moon. For sometimes people not only go wrong by adding the sorts of things (for instance, going around the earth, or being hidden at night) that can be removed from the sun without its ceasing to be the sun. (For <this sort of definition implies that> if it stops going around or shows at night, it will no longer be the sun; but that is absurd, since the sun signifies a certain sub-

stance.) They also <sometimes go wrong by mentioning only the features> that can be found in something else as well. If, for instance, something else of this sort comes to be, then clearly, <according to the alleged definition>, it will also have to be the sun, and in that case the account will be common <to the two>. *1040b*
But in fact the sun is a particular, as Cleon and Socrates are.

<These objections show why Ideas are indefinable.> For why does none of those <who believe in Ideas> present a formula of any Idea? If they tried to do so, the truth of what we have just said would become clear.

16

It is evident that even among the substances that are generally recognized to be such, most are potentialities. These include the parts of animals (for none of them is separated <as long as they remain parts of animals>; whenever they are separated, they all exist as matter),[29] and also earth, fire, and air. For none of these is one, but each is a sort of heap, until they are worked up and some one thing comes to be from them.

One would be most inclined to suppose that the parts of ensouled things that are closely <associated with> the soul are beings both in actuality and in potentiality; for they have principles of motion from some source in their joints, which is why some animals keep on living when they are divided. But nonetheless, all these things exist <only> in potentiality. They exist as long as they are one and continuous by nature, rather than by force or by growing together (that sort of thing is a deformity).

Now, one is spoken of in the same ways as being is; and the substance of one thing is one, and things whose substance is numerically one are numerically one. Evidently, then, neither one nor being can be the substance of things, just as being an element or being a principle cannot <be the substance of things>; rather, we ask 'What then is the principle?', so that we may refer <the thing> to something better known. Among these things, then, being and one are substance to a higher degree than principle, element, and cause are; but even being and one are not substance, since nothing else common is substance either. For substance belongs only to itself and to what has it, the thing whose substance

29. **(for none . . . as matter)**: See 1035b23, 1036b30, HOMONYMY.

it is. Moreover, one thing would not be in many places at once, but what is common exists in many places at once. Hence clearly no universal is found separately apart from particulars.

But those who say there are Forms are right in one way, in separating them, if they are indeed substances; but in another way they are wrong, because they say that the one over many is a Form.[30] The reason is that they cannot describe these imperishable substances apart from particular and perceptible substances, and so they make them the same in kind as perishable things (since these are the substances we know$_{o}$); they speak of man itself and horse itself, adding to perceptibles the word 'itself'.

1041a And yet even if we had not seen the stars, nonetheless, I think, they would have been everlasting substances apart from those we know; and so, as things are, it is equally true that even if we do not know what non-perceptible substances there are, there must presumably be some.

It is clear, then, that nothing said universally is a substance, and that no substance is composed of substances.

17

But let us make a sort of new beginning, and say over again what, and what sort of thing, substance should be said to be; for presumably our answer will also make things clear about the substance that is separated from perceptible substances. Since, then, substance is some sort of principle and cause, we should proceed from here.

In every case, we search for the reason why by asking why one thing belongs to another. For if we ask why a musical man is a musical man, either we are searching for what we have mentioned—for instance, why the man is musical—or else we are searching for something else. Now, to ask why something is itself is to search for nothing. For that <it is so> and its being so—I mean, for instance, that the moon is eclipsed—must be clear already; and the answer 'because it is itself' is one account and one cause applying to every case, to why a man is a man or a musician a musician. Perhaps, however, someone might answer

30. **because . . . Form**: The one over many is a universal, and (in Aristotle's view) no universal can be separated.

'because each thing is indivisible from itself, since this is what it is to be one'. But this is a short answer common to all cases.

We might, however, ask why a man is this sort of animal. Here, then, we are clearly not asking why something that is a man is a man. We are asking, then, why one thing belongs to another; that it does belong must already be clear, since otherwise we are searching for nothing. For instance, when we ask why it thunders, we are asking why there is a noise in the clouds; here we ask why one thing belongs to another. Similarly, we ask why these things—for instance, bricks and stones—are a house.

Evidently, then, we are searching for the cause; and this is the essence, to speak from a logical point of view. In some cases—for instance, presumably, a house or a bed—the cause is what something is for; sometimes it is what first initiated the motion, since this is also a cause. We search for the latter type of cause in the case of coming to be and perishing; in the case of being as well <as in the case of coming to be> we search for the former type of cause.

What we are searching for is most easily overlooked when one thing is not said of another (as when we ask, for instance, what 1041b
a man is), because we speak without qualification and do not specify that we are asking why these things are this thing.[31] Instead of speaking without qualification, we must articulate our question before we search, since otherwise we will not have distinguished a genuine search from a search for nothing. Since we must take it as given that the subject exists, clearly we search for why the matter is something. We ask, for instance, 'Why are these things a house?' Because the essence of house belongs to them. Similarly, a man is this, or rather is this body having this. Hence we search for the cause on account of which the matter is something, i.e., for the form; and this cause is the substance.

Evidently, then, there is neither searching nor teaching about incomposite things; the approach to them is different from searching.

Now, a composite is composed of something in such a way that the whole thing is one, not as a heap is, but as a syllable is. A syllable is not the same as its letters—for instance, B and A are

31. **why these things are this thing**: We answer the question 'What is a man?' by rephrasing it as 'Why are these things (the flesh, bones etc.) a man?'

not the same thing as BA, nor is flesh fire and earth. For when the components are dispersed, the flesh or syllable no longer exists, though the letters or the fire and earth still do. Hence the syllable is something, and not only the vowel and the consonant but some further thing; and similarly, flesh is not only fire and earth, or the hot and cold, but some further thing.

Now suppose that this further thing must be either an element or composed of elements. If it is an element, there will be the same argument over again; for flesh will be composed of this <new element>, plus fire and earth, plus some further thing, so that it will go on without limit. If the further thing is composed of an element, it is clearly not composed of just one (otherwise it would itself be this one), but of more than one; and then we will repeat the same argument about it as about flesh or a syllable.

It would seem, however, that this further thing is something, and not an element, and that it is the cause of one thing's being flesh and another thing's being a syllable, and similarly in the other cases.

Now this is the substance of a given thing; for this is the primary cause of the thing's being <what it is>. Some things are not substances, but the things that are substances are naturally constituted; hence this nature—the one that is not an element but a principle—will apparently be substance. An element is what is present in something as the matter into which the thing is divided—for instance, the A and the B in the syllable.

Book VIII

[*FURTHER QUESTIONS ON SUBSTANCE AND FORM*]

1

1042a3 We must, then, draw the conclusions from what has been said, gather together the main points, and so complete the discussion. Here, then, is what we have said:[1]

1. **what we have said**: The numbered points summarize the argument of most of Bk vii.

(1) We are searching for the causes, principles, and elements of substances.

(2) Some substances are agreed by everyone to be substances, while some people have held distinctive views of their own about some other things <that they count as substances>. The agreed substances are the natural ones—for instance, fire, earth, water, air, and the other simple bodies, then plants and their parts, animals and their parts, and, finally, the heaven and its parts. In some people's distinctive views, Forms and mathematical objects are substances.

(3) Some arguments imply that the essence is substance, others that the subject is substance. Other arguments imply that the genus is substance more than the species are, and that the universal is substance more than the particulars are. The Ideas are closely related to the universal and the genus, since the same argument makes all of them seem to be substances.

(4) Since the essence is substance and a definition is an account of the essence, we have discussed definition and what is in its own right.

(5) Since a definition is an account and an account has parts, we also had to consider what a part is, to see what sorts of parts are parts of the substance, and what sorts are not, and whether the same parts <that are parts of the substance> are also parts of the definition.

(6) Further, neither the universal nor the genus is substance.

(7) We should examine Ideas and mathematical objects later, since some say that these are substances apart from perceptible substances.

For now, let us proceed with a discussion of the agreed substances; these are the perceptible ones, and all perceptible substances have matter.

The subject is substance. In one way, matter <is a subject>. (By 'matter' I mean what is potentially but not actually a this.) In another way, the account and the form$_m$, which, being a this, is separable in account, <is a subject>. The third <sort of subject> is the composite of these two. Only it comes to be and perishes, and it is separable without qualification; for among substances that correspond to the account some are <separable without qualification> and some are not.

Now, clearly matter as well <as form and compound> is

substance; for in all changes between opposites there is some subject for the change. Changes in place, for instance, have a subject that is here at one time, elsewhere at another time; those involving growth have one that is this size at one time, smaller or bigger at another time; changes involving alteration
1042b have one that is, <for instance,> healthy at one time, sick at another time. Similarly, changes involving substance have a subject that is at one time in <process of> coming to be, at another time in <process of> perishing, and at one time is the sort of subject that is a this and at another time is the sort of subject that corresponds to a privation.

Coming to be and perishing imply all the other sorts of change, but one or two of the other sorts do not imply this sort. For if something has matter for change in place, it need not also have matter for coming to be and perishing. The difference between unqualified and qualified coming to be has been described in the works on nature.[2]

2

The substance that is subject and matter is agreed; this is the substance that is something potentially. It remains, then, to describe the substance of perceptible things that is actuality.

Democritus would seem to think that there are three differentiae; in his view, the body that is the subject—the matter—is one and the same, but <perceptible things> differ either by 'balance', i.e., figure, or by 'turning', i.e., position, or by 'contact', i.e., arrangement.[3] It is evident, however, that there are many differentiae. For things are differentiated by the way their matter is combined (blended together, for instance, as honey-water is); or tied together (for instance, a bundle); or glued (for instance, a book); or nailed (for instance, a box); or by more than one of these; or by having a specific position (a threshold or a lintel, for instance, since their differentia is being in a certain position); or by a specific time (for instance, dinner and breakfast); or by a specific place (for instance, the winds); or by having different perceptible attributes (for instance, hardness

2. **works on nature**: See *Phys.* i 7, COMING TO BE.

3. **'balance' . . . arrangement**: Aristotle seems to quote Democritus' actual terms.

or softness, thickness or thinness, dryness or wetness), either some or all of them, and, in general, by excess or deficiency <of them>.

Clearly, then, 'is' is also said in just as many ways.[4] Something is a threshold, for instance, because it has this position, and its being a threshold signifies its having this position; and similarly, being ice signifies <water's> having solidified in this way. The being of some things will be defined by all of these things—by some things being mixed, some blended, some bound together, some solidified, and some (a hand or foot, for instance) having the other differentiae.

We must grasp, then, what kinds of differentiae there are, since they will be the principles of <a thing's> being <what it is>. For instance, things differentiated by more and less, or thick and thin, or by other such things, are all differentiated by excess and deficiency; things differentiated by shape, or by roughness and smoothness, are all differentiated by straight and bent; and the being of other things will be being mixed, and their not being will be the opposite.

It is evident from what we have said, then, that if substance is the cause of a thing's being, we should seek the cause of the being of each of these things in these <differentiae>. Although none of these <differentiae> is substance even when combined <with matter>, still <the differentia> is in each case analogous to substance; and just as in substances what is predicated of the matter is the actuality itself, so also in other definitions what is predicated is what is closest to being the actuality. If, for instance, we have to define a threshold, we will say it is wood or stone in this position; we will define a house as bricks and timber in this position (or in some cases we mention the end as well). If we have to define ice, we will say it is water frozen or solidified in this way; we will say harmony is this sort of blending of high and low; and the same is true in the other cases.

It is evident from this that each different sort of matter has a different actuality and account. For in some cases the actuality is the composition, in some it is the mixture, and in others one of the other things we have mentioned.

4. **'is' . . . ways**: When we say that x is F, the 'is' refers to the different relations just mentioned.

That is why some people who offer definitions say what a house is by saying it is stones, bricks, and timber; in saying this, they speak of what is potentially a house, since these things are matter. Others say that a house is a container sheltering possessions and <living> bodies (or add something else of that sort); in saying this, they speak of the actuality. Others combine the matter and the actuality; in doing this, they speak of the third sort of substance, which is composed of the first two. For the account giving the differentiae would seem to be the account of the form and the actuality, and the one giving the constituents present in the house would seem to be more an account of the matter. The same is true of the sorts of formulae that Archytas used to accept; for these are accounts of the composite. What, for instance, is calm weather? Quiet in a large expanse of air; for air is the matter, and quiet is the actuality of the substance. What is calm? Smoothness of sea; the material subject is the sea, and the actuality and form$_{m}$ is the smoothness.

It is evident from what we have said, then, both what perceptible substance is and what sort of being it has; for one sort is substance as matter, another is substance as form$_{m}$ and actuality, and the third is the substance that is composed of these.

3

We must realize that it is not always obvious whether a name signifies the composite substance or signifies the actuality and form$_{m}$. Does a house, for instance, signify the combination (that it is a shelter composed of bricks and stone in this position) or does it signify the actuality and form (that it is a shelter)? Is a line twoness in length, or twoness? Is an animal a soul in a body, or a soul—since soul is the substance and actuality of the right sort of body? Now, animal might belong to both form and compound; if it does, it will be spoken of not in one account <applying to both>, but with reference to one thing.[5]

Although this question makes a difference in another area,
1043b it makes no difference to the search for perceptible substance;

5. **with reference to one thing**: See 1003a33, HOMONYMY.

for the essence belongs to the form and actuality. For soul and being soul are the same, whereas man and being man are not the same, unless the soul is also to be called the man. In the latter case, <being man> is the same as one thing, <i.e., soul>, but not the same as the other, <i.e., soul plus body>.

It is evident when we investigate that a syllable is not composed of letters plus composition, and that a house is not bricks plus composition. And this is correct; for neither composition nor mixture is composed of the things of which it is composition or mixture. The same is true in other cases. If, for instance, a threshold is <what it is> because of its position, the threshold is composed of the position, but the position is not composed of the threshold; nor is a man animal plus two-footed. On the contrary, there must be something beyond these <elements>, if they are matter; this other thing is neither an element nor composed of elements, but it is what people <mistakenly> exclude when they speak <only> of the matter. If this, then, is the cause of being, and <the cause of being> is substance, then in speaking of this they speak of the substance itself.

This substance must either be everlasting or else be perishable without <being in process of> perishing and have come to be without <being in process of> coming to be. It has been proved and shown elsewhere[6] that no one produces or generates the form; what is produced is a this, and what comes to be is what is composed <of form and matter>.

It is not yet clear whether the substances of perishable things are separable. In some cases, however, this is clearly impossible—for instance, in the case of such things as house or utensil, which cannot exist apart from the particulars. Now, presumably these are not substances at all, and neither is anything else that is not constituted by nature; for one might take nature to be the only substance found in perishable things.[7]

* * * * * * *

6. **elsewhere**: 1033a24–b19.

7. **for one . . . perishable things**: For the suggestion that artifacts are not substances cf. 1041b28–36.

Book IX

[*POTENTIALITY AND ACTUALITY*]

1

We have now discussed what is in the primary way, the being to which all the other predications of being are referred, namely substance. For it is the account of substance that determines that the other things—quantity, quality, and the other things spoken of in this way—are called beings; for, as we said in the first discussion, they all have the account of substance.

Now being is spoken of in one way as either what, or quality, or quantity; and in another way in accordance with potentiality and realization, and in accordance with activity. Let us, then, also discuss potentiality and realization.

First let us discuss the type of potentiality that is so called most fully, though it is not the most useful for our present purpose; for potentiality and actuality extend more widely than the type spoken of only in connection with motion. After we have spoken of this type of potentiality, we will define actuality, and in the course of doing so we will also clarify the other types of potentiality.

We have determined elsewhere that potentiality and being potential are spoken of in many ways. Let us ignore all those potentialities that are so called <merely> homonymously; for some things are called potentialities from some <mere> similarity—in geometry, for instance, we say that some things are or are not powers[1] of other things, by being or not being related to them in some way.

All potentialities that are spoken of with reference to the same form are principles of some sort and are called potentialities with reference to one primary sort of potentiality. This primary sort is a

1. **powers:** *Dunamis* is applied in Greek, as 'power' is in English, to numbers.

principle of change either in another subject or in the subject of the potentiality itself insofar as this subject is another thing.[2]

For one sort of potentiality is a potentiality for being affected. This is the principle of change in the very subject that is affected, causing this subject to be affected by the agency of another thing, or <by its own agency> insofar as it is another thing. Another sort of potentiality is a state of being unaffected by deterioration or perishing by the agency of a principle initiating change—either another thing or itself insofar as it is another thing. For the account of the primary sort of potentiality is present in all these formulae.

Again, these potentialities are called potentialities either for merely acting on or being affected, or for acting on or being affected well. Hence the accounts of the potentialities of the first sort are also present in a way in the accounts of those of the second sort.

Evidently, then, in a way the potentiality for acting on and for being acted on is one. For a thing is potentially <something> either by itself having the potentiality for being being acted on or by something else's having the potentiality to be acted on by it. In a way, however, the two potentialities are evidently different. For one sort of potentiality is in the subject acted on; for it is because this thing has some principle in it, and matter is also a sort of principle, that what is acted on is acted on, and one thing is acted on by another (what is oily, for instance, is combustible, what is pliable in a certain way is crushable, and so on). The other sort of potentiality is in the producer; heat, for instance, is present in the producer of heat, and the building craft in the builder. Hence insofar as something is naturally unified, it is not acted on at all by itself, since it is one and not something else.

Lack of potentiality or what lacks potentiality is the privation that is contrary to this sort of potentiality. Hence every potentiality is for the same thing and in the same respect as the corresponding lack of potentiality. Privation is spoken of in many ways. We ascribe it to what does not have something, and also to what would naturally have something but does not have it—either if it does not have it at all or if it does not have it when it would naturally have it (either because it does not have it in a given way (for instance, completely)

2. **either in . . . another thing**: If, e.g., you kick my shin, you initiate a change in another thing (in me). If I kick my own shin, I initiate (by kicking) a change in myself insofar as I am another thing (something with a shin vulnerable to being kicked).

or because it does not have it at all). In some cases, if things would naturally have something and are without it as a result of force, we say that they have been deprived.

2

Some principles of this sort are present in inanimate things, while others are present in animate things, both in the soul and in the rational part of the soul; clearly, then, some potentialities will be nonrational and others will involve reason. Hence all crafts—i.e., the productive sciences—are potentialities; for they originate change in another thing or in the subject itself insofar as it is another thing.

Every potentiality that involves reason is a potentiality for either one of a pair of contraries, whereas every nonrational potentiality is a potentiality for just one contrary; the hot, for instance, can produce only heat, whereas medical knowledge can produce either illness or health. This is because knowledge$_e$ is a rational account, and the same rational account reveals both the object <proper to the potentiality> and its privation (though not in the same way), so that in a way it is the knowledge of both contraries, but in a way it is the knowledge of the proper object rather than of the privation. And so every such science must also be of contraries, but in its own right each science must be the knowledge of the proper object, and not in its own right the knowledge of the privation. For the rational account is of the proper object in its own right, and of the privation coincidentally, in a way; for it reveals the contrary by denial and removal, since the contrary is the primary privation, and the privation is the removal of the proper object.

Since contraries do not occur in the same thing, and since knowledge is a potentiality insofar as it includes reason, and the soul has a principle of motion, it follows that, whereas a producer of health produces only health, a producer of heat produces only heat, and a producer of cold produces only cold, a knower$_e$ produces both contraries. For the rational account is of both (though not in the same way), and it is present in a soul, which has a principle of motion. And so it will initiate both motions from the same principle, by connecting them with one and the same account. Hence a rational potentiality produces contraries, since they are included under one principle, the account.

It is also evident that the potentiality of acting well or being acted on well implies the potentiality of merely acting or being acted on, but the latter potentiality does not always imply the former. For whatever acts well necessarily also acts, but what acts does not necessarily act well.

* * * * * * *

5

All potentialities either are innate (for instance, the senses) or depend on habit (for instance, flute playing) or on learning (for instance, the crafts). If a potentiality depends on habit and reason, we must actualize it before we can possess it;[3] but this does not hold for potentialities that are not of this sort, or for potentialities for being acted on. 1047b31

Now, whatever has a potentiality has a potentiality to do something, to do it at some time, and to do it in some way (and however many other conditions must be present in the definition). Further, some things have a potentiality to initiate motion in accordance with reason, and their potentialities involve reason; other things are nonrational, and their potentialities lack reason. Hence the former sort of potentialities must be in animate things, whereas the latter sort may be in both animate and inanimate things. 1048a

In the case of nonrational potentialities, it is necessary that whenever the agent and the thing acted on meet in the conditions suitable for their potentialities, the one acts and the other is acted on. But this is not necessary in the case of rational potentialities. For whereas each nonrational potentiality acts in <only> one way, each rational potentiality acts in contrary ways; and so <if rational potentialities were necessarily actualized whenever the agent and the thing acted on meet,> each would act in contrary ways at the same time, which is impossible. Something else, then, namely desire or decision, must control the action; for when the agent has an overriding desire for one alternative, that is how it will act, whenever it is in the conditions suitable for its potentiality and meets the thing that is acted on. Necessarily, then, when anything with a rational potentiality desires to act in a way for which it has a potentiality, and it is in the conditions suitable for the potentiality, it acts. It has the potentiality to act when the thing acted on is present

3. **we must . . . possess it**: Cf. *EN* ii 4.

and is in a certain state; and it will not have the potentiality to act without these conditions.

For it is not necessary to add the condition 'if nothing external prevents it'; for it has the potentiality insofar as it is a potentiality to act in a particular way, and it is a potentiality, not to act in this way in all conditions, but to act in this way in certain conditions, which exclude the presence of external hindrances; for these are excluded by the presence of some of the conditions mentioned in the definition. Hence even if one has a wish or an appetite to act in two ways or in contrary ways at the same time, one will not act in those ways. For that is not the sort of potentiality one has for them, nor is it a potentiality to act in both ways at the same time; for it will engage in its characteristic actions only in a specific way <and hence it will not engage in both at the same time>.

6

Since we have now discussed the sort of potentiality that is spoken of in relation to motion, let us discuss what, and what sort of thing, actuality is. For our distinctions will also make potentiality clear at the same time; we will see that what naturally initiates motion or is moved by something else—either without qualification or in a certain way—is not the only sort of thing that we take to have a potentiality. We also recognize another sort of potentiality; and this is why we discussed the previous cases in our investigation of it.

Actuality, then, consists in something's being present <in a subject>, but not in the same way as when we say something is present potentially. We say something is present potentially when, for instance, we say Hermes is in the block of wood, and a half-line in the whole line, because it might be separated out; and we say that we have knowledge$_e$ even if we are not attending to what we know, as long as we have the potentiality to attend to it. The other case <attending to what we know, for instance> is actuality.

What we mean to say is clear in particular cases by induction; we must not seek a formula in every case, but in some cases we must grasp the point by analogy. In this case, as the builder building is to the builder who potentially builds, or how we are when awake compared to how we are when asleep, or how we are when seeing compared to how we are when we have our eyes shut but possess sight, or as the product shaped from matter is to the matter, as the finished work is to the unworked <material>—let actuality be defined by the first part of this contrast, and the potential by the second.

Things are said to be actually <in some condition>, not all in the same way, but by analogy—as A is in B or is related to B, so C is in D or is related to D. For in some cases the actuality is that of motion in relation to potentiality, and in other cases it is the actuality of substance in relation to some matter.

The sort of potentiality or actuality that belongs to the infinite, the void, and all such things is different from the sort that belongs to many other things—to what sees or walks or is seen, for instance. For these latter things can also be truly said to be <actual> without qualification at some time—for instance, one thing is an object of sight because it is being seen, another because it can be seen. But the potentiality that belongs to the infinite <in division> is not the sort that implies that it will be actually separable; it is <separable only> in knowledge. For the fact that further division is possible at every stage ensures that this actuality is potential, not that it is <ever> separate.

* * * * * * *

7

We must distinguish when a thing is potentially <something> and *1048b37*
when it is not; for it is not potentially <something> at just any time. *1049a*
For example, is earth potentially a man or not? If not, is it potentially a man by the time it has become seed? Or perhaps not even then? Similarly, not everything can be healed by medical science or by luck; there is something which has the potentiality for it, and this is what is potentially healthy.

In cases where thought causes an agent's potentiality to be realized, the definition is this: An agent is potentially F if whenever he wants to realize F, he realizes it, provided nothing external prevents it. In the case of the subject that is acted on—healed, for instance—the definition is this: The subject is potentially F whenever nothing in it prevents it <from realizing F>. The same is true of what is potentially a house; if nothing in it—i.e., in the matter—prevents it from becoming a house, and nothing needs to be added or removed or changed, it is potentially a house. The same is true in all other cases where the principle of coming to be is external.

When the principle of coming to be is in the subject itself, the subject is potentially whatever it will be through itself if nothing external prevents it. For example, the seed is not yet <potentially the organism whose seed it is>, since it must be put in something else and changed; but whenever it is in the appropriate condition through a principle in itself, then it is potentially <the organism>. In the first condition, it needs another principle <outside itself>, just as earth is not yet potentially a statue, since it must change to become bronze.

Sometimes we call the F not G but of-G.[4] A box, for example, is not wood, but of-wood, nor is wood earth, but of-earth, and again earth, if the same applies, is not that other thing, but of-that. In all these cases <where F is of-G>, it would seem that G is without qualification potentially F; a box, for instance, is neither of-earth nor earth, but of-wood, since it is wood that is potentially a box, and this is the matter of the box—wood in general of box in general, and this wood of this box. And if there is a first thing which is no longer said of another thing or called of-that, this is the first matter; if earth, for instance, is of-air, and air is not fire but of-fire, then fire is the first matter, and the first matter is not a this.

For that of which <something else is said>, i.e., the subject, is of different sorts insofar as it is or is not a this. The subject for attributes is, for instance, a man, both body and soul, and the attributes are, for instance, musical and pale. When music is present in it, the subject is called not music but a musical thing, and the man is not paleness but a pale thing, and not walking or motion but a walking or moving thing—just as we say something is of-F, not that it is F. In these cases, then, the last thing is substance. In other cases, when the thing predicated is a form and a this, the last thing is matter, and material substance. And
1049b we find that it is correct to apply 'of-F' both to matter and to attributes, since both matter and attributes are indefinite.[5]

We have said, then, when something should be said to be potentially and when it should not.

* * * * * * *

4. **of-G**: Or 'G-en' (wooden, earthen, etc.).

5. **both . . . indefinite**. Neither matter nor an attribute satisfies the conditions for being a definite subject, i.e., a THIS.

Book XII

* * * * * * *

[*SUBSTANCE AS DIVINE INTELLECT*]

6

Since we have found that there are three types of substance, two of them natural and one unmoved, we must discuss the third kind, to show that there must be an everlasting unmoved substance. For substances are the primary beings, and if all substances are perishable, then everything is perishable. But motion cannot come to be or perish (since it has always been), nor can time (since there cannot be a before and an after if there is no time).[1] Motion is also continuous, then, in the same way that time is, since time is either the same as motion or an attribute of it. But the only continuous motion is local motion—specifically, circular motion.

Now if there is something that is capable of initiating motion or of acting, but it does not actually do so, there will be no motion; for what has a potentiality need not actualize it. It will be no use, then, to assume everlasting substances, as believers in Forms do, unless these include some principle capable of initiating change. And even this, or some other type of substance apart from the Forms, is not sufficient; for if it does not actualize its potentiality, there will be no motion. Nor yet is it sufficient if it actualizes its potentiality, but its essence$_{o}$ is potentiality; for there will be no everlasting motion, since what has a potentiality need not actualize it. There must, then, be a principle of the sort whose essence$_{o}$ is actuality. Further, these substances must be without matter; for they must be everlasting if anything else is to be everlasting, and hence they must be actuality.

Now a puzzle arises. For it seems that whatever actualizes a

1. **(since there . . . no time)**: If time came to be, then—in Aristotle's view—it must have come to be at some time, and hence there must have been some time before it existed, which is self-contradictory. See *Phys.* 251a8–252a5.

potentiality must have it, but not everything that has a potentiality also actualizes it; and so potentiality is prior. But now, if this is so, nothing that exists will exist, since things can have the potentiality to exist without actualizing it. And yet, if those who have written about the gods are right to generate everything from night,[2] or if the natural philosophers are right to say that 'all things were together',[3] the same impossibility results. For how will things be moved if there is no cause <initiating motion> in actuality? For surely matter will not initiate motion in itself, but carpentry, <for instance, must initiate the motion>; nor will the menstrual fluid or the earth initiate motion in themselves, but the semen and the seeds <must initiate the motion>.

Hence some people—Leucippus and Plato, for instance—believe in everlasting actuality; for they say that there is always motion. But they do not say why there is this motion, or what kind of motion it is, and neither do they state the cause of something's being moved in this way or that. For nothing is moved at random, but in every case there must be some <cause>—as in fact things are moved in one way by nature and in another by force or by the agency of mind or something else. Further, what sort of motion is primary? For that makes an enormous difference. Nor can Plato say that the principle is of the sort that he sometimes thinks it is—what initiates its own motion. For he also says that the soul is later <than motion> and comes into being at the same time as the universe.[4]

The view that potentiality is prior to actuality is in a way correct and in a way incorrect—we have explained how this is so. The priority of actuality is attested by Anaxagoras (since mind is actuality), and by Empedocles (who makes love and strife prior), and by those who say that there is always motion, as Leucippus does. And so chaos or night did not exist for an infinite time, but the same things have always existed (either in a cycle or in some other way), if actuality is prior to potentiality.

If, then, the same things always exist in a cycle, something must always remain actually operating in the same way. And if there is to be coming to be and perishing, then there must be

2. **from night**: HESIOD.

3. **all things were together**: ANAXAGORAS.[3]

4. **Nor can Plato . . . universe**: See Plato, *Timaeus* 34b.

something else that always actually operates, in one way at one time and in another way at another time. This <second mover>, then, must actually operate in one way because of itself and in another way because of something else, and hence either because of some third mover or because of the first mover. Hence it must be because of the first mover; for <otherwise> the first mover will cause the motion of both the second and the third. Then surely it is better if the first mover is the cause. For we have seen that it is the cause of what is always the same, and a second mover is the cause of what is different at different times. Clearly both together cause this everlasting succession. Then surely this is also how the motions occur. Why, then, do we need to search for any other principles?

7

Since it is possible for things to be as we have said they are, and since the only alternative is for everything to come to be from night and from all things being together and from what is not, this may be taken as the solution of the puzzles. There is something, then, that is always being moved in a ceaseless motion, and this motion is circular (this is clear not only from argument but also from what actually happens); and so the first heaven is everlasting. Hence there is also something that initiates motion. And since whatever both is moved and initiates motion is an intermediary, there is something that initiates motion without being moved, something that is everlasting and a substance and actuality.

This is how an object of understanding or desire initiates motion; it initiates motion without being moved. The primary objects of desire and of understanding are the same. For what appears fine is the object of appetite, and what is fine is the primary object of wish;[5] and we desire something because it seems <fine>, rather than its seeming <fine> because we desire it— for understanding is the principle.[6]

Understanding is moved by its object, and the first column <of opposites> is what is understood in its own right. In this column

5. **what appears fine . . . what is fine**: Cf. *DA* 433a26–30, *EN* 1113a15–22.

6. **understanding is the principle**: Cf. *DA* 433a21, *EN* 1139a31–6.

substance is primary; and the primary substance is the substance that is simple and actually operating. (Being one and being simple are not the same; for being one signifies a measure, while being simple signifies that something is itself in a particular condition.) Further, what is fine and what is choiceworthy for itself are in the same column; and what is primary is in every case either the best or what is analogous to the best.

Division shows that what something is for is among the things that are unmoved. For it is either the end for some <beneficiary> or the end <aimed at> in some <process>; the first of these is moved, and the second is unmoved. The <end> initiates motion by being an object of love, and it initiates motion in the other things by <something else's> being moved.

If, then, something is moved, it can be otherwise. And so, if something's actuality is the primary type of local motion, it follows that insofar as it is in motion, in this respect it admits of being otherwise, in place if not in substance. But since there is something that initiates motion without itself being moved, and this is actually operating, it cannot be otherwise in any respect at all. For local motion is the primary type of motion, and the primary type of local motion is circular motion; and this is the sort of motion that the primary mover initiates. Hence the primary mover exists necessarily; and insofar as it exists necessarily, its being is fine, and insofar as its being is fine, it is a principle.[7] For what is necessary is spoken of in a number of ways—as what is forced because it is contrary to the subject's impulse, as that without which the good cannot be, and as what cannot be otherwise but is necessary without qualification.

This, then, is the sort of principle on which the heaven and nature depend. Its way of life has the same character as our own way of life at its best has for a short time. For the primary mover is always in this state <of complete actuality>, whereas we cannot always be in it; for its actuality is also pleasure (that is why being awake, perceiving, and thinking are pleasantest, while expectations and memories are pleasant because of these).

Understanding in its own right is of what is best in its own right, and the highest degree of understanding is of what is best to the highest degree in its own right. And understanding under-

7. **it is a principle**: since it is an object of love.

stands itself by sharing the character of the object of understanding; for it becomes an object of understanding by being in contact with and by understanding its object, so that understanding and its object are the same.[8] For understanding is what is capable of receiving the object of understanding and the essence$_o$, and it is actually understanding when it possesses its object; and so it is this <actual understanding and possession> rather than <the potentiality to receive the object> that seems to be the divine aspect of understanding, and its actual attention to the object of understanding is pleasantest and best.

If, then, the god is always in the good state that we are in sometimes, that deserves wonder; if he is in a better state, that deserves still more wonder. And that is indeed the state he is in. Further, life belongs to the god. For the actuality of understanding is life, and the god is that actuality; and his actuality in its own right is the best and everlasting life. We say, then, that the god is the best and everlasting living being, so that continuous and everlasting life and duration belong to the god; for that is what the god is.

Some, however, suppose, as the Pythagoreans and Speusippus do, that what is finest and best is not present in the principle, claiming that the principles of plants and animals are their causes, whereas what is fine and complete is found in what results from these. Their view is mistaken. For the seed comes from other <principles> that are prior and complete; and what is primary is not the seed, but the complete <organism>; for instance, one would say that the man is prior to the seed (not the man who comes into being from the seed, but another one, from whom the seed comes).

It is evident from what has been said, then, that there is an everlasting, unmoved substance that is separated from perceptible things. It has also been proved that this substance cannot have any magnitude, but must be without parts and indivisible; for it initiates motion for an infinite time, but nothing finite has infinite potentiality. And since every magnitude is either infinite or finite, <the primary mover> cannot have a finite magnitude, and it cannot have an infinite magnitude, because there is no infinite magnitude at all. Besides, it has also been proved that this sub-

8. **so that . . . the same**: Cf. *DA* 430a3.

stance is not affected or altered, since all other motions depend on local motion. It is clear, then, why these things are so.

* * * * * * *

9

The nature of <divine> understanding raises a number of puzzles. For understanding seems to be the most divine of the things we observe, but many difficulties arise about what state it must be in if it is to be so divine. For if it understands nothing, what is so impressive about it? It would be like someone asleep. If, on the other hand, it does understand, but something else controls whether it understands (since its essence$_{o}$ is not actual understanding, but the potentiality for it), it is not the best substance; for what makes it valuable comes from <actual> understanding.

And in any case, whether its essence$_{o}$ is potential or actual understanding, what does it understand? It must understand either itself or something else; if something else, then either always the same thing or else different things at different times. Then does it make any difference whether the object of its understanding is fine or is just any old thing? Surely there are some things that it would be absurd for it to think about. Clearly, then, it understands what is most divine and most valuable, and it does not change; for the change would be to something worse, and it would thereby also be a motion.

First, then, if it is potential, not actual, understanding, it is reasonable to expect that the continuous <exercise of> understanding would be tiring for it. Moreover, clearly something other than understanding—namely the object of understanding—would be more valuable. For indeed both the potentiality and the activity of understanding will belong even to someone who understands the worst thing; and if this is to be avoided (since there are also some things it is better not to see than to see), then the activity of understanding is not the best thing.

<The divine understanding,> then, must understand itself, so that its understanding is an understanding of understanding. In every case, however, knowledge$_{e}$, perception, belief, and thought have something other than themselves as their object; each has itself as its object as a by-product. Further, if to understand and

to be understood are different, which is responsible for the presence of the good? For to be an act of understanding is not the same as to be understood.

Well, perhaps in some cases the knowledge is the object. In 1075a
the productive <sciences, the knowledge is> the substance and essence <of the product> without the matter, and in the theoretical sciences, the account is both the object and the understanding. In these cases, then, where the object of understanding does not differ from understanding—i.e., in cases where the object has no matter—the object and the understanding will be the same, and the activity of understanding will be one with its object.

One puzzle still remains: Is the object of understanding composite? If it were composite, understanding would change in <understanding different> parts of the whole. Perhaps we should say that whatever has no matter is indivisible. <On this view, the condition of actual understanding is> the condition that human understanding (or rather, the understanding of any composite beings) reaches over a certain length of time; for it does not possess the good at this or that time, but achieves the best, which is something other than it, in some whole <period of time>. And this is the condition the understanding that understands itself is in throughout all time.

10

We should also consider the way in which the nature of the whole <universe> possesses the good—i.e., the best good. Is this good something separated, itself in its own right, or is it the order <of the whole>? Perhaps it is present in both ways, as in an army. For there the good is in the order <of the whole army>, and it is also, and to a greater extent, the general; for he does not exist because the order exists, but the order exists because he does. All things—fishes, birds, and plants—are joined in some order, but not all in the same way. Nor are they unrelated to each other, but they have some relation; for all things are joined in some order in relation to one thing. (It is like a household, where the free members are least of all at liberty to do what they like, and all or most of what they do is ordered, whereas only a little of what slaves and beasts do promotes the common <good>, and mostly they do what they like.) For the nature of each sort of thing is such a principle <that aims at the good of the whole>.

I mean, for instance, that everything necessarily is eventually dissolved, and in this way there are other things in which everything shares for <the good of> the whole.

* * * * * * *

Book XIII

[*KNOWLEDGE, UNIVERSALS, AND SUBSTANCE*]

10

1086b14 There is a question that raises a puzzle both for those who say there are Ideas and for those who do not. We have mentioned it before, at the beginning, in the discussion of puzzles; let us discuss it now.[1]

If we do not take substances to be separated in the way in which particular beings are said to be separated, then we do away with substance as we intend to speak of it. But if we take substances to be separable, how will we regard their elements and principles? For if the elements and principles are particulars and not universals, there will be as many elements as there are beings, and the elements will not be knowable$_{e}$.

For let the syllables in speech be substances, and their letters the elements of substances. Then there must be only one BA, and only one of each of the other syllables—if they are not universals (i.e., specifically the same), but each is numerically one and a this; nor would any have the same name <as any other>. (Further, <the believers in Ideas> believe that each what-it-is-itself[2] is one.) But if each syllable is one, then so is each of the letters it is composed of. If so, there will be only one A, and only one of any given letter, by the same argument that shows that there must

1. **We have . . . discuss it now**: Bk vii might be taken to argue that (i) a primary substance is a particular form; (ii) knowledge is of universal substances; (iii) primary substances are basic objects of knowledge. This chapter might be taken to explain how these claims are consistent.

2. **what-it-is-itself**: A phrase sometimes used (as, e.g., 'what good is itself' or 'the good itself') in Plato for the FORMS.

be only one of any given syllable. But if this is so, there will be no other beings apart from the elements, but only elements.

Further, the elements will not be knowable; for they are not universals, and knowledge is of universals, as is clear from demonstrations and definitions. For there cannot be a deduction that this triangle has angles equal to two right angles, unless every triangle has its angles equal to two right angles; and there cannot be a deduction that this man is an animal, unless every man is an animal.

If, on the other hand, the principles are universals, then either the substances composed of them are also universals or else nonsubstances will be prior to substances. For no universal is a substance, but an element and principle is universal, and an element and principle is prior to those things of which it is the element and principle.

All these things follow reasonably, when they make Ideas out of elements and also claim that there is a single separated thing apart from substances that have the same form.

If, however, just as with the elements of speech, it is quite possible for there to be many As and Bs, even though there is no A-itself and B-itself apart from the many, so also (as far as this goes) there will be infinitely many similar syllables. The claim that all knowledge is universal, so that the principles of beings are also necessarily universals and not separated substances, certainly raises a greater puzzle than any other claim we have mentioned; and yet the claim is true in one way, though not in another.

For knowledge, like knowing, is of two kinds, potential and actual. Since the potentiality, as being matter, is universal and indefinite, it is of the universal and indefinite. But since the actuality is definite, it is of what is definite, and, since it is a this, it is of a this. It is <only> coincidentally that sight sees universal color; it does so because this <particular instance of> color which it sees is <an instance of> color. And similarly, this <instance of> A that the grammarian studies is <an> A.

For if the principles must be universals, what comes from them must also be universal, as in demonstrations. But if this is so, nothing will be separable or a substance. It is clear, however, that in a way knowledge is universal, and in a way it is not.

NICOMACHEAN ETHICS

Book I

[*HAPPINESS*]

1

1094a Every craft and every investigation, and likewise every action and decision, seems to aim at some good; hence the good has been well described as that at which everything aims.

However, there is an apparent difference among the ends aimed at. For the end is sometimes an activity, sometimes a product beyond the activity; and when there is an end beyond the action, the product is by nature better than the activity.

Since there are many actions, crafts and sciences, the ends turn out to be many as well; for health is the end of medicine, a boat of boatbuilding, victory of generalship, and wealth of household management.

But whenever any of these sciences are subordinate to some one capacity—as, for instance, bridlemaking and every other science producing equipment for horses are subordinate to horsemanship, while this and every action in warfare are in turn subordinate to generalship, and in the same way other sciences are subordinate to further ones—in each of these the end of the ruling science is more choiceworthy than all the ends subordinate to it, since it is the end for which those ends are also pursued. And here it does not matter whether the ends of the actions are the activities themselves, or some product beyond them, as in the sciences we have mentioned.

2

Suppose, then, that (a) there is some end of the things we pursue in our actions which we wish for because of itself, and because of which we wish for the other things; and (b) we do not choose everything because of something else, since (c) if we do, it will go on without limit, making desire empty and futile; then clearly (d) this end will be the good, i.e., the best good.

Then surely knowledge$_{g}$ of this good is also of great importance for the conduct of our lives, and if, like archers, we have a target to aim at, we are more likely to hit the right mark. If so, we should try to grasp, in outline at any rate, what the good is, and which science or capacity is concerned with it.

It seems to concern the most controlling science, the one that, more than any other, is the ruling science. And political science apparently has this character.

(1) For it is the one that prescribes which of the sciences ought 1094b
to be studied in cities, and which ones each class in the city should learn, and how far.

(2) Again, we see that even the most honored capacities—generalship, household management and rhetoric, for instance—are subordinate to it.

(3) Further, it uses the other sciences concerned with action, and moreover legislates what must be done and what avoided.

Hence its end will include the ends of the other sciences, and so will be the human good.

<This is properly called political science;> for though admittedly the good is the same for a city as for an individual, still the good of the city is apparently a greater and more complete good to acquire and preserve. For while it is satisfactory to acquire and preserve the good even for an individual, it is finer and more divine to acquire and preserve it for a people and for cities. And so, since our investigation aims at these <goods, for an individual and for a city>, it is a sort of political science.

3

Our discussion will be adequate if its degree of clarity fits the subject matter;[1] for we would not seek the same degree of exactness in all sorts of arguments alike, any more than in the products of different crafts.

Moreover, what is fine and what is just, the topics of inquiry in political science, differ and vary so much that they seem to rest on convention only, not on nature. Goods, however, also vary in the same sort of way, since they cause harm to many people;

1. **fits the subject matter:** See 1098a28, 1137b19.

for it has happened that some people have been destroyed because of their wealth, others because of their bravery.

Since these, then, are the sorts of things we argue from and about, it will be satisfactory if we can indicate the truth roughly and in outline; since <that is to say> we argue from and about what holds good usually <but not universally>, it will be satisfactory if we can draw conclusions of the same sort.

Each of our claims, then, ought to be accepted in the same way <as claiming to hold good usually>, since the educated person seeks exactness in each area to the extent that the nature of the subject allows; for apparently it is just as mistaken to demand demonstrations from a rhetorician as to accept <merely> persuasive arguments from a mathematician.

Further, each person judges well what he knows$_g$, and is a good judge about that; hence the good judge in a particular area is the person educated in that area, and the unqualifiedly good judge is the person educated in every area.

This is why a youth is not a suitable student of political science; for he lacks experience of the actions in life which political science argues from and about.

Moreover, since he tends to be guided by his feelings, his study will be futile and useless; for its end is action, not knowledge$_g$. And here it does not matter whether he is young in years or immature in character, since the deficiency does not depend on age, but results from being guided in his life and in each of his pursuits by his feelings; for an immature person, like an incontinent person, gets no benefit from his knowledge$_g$.

If, however, we are guided by reason in forming our desires and in acting, then this knowledge$_o$ will be of great benefit.

These are the preliminary points about the student, about the way our claims are to be accepted, and about what we intend to do.

4

Let us, then, begin again. Since every sort of knowledge$_g$ and decision pursues some good, what is that good which we say is the aim of political science? What <in other words> is the highest of all the goods pursued in action?

As far as its name goes, most people virtually agree <about what the good is>, since both the many and the cultivated call it happiness, and suppose that living well and doing well are the same as being happy. But they disagree about what happiness is, and the many do not give the same answer as the wise.

For the many think it is something obvious and evident—for instance, pleasure, wealth or honor—some thinking one thing, others another; and indeed the same person keeps changing his mind, since in sickness he thinks it is health, in poverty wealth. And when they are conscious of their own ignorance, they admire anyone who speaks of something grand and beyond them.

<Among the wise,> however, some used to think that apart from these many goods there is some other good that is something in itself, and also causes all these goods to be goods.

Presumably, then, it is rather futile to examine all these beliefs, and it is enough to examine those that are most current or seem to have some argument for them.

We must notice, however, the difference between arguments from principles and arguments toward principles. For indeed Plato was right to be puzzled about this, when he used to ask if <the argument> set out from the principles or led toward them— 1095b
just as on a race course the path may go from the starting-line to the far end, or back again.

For while we should certainly begin from starting points that are known$_{g}$, things are known in two ways; for some are known to us, some known without qualification <but not necessarily known to us>. Presumably, then, the starting point *we* should begin from is what is known to *us*.

This is why we need to have been brought up in fine habits if we are to be adequate students of what is fine and just, and of political questions generally. For the starting point is the belief that something is true, and if this is apparent enough to us, we will not, <,at this stage,> need the reason why it is true in addition; and if we have this good upbringing, we have the starting points, or can easily acquire them.[2] Someone who neither has them nor can acquire them should listen to Hesiod: 'He who understands everything himself is best of all; he is noble also who listens to one who has spoken well; but he who neither understands it himself nor takes to heart what he hears from another is a useless man.'

2. **For the . . . acquire them:** Both 'PRINCIPLE' and 'starting point' translate *archē*.

5

15 But let us begin again from <the common beliefs> from which
we digressed. For, it would seem, people quite reasonably reach
17 their conception of the good, i.e., of happiness, from the lives
18 <they lead>; for there are roughly three most favored lives—the
19 lives of gratification, of political activity, and, third, of study.

16 The many, the most vulgar, would seem to conceive the good
17 and happiness as pleasure, and hence they also like the life of
19 gratification. Here they appear completely slavish, since the life
20 they decide on is a life for grazing animals; and yet they have
some argument in their defense, since many in positions of power
feel the same way as Sardanapallus[3] <and also choose this life>.

The cultivated people, those active <in politics>, conceive the
good as honor, since this is more or less the end <normally pur-
sued> in the political life. This, however, appears to be too superfi-
25 cial to be what we are seeking, since it seems to depend more on
those who honor than on the one honored, whereas we intuitively
believe that the good is something of our own and hard to take
from us.

Further, it would seem, they pursue honor to convince themselves that they are good; at any rate, they seek to be honored
by intelligent people, among people who know$_g$ them, and for
30 virtue. It is clear, then, that in the view of active people at least,
virtue is superior <to honor>.

Perhaps, indeed, one might conceive virtue more than honor
to be the end of the political life. However, this also is apparently
too incomplete <to be the good>. For, it seems, someone might
1096a possess virtue but be asleep or inactive throughout his life; or,
further, he might suffer the worst evils and misfortunes; and if
this is the sort of life he leads, no one would count him happy,
except to defend a philosopher's paradox. Enough about this,
since it has been adequately discussed in the popular works also.

5 The third life is the life of study, which we will examine in
what follows.

The money-maker's life is in a way forced on him <not chosen for itself>; and clearly wealth is not the good we are seeking, since it is <merely> useful, <choiceworthy only> for some other end. Hence one would be more inclined to suppose that <any

3. **Sardanapallus:** An Assyrian king who lived in legendary luxury.

of> the goods mentioned earlier is the end, since they are liked for themselves. But apparently they are not <the end> either; and many arguments have been presented against them. Let us, then, dismiss them.

6

Presumably, though, we had better examine the universal good, and puzzle out what is meant in speaking of it. This sort of inquiry is, to be sure, unwelcome to us, when those who introduced the Forms were friends of ours; still, it presumably seems better, indeed only right, to destroy even what is close to us if that is the way to preserve truth. And we must especially do this when we are philosophers, <lovers of wisdom>; for though we love both the truth and our friends, piety requires us to honor the truth first.

Those who introduced this view did not mean to produce an Idea for any <series> in which they spoke of prior and posterior <members>; that was why they did not mean to establish an Idea <of number> for <the series of> numbers. But the good is spoken of both in what-it-is and in quality and relative;[4] and what is in itself, i.e., substance, is by nature prior to what is relative, since a relative would seem to be an appendage and coincident of being. And so there is no common Idea over these.

Further, good is spoken of in as many ways as being is spoken of. For it is spoken of in what-it-is, as god and mind; in quality, as the virtues; in quantity, as the measured amount; in relative, as the useful; in time, as the opportune moment; in place, as the <right> situation; and so on. Hence it is clear that the good cannot be some common <nature of good things> that is universal and single; for if it were, it would be spoken of in only one of the predications, not in them all.

Further, if a number of things have a single Idea, there is also a single science of them; hence <if there were an Idea of Good> there would also be some single science of all goods. But in fact there are many sciences even of the goods under one predication; for the science of the opportune moment, for instance, in war is generalship, in disease medicine. And similarly the science of the

4. **But the good . . . and relative**: The categories (see PREDICATIONS) are introduced here and in the next two paragraphs. See BE #2.

measured amount in food is medicine, in exertion gymnastics. <Hence there is no single science of the good, and so no Idea.>

One might be puzzled about what <the believers in Ideas> 1096b really mean in speaking of the So-and-So Itself, since Man Itself and man have one and the same account of man; for insofar as each is man, they will not differ at all. If that is so, then <Good Itself and good have the same account of good>; hence they also will not differ at all insofar as each is good, <hence there is no point in appealing to Good itself>.

Moreover, Good Itself will be no more of a good by being eternal; for a white thing is no whiter if it lasts a long time than if it lasts a day.

The Pythagoreans seemingly have a more plausible view about the good, since they place the One in the column of goods. Indeed, Speusippus seems to have followed them. But let us leave this for another discussion.

A dispute emerges about what we have said: 'The arguments <in favor of the Idea> are not concerned with every sort of good. Goods pursued and liked in themselves are spoken of as one species of goods, while those that in some way tend to produce or preserve these goods, or to prevent their contraries, are spoken of as goods because of these and in a different way; clearly, then, goods are spoken of in two ways, and some are goods in themselves, others goods because of these. <And it is claimed only that there is a single Form for all goods in themselves.>

Let us, then, separate the goods in themselves from the <merely> useful goods, and consider whether goods in themselves are spoken of in correspondence to a single Idea.

Well, what sorts of goods may be regarded as goods in themselves? (a) Perhaps they are those that are pursued even on their own—for instance, intelligence, seeing, some types of pleasures, and honors; for even if we also pursue these because of something else, they may still be regarded as goods in themselves. (b) Or perhaps nothing except the Idea is good in itself.

<If (b) is true>, then the Form will be futile, <since it will not explain the goodness of anything. But if (a) is true>, then, since these other things are also goods in themselves, the same account of good will have to turn up in all of them, just as the same account of whiteness turns up in snow and in chalk. In fact, however, honor, intelligence and pleasure have different and dissimilar accounts, precisely insofar as they are goods. Hence the

good is not something common which corresponds to a single Idea.

But how after all, then, is good spoken of? For <these goods have different accounts, i.e., are homonymous, and yet> are seemingly not homonymous by mere chance. Perhaps they are homonymous by all being derived from a single source, or by all referring to a single focus.[5] Or perhaps instead they are homonymous by analogy; for example, as sight is to body, so understanding is to soul, and so on for other cases.

Presumably, though, we should leave these questions for now, since their exact treatment is more appropriate for another <branch of> philosophy. And the same is true about the Idea. For even if the good predicated in common is some single thing, or something separated, itself in itself, clearly it is not the sort of good a human being can pursue in action or possess; but that is just the sort we are looking for in our present inquiry.

'But,' it might seem to some, 'it is better to get to know$_g$ the Idea with a view to the goods that we can possess and pursue in action; for if we have this as a sort of pattern, we shall also know$_o$ better about the goods that are goods for us, and if we know about them, we shall hit on them.'

This argument does indeed have some plausibility, but it would seem to clash with the sciences. For each of these, though it aims at some good and seeks to supply what is lacking, proceeds without concern for knowledge$_g$ of the Idea; and if the Idea were such an important aid, surely it would not be reasonable for all craftsmen to be ignorant and not even to look for it.

Moreover, it is a puzzle to know what the weaver or carpenter will gain for his own craft from knowing$_o$ this Good Itself, or how anyone will be better at medicine or generalship from having gazed on the Idea Itself. For what the doctor appears to consider is not even health <universally, let alone good universally>, but human beings' health, since it is particular patients he treats.

So much, then, for these questions.

7

But let us return once again to the good we are looking for, and consider just what it could be, since it is apparently one thing in

5. **All referring . . .**: See HOMONYMY.

one action or craft, and another thing in another; for it is one thing in medicine, another in generalship, and so on for the rest.

What, then, is the good in each of these cases? Surely it is that for the sake of which the other things are done; and in medicine this is health, in generalship victory, in housebuilding a house, in another case something else, but in every action and decision it is the end, since it is for the sake of the end that everyone does the other things.

And so, if there is some end of everything that is pursued in action, this will be the good pursued in action; and if there are more ends than one, these will be the goods pursued in action.

Our argument has progressed, then, to the same conclusion <as before, that the highest end is the good>; but we must try to clarify this still more.

Though apparently there are many ends, we choose some of them—for instance, wealth, flutes and, in general, instruments—because of something else; hence it is clear that not all ends are complete. But the best good is apparently something complete. Hence, if only one end is complete, this will be what we are looking for; and if more than one are complete, the most complete of these will be what we are looking for.

An end pursued in itself, we say, is more complete than an end pursued because of something else; and an end that is never choiceworthy because of something else is more complete than ends that are choiceworthy both in themselves and because of this end; and hence an end that is always <choiceworthy, and also> choiceworthy in itself, never because of something else, is complete without qualification.

Now happiness more than anything else seems complete without qualification, since we always <choose it, and also> choose it because of itself, never because of something else.

Honour, pleasure, understanding and every virtue we certainly choose because of themselves, since we would choose each of them even if it had no further result; but we also choose them for the sake of happiness, supposing that through them we shall be happy. Happiness, by contrast, no one ever chooses for their sake, or for the sake of anything else at all.

The same conclusion <that happiness is complete> also appears to follow from self-sufficiency, since the complete good seems to be self-sufficient.

Now what we count as self-sufficient is not what suffices for a solitary person by himself, living an isolated life, but what suffices also for parents, children, wife and in general for friends and fellow-citizens, since a human being is a naturally political <animal>.[6] Here, however, we must impose some limit; for if we extend the good to parents' parents and children's children and to friends of friends, we shall go on without limit; but we must examine this another time.

Anyhow, we regard something as self-sufficient when all by itself it makes a life choiceworthy and lacking nothing; and that is what we think happiness does.

Moreover, we think happiness is most choiceworthy of all goods, since it is not counted as one good among many. If it were counted as one among many, then, clearly, we think that the addition of the smallest of goods would make it more choiceworthy;[7] for <the smallest good> that is added becomes an extra quantity of goods <so creating a good larger than the original good>, and the larger of two goods is always more choiceworthy. <But we do not think any addition can make happiness more choiceworthy; hence it is most choiceworthy.>

Happiness, then, is apparently something complete and self-sufficient, since it is the end of the things pursued in action.

But presumably the remark that the best good is happiness is apparently something <generally> agreed, and what we miss is a clearer statement of what the best good is.

Well, perhaps we shall find the best good if we first find the function of a human being. For just as the good, i.e., <doing> well, for a flautist, a sculptor, and every craftsman, and, in general, for whatever has a function and <characteristic> action, seems to depend on its function, the same seems to be true for a human being, if a human being has some function.

Then do the carpenter and the leatherworker have their functions and actions, while a human being has none, and is by nature idle, without any function? Or, just as eye, hand, foot and, in general, every <bodily> part apparently has its functions, may

6. **solitary . . . political <animal>**: Cf. 1142a9, 1157b18, 1158a23, 1169b16, 1170b12, 1172a6, 1178b5, *Pol.* 1253a7, 1280b33.

7. **of all goods . . . more choiceworthy**: Alternative rendering: '. . . of all goods, when it is not counted with other goods. When it is so counted, then, clearly, we think the addition of the smallest good to it makes it more choiceworthy. . . .'

we likewise ascribe to a human being some function apart from all of theirs?

What, then, could this be? For living is apparently shared with 1098a plants, but what we are looking for is the special function of a human being; hence we should set aside the life of nutrition and growth. The life next in order is some sort of life of sense-perception; but this too is apparently shared, with horse, ox and every animal. The remaining possibility, then, is some sort of life of action of the <part of the soul> that has reason.

Now this <part has two parts, which have reason in different ways>, one as obeying the reason[8] <in the other part>, the other as itself having reason and thinking. <We intend both.> Moreover, life is also spoken of in two ways <as capacity and as activity>, and we must take <a human being's special function to be> life as activity, since this seems to be called life to a fuller extent.

(a) We have found, then, that the human function is the soul's activity that expresses reason <as itself having reason> or requires reason <as obeying reason>. (b) Now the function of F, of a harpist, for instance, is the same in kind, so we say, as the function of an excellent F, an excellent harpist, for instance. (c) The same is true without qualification in every case, when we add to the function the superior achievement that expresses the virtue; for a harpist's function, for instance, is to play the harp, and a good harpist's is to do it well. (d) Now we take the human function to be a certain kind of life, and take this life to be the soul's activity and actions that express reason. (e) Hence by (c) and (d)> the excellent man's function is to do this finely and well. (f) Each function is completed well when its completion expresses the proper virtue. (g) Therefore <by (d), (e) and (f)> the human good turns out to be the soul's activity that expresses virtue.

And if there are more virtues than one, the good will express the best and most complete virtue. Moreover, it will be in a complete life.[9] For one swallow does not make a spring, nor does one day; nor, similarly, does one day or a short time make us blessed and happy.

This, then, is a sketch of the good; for, presumably, the outline

8. **obeying the reason:** Cf. 1102b26.

9. **complete life**: See 1101a6, 1177b25.

must come first, to be filled in later. If the sketch is good, then anyone, it seems, can advance and articulate it, and in such cases time is a good discoverer or <at least> a good coworker. That is also how the crafts have improved, since anyone can add what is lacking <in the outline>.

However, we must also remember our previous remarks, so that we do not look for the same degree of exactness in all areas, but the degree that fits the subject matter in each area and is proper to the investigation. For the carpenter's and the geometer's inquiries about the right angle are different also; the carpenter's is confined to the right angle's usefulness for his work, whereas the geometer's concerns what, or what sort of thing, the right angle is, since he studies the truth. We must do the same, then, in other areas too, <seeking the proper degree of exactness>, so that digressions do not overwhelm our main task.

Nor should we make the same demand for an explanation in all cases. Rather, in some cases it is enough to prove that something is true without explaining why it is true. This is so, for instance, with principles, where the fact that something is true is the first thing, i.e., the principle.[10]

Some principles are studied by means of induction, some by means of perception, some by means of some sort of habituation, and others by other means. In each case we should try to find them out by means suited to their nature, and work hard to define them well. For they have a great influence on what follows; for the principle seems to be more than half the whole, and makes evident the answer to many of our questions.

[8]

However, we should examine the principle not only from the conclusion and premisses <of a deductive argument>, but also from what is said about it; for all the facts harmonize with a true account, whereas the truth soon clashes with a false one.

Goods are divided, then, into three types, some called external, some goods of the soul, others goods of the body; and the goods of the soul are said to be goods to the fullest extent and most of

10. **Rather, in some . . . i.e., the principle**: The principles provide the explanation (or reason), and so a further explanation cannot be given for them.

all, and the soul's actions and activities are ascribed to the soul. Hence the account <of the good> is sound, to judge by this belief anyhow—and it is an ancient belief agreed on by philosophers.

Our account is also correct in saying that some sort of actions and activities are the end; for then the end turns out to be a good of the soul, not an external good.

The belief that the happy person lives well and does well in action also agrees with our account, since we have virtually said that the end is a sort of living well and doing well in action.

Further, all the features that people look for in happiness appear to be true of the end described in our account. For to some people it seems to be virtue; to others intelligence; to others some sort of wisdom; to others again it seems to be these, or one of these, involving pleasure or requiring its addition; and others add in external prosperity as well.

Some of these views are traditional, held by many, while others are held by a few reputable men; and it is reasonable for each group to be not entirely in error, but correct on one point at least, or even on most points.

First, our account agrees with those who say happiness is virtue <in general> or some <particular> virtue; for activity expressing virtue is proper to virtue. Presumably, though, it matters quite a bit whether we suppose that the best good consists in possessing or in using, i.e., in a state or in an activity <that actualizes the state>. For while someone may be in a state that achieves no good, if, for instance, he is asleep or inactive in some other way, this cannot be true of the activity; for it will necessarily do actions and do well in them. And just as Olympic prizes are not for the finest and strongest, but for the contestants, since it is only these who win; so also in life <only> the fine and good people who act correctly win the prize.

Moreover, the life of these <active people> is also pleasant in itself. For being pleased is a condition of the soul, <hence included in the activity of the soul>. Further, each type of person finds pleasure in whatever he is called a lover of, so that a horse, for instance, pleases the horse-lover, a spectacle the lover of spectacles, and similarly what is just pleases the lover of justice, and in general what expresses virtue pleases the lover of virtue. Hence the things that please most people conflict, because they are not pleasant by nature, whereas the things that please lovers of what is fine are things pleasant by nature; and actions expressing virtue are pleasant in this way; and so they both please lovers of what is fine and are pleasant in themselves.

Hence their life does not need pleasure to be added <to virtuous activity> as some sort of ornament; rather, it has its pleasure within itself. For besides the reasons already given, someone who does not enjoy fine actions is not good; for no one would call him just, for instance, if he did not enjoy doing just actions, or generous if he did not enjoy generous actions, and similarly for the other virtues. If this is so, then actions expressing the virtues are pleasant in themselves.

Moreover, these actions are good and fine as well as pleasant; indeed, they are good, fine and pleasant more than anything else, since on this question the excellent person has good judgment, and his judgment agrees with our conclusions.

Happiness, then, is best, finest and most pleasant, and these three features are not distinguished in the way suggested by the Delian inscription: 'What is most just is finest; being healthy is most beneficial; but it is most pleasant to win our heart's desire.' For all three features are found in the best activities, and happiness we say is these activities, or <rather> one of them, the best one.

Nonetheless, happiness evidently also needs external goods to be added <to the activity>, as we said, since we cannot, or cannot easily, do fine actions if we lack the resources.

For, first of all, in many actions we use friends, wealth and political power just as we use instruments. Further, deprivation of certain <externals>—for instance, good birth, good children, beauty—mars our blessedness; for we do not altogether have the character of happiness if we look utterly repulsive or are ill-born, solitary or childless, and have it even less, presumably, if our children or friends are totally bad, or were good but have died.

And so, as we have said, happiness would seem to need this sort of prosperity added also; that is why some people identify happiness with good fortune, while others <reacting from one extreme to the other> identify it with virtue.

9

This <question about the role of fortune> raises a puzzle: Is happiness acquired by learning, or habituation, or by some other form of cultivation? Or is it the result of some divine fate, or even of fortune?

First, then, if the gods give any gift at all to human beings, it is reasonable to give happiness more than any other human <good>, insofar as it is the best of human <goods>. Presumably, however, this question is more suitable for a different inquiry.

But even if it is not sent by the gods, but instead results from virtue and some sort of learning or cultivation, happiness appears to be one of the most divine things, since the prize and goal of virtue appears to be the best good, something divine and blessed.

Moreover <if happiness comes in this way> it will be widely shared; for anyone who is not deformed <in his capacity> for virtue will be able to achieve happiness through some sort of learning and attention.

And since it is better to be happy in this way than because of fortune, it is reasonable for this to be the way <we become> happy. For whatever is natural is naturally in the finest state possible, and so are the products of crafts and of every other cause, especially the best cause; and it would be seriously inappropriate to entrust what is greatest and finest to fortune.

The answer to our question is also evident from our account <of happiness>. For we have said it is a certain sort of activity of the soul expressing virtue, <and hence not a product of fortune>; and some of the other goods are necessary conditions of happiness>, others are naturally useful and cooperative as instruments <but are not parts of it>.

Further, this conclusion agrees with our opening remarks. For we took the goal of political science to be the best good; and most of its attention is devoted to the character of the citizens, to make them good people who do fine actions, <which is reasonable if happiness depends on virtue, not on fortune>.

It is not surprising, then, that we regard neither ox nor horse nor any other kind of animal as happy, since none of them can share in this sort of activity. And for the same reason a child is not happy either,[11] since his age prevents him from doing these sorts of actions; and if he is called happy, he is being congratulated because of anticipated blessedness, since, as we have said, happiness requires both complete virtue and a complete life.

<Happiness needs a complete life.> For life includes many reversals of fortune, good and bad, and the most prosperous

11. **we regard neither . . . happy either**: Cf. 1177a8, 1178b27, *Phys.* 197b6.

person may fall into a terrible disaster in old age, as the Trojan stories tell us about Priam; but if someone has suffered these sorts of misfortunes and comes to a miserable end, no one counts him happy.

10

Then should we count no human being happy during his lifetime, but follow Solon's advice to wait to see the end? And if we should hold that, can he really be happy during the time after he has died? Surely that is completely absurd, especially when we say happiness is an activity.

We do not say, then, that someone is happy during the time he is dead, and Solon's point is not this <absurd one>, but rather that when a human being has died, we can safely pronounce <that he was> blessed <before he died>, on the assumption that he is now finally beyond evils and misfortunes.

Still, even this claim is disputable. For if a living person has good or evil of which he is not aware, then a dead person also, it seems, has good or evil when, for instance, he receives honors or dishonors, and his children, and descendants in general, do well or suffer misfortune. <Hence, apparently, what happens after his death can affect whether or not he was happy before his death.>

However, this view also raises a puzzle. For even if someone has lived in blessedness until old age, and has died appropriately, many fluctuations of his descendants' fortunes may still happen to him; for some may be good people and get the life they deserve, while the contrary may be true of others, and clearly they may be as distantly related to their ancestor as you please. Surely, then, it would be an absurd result if the dead person's condition changed along with the fortunes of his descendants, so that at one time he became happy <in his lifetime> and at another time miserable. But it would also be absurd if the condition of descendants did not affect their ancestors at all or for any length of time.

But we must return to the previous puzzle, since that will perhaps also show us the answer to our present question.

If, then, we must wait to see the end, and must then count someone blessed, not as being blessed <during the time he is dead> but because he previously was blessed, surely it is absurd if at the time when he is happy we will not truly ascribe to him the happiness he has.

1100b <We hesitate> out of reluctance to call him happy during his lifetime, because of the variations, and because we suppose happiness is enduring and definitely not prone to fluctuate, whereas the same person's fortunes often turn to and fro. For clearly, if we are guided by his fortunes, so that we often call him happy and then miserable again, we will be representing the happy person as a kind of chameleon insecurely based.

But surely it is quite wrong to be guided by someone's fortunes. For his doing well or badly does not rest on them; though a human life, as we said, needs these added, it is the activities expressing virtue that control happiness, and the contrary activities that control its contrary.

Indeed, the present puzzle is further evidence for our account <of happiness>. For no human achievement has the stability of activities that express virtue, since these seem to be more enduring even than our knowledge of the sciences; and the most honorable of the virtues themselves are more enduring <than the others> because blessed people devote their lives to them more fully and more continually than to anything else—for this <continual activity> would seem to be the reason we do not forget them.

It follows, then, that the happy person has the <stability> we are looking for and keeps the character he has throughout his life. For always, or more than anything else, he will do and study the actions expressing virtue, and will bear fortunes most finely, in every way and in all conditions appropriately, since he is truly 'good, foursquare and blameless'. However, many events are matters of fortune, and some are smaller, some greater. Hence, while small strokes of good or ill fortune clearly will not influence his life, many great strokes of good fortune will make it more blessed, since in themselves they naturally add adornment to it, and his use of them proves to be fine and excellent. Conversely, if they are great misfortunes, they oppress and spoil his blessedness, since they involve pain and impede many activities.

And yet, even here what is fine shines through, whenever someone bears many severe misfortunes with good temper, not because he feels no distress, but because he is noble and magnanimous.

And since it is activities that control life, as we said, no blessed person could ever become miserable, since he will never do hateful and base actions. For a truly good and intelligent person, we suppose, will bear strokes of fortune suitably, and from his resources at any time will do the finest actions, just as a good general will make the best use of his forces in war, and a good shoemaker will produce the finest shoe from the hides given to him, and similarly for all other craftsmen.

If this is so, then the happy person could never become miserable. Still, he will not be blessed either, if he falls into misfortunes as bad as Priam's. Nor, however, will he be inconstant and prone to fluctuate, since he will neither be easily shaken from his happiness nor shaken by just any misfortunes. He will be shaken from it, though, by many serious misfortunes, and from these a return to happiness will take no short time; at best, it will take a long and complete length of time that includes great and fine successes.

Then why not say that the happy person is the one who expresses complete virtue in his activities, with an adequate supply of external goods, not for just any time but for a complete life? Or should we add that he will also go on living this way and will come to an appropriate end?

The future is not apparent to us, and we take happiness to be the end, and altogether complete in every way; hence we will say that a living person who has, and will keep, the goods we mentioned is blessed, but blessed as a human being is. So much for a determination of this question.

* * * * * * *

13

Since happiness is an activity of the soul expressing complete virtue, we must examine virtue; for that will perhaps also be a way to study happiness better.

Moreover, the true politician seems to have spent more effort on virtue than on anything else, since he wants to make the citizens good and law-abiding. We find an example of this in the Spartan and Cretan legislators and in any others with their concerns. Since, then, the examination of virtue is proper for political science, the inquiry clearly suits our original decision <to pursue political science>.

It is clear that the virtue we must examine is human virtue, since we are also seeking the human good and human happiness. And by human virtue we mean virtue of the soul, not of the body, since we also say that happiness is an activity of the soul. If this is so, then it is clear that the politician must acquire some knowledge$_o$ about the soul, just as someone setting out to heal the eyes must acquire knowledge about the whole body as well. This is all the more true to the extent that political science is better and more honorable than medicine—and even among doctors the cultivated ones devote a lot of effort to acquiring knowledge$_g$ about the body. Hence the politician as well <as the student of nature> must study the soul.

But he must study it for the purpose <of inquiring into virtue>, as far as suffices for what he seeks; for a more exact treatment would presumably take more effort than his purpose requires. <We> have discussed the soul sufficiently <for our purposes> in <our> popular works as well <as our less popular>, and we should use this discussion.

We have said, for instance, that one <part> of the soul is nonrational, while one has reason. Are these distinguished as parts of a body and everything divisible into parts are? Or are they two only in account,[12] and inseparable by nature, as the convex and the concave are in a surface? It does not matter for present purposes.

Consider the nonrational <part>. One <part> of it, i.e., the cause of nutrition and growth, is seemingly plant-like and shared <with other living things>: for we can ascribe this capacity of the soul to everything that is nourished, including embryos, and the same one to complete living things, since this is more reasonable than to ascribe another capacity to them.

Hence the virtue of this capacity is apparently shared, not <specifically> human. For this part and capacity more than others seem to be active in sleep, and here the good and the bad person are least distinct, which is why happy people are said to be no better off than miserable people for half their lives.

And this lack of distinction is not surprising, since sleep is inactivity of the soul insofar as it is called excellent or base, unless to some small extent some movements penetrate <to our awareness>, and in this way the decent person comes to have better images <in dreams> than just any random person has. Enough

12. **two only in account**: Cf. *DA* 413b13–32, 432a15–b8, 433a31–b13.

about this, however, and let us leave aside the nutritive part, since by nature it has no share in human virtue.

Another nature in the soul would also seem to be nonrational, though in a way it shares in reason.

<Clearly it is nonrational.> For in the continent and the incontinent person we praise their reason, i.e., the <part> of the soul that has reason, because it exhorts them correctly and toward what is best; but they evidently also have in them some other <part> that is by nature something apart from reason, conflicting and struggling with reason.

For just as paralyzed parts of a body, when we decide to move them to the right, do the contrary and move off to the left, the same is true of the soul; for incontinent people have impulses in contrary directions. In bodies, admittedly, we see the part go astray, whereas we do not see it in the soul; nonetheless, presumably, we should suppose that the soul also has something apart from reason, contrary to and countering reason. The <precise> way it is different does not matter.

However, this <part> as well <as the rational part> appears, as we said, to share in reason. At any rate, in the continent person it obeys reason; and in the temperate and the brave person it presumably listens still better to reason, since there it agrees with reason in everything.

The nonrational <part>, then, as well <as the whole soul> apparently has two parts. For while the plant-like <part> shares in reason not at all, the <part> with appetites and in general desires shares in reason in a way, insofar as it both listens to reason and obeys it.

It listens in the way in which we are said to 'listen to reason' from father or friends, not in the way in which we <'give the reason'> in mathematics.

The nonrational part also <obeys and> is persuaded in some way by reason, as is shown by chastening, and by every sort of reproof and exhortation.

If we ought to say, then, that this <part> also has reason, then the <part> that has reason, as well <as the nonrational part> will have two parts, one that has reason to the full extent by having it within itself, and another <that has it> by listening to reason as to a father.

The division between virtues also reflects this difference. For some virtues are called virtues of thought, others virtues of character; wisdom, comprehension and intelligence are called virtues of thought, generosity and temperance virtues of character.

For when we speak of someone's character we do not say that he is wise or has good comprehension, but that he is gentle or temperate. <Hence these are the virtues of character.> And yet, we also praise the wise person for his state, and the states that are praiseworthy are the ones we call virtues. <Hence wisdom is also a virtue.>

Book II

[*VIRTUES OF CHARACTER*]

1

Virtue, then, is of two sorts, virtue of thought and virtue of character. Virtue of thought arises and grows mostly from teaching, and hence needs experience and time. Virtue of character results from habit; hence its name[1] 'ethical', slightly varied from 'ethos'.

Hence it is also clear that none of the virtues of character arises in us naturally.

For if something is by nature <in one condition>, habituation cannot bring it into another condition. A stone, for instance, by nature moves downward, and habituation could not make it move upward, not even if you threw it up ten thousand times to habituate it; nor could habituation make fire move downward, or bring anything that is by nature in one condition into another condition. Thus the virtues arise in us neither by nature nor against nature. Rather, we are by nature able to acquire them, and reach our complete perfection through habit.

Further, if something arises in us by nature, we first have the capacity for it, and later display the activity. This is clear in the case of the senses; for we did not acquire them by frequent seeing or hearing, but already had them when we exercised them, and did not get them by exercising them.

1. **hence its name**: Aristotle plays on the similarity between *ēthos* (long e: 'character') and *ethos* (short e: 'habit').

Virtues, by contrast, we acquire, just as we acquire crafts, by having previously activated them. For we learn a craft by producing the same product that we must produce when we have learned it, becoming builders, for instance, by building and harpists by playing the harp; so also, then, we become just by doing just 1103b actions, temperate by doing temperate actions, brave by doing brave actions.

What goes on in cities is evidence for this also. For the legislator makes the citizens good by habituating them, and this is the wish of every legislator; if he fails to do it well he misses his goal. <The right> habituation is what makes the difference between a good political system and a bad one.

Further, just as in the case of a craft, the sources and means that develop each virtue also ruin it. For playing the harp makes both good and bad harpists, and it is analogous in the case of builders and all the rest; for building well makes good builders, building badly, bad ones. If it were not so, no teacher would be needed, but everyone would be born a good or a bad craftsman.

It is the same, then, with the virtues. For actions in dealings with <other> human beings make some people just, some unjust; actions in terrifying situations and the acquired habit of fear or confidence make some brave and others cowardly. The same is true of situations involving appetites and anger; for one or another sort of conduct in these situations makes some people temperate and gentle, others intemperate and irascible.

To sum up, then, in a single account: A state <of character> arises from <the repetition of> similar activities. Hence we must display the right activities, since differences in these imply corresponding differences in the states. It is not unimportant, then, to acquire one sort of habit or another, right from our youth; rather, it is very important, indeed all-important.

2

Our present inquiry does not aim, as our others do, at study; for the purpose of our examination is not to know$_{o}$ what virtue is, but to become good, since otherwise the inquiry would be of no benefit to us. Hence we must examine the right way to act, since, as we have said, the actions also control the character of the states we acquire.

First, then, actions should express correct reason. That is a common <belief>, and let us assume it; later we will say what correct reason is and how it is related to the other virtues.

1104a But let us take it as agreed in advance that every account of the actions we must do has to be stated in outline, not exactly. As we also said at the start, the type of accounts we demand should reflect the subject matter; and questions about actions and expediency, like questions about health, have no fixed <and invariable answers>.

And when our general account is so inexact, the account of particular cases is all the more inexact. For these fall under no craft or profession, and the agents themselves must consider in each case what the opportune action is, as doctors and navigators do.

The account we offer, then, in our present inquiry is of this inexact sort; still, we must try to offer help.

First, then, we should observe that these sorts of states naturally tend to be ruined by excess and deficiency. We see this happen with strength and health, which we mention because we must use what is evident as a witness to what is not. For both excessive and deficient exercises ruin strength; and likewise, too much or too little eating or drinking ruins health, while the proportionate amount produces, increases and preserves it.

The same is true, then, of temperance, bravery and the other virtues. For if, for instance, someone avoids and is afraid of everything, standing firm against nothing, he becomes cowardly, but if he is afraid of nothing at all and goes to face everything, he becomes rash. Similarly, if he gratifies himself with every pleasure and refrains from none, he becomes intemperate, but if he avoids them all, as boors do, he becomes some sort of insensible person. Temperance and bravery, then, are ruined by excess and deficiency but preserved by the mean.

The same actions, then, are the sources and causes both of the emergence and growth of virtues and of their ruin; but further, the activities of the virtues will be found in these same actions. For this is also true of more evident cases; strength, for instance, arises from eating a lot and from withstanding much hard labor, and it is the strong person who is most able to do these very things. It is the same with the virtues. Refraining from pleasures makes us become temperate, and when we have become temper-
1104b ate we are most able to refrain from pleasures. And it is similar with bravery; habituation in disdaining what is fearful and in

standing firm against it makes us become brave, and when we have become brave we shall be most able to stand firm.

3

But <actions are not enough>; we must take as a sign of someone's state his pleasure or pain in consequence of his action. For if someone who abstains from bodily pleasures enjoys the abstinence itself, then he is temperate, but if he is grieved by it, he is intemperate. Again, if he stands firm against terrifying situations and enjoys it, or at least does not find it painful, then he is brave, and if he finds it painful, he is cowardly.

<Pleasures and pains are appropriately taken as signs> because virtue of character is concerned with pleasures and pains.

(1) For it is pleasure that causes us to do base actions, and pain that causes us to abstain from fine ones. Hence we need to have had the appropriate upbringing—right from early youth, as Plato says—to make us find enjoyment or pain in the right things; for this is the correct education.

(2) Further, virtues are concerned with actions and feelings; but every feeling and every action implies pleasure or pain; hence, for this reason too, virtue is concerned with pleasures and pains.

(3) Corrective treatment <for vicious actions> also indicates <the relevance of pleasure and pain>, since it uses pleasures and pains; it uses them because such correction is a form of medical treatment, and medical treatment naturally operates through contraries.

(4) Further, as we said earlier, every state of soul is naturally related to and concerned with whatever naturally makes it better or worse; and pleasures and pains make people worse, from pursuing and avoiding the wrong ones, at the wrong time, in the wrong ways, or whatever other distinctions of that sort are needed in an account.

These <bad effects of pleasure and pain> are the reason why people actually define the virtues as ways of being unaffected and undisturbed <by pleasures and pains>. They are wrong, however, because they speak <of being unaffected> without qualification, not of being unaffected in the right or wrong way, at the right or wrong time, and the added specifications.

We assume, then, that virtue is the sort of state <with the

appropriate specifications> that does the best actions concerned with pleasures and pains, and that vice is the contrary. The following points will also make it evident that virtue and vice are concerned with the same things.

(5) There are three objects of choice—fine, expedient and pleasant—and three objects of avoidance—their contraries, shameful, harmful and painful. About all these, then, the good person is correct and the bad person is in error, and especially about pleasure. For pleasure is shared with animals, and implied by every object of choice, since what is fine and what is expedient appear pleasant as well.

(6) Further, since pleasure grows up with all of us from infancy on, it is hard to rub out this feeling that is dyed into our lives; and we estimate actions as well <as feelings>, some of us more, some less, by pleasure and pain. Hence, our whole inquiry must be about these, since good or bad enjoyment or pain is very important for our actions.

(7) Moreover, it is harder to fight pleasure than to fight emotion, <though that is hard enough>, as Heracleitus says. Now both craft and virtue are concerned in every case with what is harder, since a good result is even better when it is harder. Hence, for this reason also, the whole inquiry, for virtue and political science alike, must consider pleasures and pains; for if we use these well, we shall be good, and if badly, bad.

In short, virtue is concerned with pleasures and pains; the actions that are its sources also increase it or, if they are done differently, ruin it; and its activity is concerned with the same actions that are its sources.

4

However, someone might raise this puzzle: 'What do you mean by saying that to become just we must first do just actions and to become temperate we must first do temperate actions? For if we do what is grammatical or musical, we must already be grammarians or musicians. In the same way, then, if we do what is just or temperate, we must already be just or temperate.'

But surely this is not so even with the crafts, for it is possible to produce something grammatical by chance or by following someone else's instructions. To be a grammarian, then, we must both produce something grammatical and produce it in the way in which the grammarian produces it, i.e., expressing grammatical knowledge that is in us.

Moreover, in any case what is true of crafts is not true of virtues. For the products of a craft determine by their own character whether they have been produced well;[2] and so it suffices that they are in the right state when they have been produced. But for actions expressing virtue to be done temperately or justly <and hence well> it does not suffice that they are themselves in the right state. Rather, the agent must also be in the right state when he does them. First, he must know$_o$ <that he is doing virtuous actions>; second, he must decide on them, and decide on them for themselves; and, third, he must also do them from a firm and unchanging state.

As conditions for having a craft these three do not count, except for the knowing itself. As a condition for having a virtue, however, the knowing counts for nothing, or <rather> for only a little, whereas the other two conditions are very important, indeed all-important. And these other two conditions are achieved by the frequent doing of just and temperate actions.

Hence actions are called just or temperate when they are the sort that a just or temperate person would do. But the just and temperate person is not the one who <merely> does these actions, but the one who also does them in the way in which just or temperate people do them.

It is right, then, to say that a person comes to be just from doing just actions and temperate from doing temperate actions; for no one has even a prospect of becoming good from failing to do them.

The many, however, do not do these actions but take refuge in arguments, thinking that they are doing philosophy, and that this is the way to become excellent people. In this they are like a sick person who listens attentively to the doctor, but acts on none of his instructions. Such a course of treatment will not improve the state of his body; any more than will the many's way of doing philosophy improve the state of their souls.

2. **For the products . . . produced well**: A better method of production is better because it is better at producing the right sort of product.

5

Next we must examine what virtue is. Since there are three conditions arising in the soul—feelings, capacities and states—virtue must be one of these.

By feelings I mean appetite, anger, fear, confidence, envy, joy, love, hate, longing, jealousy, pity, in general whatever implies pleasure or pain.

By capacities I mean what we have when we are said to be capable of these feelings—capable of being angry, for instance, or afraid or feeling pity.

By states I mean what we have when we are well or badly off in relation to feelings. If, for instance, our feeling is too intense or slack, we are badly off in relation to anger, but if it is intermediate, we are well off;[3] and the same is true in the other cases.

First, then, neither virtues nor vices are feelings. (a) For we are called excellent or base insofar as we have virtues or vices, not insofar as we have feelings. (b) We are neither praised nor blamed insofar as we have feelings; for we do not praise the angry or the frightened person, and do not blame the person who is simply angry, but only the person who is angry in a particular way. But we are praised or blamed insofar as we have virtues or vices. (c) We are angry and afraid without decision; but the virtues are decisions of some kind, or <rather> require decision. (d) Besides, insofar as we have feelings, we are said to be moved; but insofar as we have virtues or vices, we are said to be in some condition rather than moved.

For these reasons the virtues are not capacities either; for we are neither called good nor called bad insofar as we are simply capable of feelings. Further, while we have capacities by nature, we do not become good or bad by nature; we have discussed this before.

If, then, the virtues are neither feelings nor capacities, the remaining possibility is that they are states. And so we have said what the genus of virtue is.

6

But we must say not only, as we already have, that it is a state, but also what sort of state it is.

3. **By states . . . well off**: A STATE is not *merely* a capacity (see POTENTIALITY). Aristotle does not deny that a state is a *type* of capacity.

It should be said, then, that every virtue causes its possessors to be in a good state and to perform their functions well; the virtue of eyes, for instance, makes the eyes and their functioning excellent, because it makes us see well; and similarly, the virtue of a horse makes the horse excellent, and thereby good at galloping, at carrying its rider and at standing steady in the face of the enemy. If this is true in every case, then the virtue of a human being will likewise be the state that makes a human being good and makes him perform his function well.[4]

We have already said how this will be true, and it will also be evident from our next remarks, if we consider the sort of nature that virtue has.

In everything continuous and divisible we can take more, less and equal, and each of them either in the object itself or relative to us; and the equal is some intermediate between excess and deficiency.

By the intermediate in the object I mean what is equidistant from each extremity; this is one and the same for everyone. But relative to us the intermediate is what is neither superfluous nor deficient; this is not one, and is not the same for everyone.[5]

If, for instance, ten are many and two are few, we take six as intermediate in the object, since it exceeds <two> and is exceeded <by ten> by an equal amount, <four>; this is what is intermediate by numerical proportion. But that is not how we must take the 1106b intermediate that is relative to us. For if, for instance, ten pounds <of food> are a lot for someone to eat, and two pounds a little, it does not follow that the trainer will prescribe six, since this might also be either a little or a lot for the person who is to take it—for Milo <the athlete> a little, but for the beginner in gymnastics a lot; and the same is true for running and wrestling. In this way every scientific expert avoids excess and deficiency and seeks and chooses what is intermediate—but intermediate relative to us, not in the object.

This, then, is how each science produces its product well, by

4. **then the virtue . . . function well**: On VIRTUE and FUNCTION see 1098a7, 1139a16.

5. **But relative . . . for everyone**: The appeal to a mean does not provide a precise, quantitative test. To find the mean relative to us is to find the state of character that correct reason requires, neither suppressing nor totally indulging nonrational desires.

focusing on what is intermediate and making the product conform to that. This, indeed, is why people regularly comment on well-made products that nothing could be added or subtracted, since they assume that excess or deficiency ruins a good <result> while the mean preserves it. Good craftsmen also, we say, focus on what is intermediate when they produce their product. And since virtue, like nature, is better and more exact than any craft, it will also aim at what is intermediate.

By virtue I mean virtue of character; for this <pursues the mean because> it is concerned with feelings and actions, and these admit of excess, deficiency and an intermediate condition. We can be afraid, for instance, or be confident, or have appetites, or get angry, or feel pity, in general have pleasure or pain, both too much and too little, and in both ways not well; but <having these feelings> at the right times, about the right things, toward the right people, for the right end, and in the right way, is the intermediate condition.

Now virtue is concerned with feelings and actions, in which excess and deficiency are in error and incur blame, while the intermediate condition is correct and wins praise, which are both proper features of virtue. Virtue, then, is a mean, insofar as it aims at what is intermediate.

Moreover, there are many ways to be in error, since badness is proper to what is unlimited, as the Pythagoreans pictured it, and good to what is limited; but there is only one way to be correct. That is why error is easy and correctness hard, since it is easy to miss the target and hard to hit it. And so for this reason also excess and deficiency are proper to vice, the mean to virtue; 'for we are noble in only one way, but bad in all sorts of ways.'

1107a Virtue, then, is (a) a state that decides, (b) <consisting> in a mean, (c) the mean relative to us, (d) which is defined by reference to reason, (e) i.e., to the reason by reference to which the intelligent person would define it. It is a mean between two vices, one of excess and one of deficiency.

It is a mean for this reason also: Some vices miss what is right because they are deficient, others because they are excessive, in feelings or in actions, while virtue finds and chooses what is intermediate.

Hence, as far as its substance and the account stating its essence are concerned, virtue is a mean; but as far as the best <condition> and the good <result> are concerned, it is an extremity.

But not every action or feeling admits of the mean. For the names of some automatically include baseness—for instance, spite, shamelessness, envy <among feelings>, and adultery, theft, murder, among actions. All of these and similar things are called by these names because they themselves, not their excesses or deficiencies, are base.

Hence in doing these things we can never be correct, but must invariably be in error. We cannot do them well or not well—by committing adultery, for instance, with the right woman at the right time in the right way; on the contrary, it is true without qualification that to do any of them is to be in error.

<To think these admit of a mean>, therefore, is like thinking that unjust or cowardly or intemperate action also admits of a mean, an excess and a deficiency. For then there would be a mean of excess, a mean of deficiency, an excess of excess and a deficiency of deficiency.

Rather, just as there is no excess or deficiency of temperance or of bravery, since the intermediate is a sort of extreme <in achieving the good>, so also there is no mean of these <vicious actions> either, but whatever way anyone does them, he is in error. For in general there is no mean of excess or of deficiency, and no excess or deficiency of a mean.

7

However, we must not only state this general account but also apply it to the particular cases. For among accounts concerning actions, though the general ones are common to more cases, the specific ones are truer, since actions are about particular cases, and our account must accord with these. Let us, then, find these from the chart.[6]

(1) First, in feelings of fear and confidence the mean is bravery. 1107b
The excessively fearless person is nameless (and in fact many cases are nameless), while the one who is excessively confident is rash; the one who is excessively afraid and deficient in confidence is cowardly.

(2) In pleasures and pains, though not in all types, and in pains less than in pleasures, the mean is temperance and the

6. **chart**: Presumably in Aristotle's lecture room.

excess intemperance. People deficient in pleasure are not often found, which is why they also lack even a name; let us call them insensible.

(3) In giving and taking money the mean is generosity, the excess wastefulness and the deficiency ungenerosity. Here the vicious people have contrary excesses and defects; for the wasteful person spends to excess and is deficient in taking, whereas the ungenerous person takes to excess and is deficient in spending. At the moment we are speaking in outline and summary, and that suffices; later we shall define these things more exactly.

(4) In questions of money there are also other conditions. Another mean is magnificence; for the magnificent person differs from the generous by being concerned with large matters, while the generous person is concerned with small. The excess is ostentation and vulgarity, and the deficiency niggardliness, and these differ from the vices related to generosity in ways we shall describe later.

(5) In honor and dishonor the mean is magnanimity, the excess something called a sort of vanity, and the deficiency pusillanimity.

(6) And just as we said that generosity differs from magnificence in its concern with small matters, similarly there is a virtue concerned with small honors, differing in the same way from magnanimity, which is concerned with great honors. For honor can be desired either in the right way or more or less than is right. If someone desires it to excess, he is called an honor-lover, and if his desire is deficient he is called indifferent to honor, but if he is intermediate he has no name. The corresponding conditions have no name either, except the condition of the honor-lover, which is called honor-loving.

This is why people at the extremes claim the intermediate area. Indeed, we also sometimes call the intermediate person an honor-lover, and sometimes call him indifferent to honor; and sometimes we praise the honor-lover, sometimes the person indifferent to honor. We will mention later the reason we do this; for the moment, let us speak of the other cases in the way we have laid down.

(7) Anger also admits of an excess, deficiency and mean. These are all practically nameless; but since we call the intermediate person mild, let us call the mean mildness. Among the extreme people let the excessive person be irascible, and the vice be irasci-

bility, and let the deficient person be a sort of inirascible person, and the deficiency be inirascibility.

There are three other means, somewhat similar to one another, but different. For they are all concerned with association in conversations and actions, but differ insofar as one is concerned with truth-telling in these areas, the other two with sources of pleasure, some of which are found in amusement, and the others in daily life in general. Hence we should also discuss these states, so that we can better observe that in every case the mean is praiseworthy, while the extremes are neither praiseworthy nor correct, but blameworthy. Most of these cases are also nameless, and we must try, as in the other cases also, to make names ourselves, to make things clear and easy to follow.

(8) In truth-telling, then, let us call the intermediate person truthful, and the mean truthfulness; pretense that overstates will be boastfulness, and the person who has it boastful; pretense that understates will be self-deprecation, and the person who has it self-deprecating.

(9) In sources of pleasure in amusements let us call the intermediate person witty, and the condition wit; the excess buffoonery and the person who has it a buffoon; and the deficient person a sort of boor and the state boorishness.

(10) In the other sources of pleasure, those in daily life, let us call the person who is pleasant in the right way friendly, and the mean state friendliness. If someone goes to excess with no <further> aim he will be ingratiating; if he does it for his own advantage, a flatterer. The deficient person, unpleasant in everything, will be a sort of quarrelsome and ill-tempered person.

(11) There are also means in feelings and concerned with feelings: shame, for instance, is not a virtue, but the person prone to shame as well as the virtuous person we have described receives praise. For here also one person is called intermediate, and another—the person excessively prone to shame, who is ashamed about everything—is called excessive; the person who is deficient in shame or never feels shame at all is said to have no sense of disgrace; and the intermediate one is called prone to shame.

(12) Proper indignation is the mean between envy and spite; these conditions are concerned with pleasure and pain at what happens to our neighbors. For the properly indignant person feels pain when someone does well undeservedly; the envious person exceeds him by feeling pain when anyone does well, while the

spiteful person is so deficient in feeling pain that he actually enjoys <other people's misfortunes>.

There will also be an opportunity elsewhere to speak of these <means that are not virtues>.

We must consider justice after these other conditions, and, because it is not spoken of in one way only, we shall distinguish its two types and say how each of them is a mean.

10 Similarly, we must consider the virtues that belong to reason.

* * * * * * *

Book III

[*VIRTUE, PRAISE, AND BLAME*]

1

1109b30 Virtue, then, is about feelings and actions. These receive praise or blame when they are voluntary, but pardon, sometimes even pity, when they are involuntary. Hence, presumably, in examining virtue we must define the voluntary and the involuntary. This
1110a is also useful to legislators, both for honors and for corrective treatments.

What comes about by force or because of ignorance seems to be involuntary. What is forced has an external principle, the sort of principle in which the agent or victim contributes nothing—if, for instance, a wind or human beings who control him were to carry him off.

5 But now consider actions done because of fear of greater evils, or because of something fine. Suppose, for instance, a tyrant tells you to do something shameful, when he has control over your parents and children, and if you do it, they will live, but if not, they will die. These cases raise dispute about whether they are voluntary or involuntary.

10 However, the same sort of thing also happens with throwing cargo overboard in storms; for no one willingly throws cargo

overboard, without qualification,[1] but anyone with any sense throws it overboard <under some conditions> to save himself and the others.

These sorts of actions, then, are mixed. But they would seem to be more like voluntary actions. For at the time they are done they are choiceworthy, and the goal of an action reflects the occasion; hence also we should call the action voluntary or involuntary with reference to the time when he does it. Now in fact he does it willingly; for in these sorts of actions he has within him the principle of the movement of the limbs that are the instruments <of the action>, and when the principle of the actions is in him, it is also up to him to do them or not to do them. Hence actions of this sort are voluntary, though presumably the actions without <the appropriate> condition are involuntary, since no one would choose any action of this sort in itself.

For such <mixed> actions people are sometimes actually praised, whenever they endure something shameful or painful as the price of great and fine results; and if they do the reverse, they are blamed, since it is a base person who endures what is most shameful for nothing fine or for only some moderately fine result.

In some cases there is no praise, but there is pardon, whenever someone does a wrong action because of conditions of a sort that overstrain human nature, and that no one would endure. But presumably there are some things we cannot be compelled[2] to do, and rather than do them we should suffer the most terrible consequences and accept death; for the things that <allegedly> compelled Euripides' Alcmaeon to kill his mother appear ridiculous.

It is sometimes hard, however, to judge what <goods> should be chosen at the price of what <evils>, and what <evils> should be endured as the price of what <goods>. And it is even harder to abide by our judgment, since the results we expect <when we endure> are usually painful, and the actions we are compelled
<to endure, when we choose> are usually shameful. That is why 1110b
those who have been compelled or not compelled receive praise or blame.

1. **without qualification**: Here and in a18 and b1 Aristotle contrasts simply doing F with doing F in specific conditions in which it is reasonable to do F. See WITHOUT QUALIFICATION #4. 'In itself' (see IN ITS OWN RIGHT), a19, b3, marks the same contrast.

2. **compelled**: Compulsion (or necessitation; see NECESSARY) is contrasted with FORCE.

What sorts of things, then, should we say are forced? Perhaps we should say that something is forced without qualification whenever its cause is external and the agent contributes nothing. Other things are involuntary in themselves, but choiceworthy on this occasion and as the price of these <goods>, and their principle is in the agent. These are involuntary in themselves, but, on this occasion and as the price of these <goods>, voluntary. Still, they would seem to be more like voluntary actions, since actions involve particular <conditions>, and <in mixed actions> these <conditions> are voluntary. But what sort of thing should be chosen as the price of what <good> is not easy to answer, since there are many differences in particular <conditions>.

But suppose someone says that pleasant things and fine things force us, since they are outside us and compel us. It will follow that for him everything is forced, since everyone in every action aims at something fine or pleasant.

Moreover, if we are forced and unwilling to act, we find it painful; but if something pleasant or fine is its cause, we do it with pleasure.

It is ridiculous, then, for <our opponent> to ascribe responsibility to external <causes> and not to himself, when he is easily snared by such things; and ridiculous to take responsibility for fine actions himself, but to hold pleasant things responsible for his shameful actions.

What is forced, then, would seem to be what has its principle outside the person forced, who contributes nothing.

Everything caused by ignorance is nonvoluntary, but what is involuntary also causes pain and regret. For if someone's action was caused by ignorance, but he now has no objection to the action, he has done it neither willingly, since he did not know$_{o}$ what it was, nor unwillingly, since he now feels no pain. Hence, among those who act because of ignorance, the agent who now regrets his action seems to be unwilling, while the agent with no regrets may be called nonwilling, since he is another case—for since he is different, it is better if he has his own special name.

Further, action caused by ignorance would seem to be different from action done in ignorance. For if the agent is drunk or angry, his action seems to be caused by drunkenness or anger, not by ignorance, though it is done in ignorance, not in knowledge.

<This ignorance does not make an action involuntary.> Certainly every vicious person is ignorant of the actions he must do

or avoid, and this sort of error makes people unjust, and in general bad. But talk of involuntary action is not meant to apply to <this> ignorance of what is beneficial.[3]

For the cause of involuntary action is not <this> ignorance in the decision, which causes vice; it is not <in other words> ignorance of the universal, since that is a cause for blame. Rather, the cause is ignorance of the particulars which the action consists in and is concerned with; for these allow both pity and pardon, since an agent acts involuntarily if he is ignorant of one of these particulars.

Presumably, then, it is not a bad idea to define these particulars, and say what they are, and how many. They are: (1) who is doing it; (2) what he is doing; (3) about what or to what he is doing it; (4) sometimes also what he is doing with it—with the instrument, for example; (5) for what result—safety, for example; (6) in what way—gently or hard, for example.

Now certainly someone could not be ignorant of *all* of these unless he were mad. Nor, clearly, (1) could he be ignorant of who is doing it, since he could hardly be ignorant of himself. But (2) he might be ignorant of what he is doing, as when someone says that <the secret> slipped out while he was speaking, or, as Aeschylus said about the mysteries, that he did not know it was forbidden to reveal it; or, like the person with the catapult, that he let it go when he <only> wanted to demonstrate it. (3) Again, he might think that his son is an enemy, as Merope did; or (4) that the barber spear has a button on it, or that the stone is pumice-stone. (5) By giving someone a drink to save his life we might kill him; (6) and wanting to touch someone, as they do in sparring, we might wound him.

There is ignorance about all of these <particulars> that the action consists in. Hence someone who was ignorant of one of these seems to have done an action unwillingly, especially when he was ignorant of the most important of them; these seem to be (2) what he is doing, and (5) the result for which he does it.

Hence it is action called involuntary with reference to *this* sort of ignorance <that we meant when we said that> the agent must, in addition, feel pain and regret for his action.

3. **But talk . . . beneficial**: Probably 'ignorance of what is beneficial', 'ignorance in the decision' and ignorance of the universal' all refer to the same thing.

Since, then, what is involuntary is what is forced or is caused by ignorance, what is voluntary seems to be what has its principle in the agent himself when he knows the particulars that the action consists in.

<Our definition is sound.> For, presumably, it is not correct to say that action caused by emotion or appetite is involuntary.

For, first of all, on this view none of the other animals will ever act voluntarily; nor will children. <But clearly they do.>

Next, among all the actions caused by appetite or emotion do we do none of them voluntarily? Or do we do the fine actions voluntarily and the shameful involuntarily? Surely <the second answer> is ridiculous when one and the same thing <i.e., appetite or emotion> causes <both fine and shameful actions>. And presumably it is also absurd to say <as the first answer implies> that things we ought to desire are involuntary; and in fact we ought both to be angry at some things and to have appetite for some things—for health and learning, for instance.

Again, what is involuntary seems to be painful, whereas what expresses our appetite seems to be pleasant.

Moreover, how are errors that express emotion any less volun-
1111b tary than those that express rational calculation? For both sorts of errors are to be avoided; and since nonrational feelings seem to be no less human <than rational calculation>, actions resulting from emotion or appetite are also proper to a human being; it is absurd, then, to regard them as involuntary.

2

Now that we have defined what is voluntary and what involuntary, the next task is to discuss decision; for decision seems to be most proper to virtue, and to distinguish characters from one another better than actions do.

Decision, then, is apparently voluntary, but not the same as what is voluntary, which extends more widely. For children and the other animals share in what is voluntary, but not in decision; and the actions we do on the spur of the moment are said to be voluntary, but not to express decision.

Those who say decision is appetite or emotion or wish or some sort of belief would seem to be wrong.

For decision is not shared with nonrational <animals>, but appetite and emotion are shared with them.

Further, the incontinent person acts on appetite, not on decision, but the continent person does the reverse and acts on decision, not on appetite.

Again, appetite is contrary to decision, but not to appetite.

Further, appetite's concern is what is pleasant and what is painful, but neither of these is the concern of decision.

Still less is emotion decision; for actions caused by emotion seem least of all to express decision.

But further, it is not wish either, though it is apparently close to it.

For, first, we do not decide to do what is impossible, and anyone claiming to decide to do it would seem a fool; but we do wish for what is impossible—for immortality, for instance—as well <as for what is possible>.

Further, we wish <not only for results we can achieve>, but also for results that are <possible, but> not achievable through our own agency—victory for some actor or athlete, for instance. But what we decide to do is never anything of that sort, but what we think would come about through our own agency.

Again, we wish for the end more <than for what promotes it>, but we decide to do what promotes the end. We wish, for instance, to be healthy, but decide to do what will make us healthy; and we wish to be happy, and say so, but could not appropriately say we decide to be happy, since in general what we decide to do would seem to be what is up to us.

Nor is it belief.

For, first, belief seems to be about everything, no less about what is eternal and what is impossible <for us> than about what is up to us.

Moreover, beliefs are divided into true and false, not into good and bad, but decisions are divided into good and bad more than into true and false.

Now presumably no one even claims that decision is the same 1112a
as belief in general. But it is not the same as any kind of belief either.

For it is our decisions to do what is good or bad, not our beliefs, that make the characters we have.

Again, we decide to take or avoid something good or bad. We believe what it is, whom it benefits or how; but we do not exactly believe to take or avoid.

Further, decision is praised more for deciding on what is right, whereas belief is praised for believing rightly.

Moreover, we decide on something <even> when we know$_o$ most completely that it is good; but <what> we believe <is> what we do not quite know.

Again, those who make the best decisions do not seem to be the same as those with the best beliefs; on the contrary, some seem to have better beliefs, but to make the wrong decisions because of vice.

We can agree that decision follows or implies belief. But that is irrelevant, since it is not the question we are asking; our question is whether decision is the *same* as some sort of belief.

Then what, or what sort of thing, is decision, since it is none of the things mentioned? Well, apparently it is voluntary, but not everything voluntary is decided. Then perhaps what is decided is the result of prior deliberation. For decision involves reason and thought, and even the name itself would seem to indicate that <what is decided, *prohaireton*> is chosen <*haireton*> before <*pro*> other things.

3

But do we deliberate about everything, and is everything open to deliberation, or is there no deliberation about some things? By 'open to deliberation', presumably, we should mean what someone with some sense, not some fool or madman, might deliberate about.

Now no one deliberates about eternal things—about the universe, for instance, or about the incommensurability of the sides and the diagonal; nor about things that are in movement but always come about the same way, either from necessity or by nature or by some other cause—the solstices, for instance, or the rising of the stars; nor about what happens different ways at different times—droughts and rains, for instance; nor about what results from fortune—the finding of a treasure, for instance.[4] For none of these results could be achieved through our agency.

We deliberate about what is up to us, i.e., about the actions we can do; and this is what is left <besides the previous cases>. For
33 causes seem to include nature, necessity and fortune, but besides them mind and everything <operating> through human agency.

28 However, we do not deliberate about all human affairs; no

4. **treasure, for instance**: Here the mss have b28–9 'However, we do not . . . best political system', which we have placed after b33 below.

Spartan, for instance, deliberates about how the Scythians might 29
have the best political system. Rather, each group of human beings 33
deliberates about the actions *they* can do.

Now there is no deliberation about the sciences that are exact 1112b
and self-sufficient, as, for instance, about letters, since we are in no doubt about how to write them <in spelling a word>. Rather, we deliberate about what results through our agency, but in different ways on different occasions, as, for instance, about questions of medicine and money-making; more about navigation than about gymnastics, to the extent that it is less exactly worked out, and similarly with other <crafts>; and more about beliefs than about sciences, since we are more in doubt about them.

Deliberation concerns what is usually <one way rather than another>, where the outcome is unclear and the right way to act is undefined. And we enlist partners in deliberation on large issues when we distrust our own ability to discern <the right answer>.

We deliberate not about ends, but about what promotes ends; a doctor, for instance, does not deliberate about whether he will cure, or an orator about whether he will persuade, or a politician about whether he will produce good order, or any other <expert> about the end <that his science aims at>.

Rather, we first lay down the end, and then examine the ways and means to achieve it. If it appears that any of several <possible> means will reach it, we consider which of them will reach it most easily and most finely; and if only one <possible> means reaches it, we consider how that means will reach it, and how the means itself is reached, until we come to the first cause, the last thing to be discovered.

For a deliberator would seem to inquire and analyze in the way described, as though analyzing a diagram.[5] <The comparison is apt, since>, apparently, all deliberation is inquiry, though not all inquiry—in mathematics, for instance—is deliberation. And the last thing <found> in the analysis is the first that comes to be.

If we encounter an impossible step—for instance, we need money but cannot raise it—we desist; but if the action appears possible, we undertake it. What is possible is what we could

5. **analyzing a diagram**: The geometer considers how to construct a complex figure by analyzing it into simpler figures, until he finds the first one that he should draw.

achieve through our agency <including what our friends could achieve for us>; for what our friends achieve is, in a way, achieved through our agency, since the principle is in us. <In crafts> we sometimes look for instruments, sometimes <for the way> to use them; so also in other cases we sometimes look for the means to the end, sometimes for the proper use of the means or for the means to that proper use.

As we have said, then, a human being would seem to be the principle of action; deliberation is about the actions he can do; and actions are for the sake of other things; hence we deliberate about what promotes an end, not about the end.

1113a Nor do we deliberate about particulars, about whether this is a loaf, for instance, or is cooked the right amount; for these are questions for perception, and if we keep on deliberating at each stage we shall go on without end.

What we deliberate about is the same as what we decide to do, except that by the time we decide to do it, it is definite; for what we decide to do is what we have judged <to be right> as a result of deliberation. For each of us stops inquiring how to act as soon as he traces the principle to himself, and within himself to the dominant part; for this is the part that decides. This is also clear from the ancient political systems described by Homer; there the kings would first decide and then announce their decision to the people.

We have found, then, that what we decide to do is whatever action among those up to us we deliberate about and desire to do. Hence also decision will be deliberative desire to do an action that is up to us; for when we have judged <that it is right> as a result of deliberation, our desire to do it expresses our wish.

So much, then, for an outline of the sort of thing decision is about; it is about what promotes the end.

4

Wish, we have said, is for the end. But to some it seems that wish is for the good, to others that it is for the apparent good.[6]

6. **Wish . . . apparent good**: 'Wished' may mean (a) what is wished or (b) what deserves to be wished. The proper object of wish is the good (i.e., the suitable object for the well-informed person) just as what is known by nature (1095b3) is what is true (i.e., what the fully informed person thinks he knows).

For those who say the good is what is wished, it follows that what someone wishes if he chooses incorrectly is not wished at all. For if it is wished, then <on this view> it is good; but what he wishes is in fact bad, if it turns out that way. <Hence what he wishes is not wished, which is self-contradictory.>

For those, on the other hand, who say the apparent good is wished, it follows that there is nothing wished by nature. To each person what is wished is what seems <good to him>; but different things, and indeed contrary things, if it turns out that way, appear good to different people. <Hence contrary things will be wished and nothing will be wished by nature.>

If, then, these views do not satisfy us, should we say that, without qualification and in reality, what is wished is the good, but to each person what is wished is the apparent good?

To the excellent person, then, what is wished will be what is wished in reality, while to the base person what is wished is whatever it turns out to be <that appears good to him>. Similarly in the case of bodies, really healthy things are healthy to people in good condition, while other things are healthy to sickly people, and the same is true of what is bitter, sweet, hot, heavy and so on.

For the excellent person judges each sort of thing correctly, and in each case what is true appears to him. For each state <of character> has its own special <view of> what is fine and pleasant, and presumably the excellent person is far superior because he sees what is true in each case, being a sort of standard and measure of what is fine and pleasant.

In the many, however, pleasure would seem to cause deception, 1113b
since it appears good when it is not; at any rate, they choose what is pleasant because they assume it is good, and avoid pain because they assume it is evil.

5

We have found, then, that we wish for the end, and deliberate and decide about what promotes it; hence the actions concerned with what promotes the end will express a decision and will be voluntary. Now the activities of the virtues are concerned with <what promotes the end>; hence virtue is also up to us, and so is vice.

For when acting is up to us, so is not acting, and when No is up to us, so is Yes. Hence if acting, when it is fine, is up to us, then not acting, when it is shameful, is also up to us; and if not acting, when it is fine, is up to us, then acting, when it is shameful, is also up to us. Hence if doing, and likewise not doing, fine or shameful actions is up to us; and if, as we saw, <doing or not doing them> is <what it is> to be a good or bad person; then it follows that being decent or base is up to us.

The claim that no one is willingly bad or unwillingly blessed would seem to be partly true but partly false. For while certainly no one is unwillingly blessed, vice is voluntary. If it is not, we must dispute the conclusion just reached, that a human being originates and fathers his own actions as he fathers his children. But if our conclusion appears true, and we cannot refer <actions> back to other principles beyond those in ourselves, then it follows that whatever has its principle in us is itself up to us and voluntary.

There would seem to be testimony in favor of our view not only in what each of us does as a private citizen, but also in what legislators themselves do. For they impose corrective treatments and penalties on anyone who does vicious actions, unless his action is forced or is caused by ignorance that he is not responsible for; and they honor anyone who does fine actions; they assume that they will encourage the one and restrain the other. But no one encourages us to do anything that is not up to us and voluntary; people assume it is pointless to persuade us not to get hot or distressed or hungry or anything else of that sort, since persuasion will not stop it happening to us.

Indeed, legislators also impose corrective treatments for the ignorance itself, if the person seems to be responsible for the ignorance. A drunk, for instance, pays a double penalty; for the principle is in him, since he controls whether he gets drunk, and his getting drunk is responsible for his ignorance.

They also impose corrective treatment on someone who <does a vicious action> in ignorance of some provision of law that he is required to know[e] and that is not hard <to know>. And they impose it in other cases likewise for any other ignorance that seems to be caused by the agent's inattention; they assume it is up to him not to be ignorant, since he controls whether he pays attention.

But presumably his character makes him inattentive. Still, he is himself responsible for having this character, by living carelessly, and similarly for being unjust by cheating, or being intemperate by passing his time in drinking and the like; for each type of activity produces the corresponding character. This is clear from those who train for any contest or action, since they continually practice the

appropriate activities. <Only> a totally insensible person would 10
not know$_g$ that each type of activity is the source of the corresponding state; hence if someone does what he knows will make him 12
unjust, he is willingly unjust.[7] 13

Moreover, it is unreasonable for someone doing injustice not to 11
wish to be unjust, or for someone doing intemperate action not to 12
wish to be intemperate. This does not mean, however, that if he is 13
unjust and wishes to stop, he will stop and will be just.

For neither does a sick person recover his health <simply by 15
wishing>; nonetheless, he is sick willingly, by living incontinently and disobeying the doctors, if that was how it happened. At that time, then, he was free not to be sick, though no longer free once he has let himself go, just as it was up to us to throw a stone, since the principle was in us, though we can no longer take it back once we have thrown it.

Similarly, then, the person who is <now> unjust or intemperate 20
was originally free not to acquire this character, so that he has it willingly, though once he has acquired the character, he is no longer free not to have it <now>.

It is not only vices of the soul that are voluntary; vices of the body are also voluntary for some people, and we actually censure them. For we never censure someone if nature causes his ugliness; but if
his lack of training or attention causes it, we do censure him. The 25
same is true for weakness of maiming; for everyone would pity, not reproach someone if he were blind by nature or because of a disease or a wound, but would censure him if his heavy drinking or some other form of intemperance made him blind.

Hence bodily vices that are up to us are censured, while those 30
not up to us are not censured. If so, then in the other cases also the vices that are censured will be up to us.

But someone may say, 'Everyone aims at the apparent good, and 1114b
does not control how it appears; on the contrary, his character controls how the end appears to him.'

First, then, if each person is in some way responsible for his own state <of character>, then he is also himself in some way responsible for how <the end> appears.

Suppose, on the other hand, that no one is responsible for acting
badly, but one does so because one is ignorant of the end, and thinks 5

7. **hence if someone . . . willingly unjust**: The mss have this after 'unjust or intemperate' in the next paragraph.

this is the way to gain what is best for oneself. One's aiming at the end will not be one's own choice, but one needs a sort of natural, inborn sense of sight, to judge finely and to choose what is really good. Whoever by nature has this sense in a fine condition has a good nature. For this sense is the greatest and finest thing, and one cannot acquire it or learn it from another; rather, its natural character determines his later condition, and when it is naturally good and fine, that is true and complete good nature.

If all this is true, then, surely virtue will be no more voluntary than vice? For how the end appears is laid down, by nature or in whatever way, for the good and the bad person alike, and they trace all the other things back to the end in doing whatever actions they do.

Suppose, then, that it is not nature that makes the end appear however it appears to each person, but something also depends on him; or, alternatively, suppose that <how> the end <appears> is natural, but virtue is voluntary because the virtuous person does the other things voluntarily. In either case vice will be no less voluntary than virtue; for the bad person, no less than the good, is responsible for his own actions, even if not for <how> the end <appears>.

Now the virtues, as we say, are voluntary, since in fact we are ourselves in a way jointly responsible for our states of character, and by having the sort of character we have we lay down the sort of end we do. Hence the vices will also be voluntary, since the same is true of them.

We have now discussed the virtues in general. We have described their genus in outline; they are means, and they are states. Certain actions produce them, and they cause us to do these same actions, expressing the virtues themselves, in the way that correct reason prescribes.[8] They are up to us and voluntary.

Actions and states, however, are not voluntary in the same way. For we are in control of actions from the beginning to the 1115a end, when we know$_{o}$ the particulars. With states, however, we are in control of the beginning, but do not know$_{g}$, any more than with sicknesses, what the cumulative effect of particular actions will be; nonetheless, since it was up to us to exercise a capacity either this way or another way, states are voluntary.

8. **in the way . . . prescribes**: The mss place this at the end of the next sentence.

Let us now take up the virtues again, and discuss each singly. Let us say what they are, what sorts of thing they are concerned with, and how they are concerned with them; it will also be clear at the same time how many virtues there are.

* * * * * * *

Book V

[Justice]

1

The questions we must examine about justice and injustice are 1129a
these: What sorts of actions are they concerned with? What sort of mean is justice? What are the extremes between which justice is intermediate? Let us examine them by the same type of investigation that we used in the topics discussed before.

We see that the state everyone means in speaking of justice is the state that makes us doers of just actions, that makes us do justice and wish what is just. In the same way they mean by injustice the state that makes us do injustice and wish what is unjust. Let us also, then, <follow the common beliefs and> begin by assuming this in outline.

For what is true of sciences and capacities is not true of states. For while one and the same capacity or science seems to have contrary activities, a state that is a contrary has no contrary activities. Health, for instance, only makes us do healthy actions, not their contraries; for we say we are walking in a healthy way if <and only if> we are walking in the way a healthy person would.

Often one of a pair of contrary states is recognized from the other contrary; and often the states are recognized from their subjects. For if, for instance, the good state is evident, the bad state becomes evident too; and moreover the good state becomes evident from the things that have it, and the things from the state. For if, for instance, the good state is thickness of flesh, then the bad state will necessarily be thinness of flesh, and the thing that produces the good state will be what produces thickness of flesh.

It follows, usually, that if one of a pair of contraries is spoken of in more ways than one, so is the other; if, for instance, what is just is spoken of in more ways than one, so is what is unjust.

Now it would seem that justice and injustice are both spoken of in more ways than one, but since the different ways are closely related, their homonymy is unnoticed, and is less clear than it is with distant homonyms where the distance in appearance is wide (for instance, the bone below an animal's neck and what we lock doors with are called keys homonymously).

Let us, then, find the number of ways an unjust person is spoken of. Both the lawless person and the greedy and unfair person seem to be unjust; and so, clearly, both the lawful and the
1129b fair[1] person will be just. Hence what is just will be both what is lawful and what is fair, and what is unjust will be both what is lawless and what is unfair.

Since the unjust person is greedy, he will be concerned with goods[2]—not with all goods, but only with those involved in good and bad fortune, goods which are, <considered> without qualification, always good, but for this or that person not always good. Though human beings pray for these and pursue them, they are wrong; the right thing is to pray that what is good without qualification will also be good for us, but to choose <only> what is good for us.

Now the unjust person <who chooses these goods> does not choose more in every case; in the case of what is bad without qualification he actually chooses less. But since what is less bad also seems to be good in a way, and greed aims at more of what is good, he seems to be greedy. In fact he is unfair; for unfairness includes <all these actions>, and is a common feature <of his choice of the greater good and of the lesser evil>.

Since, as we saw, the lawless person is unjust and the lawful person is just, it clearly follows that whatever is lawful is in some way just;[3] for the provisions of legislative science are lawful, and

1. **fair**: *ison*. See EQUAL.

2. **goods**: Wealth, e.g., is GOOD for a human being, not because it is good for every human being, but because a human being can use wealth well, and, if he uses it well, it will promote his happiness. See WITHOUT QUALIFICATION #3.

3. **whatever . . . some way just**: Aristotle does not say here that every system of positive LAW is just. His reference to 'legislative science' shows that he has in mind only correct laws.

we say that each of them is just. Now in every matter they deal with the laws aim either at the common benefit of all, or at the benefit of those in control, whose control rests on virtue or on some other such basis. And so in one way what we call just is whatever produces and maintains happiness and its parts for a political community.

Now the law instructs us to do the actions of a brave person—not to leave the battle-line, for instance, or to flee, or to throw away our weapons; of a temperate person—not to commit adultery or wanton aggression; of a mild person—not to strike or revile another; and similarly requires actions that express the other virtues, and prohibits those that express the vices. The correctly established law does this correctly, and the less carefully framed one does this worse.

This type of justice, then, is complete virtue, not complete virtue without qualification but complete virtue in relation to another. And this is why justice often seems to be supreme among the virtues, and 'neither the evening star nor the morning star is so marvelous', and the proverb says 'And in justice all virtue is summed up.'

Moreover, justice is complete virtue to the highest degree because it is the complete exercise of complete virtue. And it is the complete exercise because the person who has justice is able to exercise virtue in relation to another, not only in what concerns himself; for many are able to exercise virtue in their own concerns but unable in what relates to another.

And hence Bias seems to have been correct in saying that ruling will reveal the man, since a ruler is automatically related to another, and in a community. And for the same reason justice is the only virtue that seems to be another person's good,[4] because it is related to another; for it does what benefits another, either the ruler or the fellow-member of the community.

The worst person, therefore, is the one who exercises his vice toward himself and his friends as well <as toward others>. And the best person is not the one who exercises virtue <only> toward himself, but the one who <also> exercises it in relation to another, since this is a difficult task.

This type of justice, then, is the whole, not a part, of virtue, and the injustice contrary to it is the whole, not a part, of vice.

At the same time our discussion makes clear the difference

4. **another person's good**: See Plato, *Republic* 343c.

between virtue and this type of justice. For virtue is the same as justice, but what it is to be virtue is not the same as what it is to be justice. Rather, insofar as virtue is related to another, it is justice, and insofar as it is a certain sort of state without qualification, it is virtue.

2

But we are looking for the type of justice, since we say there is one, that consists in a part of virtue, and correspondingly for the type of injustice that is a part <of vice>.

Here is evidence that there is this type of justice and injustice:

First, if someone's activities express the other vices—if, for instance, cowardice made him throw away his shield, or irritability made him revile someone, or ungenerosity made him fail to help someone with money—what he does is unjust, but not greedy. But when one acts from greed, in many cases his action expresses none of these vices—certainly not all of them; but it still expresses some type of wickedness, since we blame him, and <in particular> it expresses injustice. Hence there is another type of injustice that is a part of the whole, and a way for a thing to be unjust that is a part of the whole that is contrary to law.

Moreover, if A commits adultery for profit and makes a profit, while B commits adultery because of his appetite, and spends money on it to his own loss, B seems intemperate rather than greedy, while A seems unjust, not intemperate. Clearly, then, this is because A acts to make a profit.

Further, we can refer every other unjust action to some vice—to intemperance if he committed adultery, to cowardice if he deserted his comrade in the battle-line, to anger if he struck someone. But if he made an <unjust> profit, we can refer it to no other vice except injustice.

Hence evidently (a) there is another type of injustice, special injustice, apart from the whole of injustice; and (b) it is synony-
1130b mous with the whole, since the definition is in the same genus. For (b) both have their area of competence in relation to another. But (a) special injustice is concerned with honor or wealth or safety, or whatever single name will include all these, and aims at the pleasure that results from making a profit; but the concern of injustice as a whole is whatever concerns the excellent person.

Clearly, then, there is more than one type of justice, and there is another type apart from <the type that is> the whole of virtue; but we must still grasp what it is, and what sort of thing it is.

What is unjust is divided into what is lawless and what is unfair, and what is just into what is lawful and what is fair. The <general> injustice previously described, then, is concerned with what is lawless. But what is unfair is not the same as what is lawless, but related to it as part to whole, since whatever is unfair is lawless, but not everything lawless is unfair. Hence also the type of injustice and the way for a thing to be unjust <that expresses unfairness> are not the same as the type <that exprsses lawlessness>, but differ as parts from wholes. For this injustice <as unfairness> is a part of the whole of injustice, and similarly justice <as fairness> is a part of the whole of justice.

Hence we must describe special <as well as general> justice and injustice, and equally this way for a thing to be just or unjust.

Let us, then, set to one side the type of justice and injustice that corresponds to the whole of virtue, justice being the exercise of the whole of virtue, and injustice of the whole of vice, in relation to another.

And it is evident how we must distinguish the way for a thing to be just or unjust that expresses this type of justice and injustice; for the majority of lawful actions, we might say, are the actions resulting from virtue as a whole. For the law instructs us to express each virtue, and forbids us to express each vice, in how we live. Moreover, the actions producing the whole of virtue are the lawful actions that the laws prescribe for education promoting the common good.

We must wait till later,[5] however, to determine whether the education that makes an individual an unqualifiedly good man is a task for political science or for another science; for, presumably, being a good man is not the same as being every sort of good citizen.[6]

Special justice, however, and the corresponding way for something to be just <must be divided>.

One species is found in the distribution of honors or wealth or anything else that can be divided among members of a community who share in a political system; for here it is possible for one member to have a share equal or unequal to another's.

5. **later**: See x 9, *Pol.* vii.
6. **for, presumably . . . good citizen**: See *Pol.* iii 4.

1131a Another species concerns rectification in transactions. This species has two parts, since one sort of transaction is voluntary, and one involuntary. Voluntary transactions include selling, buying, lending, pledging, renting, depositing, hiring out—these are called voluntary because the principle of these transactions is voluntary. Some involuntary ones are secret, such as theft, adultery, poisoning, pimping, slave-deception, murder by treachery, false witness; others are forcible, such as assault, imprisonment, murder, plunder, mutilation, slander, insult.

* * * * * * *

7

1134b18 One part of what is politically just is natural, and the other part legal.[7] What is natural is what has the same validity everywhere alike, independent of its seeming so or not. What is legal is what originally makes no difference <whether it is done> one way or another, but makes a difference whenever people have laid down the rule—that a mina is the price of a ransom, for instance, or that a goat rather than two sheep should be sacrificed; and also laws passed for particular cases—that sacrifices should be offered to Brasidas,[8] for instance; and enactments by decree.

Now it seems to some people that everything just is merely legal, since what is natural is unchangeable and equally valid everywhere—fire, for instance, burns both here and in Persia—while they see that what is just changes <from city to city>.

This is not so, though in a way it is so. With us, though presumably not at all with the gods, there is such a thing as what is natural, but still all is changeable; despite the change there is such a thing as what is natural and what is not.

What sort of thing that <is changeable and hence> admits of being otherwise is natural, and what sort is not natural, but legal and conventional, if both natural and legal are changeable?

7. **One part . . . other part legal**: On LAW (here related to convention) and NATURE cf. 1094b16.

8. **Brasidas**: A Spartan general who after his death received sacrifices in Amphipolis as a liberator. His cult was a strictly local observance initiated by decree.

It is clear in other cases also, and the same distinction <between the natural and the unchangeable> will apply; for the right hand, for instance, is naturally superior, even though it is possible for everyone to become ambidextrous.

The sorts of things that are just by convention and expediency are like measures. For measures for wine and for corn are not of equal size everywhere, but in wholesale markets they are bigger, and in retail smaller. Similarly, the things that are just by human <enactment> and not by nature differ from place to place, since political systems also differ; still, only one system is by nature the best everywhere.

* * * * * * *

Book VI

[*VIRTUES OF THOUGHT*]

1

Since we have said previously that we must choose the intermediate condition, not the excess or the deficiency, and that the intermediate condition is as correct reason says, let us now determine this <i.e., what it says>.[1]

For in all the states of character we have mentioned, as well as in the others, there is a target which the person who has reason focuses on and so tightens or relaxes; and there is a definition of the means, which we say are between excess and deficiency because they express correct reason.

To say this is admittedly true, but it is not at all clear. For in other pursuits directed by a science it is equally true that we must labor and be idle neither too much nor too little, but the intermediate amount prescribed by correct reason. But knowing only this, we would be none the wiser about, for instance, the medicines to be applied to the body, if we were told we must

1. **let us . . . it says>**: Cf. 1103b21, 1107a1.

apply the ones that medical science prescribes and in the way that the medical scientist applies them.

Similarly, then, our account of the states of the soul must not only be true up to this point; we must also determine what correct reason is, i.e., what its definition is.

After we divided the virtues of the soul we said that some are 1139a virtues of character and some of thought. And so, having finished our discussion of the virtues of character, let us now discuss the others as follows, after speaking first about the soul.

Previously, then, we said there are two parts of the soul, one that has reason, and one nonrational. Now we should divide in the same way the part that has reason.

Let us assume there are two parts that have reason: one with which we study beings whose principles do not admit of being otherwise than they are, and one with which we study beings whose principles admit of being otherwise. For when the beings are of different kinds, the parts of the soul naturally suited to each of them are also of different kinds, since the parts possess knowledge$_g$ by being somehow similar and appropriate <to their objects>.

Let us call one of these the scientific part, and the other the rationally calculating part, since deliberating is the same as rationally calculating, and no one deliberates about what cannot be otherwise. Hence the rationally calculating part is one part of the part of the soul that has reason.

Hence we should find the best state of the scientific and the best state of the rationally calculating part; for this state is the virtue of each of them. And since something's virtue is relative to its own proper function[2] <we must consider the function of each part>.

2

There are three <capacities> in the soul—perception, understanding, desire—that control action and truth. Of these three perception clearly originates no action, since beasts have perception, but no share in action.

As assertion and denial are to thought, so pursuit and avoidance are to desire. Now virtue of character is a state that decides;

2. **function**: See 1106a15.

and decision is a deliberative desire. If, then, the decision is excellent, the reason must be true and the desire correct, so that what reason asserts is what desire pursues.

This, then, is thought and truth concerned with action. By contrast, when thought is concerned with study, not with action or production, its good or bad state consists <simply> in being true or false. For truth is the function of whatever thinks; but the function of what thinks about action is truth agreeing with correct desire.

Now the principle of an action—the source of motion, not the action's goal—is decision, and the principle of decision is desire together with reason that aims at some goal. Hence decision requires understanding and thought, and also a state of character, since doing well or badly in action requires both thought and character.

Thought by itself, however, moves nothing; what moves us is thought aiming at some goal and concerned with action. For this is the sort of thought that also originates productive thinking; for every producer in his production aims at some <further> goal, and the goal without qualification is not the product, which is only the <conditional> goal of some <production>, and aims at some <further> goal. <A goal without qualification is> what we achieve in *action*, since doing well in action is the goal.

Now desire is for the goal. Hence decision is either understanding combined with desire or desire combined with thought; and what originates movement in this way is a human being.

We do not decide to do what is already past; no one decides, e.g., to have sacked Troy. For neither do we deliberate about what is past, but only about what will be and admits <of being or not being>; and what is past does not admit of not having happened. Hence Agathon is correct to say 'Of this alone even a god is deprived—to make what is all done to have never happened.'

Hence the function of each of the understanding parts is truth; and so the virtue of each part will be the state that makes that part grasp the truth most of all.

* * * * * * *

5

To grasp what intelligence is we should first study the sort of people we call intelligent.

It seems proper, then, to an intelligent person to be able to deliberate finely about what is good and beneficial for himself, not about some restricted area—about what promotes health or strength, for instance—but about what promotes living well in general.

A sign of this is the fact that we call people intelligent about some <restricted area> whenever they calculate well to promote some excellent end, in an area where there is no craft. Hence where <living well> as a whole is concerned, the deliberative person will also be intelligent.

Now no one deliberates about what cannot be otherwise or about what cannot be achieved by his action. Hence, if science involves demonstration, but there is no demonstration of anything whose principles admit of being otherwise, since every such thing itself admits of being otherwise; and if we cannot deliberate about what is by necessity; it follows that intelligence is not science nor yet craft-knowledge. It is not science, because what is done in action admits of being otherwise; and it is not craft-knowledge, because action and production belong to different kinds.

The remaining possibility, then, is that intelligence is a state grasping the truth, involving reason, concerned with action about what is good or bad for a human being.

For production has its end beyond it; but action does not, since its end is doing well itself, <and doing well is the concern of intelligence>.

Hence Pericles and such people are the ones whom we regard as intelligent, because they are able to study what is good for themselves and for human beings; and we think that household managers and politicians are such people.

This is also how we come to give temperance (*sophrosune*) its name, because we think that it preserves intelligence, (*sozousan ten phronesin*). This is the sort of supposition that it preserves. For the sort of supposition that is corrupted and perverted by what is pleasant or painful is not every sort—not, for instance, the supposition that the triangle does or does not have two right angles—but suppositions about what is done in action.

For the principle of what is done in action is the goal it aims at; and if pleasure or pain has corrupted someone, it follows that the principle will not appear to him. Hence it will not be apparent that this must be the goal and cause of all his choice and action; for vice corrupts the principle.

Hence <since intelligence is what temperance preserves, and what temperance preserves is a true supposition about action>, intelligence must be a state grasping the truth, involving reason, and concerned with action about human goods.

Moreover, there is virtue <or vice in the use> of craft, but not <in the use> of intelligence. Further, in a craft, someone who makes errors voluntarily is more choiceworthy; but with intelligence, as with the virtues, the reverse is true. Clearly, then, intelligence is a virtue, not craft-knowledge.

There are two parts of the soul that have reason. Intelligence is a virtue of one of them, of the part that has belief; for belief is concerned, as intelligence is, with what admits of being otherwise.

Moreover, it is not only a state involving reason. A sign of this is the fact that such a state can be forgotten, but intelligence cannot.

* * * * * * *

8

Political science and intelligence are the same state, but their being is not the same. 1141b23

One part of intelligence about the city is the ruling part; this is legislative science.

The part concerned with particulars <often> monopolizes the name 'political science' that <properly> applies to both parts in common. This part is concerned with action and deliberation, since <it is concerned with decrees and> the decree is to be acted on as the last thing <reached in deliberation>. Hence these people are the only ones who are said to be politically active; for these are the only ones who practice <politics> in the way that handcraftsmen practice <their craft>.

Now likewise intelligence concerned with the individual himself seems most of all to be counted as intelligence; and this <part of intelligence often> monopolizes the name 'intelligence' that

<properly> applies <to all parts> in common. Of the other parts one is household science, another legislative, another political, one part of which is deliberative and another judicial.

In fact knowledge$_o$ of what is <good> for oneself is one species <of intelligence>. But there is much difference <in opinions> about it.

1142a Someone who knows about himself, and spends his time on his own concerns, seems to be intelligent, while politicians seem to be too active. Hence Euripides says, 'Surely I cannot be intelligent, when I could have been inactive, numbered among all the many in the army, and have had an equal share. . . . For those who go too far and are too active. . . .'

For people seek what is good for themselves, and suppose that this <inactivity> is the action required <to achieve their good>. Hence this belief has led to the view that these are the intelligent people.

Presumably, however, one's own welfare requires household management and a political system.

Moreover, <another reason for the difference of opinion is this>: it is unclear, and should be examined, how one must manage one's own affairs.

A sign of what has been said <about the unclarity of what intelligence requires> is the fact that whereas young people become accomplished in geometry and mathematics, and wise within these limits, intelligent young people do not seem to be found. The reason is that intelligence is concerned with particulars as well as universals, and particulars become known$_g$ from experience, but a young person lacks experience, since some length of time is needed to produce it.

Indeed <to understand the difficulty and importance of experience> we might consider why a boy can become accomplished in mathematics, but not in wisdom or natural science. Surely it is because mathematical objects are reached through abstraction, whereas the principles in these other cases are reached from experience. Young people, then, <lacking experience>, have no real conviction in these other sciences, but only say the words, whereas the nature of mathematical objects is clear to them.

Moreover <intelligence is difficult because it is deliberative and> deliberation may be in error about either the universal or the particular. For <we may wrongly suppose> either that all sorts of heavy water are bad or that this water is heavy.

Intelligence is evidently not scientific knowledge; for, as we 25
said, it concerns the last thing <i.e., the particular>, since this is what is done in action. Hence it is opposed to understanding. For understanding is about the <first> terms, <those> that have no account of them; but intelligence is about the last thing, an object of perception, not of scientific knowledge.

This is not the perception of proper objects,[3] but the sort by which we perceive that the last among mathematical objects is a
triangle; for it will stop here too. This is another species <of 30
perception than perception of proper objects>; but it is still perception more than intelligence is.

* * * * * * *

12

Someone might, however, be puzzled about what use they 1143b18
<—wisdom and intelligence—> are.

For wisdom is not concerned with any sort of coming into 20
being, and hence will not study any source of human happiness.

Admittedly intelligence will study this; but what do we need 25
it for?

For knowledge$_{o}$ of what is healthy or fit—i.e., of what results 26
from the state of health, not of what produces it—makes us no
readier to act appropriately if we are already healthy; for having 27
the science of medicine or gymnastics makes us no readier to act 21
appropriately. Similarly, intelligence is the science of what is just and what is fine, and what is good for a human being; but this
is how the good man acts; and if we are already good, knowledge 25
of them makes us no readier to act appropriately, since virtues are states <activated in actions>.

If we concede that intelligence is not useful for this, should 28
we say it is useful for becoming good? In that case it will be no 30
use to those who are already excellent. Nor, however, will it be any use to those who are not. For it will not matter to them whether they have it themselves or take the advice of others who have it. The advice of others will be quite adequate for us, just

3. **proper objects**: See *DA* ii 6.

as it is with health: we wish to be healthy, but still do not learn medical science.

Besides, it would seem absurd for intelligence, inferior as it is to wisdom, to control it <as a superior. But this will be the result>, since the science that produces also rules and prescribes about its product.

We must discuss these questions; for so far we have only gone through the puzzles about them.

First of all, let us state that both intelligence and wisdom must be choiceworthy in themselves, even if neither produces anything at all; for each is the virtue of one of the two <rational> parts <of the soul>.

Second, they do produce something. Wisdom produces happiness, not in the way that medical science produces health, but in the way that health produces <health>. For since wisdom is a part of virtue as a whole, it makes us happy because it is a state that we possess and activate.

Further, we fulfill our function insofar as we have intelligence and virtue of character; for virtue makes the goal correct, and intelligence makes what promotes the goal <correct>. The fourth part of the soul, the nutritive part, has no such virtue <related to our function>, since no action is up to it to do or not to do.

To answer the claim that intelligence will make us no readier to do fine and just actions, we must begin from a little further back <in our discussion>.

Here is where we begin. We say that some people who do just actions are not yet thereby just, if, for instance, they do the actions prescribed by the laws, either unwillingly or because of ignorance or because of some other end, not because of the actions themselves, even though they do the right actions, those that the excellent person ought to do. Equally, however, it would seem to be possible for someone to do each type of action in the state that makes him a good person, i.e., because of decision and for the sake of the actions themselves.[4]

Now virtue makes the decision correct; but the actions that are naturally to be done to fulfill the decision are the concern not of virtue, but of another capacity. We must get to know$_{o}$ them more clearly before continuing our discussion.

There is a capacity, called cleverness, which is such as to be

4. **because of . . . themselves**: See 1105a32.

able to do the actions that tend to promote whatever goal is assumed and to achieve it. If, then, the goal is fine, cleverness is praiseworthy, and if the goal is base, cleverness is unscrupulousness; hence both intelligent and unscrupulous people are called clever.

Intelligence is not the same as this capacity <of cleverness>, though it requires it. Intelligence, this eye of the soul, cannot reach its fully developed state without virtue, as we have said and as is clear. For inferences about actions have a principle, 'Since the end and the best good is this sort of thing', whatever it actually is—let it be any old thing for the sake of argument. And this <best good> is apparent only to the good person; for vice perverts us and produces false views about the principles of actions.

Evidently, then, we cannot be intelligent without being good. 1144b

13

We must, then, also examine virtue over again. For virtue is similar <in this way> to intelligence; as intelligence is related to cleverness, not the same but similar, so natural virtue is related to full virtue.

For each of us seems to possess his type of character to some extent by nature, since we are just, brave, prone to temperance, or have another feature, immediately from birth. However, we still search for some other condition as full goodness, and expect to possess these features in another way.

For these natural states belong to children and to beasts as well <as to adults>, but without understanding they are evidently harmful. At any rate, this much would seem to be clear: just as a heavy body moving around unable to see suffers a heavy fall because it has no sight, so it is with virtue. <A naturally well-endowed person without understanding will harm himself.> But if someone acquires understanding, he improves in his actions; and the state he now has, though still similar <to the natural one>, will be virtue to the full extent.

And so, just as there are two sorts of conditions, cleverness and intelligence, in the part of the soul that has belief, so also there are two in the part that has character, natural virtue and full virtue. And of these full virtue cannot be acquired without intelligence.

This is why some say that all the virtues are <instances of> intelligence, and why Socrates' inquiries were in one way correct, and in another way in error. For in that he thought all the virtues are <instances of> intelligence, he was in error; but in that he thought they all require intelligence, he was right.

Here is a sign of this: Whenever people now define virtue, they all say what state it is and what it is related to, and then add that it is the state that expresses correct reason. Now correct reason is reason that expresses intelligence; it would seem, then, that they all in a way intuitively believe that the state expressing intelligence is virtue.

But we must make a slight change. For it is not merely the state expressing correct reason, but the state involving correct reason, that is virtue. And it is intelligence that is correct reason in this area. Socrates, then, thought that the virtues are <instances of> reason because he thought they are all <instances of> knowledge$_e$, whereas we think they involve reason.

What we have said, then, makes it clear that we cannot be fully good without intelligence, or intelligent without virtue of character.

In this way we can also solve the dialectical argument that someone might use to show that the virtues are separated from each other. For, <it is argued>, since the same person is not naturally best suited for all the virtues, someone will already have one virtue before he has got another.

This is indeed possible with the natural virtues. It is not possible, however, with the <full> virtues that someone must have to be called good without qualification; for as soon as he has intelligence, which is a single state, he has all the virtues as well.

And clearly, even if intelligence were useless in action, we would need it because it is the virtue of this part of the soul, and because the decision will not be correct without intelligence or without virtue. For virtue makes us reach the end in our action, while intelligence makes us reach what promotes the end.

Moreover, intelligence does not control wisdom or the better part of the soul, just as medical science does not control health. For it does not use health, but only aims to bring health into being; hence it prescribes for the sake of health, but does not prescribe to health. Besides, <saying that intelligence controls wisdom> would be like saying that political science rules the gods because it prescribes about everything in the city.

Book VII

[*CONTINENCE AND INCONTINENCE*]

1

* * * * * * *

We must now discuss incontinence, softness and self-indulgence, and also continence and resistance; for we must not suppose that continence and incontinence are concerned with the same states as virtue and vice, or that they belong to a different kind.

As in the other cases we must set out the appearances, and first of all go through the puzzles. In this way we must prove the common beliefs about these ways of being affected—ideally, all the common beliefs, but if not all, then most of them, and the most important. For if the objections are solved, and the common beliefs are left, it will be an adequate proof.[1]

Continence and resistance seem to be good and praiseworthy conditions, while incontinence and softness seem to be base and blameworthy conditions.

The continent person seems to be the same as one who abides by his rational calculation; and the incontinent person seems to be the same as one who abandons it.

The incontinent person knows$_o$ that his actions are base, but does them because of his feelings, while the continent person knows that his appetites are base, but because of reason does not follow them.

People think the temperate person is continent and resistant. Some think that every continent and resistant person is temperate, while others do not. Some people say the incontinent person is intemperate and the intemperate incontinent, with no distinction; others say they are different.

Sometime it is said that an intelligent person cannot be incontinent; but sometimes it is said that some people are intelligent and clever, but still incontinent.

1. **As in the other . . . adequate proof**: Aristotle describes DIALECTICAL method.

Further, people are called incontinent about emotion, honor and gain.

These, then, are the things that are said.

2

We might be puzzled about the sort of correct supposition someone has when he acts incontinently.

First of all, some say he cannot have knowledge$_e$ <at the time he acts>. For it would be terrible, Socrates[2] thought, for knowledge to be in someone, but mastered by something else, and dragged around like a slave. For Socrates fought against the account <of incontinence> in general, in the belief that there is no incontinence; for no one, he thought, supposes while he acts that his action conflicts with what is best; our action conflicts with what is best only because we are ignorant <of the conflict>.

This argument, then, contradicts things that appear manifestly. If ignorance causes the incontinent person to be affected as he is, then we must look for the type of ignorance that it turns out to be; for it is evident, at any rate, that before he is affected the person who acts incontinently does not think <he should do the action he eventually does>.

Some people concede some of <Socrates' points>, but reject some of them. For they agree that nothing is superior to knowledge, but deny that no one's action conflicts with what has seemed better to him. Hence they say that when the incontinent person is overcome by pleasure he has only belief, not knowledge.

In that case, however, if he has belief, not knowledge, and what resists is not a strong supposition, but only a mild one, such as people have when they are in doubt, we will pardon failure to abide by these beliefs against strong appetites. In fact, however, we do not pardon vice, or any other blameworthy condition <and incontinence is one of these>.

Then is it intelligence that resists, since it is the strongest? This is absurd. For on this view the same person will be both intelligent and incontinent; and no one would say that the intelligent person is the sort to do the worst actions willingly.

Besides, we have shown earlier that the intelligent person acts

2. **Socrates**: See Plato, *Protagoras* 352–7.

<on his knowledge>, since he is concerned with the last things, <i.e., particulars>, and that he has the other virtues.

Further, if the continent person must have strong and base appetites, the temperate person will not be continent nor the continent person temperate. For the temperate person is not the sort to have either excessive or base appetites; but <the continent person> must have both.

For if his appetites are good, the state that prevents him from following them must be base, so that not all continence is excellent. If, on the other hand, the appetites are weak and not base, continence is nothing impressive; and if they are base and weak, it is nothing great.

Besides, if continence makes someone prone to abide by every belief, it is bad, if, for instance, it makes him abide by a false as well <as true> belief.

And if incontinence makes someone prone to abandon every belief, there will be an excellent type of incontinence. Neoptolemus, for instance, in Sophocles' *Philoctetes* is praiseworthy when, after being persuaded by Odysseus, he does not abide by his resolve, because he feels pain at lying.

Besides, the sophistical argument is a puzzle. For <the sophists> wish to refute an <opponent, by showing> that his views have paradoxical results, so that they will be clever in encounters. Hence the inference that results is a puzzle; for thought is tied up, since it does not want to stand still because the conclusion is displeasing, but it cannot advance because it cannot solve the argument.

A certain argument, then, concludes that foolishness combined with incontinence is virtue. For incontinence makes someone act contrary to what he supposes <is right>; but since he supposes that good things are bad and that it is wrong to do them, he will do the good actions, not the bad.

Further, someone who acts to pursue what is pleasant because this is what he is persuaded and decides[3] to do, seems to be better than someone who acts not because of rational calculation, but because of incontinence.

For the first person is the easier to cure, because he might be persuaded otherwise; but the incontinent person illustrates the proverb 'If water chokes us, what must we drink to wash it down?' *1146b*

3. **decides**: This is the intemperate person.

For if he had been persuaded to do the action he does, he would have stopped when he was persuaded to act otherwise; but in fact, though already persuaded to act otherwise, he still acts <wrongly>.

Further, is there incontinence and continence about everything? If so, who is simply incontinent? For no one has all the types of incontinence, but we say that some people are simply incontinent.

These, then, are the sorts of puzzles that arise. We must undermine some of these claims, and leave others intact; for the solution of the puzzle is the discovery <of what we are seeking>.

3

First, then, we must examine whether the incontinent has knowledge$_o$ or not, and in what way he has it. Second, what should we take to be the incontinent and the continent person's area of concern—every pleasure and pain, or some definite subclass? Are the continent and the resistant person the same or different? Similarly we must deal with the other questions that are relevant to this study.

We begin the examination with this question: Are the continent and the incontinent person distinguished <from others> (i) by their concerns, or (ii) by their attitudes to them? In other words, is the incontinent person incontinent (i) only by having these concerns, or instead (ii) by having this attitude: or instead (iii) by both? Next, is there continence and incontinence about everything, or not?

<Surely (iii) is right.> For <(i) is insufficient> since the simple incontinent is not concerned with everything, but with the same things as the intemperate person. Moreover, <(ii) is insufficient> since he is not incontinent simply by being inclined toward these things—that would make incontinence the same as intemperance. Rather <as (iii) implies>, he is incontinent by being inclined toward them in this way. For the intemperate person acts on decision when he is led on, since he thinks it is right in every case to pursue the pleasant thing at hand; but the incontinent person thinks it is wrong to pursue it, yet still pursues it.

It is claimed that the incontinent person's action conflicts with the true belief, not with knowledge$_e$. But whether it is knowledge or belief that he has does not matter for this argument. For some people with belief are in no doubt, but think they have exact knowledge$_o$.

If, then, it is the weakness of their conviction that makes people with belief, not people with knowledge$_e$, act in conflict with their supposition, it follows that knowledge will <for these purposes> be no different from belief; for, as Heracleitus makes clear, some people's convictions about what they believe are no weaker than other people's convictions about what they know.

But we speak of knowing in two ways, and ascribe it both to someone who has it without using it and to someone who is using it. Hence it will matter whether someone has the knowledge that his action is wrong, without attending to his knowledge, or both has and attends to it. For this second case seems extraordinary, but wrong action when he does not attend to his knowledge does not seem extraordinary.

Besides, since there are two types of premisses, someone's action may well conflict with his knowledge if he has both types of premisses, but uses only the universal premiss and not the particular premiss. For <the particular premiss states the particulars and> it is particular actions that are done.

Moreover, <in both types of premisses> there are different types of universal, (a) one type referring to the agent himself, and (b) the other referring to the object. Perhaps, for instance, someone knows that (a1) dry things benefit every human being, and that (a2) he himself is a human being, or that (b1) this sort of thing is dry; but he either does not have or does not activate the knowledge that (b2) this particular thing is of this sort.

Hence these ways <of knowing and not knowing> make such a remarkable difference that it seems quite intelligible <for someone acting against his knowledge> to have the one sort of knowledge$_o$ <i.e., without (b2)>, but astounding if he has the other sort <including (b2)>.

Besides, human beings may have knowledge$_e$ in a way different from those we have described. For we see that having without using includes different types of having; hence in some people, such as those asleep or mad or drunk, both have knowledge in a way and do not have it.

Moreover, this is the condition of those affected by strong feelings. For emotions, sexual appetites and some conditions of this sort clearly <both disturb knowledge and> disturb the body as well, and even produce fits of madness in some people.

Clearly, then <since incontinents are also affected by strong feelings>, we should say that they have knowledge in a way similar to these people.

Saying the words that come from knowledge$_e$ is no sign <of fully having it>. For people affected in these ways even recite demonstrations and verses of Empedocles. Further, those who have just learned something do not yet know$_o$ it, though they string the words together; for it must grow into them, and this needs time.

Hence we must suppose that incontinents say the words in the way that actors do.

Further, we may also look at the cause in the following way, referring to <human> nature.[4] One belief (a) is universal; the other (b) is about particulars, and because they are particulars perception controls them. And in the cases where these two beliefs result in (c) one belief, it is necessary in purely theoretical beliefs for the soul to affirm what has been concluded, and in beliefs about production (d) to act at once on what has been concluded.

If, for instance, (a) everything sweet must be tasted, and (b) this, some one particular thing, is sweet, it is necessary (d) for someone who is able and unhindered also to act on this at the same time.

Suppose, then, that someone has (a) the universal belief, and it hinders him from tasting; he has (b) the second belief, that everything sweet is pleasant and this is sweet, and this belief (b) is active; and he also has appetite. Hence the belief (c) tells him to avoid this, but appetite leads him on, since it is capable of moving each of the <bodily> parts.

1147b The result, then, is that in a way reason and belief make him act incontinently. The belief (b) is contrary to correct reason (a), but only coincidentally, not in itself. For it is the appetite, not the belief, that is contrary <in itself to correct reason>.

Hence beasts are not incontinent, because they have no universal supposition, but <only> appearance and memory of particulars.

How is the ignorance resolved, so that the incontinent person

4. **nature**: Aristotle discusses the question from a natural (i.e., specific to psychology, not merely LOGICAL) point of view, referring to the structure of practical inference; cf. *DA* 431a15. The letters interpolated in the translation express some controversial decisions about interpretation.

recovers his knowledge$_e$? The same account that applies to someone drunk or asleep applies here too, and is not special to this way of being affected. We must hear it from the natural scientists.

And since the last premiss[5] (b) is a belief about something perceptible, and controls action, this must be what the incontinent person does not have when he is being affected. Or rather the way he has it is not knowledge of it, but, as we saw, <merely> saying the words, as the drunk says the words of Empedocles.

Further, since the last term does not seem to be universal, or expressive of knowledge in the same way as the universal term, even the result Socrates was looking for would seem to come about. For the knowledge that is present when someone is affected by incontinence, and that is dragged about because he is affected, is not the sort that seems to be knowledge to the full extent <in (c)>, but only perceptual knowledge <in (b)>.

So much, then, for knowing$_o$ and not knowing, and for how it is possible to know and still to act incontinently.

* * * * * * *

Book VIII

[*VARIETIES OF FRIENDSHIP*]

1

After that the next topic is friendship; for it is a virtue, or involves virtue, and besides is most necessary for our life. 1155a

For no one would choose to live without friends even if he had all the other goods. For in fact rich people and holders of powerful positions, even more than other people, seem to need friends. For how would one benefit from such prosperity if one had no opportunity for beneficence, which is most often displayed, and most highly praised, in relation to friends? And how would one guard and protect prosperity without friends, when

5. **premiss**: Or (less probably) 'proposition'—in which case (c) would be intended.

it is all the more precarious the greater it is? In poverty also, and in the other misfortunes, people think friends are the only refuge.

Moreover, the young need it to keep them from error. The old need it to care for them and support the actions that fail because of weakness. And those in their prime need it, to do fine actions; for 'when two go together . . .', they are more capable of understanding and acting.

Further, a parent would seem to have a natural friendship for a child, and a child for a parent, not only among human beings but also among birds and most kinds of animals. Members of the same race, and human beings most of all, have a natural friendship for each other; that is why we praise friends of humanity. And in our travels we can see how every human being is akin and beloved to a human being.

Moreover, friendship would seem to hold cities together, and legislators would seem to be more concerned about it than about justice. For concord would seem to be similar to friendship and they aim at concord among all, while they try above all to expel civil conflict, which is enmity.

Further, if people are friends, they have no need of justice, but if they are just they need friendship in addition; and the justice that is most just seems to belong to friendship.

However, friendship is not only necessary, but also fine. For we praise lovers of friends, and having many friends seems to be a fine thing. Moreover, people think that the same people are good and also friends.

Still, there are quite a few disputed points about friendship.

For some hold it is a sort of similarity and that similar people are friends. Hence the saying 'Similar to similar', and 'Birds of a feather', and so on. On the other hand it is said that similar people are all like the proverbial potters, quarreling with each other.

1155b On these questions some people inquire at a higher level, more proper to natural science. Euripides says that when earth gets dry it longs passionately for rain, and the holy heaven when filled with rain longs passionately to fall into the earth; and Heracleitus says that the opponent cooperates, the finest harmony arises from discordant elements, and all things come to be in struggle. Others, such as Empedocles, oppose this view, and say that similar aims for similar.

Let us, then, leave aside the puzzles proper to natural science, since they are not proper to the present examination; and let us examine the puzzles that concern human <nature>, and bear on characters and feelings.

For instance, does friendship arise among all sorts of people, or can people not be friends if they are vicious?

Is there one species of friendship, or are there more? Some people think there is only one species because friendship allows more and less. But here their confidence rests on an inadequate sign; for things of different species also allow more and less.

2

Perhaps these questions will become clear once we find out what it is that is lovable. For, it seems, not everything is loved, but <only> what is lovable, and this is either good or pleasant or useful. However, it seems that what is useful is the source of some good or some pleasure; hence what is good and what is pleasant are lovable as ends.

Do people love what is good, or what is good for them? For sometimes these conflict; and the same is true of what is pleasant. Each one, it seems, loves what is good for him; and while what is good is lovable without qualification, what is lovable for each one is what is good for him. In fact each one loves not what *is* good for him, but what *appears* good for him; but this will not matter, since <what appears good for him> will be what appears lovable.

Hence there are these three causes of love.

Love for a soulless thing is not called friendship, since there is no mutual loving, and you do not wish good to it. For it would presumably be ridiculous to wish good things to wine; the most you wish is its preservation so that you can have it. To a friend, however, it is said, you must wish goods for his own sake.

If you wish good things in this way, but the same wish is not returned by the other, you would be said to have <only> goodwill for the other. For friendship is said to be *reciprocated* goodwill.

But perhaps we should add that friends are aware of the reciprocated goodwill. For many a one has goodwill to people whom he has not seen but supposes to be decent or useful, and one of these might have the same goodwill toward him. These people, then, apparently have goodwill to each other, but how could we call them friends when they are unaware of their attitude to each other?

Hence, <to be friends> they must have goodwill[1] to each other, wish goods and be aware of it, from one of the causes mentioned above.

3

Now since these causes differ in species, so do the types of loving and types of friendship. Hence friendship has three species, corresponding to the three objects of love. For each object of love has a corresponding type of mutual loving, combined with awareness of it, and those who love each other wish goods to each other insofar as they love each other.

Those who love each other for utility love the other not in himself, but insofar as they gain some good for themselves from him. The same is true of those who love for pleasure; for they like a witty person not because of his character, but because he is pleasant to themselves.

And so those who love for utility or pleasure are fond of a friend because of what is good or pleasant for themselves, not insofar as the beloved is who he is, but insofar as he is useful or pleasant.

Hence these friendships as well <as the friends> are coincidental, since the beloved is loved not insofar as he is who he is, but insofar as he provides some good or pleasure.

And so these sorts of friendships are easily dissolved, when the friends do not remain similar <to what they were>; for if someone is no longer pleasant or useful, the other stops loving him.

What is useful does not remain the same, but is different at different times. Hence, when the cause of their being friends is removed, the friendship is dissolved too, on the assumption that the friendship aims at these <useful results>. This sort of friendship seems to arise especially among older people, since at that age they pursue what is advantageous, not what is pleasant, and also among those in their prime or youth who pursue what is expedient.

Nor do such people live together very much. For sometimes they do not even find each other pleasant. Hence they have no

1. **goodwill**: The definition of goodwill implies that in all friendships A must wish good for B for B's sake. Contrast 1156a10.

further need to meet in this way if they are not advantageous <to each other>; for each finds the other pleasant <only> to the extent that he expects some good from him. The friendship of hosts and guests[2] is taken to be of this type too.

The cause of friendship between young people seems to be pleasure. For their lives are guided by their feelings, and they pursue above all what is pleasant for themselves and what is near at hand. But as they grow up <what they find> pleasant changes too. Hence they are quick to become friends, and quick to stop; for their friendship shifts with <what they find> pleasant, and the change in such pleasure is quick. Young people are prone to erotic passion, since this mostly follows feelings, and is caused by pleasure; that is why they love and quickly stop, often changing in a single day.

These people wish to spend their days together and to live together; for this is how they gain <the good things> corresponding to their friendship.

But complete friendship is the friendship of good people similar in virtue; for they wish goods in the same way to each other insofar as they are good, and they are good in themselves. <Hence they wish goods to each other for each other's own sake.> Now those who wish goods to their friend for the friend's own sake are friends most of all; for they have this attitude because of the friend himself, not coincidentally. Hence these people's friendship lasts as long as they are good; and virtue is enduring.

Each of them is both good without qualification and good for his friend, since good people are both good without qualification and advantageous for each other. They are pleasant in the same ways too, since good people are pleasant both without qualification and for each other. <They are pleasant for each other> because each person finds his own actions and actions of that kind pleasant, and the actions of good people are the same or similar.

It is reasonable that this sort of friendship is enduring, since it embraces in itself all the features that friends must have. For the cause of every friendship is good or pleasure, either unqualified or

2. **of hosts and guests**: *xenikē*. If A is an Athenian and B is a Spartan, each is the *xenos* of the other if A provides B with hospitality in Athens and B does the same for A in Sparta, and they provide each other with other sorts of reciprocal mutual aid.

for the lover; and every friendship reflects some similarity. And all the features we have mentioned are found in this friendship because of <the nature of> the friends themselves. For they are similar in this way <i.e., in being good>. Moreover, their friendship also has the other things—what is good without qualification and what is pleasant without qualification; and these are lovable most of all. Hence loving and friendship are found most of all and at their best in these friends.

These kinds of friendships are likely to be rare, since such people are few. Moreover, they need time to grow accustomed to each other; for, as the proverb says, they cannot know$_o$ each other before they have shared the traditional <peck of> salt, and they cannot accept each other or be friends until each appears lovable to the other and gains the other's confidence. Those who are quick to treat each other in friendly ways wish to be friends, but are not friends, unless they are also lovable, and know this. For though the wish for friendship comes quickly, friendship does not.

Book IX

* * * * * * *

[THE SOURCES AND JUSTIFICATION OF FRIENDSHIP]

8

There is also a puzzle about whether one ought to love oneself or someone else most of all; for those who like themselves most are criticized and denounced as self-lovers, as though this were something shameful.

Indeed, the base person does seem to go to every length for his own sake, and all the more the more vicious he is; hence he is accused, for instance, of doing nothing of his own accord. The decent person, on the contrary, acts for what is fine, all the more the better he is, and for his friend's sake, disregarding his own good.

The facts, however, conflict with these claims, and that is 1168b not unreasonable.

For it is said that we must love most the friend who is most a friend; and one person is most a friend to another if he wishes goods to the other for the other's sake, even if no one will know$_{o}$ about it. But these are features most of all of one's relation to oneself; and so too are all the other defining features of a friend, since we have said that all the features of friendship extend from oneself to others.

All the proverbs agree with this too, speaking, for instance, of 'one soul', 'what friends have is common', 'equality is friendship' and 'the knee is closer than the shin'. For all these are true most of all in someone's relations with himself, since one is a friend to himself most of all. Hence he should also love himself most of all.

It is not surprising that there is a puzzle about which view we ought to follow, since both inspire some confidence; hence we must presumably divide these sorts of arguments, and distinguish how far and in what ways those on each side are true.

Perhaps, then, it will become clear, if we grasp how those on each side understand self-love.

Those who make self-love a matter for reproach ascribe it to those who award the biggest share in money, honors and bodily pleasures to themselves. For these are the goods desired and eagerly pursued by the many on the assumption that they are best; and hence they are also contested.[1]

Those who are greedy for these goods gratify their appetites and in general their feelings and the nonrational part of the soul; and since this is the character of the many, the application of the term <'self-love'> is derived from the most frequent <kind of self-love>, which is base. This type of self-lover, then, is justifiably reproached.

And plainly it is the person who awards himself these goods whom the many habitually call a self-lover. For if someone is always eager to excel everyone in doing just or temperate

1. **contested**: Or 'fought over', i.e., the objects pursued in competition. See Plato, *Republic*. 586b–c.

actions or any others expressing the virtues, and in general always gains for himself what is fine, no one will call him a self-lover or blame him for it.

However, it is this more than the other sort of person who seems to be a self-lover. At any rate he awards himself what is finest and best of all, and gratifies the most controlling part of himself, obeying it in everything. And just as a city and every other composite system seems to be above all its most controlling part, the same is true of a human being;[2] hence someone loves himself most if he likes and gratifies this part.

Similarly, someone is called continent or incontinent because his understanding is or is not the master, on the assumption that this is what each person is. Moreover, his own voluntary actions seem above all to be those involving reason. Clearly, then, this, or this above all, is what each person is, and the decent person likes this most of all.

Hence he most of all is a self-lover, but a different kind from the self-lover who is reproached, differing from him as much as the life guided by reason differs from the life guided by feelings, and as much as the desire for what is fine differs from the desire for what seems advantageous.

Those who are unusually eager to do fine actions are welcomed and praised by everyone. And when everyone contends to achieve what is fine and strains to do the finest actions, everything that is right will be done for the common good, and each person individually will receive the greatest of goods, since that is the character of virtue.

Hence the good person must be a self-lover, since he will both help himself and benefit others by doing fine actions. But the vicious person must not love himself, since he will harm both himself and his neighbors by following his base feelings.

For the vicious person, then, the right actions conflict with those he does. The decent person, however, does the right actions, since every understanding chooses what is best for itself and the decent person obeys his understanding.

Besides, it is true that, as they say, the excellent person labors for his friends and for his native country, and will die

2. **And just . . . human being**: Cf. 1178a2. A complex system is most of all its most CONTROLLING (or important) part because this part represents the interests of the whole.

for them if he must; he will sacrifice money, honors and contested goods in general, in achieving what is fine for himself. For he will choose intense pleasure for a short time over mild pleasure for a long time; a year of living finely over many years of undistinguished life; and a single fine and great action over many small actions.

This is presumably true of one who dies for others; he does indeed choose something great and fine for himself. He is ready to sacrifice money as long as his friends profit; for the friends gain money, while he gains what is fine, and so he awards himself the greater good. He treats honors and offices the same way; for he will sacrifice them all for his friends, since this is fine and praiseworthy for him. It is not surprising, then, that he seems to be excellent, when he chooses what is fine at the cost of everything. It is also possible, however, to sacrifice actions to his friend, since it may be finer to be responsible for his friend's doing the action than to do it himself. In everything praiseworthy, then, the excellent person awards himself what is fine.

In this way, then, we must be self-lovers, as we have said. 1169b
But in the way the many are, we ought not to be.

9

There is also a dispute about whether the happy person will need friends or not.

For it is said that blessedly happy and self-sufficient people have no need of friends. For they already have <all> the goods, and hence, being self-sufficient, need nothing added. But your friend, since he is another yourself, supplies what your own efforts cannot supply. Hence it is said, 'When the god gives well, what need is there of friends?'

However, in awarding the happy person all the goods it would seem absurd not to give him friends; for having friends seems to be the greatest external good.

And it is more proper to a friend to confer benefits than to receive them, and proper to the good person and to virtue to do good; and it is finer to benefit friends than to benefit strangers. Hence the excellent person will need people for him to benefit. Indeed, that is why there is a question about whether friends are needed more in good fortune than in ill-fortune; for it is assumed that in ill-fortune we need people to benefit us, and in good fortune we need others for us to benefit.

Surely it is also absurd to make the blessed person solitary.[3] For no one would choose to have all <other> goods and yet be alone, since a human being is political, tending by nature to live together with others. This will also be true, then, of the happy person; for he has the natural goods, and clearly it is better to spend his days with decent friends than with strangers of just any character. Hence the happy person will need friends.

Then what are the other side saying, and in what way is it true? Surely they say what they say because the many think that it is the useful people who are friends. Certainly the blessedly happy person will have no need of these, since he has <all> goods. Similarly, he will have no need, or very little, of friends for pleasure; for since his life is pleasant, it has no need of imported pleasures. Since he does not need these sorts of friends, he does not seem to need friends at all.

However, this conclusion is presumably not true:

(1) For we said at the beginning that happiness is a kind of activity; and clearly activity comes into being, and does not belong <to someone all the time>, as a possession does. Being happy, then, is found in living and being active.

(2) The activity of the good person is excellent, and <hence> pleasant in itself, as we said at the beginning.

(3) Moreover, what is our own is pleasant.

(4) We are able to observe our neighbors more than ourselves, and to observe their actions more than our own.

1170a (5) Hence a good person finds pleasure in the actions of excellent people who are his friends, since these actions have both the naturally pleasant <features, i.e., they are good, and they are his own>.

(6) The blessed person decides to observe virtuous actions that are his own; and the actions of a virtuous friend are of this sort.

(7) Hence he will need virtuous friends.

3. **solitary**: See 1097b9.

Further, it is thought that the happy person must live pleasantly. But the solitary person's life is hard, since it is not easy for him to be continuously active all by himself; but in relation to others and in their company it is easier, and hence his activity will be more continuous. It is also pleasant in itself, as it must be in the blessedly happy person's case. For the excellent person, insofar as he is excellent, enjoys actions expressing virtue, and objects to actions caused by vice, just as the musician enjoys fine melodies and is pained by bad ones.

Further, good people's life together allows the cultivation of virtue, as Theognis says.

If we examine the question more from the point of view of <human> nature, an excellent friend would seem to be choiceworthy by nature for an excellent person.

(1) For, as we have said, what is good by nature is good and pleasant in itself for an excellent person.

(2) For animals life is defined by the capacity for perception; for human beings it is defined by the capacity for perception of understanding.

(3) Every capacity refers to an activity, and a thing is present to its full extent in its activity.

(4) Hence living to its full extent would seem to be perceiving or understanding.

(5) Life is good and pleasant in itself. For it has definite order, which is proper to the nature of what is good.

(6) What is good by nature is also good for the decent person. That is why life would seem to be pleasant for everyone. Here, however, we must not consider a life that is vicious and corrupted, or filled with pains; for such a life lacks definite order, just as its proper features do. (The truth about pain will be more evident in what follows.)

(7) Life itself, then, is good and pleasant. So it looks, at any rate, from the fact that everyone desires it, and decent and blessed people desire it more than others do; for their life is most choiceworthy for them, and their living is most blessed.

(8) Now someone who sees perceives that he sees; one who hears perceives that he hears; and one who walks perceives that he walks.

(9) Similarly in the other cases also there is some <element> that perceives that we are active.

(10) Hence, if we are perceiving, we perceive that we are perceiving; and if we are understanding, we perceive that we are understanding.

(11) Now perceiving that we are perceiving or understanding is the same as perceiving that we are, since we agreed <in (4)> that being is perceiving or understanding.

1170b (12) Perceiving that we are alive is pleasant in itself. For life is by nature a good <from (5)>, and it is pleasant to perceive that something good is present in us.

(13) And living is choiceworthy, for a good person most of all, since being is good and pleasant for him; for he is pleased to perceive something good in itself together <with his own being>.

(14) The excellent person is related to his friend in the same way as he is related to himself, since a friend is another himself.

(15) Therefore, just as his own being is choiceworthy for him, his friend's being is choiceworthy for him in the same or a similar way.

We agreed that someone's own being is choiceworthy because he perceives that he is good, and this sort of perception is pleasant in itself. He must, then, perceive his friend's being together <with his own>, and he will do this when they live together[4] and share conversation and thought. For in the case of human beings what seems to count as living together is this sharing of conversation and thought, not sharing the same pasture, as in the case of grazing animals.

If, then, for the blessedly happy person, being is choiceworthy, since it is naturally good and pleasant; and if the being of his friend is closely similar to his own; then his friend will also be choiceworthy. Whatever is choiceworthy for him he must possess, since otherwise he will to this extent lack something, <and hence will not be self-sufficient>.[5] Anyone who is to be happy, then, must have excellent friends.

* * * * * * *

4. **live together**: See 1095b30, 1097b9.
5. **Whatever . . . self-sufficient>**: Cf. 1097b6, 1097b16–20.

Book X

* * * * * * *

[*HAPPINESS AND INTELLECTUAL ACTIVITY*]

6

We have now finished our discussion of the types of virtue; of friendship; and of pleasure. It remains for us to discuss happiness in outline, since we take this to be the end of human <aims>. Our discussion will be shorter if we first take up again what we said before.

We said, then, that happiness is not a state.[1] For if it were, someone might have it and yet be asleep for his whole life, living the life of a plant, or suffer the greatest misfortunes. If we do not approve of this, we count happiness as an activity rather than a state, as we said before.

Some activities are necessary, i.e., choiceworthy for some other end, while others are choiceworthy in themselves. Clearly, then, we should count happiness as one of those activities that are choiceworthy in themselves, not as one of those choiceworthy for some other end. For happiness lacks nothing, but is self-sufficient; and an activity is choiceworthy in itself when nothing further beyond it is sought from it.

This seems to be the character of actions expressing virtue; for doing fine and excellent actions is choiceworthy for itself.

But pleasant amusements also <seem to be choiceworthy in themselves>. For they are not chosen for other ends, since they actually cause more harm than benefit, by causing neglect of our bodies and possessions.

Moreover, most of those people congratulated for their happiness resort to these sorts of pastimes. Hence people who are witty participants in them have a good reputation with tyrants, since they offer themselves as pleasant <partners> in the tyrant's aims, and these are the sort of people the tyrant requires. And so these amusements seem to have the character of happiness because people in supreme power spend their leisure in them.

1. **not a state**: See 1095b31.

However, these sorts of people are presumably no evidence. For virtue and understanding, the sources of excellent activities, do not depend on holding supreme power. Further, these powerful people have had no taste of pure and civilized pleasure, and so they resort to bodily pleasures. But that is no reason to think these pleasures are most choiceworthy, since boys also think that what they honor is best. Hence, just as different things appear honorable to boys and to men, it is reasonable that in the same way different things appear honorable to base and to decent people.

As we have often said, then, what is honorable and pleasant is what is so to the excellent person; and to each type of person the activity expressing his own proper state is most choiceworthy; hence the activity expressing virtue is most choiceworthy to the excellent person <and hence is most honorable and pleasant>.

Happiness, then, is not found in amusement; for it would be absurd if the end were amusement, and our lifelong efforts and sufferings aimed at amusing ourselves. For we choose practically everything for some other end—except for happiness, since it is <the> end; but serious work and toil aimed <only> at amusement appears stupid and excessively childish. Rather, it seems correct to amuse ourselves so that we can do something serious, as Anacharsis says; for amusement would seem to be relaxation, and it is because we cannot toil continuously that we require relaxation. Relaxation, then, is not <the> end, since we pursue it <to prepare> for activity.

Further, the happy life seems to be a life expressing virtue, which is a life involving serious actions, and not consisting in amusement.

Besides, we say that things to be taken seriously are better than funny things that provide amusement, and that in each case the activity of the better part and the better person is more serious and excellent; and the activity of what is better is superior, and thereby has more the character of happiness.

Moreover, anyone at all, even a slave, no less than the best person, might enjoy bodily pleasures; but no one would allow that a slave shares in happiness, if one does not <also allow that the slave shares in the sort of> life <needed for happiness>. Happiness, then, is found not in these pastimes, but in the activities expressing virtue, as we also said previously.

7

If happiness, then, is activity expressing virtue, it is reasonable for it to express the supreme virtue, which will be the virtue of the best thing.

The best is understanding, or whatever else seems to be the natural ruler and leader, and to understand what is fine and divine, by being itself either divine or the most divine element in us.

Hence complete happiness will be its activity expressing its proper virtue; and we have said that this activity is the activity of study. This seems to agree with what has been said before, and also with the truth.

For this activity is supreme, since understanding is the supreme element in us, and the objects of understanding are the supreme objects of knowledge$_g$.

Besides, it is the most continuous activity, since we are more capable of continuous study than any continuous action.

We think pleasure must be mixed into happiness; and it is agreed that the activity expressing wisdom is the pleasantest of the activities expressing virtue. At any rate, philosophy seems to have remarkably pure and firm pleasures; and it is reasonable for those who have knowledge$_o$ to spend their lives more pleasantly than those who seek it.

Moreover, the self-sufficiency we spoke of will be found in study above all.

For admittedly the wise person, the just person and the other virtuous people all need the good things necessary for life. Still, when these are adequately supplied, the just person needs other people as partners and recipients of his just actions; and the same is true of the temperate person and the brave person and each of the others.

But the wise person is able, and more able the wiser he is, to study even by himself; and though he presumably does it better 1177b
with colleagues, even so he is more self-sufficient than any other <virtuous person>.

Besides, study seems to be liked because of itself alone,[2] since it has no result beyond having studied. But from the virtues

2. **because of itself alone**: Cf. 1176b2. Less probably, 'it is the only virtue chosen because of itself'.

concerned with action we try to a greater or lesser extent to gain something beyond the action itself.

Happiness seems to be found in leisure, since we accept trouble so that we can be at leisure, and fight wars so that we can be at peace. Now the virtues concerned with action have their activities in politics or war, and actions here seem to require trouble.

This seems completely true for actions in war, since no one chooses to fight a war, and no one continues it, for the sake of fighting a war; for someone would have to be a complete murderer if he made his friends his enemies so that there could be battles and killings.

But the actions of the politician require trouble also. Beyond political activities themselves those actions seek positions of power and honors; or at least they seek happiness for the politician himself and for his fellow-citizens, which is something different from political science itself, and clearly is sought on the assumption that it is different.

Hence among actions expressing the virtues those in politics and war are pre-eminently fine and great; but they require trouble, aim at some <further> end, and are choiceworthy for something other than themselves.[3]

But the activity of understanding, it seems, is superior in excellence because it is the activity of study, aims at no end beyond itself and has its own proper pleasure, which increases the activity. Further, self-sufficiency, leisure, unwearied activity (as far as is possible for a human being), and any other features ascribed to the blessed person, are evidently features of this activity.

Hence a human being's complete happiness will be this activity, if it receives a complete span of life, since nothing incomplete is proper to happiness.

Such a life would be superior to the human level. For someone will live it not insofar as he is a human being, but insofar as he has some divine element in him. And the activity of this divine element is as much superior to the activity expressing the rest of virtue as this element is superior to the compound. Hence if understanding is something divine in comparison with a human being, so also will the life that expresses understanding be divine in comparison with human life.

3. **and are . . . themselves**: Less probably, 'and are not choiceworthy because of themselves'.

We ought not to follow the proverb-writers, and 'think human, since you are human', or 'think mortal, since you are mortal.' Rather, as far as we can, we ought to be pro-immortal,[4] and go to all lengths to live a life that expresses our supreme element; 1178a for however much this element may lack in bulk, by much more it surpasses everything in power and value.

Moreover, each person seems to be his understanding, if he is his controlling and better element; it would be absurd, then, if he were to choose not his own life, but something else's.

And what we have said previously will also apply now. For what is proper to each thing's nature is supremely best and pleasantest for it; and hence for a human being the life expressing understanding will be supremely best and pleasantest, if understanding above all is the human being. This life, then, will also be happiest.

8

The life expressing the other kind of virtue <i.e., the kind concerned with action> is <happiest> in a secondary way because the activities expressing this virtue are human.

For we do just and brave actions, and the others expressing the virtues, in relation to other people, by abiding by what fits each person in contracts, services, all types of actions, and also in feelings; and all these appear to be human conditions.

Indeed, some feelings actually seem to arise from the body; and in many ways virtue of character seems to be proper to feelings.

Besides, intelligence is yoked together with virtue of character, and so is this virtue with intelligence.[5] For the principles of intelligence express the virtues of character; and correctness in virtues of character expresses intelligence. And since these virtues are also connected to feelings, they are concerned with the compound. Since the virtues of the compound are human virtues, the life and the happiness expressing these virtues is also human.

The virtue of understanding, however, is separated <from the compound>. Let us say no more about it, since an exact account would be too large a task for our present project.

4. **to be pro-immortal**: Or 'to make ourselves immortal'.

5. **Besides . . . with intelligence**: See 1145a4.

Moreover, it seems to need external supplies very little, or <at any rate> less than virtue of character needs them. For grant that they both need necessary goods, and to the same extent, since there will be only a very small difference even though the politician labors more about the body and suchlike. Still, there will be a large difference in <what is needed> for the <proper> activities <of each type of virtue>.

For the generous person will need money for generous actions; and the just person will need it for paying debts, since wishes are not clear, and people who are not just pretend to wish to do justice. Similarly, the brave person will need enough power, and the temperate person will need freedom <to do intemperate actions>, if they are to achieve anything that the virtue requires. For how else will they, or any other virtuous people, make their virtue clear?

Moreover, it is disputed whether it is decision or actions that is more in control of virtue, on the assumption that virtue depends on both. Well, certainly it is clear that what is complete depends on both; but for actions many external goods are needed, and the greater and finer the actions the more numerous are the external goods needed.

But someone who is studying needs none of these goods, for that activity at least; indeed, for study at least, we might say they are even hindrances.

Insofar as he is a human being, however, and <hence> lives together with a number of other human beings, he chooses to do the actions expressing virtue. Hence he will need the sorts of external goods <that are needed for the virtues>, for living a human life.

In another way also it appears that complete happiness is some activity of study. For we traditionally suppose that the gods more than anyone are blessed and happy; but what sorts of actions ought we to ascribe to them? Just actions? Surely they will appear ridiculous making contracts, returning deposits and so on. Brave actions? Do they endure what <they find> frightening and endure dangers because it is fine? Generous actions? Whom will they give to? And surely it would be absurd for them to have currency or anything like that. What would their temperate actions be? Surely it is vulgar praise to say that they do not have base appetites. When we go through them all, anything that concerns actions appears trivial and unworthy of the gods.

However, we all traditionally suppose that they are alive and active, since surely they are not asleep like Endymion. Then if someone is alive, and action is excluded, and production even more, what is left but study? Hence the gods' activity that is superior in blessedness will be an activity of study. And so the human activity that is most akin to the gods' will, more than any others, have the character of happiness.

A sign of this is the fact that other animals have no share in happiness, being completely deprived of this activity of study. For the whole life of the gods is blessed, and human life is blessed to the extent that it has something resembling this sort of activity; but none of the other animals is happy, because none of them shares in study at all. Hence happiness extends just as far as study extends, and the more someone studies, the happier he is, not coincidentally but insofar as he studies, since study is valuable in itself. And so <on this argument> happiness will be some kind of study.

However, the happy person is a human being, and so will need external prosperity also; for his nature is not self-sufficient for study, but he needs a healthy body, and needs to have food and the other services provided.

Still, even though no one can be blessedly happy without external goods, we must not think that to be happy we will need many large goods. For self-sufficiency and action do not depend on excess, and we can do fine actions even if we do not rule earth and sea; for even from moderate resources we can do the actions expressing virtue. This is evident to see, since many private citizens seem to do decent actions no less than people in power do—even more, in fact. It is enough if moderate resources are provided; for the life of someone whose activity expresses virtue will be happy.

Solon surely described happy people well, when he said they had been moderately supplied with external goods, had done what he regarded as the finest actions, and had lived their lives temperately. For it is possible to have moderate possessions and still to do the right actions.

And Anaxagoras would seem to have supposed that the happy person was neither rich nor powerful, since he said he would not be surprised if the happy person appeared an absurd sort of person to the many. For the many judge by externals, since these are all they perceive.

Hence the beliefs of the wise would seem to accord with our arguments.

These considerations do indeed produce some confidence. The truth, however, in questions about action is judged from what we do and how we live, since these are what control <the answers to such questions>. Hence we ought to examine what has been said by applying it to what we do and how we live; and if it harmonizes with what we do, we should accept it, but if it conflicts we should count it <mere> words.

The person whose activity expresses understanding and who takes care of understanding would seem to be in the best condition, and most loved by the gods. For if the gods pay some attention to human beings, as they seem to, it would be reasonable for them to take pleasure in what is best and most akin to them, namely understanding; and reasonable for them to benefit in return those who most of all like and honor understanding, on the assumption that these people attend to what is beloved by the gods, and act correctly and finely.

Clearly, all this is true of the wise person more than anyone else; hence he is most loved by the gods. And it is likely that this same person will be happiest; hence the wise person will be happier than anyone else on this argument too.

[*ETHICS AND POLITICS*]

9

We have now said enough in outlines about happiness and the virtues, and about friendship and pleasure also. Should we then think that our decision <to study these> has achieved its end? On the contrary, the aim of studies about action, as we say, is surely not to study and know$_o$ about each thing, but rather to act on our knowledge. Hence knowing about virtue is not enough, but we must also try to possess and exercise virtue, or become good in any other way.

Now if arguments were sufficient by themselves to make people decent, the rewards they would command would justifiably have been many and large, as Theognis says, and rightly bestowed. In fact, however, arguments seem to have enough influence to stimulate and encourage the civilized ones among the young people, and perhaps to make virtue take possession of a well-born character that truly loves what is fine; but they seem unable to stimulate the many toward being fine and good.

For the many naturally obey fear, not shame; they avoid what is base because of the penalties, not because it is disgraceful. For since they live by their feelings, they pursue their proper pleasures and the sources of them, and avoid the opposed pains, and have not even a notion of what is fine and <hence> truly pleasant, since they have had no taste of it.

What argument could reform people like these? For it is impossible, or not easy, to alter by argument what has long been absorbed by habit; but, presumably, we should be satisfied to achieve some share in virtue when we already have what we seem to need to become decent.

Some think it is nature that makes people good; some think it is habit; some that it is teaching.

The <contribution> of nature clearly is not up to us, but results from some divine cause in those who have it, who are the truly fortunate ones.

Arguments and teaching surely do not influence everyone, but the soul of the student needs to have been prepared by habits for enjoying and hating finely, like ground that is to nourish seed. For someone whose life follows his feelings would not even listen to an argument turning him away, or comprehend it <if he did listen>; and in that state how could he be persuaded to change? And in general feelings seem to yield to force, not to argument.

Hence we must already in some way have a character suitable for virtue, fond of what is fine and objecting to what is shameful.

But it is hard for someone to be trained correctly for virtue from his youth if he has not been brought up under correct laws, since the many, especially the young, do not find it pleasant to live in a temperate and resistant way. Hence laws must prescribe their upbringing and practices; for they will not find these things painful when they get used to them.

Presumably, however, it is not enough to get the correct upbringing and attention when they are young; rather, they must continue the same practices and be habituated to them when they become men. Hence we need laws concerned with these things also, and in general with all of life. For the many yield to compulsion more than to argument, and to sanctions more than to what is fine.

This, some think, is why legislators should urge people toward virtue and exhort them to aim at what is fine, on the assumption that anyone whose good habits have prepared him decently will listen to them, but should impose corrective treatments and penalties on anyone who disobeys or lacks the right nature, and completely expel an incurable. For the decent person, it is assumed, will attend to reason because his life aims at what is fine, while the base person, since he desires pleasure, has to receive corrective treatment by pain, like a beast of burden; that is why it is said that the pains imposed must be those most contrary to the pleasures he likes.

As we have said, then, someone who is to be good must be finely brought up and habituated, and then must live in decent practices, doing nothing base either willingly or unwillingly. And this will be true if his life follows some sort of understanding and correct order that has influence over him.

A father's instructions, however, lack this influence and compelling power; and so in general do the instructions of an individual man, unless he is a king or someone like that. Law, however, has the power that compels; and law is reason that proceeds from a sort of intelligence and understanding. Besides, people become hostile to an individual human being who opposes their impulses even if he is correct in opposing them; whereas a law's prescription of what is decent is not burdensome.

And yet, only in Sparta, or in a few other cities as well, does the legislator seem to have attended to upbringing and practices. In most other cities they are neglected, and each individual citizen lives as he wishes, 'laying down the rules for his children and wife', like a Cyclops.

It is best, then, if the community attends to upbringing, and attends correctly. If, however, the community neglects it, it seems fitting for each individual to promote the virtue of his children and his friends—to be able to do it, or at least to decide to do it.

[*LEGISLATIVE SCIENCE*]

From what we have said, however, it seems he will be better able to do it if he acquires legislative science. For, clearly, attention
1180b by the community works through laws, and decent attention works through excellent laws; and whether the laws are written or unwritten, for the education of one or of many, seems unimportant, as it is in music, gymnastics and other practices. For just

as in cities the provisions of law and the <prevailing> types of character have influence, similarly a father's words and habits have influence, and all the more because of kinship and because of the benefits he does; for his children are already fond of him and naturally ready to obey.

Moreover, education adapted to an individual is actually better than a common education for everyone, just as individualized medical treatment is better. For though generally a feverish patient benefits from rest and starvation, presumably some patient does not; nor does the boxing instructor impose the same way of fighting on everyone. Hence it seems that treatment in particular cases is more exactly right when each person gets special attention, since he then more often gets the suitable treatment.

Nonetheless a doctor, a gymnastics trainer and everyone else will give the best individual attention if they also know$_{o}$ universally what is good for all, or for these sorts. For sciences are said to be, and are, of what is common <to many particular cases>.

Admittedly someone without scientific knowledge may well attend properly to a single person, if his experience has allowed him to take exact note of what happens in each case, just as some people seem to be their own best doctors, though unable to help anyone else at all. Nonetheless, presumably, it seems that someone who wants to be an expert in a craft and a branch of study should progress to the universal, and come to know$_{g}$ that, as far as possible; for that, as we have said, is what the sciences are about.

Then perhaps also someone who wishes to make people better by his attention, many people or few, should try to acquire legislative science, if we will become good through laws. For not just anyone can improve the condition of just anyone, or the person presented to him; but if anyone can it is the person with knowledge$_{o}$, just as in medical science and the others that require attention and intelligence.

Next, then, should we examine whence and how someone might acquire legislative science? Just as in other cases <we go to the practitioner>, should we go to the politicians? For, as we saw, legislative science seems to be a part of political science.

But is the case of political science perhaps apparently different from the other sciences and capacities? For evidently in others the same people, such as doctors or painters, who transmit the capacity to others actively practice it themselves. By contrast, it

1181a is the sophists who advertise that they teach politics but none of them practices it. Instead, those who practice it are the political activists, and they seem to act on some sort of capacity and experience rather than thought.

For evidently they neither write nor speak on such questions, though presumably it would be finer to do this than to compose speeches for the law courts or the Assembly; nor have they made politicians out of their own sons or any other friends of theirs. And yet it would be reasonable for them to do this if they were able; for there is nothing better than the political capacity that they could leave to their cities, and nothing better that they could decide to produce in themselves, or, therefore, in their closest friends.

Certainly experience would seem to contribute quite a lot; otherwise people would not have become better politicians by familiarity with politics. Hence those who aim to know$_{o}$ about political science would seem to need experience as well.

By contrast, those of the sophists who advertise <that they teach political science> appear to be a long way from teaching; for they are altogether ignorant about the sort of thing political science is, and the sorts of things it is about. For if they had known$_{o}$ what it is, they would not have taken it to be the same as rhetoric, or something inferior to it, or thought it an easy task to assemble the laws with good reputations and then legislate. For they think they can select the best laws, as though the selection itself did not require comprehension, and as though correct judgment were not the most important thing, as it is in music.

It is those with experience in each area who judge the products correctly and who comprehend the method or way of completing them, and what fits with what; for if we lack experience, we must be satisfied with noticing that the product is well or badly made, 1181b as with painting. Now laws would seem to be the products of political science; how, then, could someone acquire legislative science, or judge which laws are best, from laws alone? For neither do we appear to become experts in medicine by reading textbooks.

And yet doctors not only try to describe the <recognized> treatments, but also distinguish different <physical> states, and try to say how each type of patient might be cured and must be treated. And what they say seems to be useful to the experienced, though useless to the ignorant.

Similarly, then, collections of laws and political systems might also, presumably, be most useful if we are capable of studying them and of judging what is done finely or in the contrary way, and what sorts of <elements> fit with what. Those who lack the <proper> state <of experience> when they go through these collections will not manage to judge finely, unless they can do it all by themselves <without training>, though they might come to comprehend them better by going through them.

Since, then, our predecessors have left the area of legislation uncharted, it is presumably better to examine it ourselves instead, and indeed to examine political systems in general, and so to complete the philosophy of human affairs, as far as we are able.

First, then, let us try to review any sound remarks our predecessors have made on particular topics. Then let us study the collected political systems,[6] to see from them what sorts of things preserve and destroy cities, and political systems of different types; and what causes some cities to conduct politics well, and some badly.

For when we have studied these questions, we will perhaps grasp better what sort of political system is best; how each political system should be organized so as to be best; and what habits and laws it should follow.[7]

Let us discuss this, then, starting from the beginning.

6. **collected political systems**: Aristotle and his students collected 158 of them. Only one, the *Constitution of Athens*, largely survives.

7. **For when . . . should follow**: In this and the previous paragraph Aristotle outlines the *Pol.*, as the natural completion of the *EN*.

POLITICS

Book I

[*THE HUMAN GOOD AND THE POLITICAL COMMUNITY*]

1

We see that every city is some sort of community, and that every community is constituted for the sake of some good, since everyone does everything for the sake of what seems good.[1] Clearly, then, while all communities aim at some good, the community that aims most of all at the good—at the good that most of all controls all the other goods—is the one that most of all controls and includes the others; and this is the one called the city, the political community.

It is wrong, then, to suppose, as some do,[2] that the character of the politician, the king, the household manager, and the slave-master is the same. People suppose this because they think the difference is not a difference in kind, but only in the number who are ruled, so that the ruler of a few is a master, the ruler of more people is a household-manager, and the ruler of still more people is a politician or a king—on the assumption that a large household is no different from a small city. And all they can say to distinguish a king from a politician is that someone who directs things himself is a king, whereas someone who follows the principles of political science, ruling and being ruled in turn, is a politician. These views are not true.

What we mean will be clear if the investigation follows our recognized line of inquiry. Just as in other cases we must divide the composite into incomposites, since these are the smallest parts of the whole, so also in this case we must investigate the components of the city; for then we will also see better the difference between these rulers, and the prospect of finding any sort of scientific treatment of the questions we have mentioned.

1. **everyone . . . what seems good**: Cf. *EN* 1094a1–3, 1102a2–3.
2. **as some do**: See Plato, *Statesman* 259b.

2

The best way to study this as well as other matters is to trace things back to their beginnings and observe their growth. First, then, those who cannot exist without each other have to form pairs, as female and male do for reproduction. And they do this not because of any decision, but from the natural impulse that they share with other animals and with plants to leave behind another of the same kind as oneself.[3]

Self-preservation <rather than reproduction> is the basis of the natural division between ruler and subject. For the capacity for rational foresight makes one a natural ruler and natural master, and the capacity to execute this foresight by bodily labor makes another a subject and a natural slave; that is why the interests of master and slave coincide.

Now there is a natural distinction between the female and the 1252b
slave. For nature makes nothing stingily, like a smith making a Delphic knife,[4] but makes one thing for one function, since the best instrument for a particular function is made exclusively for it, not for many others. Among foreigners, however, female and slave have the same rank; the reason is that no foreigners are natural rulers, and so their community consists of a female slave and a male slave. Hence the poets say 'It is to be expected that Greeks rule over foreigners', assuming that the foreigner and the slave are naturally the same.

And so from these two communities <between female and male and between slave and master> the first community that results is the household. Hesiod was right when he said 'Get first of all a house, a wife, and a plough-ox'—for the poor use an ox in place of a slave. Hence the community naturally formed for every day is a household of 'breadbin-mates' (as Charondas calls them) or (as Epimenides the Cretan says) 'manger-mates'.

The first community formed from a number of households for long-term advantage is a village, and the most natural type of village would seem to be an extension of a household, including children and grandchildren, sometimes called 'milkmates'. That is why cities were also originally ruled by kings and some nations are ruled

3. **natural impulse . . . oneself**: Cf. *DA* 415a26.

4. **a Delphic knife**: made for several different tasks (like a Swiss Army knife).

by kings even at present; they were formed from communities ruled by kings—for in every household the oldest member rules as its king, and the same is true in its extensions, because the villagers are related by kinship. Homer describes this when he says 'Each rules over his children and wives', because they were isolated, as households were in ancient times. And for the same reason everyone says the gods are ruled by a king; it is because we were all ruled by kings in ancient times, and some still are, and human beings ascribe to the gods a human way of life, as well as a human form.

The complete community, formed from a number of villages, is a city. Unlike the others, it has the full degree of practically every sort of self-sufficiency; it comes to be for the sake of living, but remains in being for the sake of living well. That is why every city is natural, since the previous communities are natural. For the city is their end, and nature is an end; for we say that something's nature (for instance, of a human being, a horse, or a household) is the character it has when its coming to be is complete.[5] Moreover, the final
1253a cause and end is the best <good>, and self-sufficiency is both the end and the best <good>.

It is evident, then, that the city exists by nature, and that a human being is by nature a political animal. Anyone without a city because of his nature rather than his fortune is either worthless or superior to a human being. Like the man reviled by Homer, 'he has no kin, no law, no home'. For his natural isolation from a city gives him an appetite for war, since, like <a solitary piece> in a game of checkers, he has no partner.

It is evident why a human being is more of a political animal than is any bee or any gregarious animal; for nature, we say, does nothing pointlessly, and a human being is the only animal with rational discourse. A voice signifies pleasure and pain, and so the other animals, as well as human beings, have it, since their nature is far enough advanced for them to perceive pleasure and pain and to signify them to one another. But rational discourse is for making clear what is expedient or harmful, and hence what is just or unjust. For this is distinctive of human beings in contrast to the other animals, that they are the only ones with a perception of good and evil, and of just and unjust, and so on; and it is community in these that produces a household and a city.

Further, the city is naturally prior to the household and to the

5. **for we say . . . is complete**: Cf. *Phys.* 193b12n.

individual, since the whole is necessarily prior to the part. For if the whole animal is dead, neither foot nor hand will survive, except homonymously, as if we were speaking of a stone hand—for that is what a dead hand will be like. Now everything is defined by its function[6] and potentiality; and so anything that has lost them should not be called the same thing, but a homonymous thing.

Clearly, then, the city is also natural and is prior to the individual. For if the individual separated from the city is not self-sufficient, his relation to it corresponds to that of parts to wholes in other cases; and anyone who is incapable of membership in a community, or who has no need of it because he is self-sufficient, is no part of a city, and so is either a beast or a god.

Everyone has a natural impulse, then, toward this sort of community, and whoever first constituted it is the cause of the greatest goods. For just as a human being is the best of the animals if he has been completed, he is also the worst of them if he is separated from law and the rule of justice. For injustice is most formidable when it is armed, and a human being naturally grows up armed and equipped for intelligence and virtue, but can most readily use this equipment for ends that are contrary to intelligence and virtue;[7] hence without virtue he is the most unscrupulous and savage of animals, the most excessive in pursuit of sex and food. Justice, however, is political; for the rule of justice is an order in the political community, and justice is the judgment of what is just.

* * * * * * *

BOOK II

[*CRITICISMS OF PROPOSALS FOR IDEAL STATES*][1]

1

Our decision is to study the best political community for those 1260b27
who are capable of living, as far as possible, in the conditions they would aspire to live in; hence we must also investigate

6. **everything . . . function**: Cf. *EN* 1097b24.
7. **contrary . . . virtue**: Cf. *EN* 1103a23–6, 1144b1–14.
1. The extracts from Bk ii come from the criticism of Plato's *Republic*.

the political systems that are found in cities said to be well governed, and also any systems other people have proposed that seem well conceived. Our aim is to see what the correct condition is for a city and what is useful, and also to show that, in searching for something different from these systems, we are not behaving like people who want above all to play the sophist, but are undertaking this line of inquiry in response to the inadequacies of current systems.

* * * * * * *

2

The proposal that all <the rulers'> women should be shared[2] raises many objections. In particular Socrates' arguments do not make it apparent why he thinks this legislation is needed. Moreover, the end he prescribes for the city is impossible, taken literally, and he has not explained how else we should take it. I refer to Socrates' assumption that it is best if all the city is as unified as possible. It is evident, on the contrary, that as the city goes further and further in the direction of unity, it will finally not even be a city. For a city is by nature a mass of people; as it becomes more and more unified, first the city will turn into a household, and then the household will turn into just one person—for we would say that a household is more unified than a city, and one person more unified than a household. And so, even if someone were capable of completely unifying a city, he should not do it, since he would destroy the city.

Besides, a city is composed, not merely of a number of human beings, but of those different in kind—for similar people do not constitute a city. For a city is different from an alliance; for since an alliance naturally aims at assistance, the added quantity, even of something the same in kind, makes the ally useful (like a weight that pulls a balance down further). A city differs in the same way from a nation that is not scattered in

2. **The proposal . . . shared**: Plato, *Republic* 457d.

separate villages but <is all together>, as the Arcadians[3] are. <In contrast to these cases,> the parts from which a unity[4] comes to be must differ in kind.

This is why reciprocal equality preserves a city, as we said before in the *Ethics*.[5] Even free and equal people need this, since they cannot all rule at the same time, but must rule for a year, or some other fixed length of time. Such an arrangement ensures that they all rule—just as if cobblers and carpenters were to change occupations, and the same people were not cobblers or carpenters all the time. Since <the normal practice in the crafts> is also better in the political community, it is clearly better if the same people are, if possible, always rulers.
But in some circumstances this is not possible, because all are 1261b
naturally equal, and moreover it is just for all to take part in ruling—whether it is a benefit or a burden. This arrangement—where equals yield office to each other in turn and are similar when they are not holding office—at least imitates <the practice of the crafts>; some rule and others are ruled, taking turns, as though they had become other people. In the same way, among the rulers themselves, different ones rule in different ruling offices.

It is evident, then, from what we have said, that a city is not naturally unified in the way that some claim it is and that the unity alleged to be the greatest good for cities in fact destroys them, whereas a thing's good preserves it.

It is evident in another way too that attempts at excessive unification do not benefit a city. For a household is more self-sufficient than an individual person is; and a community of a mass of people counts as a city only if it proves to be self-sufficient. Since, then, what is more self-sufficient is more choiceworthy, what is less unified is <in this case> more choiceworthy than what is more unified.

3

But even if it is indeed best if the community is as unified as possible, <Socrates'> argument does not seem to demonstrate

3. **Arcadians**: Their villages formed a federation, not a *polis*.
4. **a unity**: Cf. *Met*. 1040b5–16.
5. ***Ethics***: 1132b33.

that this will be the effect of agreement in saying 'mine' and 'not mine'[6]—though Socrates regards this agreement as a sign of the city's being completely unified.

For 'all' is said in two ways. If all, taken each one at a time, <speak of what is 'mine'>, then perhaps the <unity> that Socrates wants to produce would be more likely to result; for each one will call the same person his own son, and the same person his own wife, and will speak in the same way of property, and whatever else he has. In fact, however, those who share wives and children will not speak in this way. They will, all together, not each taken one at a time, regard <wives and children as theirs>; and similarly, all together, not each taken one at a time, will regard property <as theirs>. Evidently, then, speaking of 'all' is a fallacious inference;[7] for 'all', 'both', 'odd', and 'even' also produce contentious deductions in discussions, because they are spoken of in these two ways. Hence if all say the same thing, the result is in one case fine, but not possible, and in the other case contributes nothing to concord.

Besides this, the proposal mentioned involves a further harm. For what is common to the largest number of people gets least attention, since people think most about what is private to them and think less about what is common, or else think about what is common only to the extent that it applies to each of them. They care less about it because, in addition to other reasons, they assume that someone else is thinking about it—as in household service many attendants sometimes serve worse than a few. <In Socrates' city> each citizen will have a thousand sons, but not as sons of each taken one at a time; any given son will be the son of this father no more than of any other, and so all the fathers alike will care little about them.

* * * * * * *

6. **agreement . . . 'not mine'**: See Plato, *Rep.* 462c.

7. **fallacious inference**: The fallacy Aristotle has in mind is illustrated by the difference between: (a) If all ('taken each one at a time') are human beings, each is a human being; and (b) If all ('all together') fill an airplane, each fills an airplane.

4

And in general the results of this sort of law <eliminating private property> are bound to be contrary to the results to be expected from correctly established laws, and contrary to Socrates' aim in prescribing these arrangements about children and women. For we think friendship is the greatest good for cities, since it best prevents civil conflict in them;[8] indeed Socrates himself praises the unity of the city more than anything else, and, like other people, he takes unity to be the result of friendship. In the same way, as we know, in the discussions of erotic love,[9] Aristophanes says that erotic lovers love so intensely that they long to grow together and make one person out of two. But whereas this union requires the perishing of one or both of the lovers, sharing of wives and children will merely make friendship in the city watery, and it will be least true that a father speaks of 'my son' or a son of 'my father'. For just as a little of something sweet mixed into a lot of water makes the mixture imperceptible, the same is true of the mutual closeness resulting from these names <'father' and 'son'>, since this sort of political system is the least likely to ensure that a father is especially concerned for his son, or a son for his father, or one brother for another. For the two most important sources of care and friendship among human beings are the fact that something is one's own and the fact that one likes it; neither can be true of those living under such a political system. 1262b3

* * * * * * *

5

These, then, and others like them, are the disagreeable results of common ownership. The present arrangement would be far better, if it were improved by good habits and ordered by correct laws. For in that case it would have the advantages of both arrangements, i.e., of common and of private ownership. 1263a21

8. **For we . . . in them**: Cf. *EN* 1155a22–8.
9. **erotic love**: See Plato, *Symposium* 192de.

For ownership ought to be common in a way, but basically private; if different people attend to different things, no mutual accusations result, and they will together contribute more, since each person keeps his mind on his own proper concerns. On the other hand, virtue will make friends' possessions common (as the proverb says) for their use.

Even now there are traces of this arrangement in outline in some cities, suggesting that it is not impossible, and, especially in well-managed cities, some aspects are already there, and others might arise. For while each has his own possessions, he offers his own for his friends to use and uses <his friends'> possessions as common possessions. In Sparta, for instance, they use one another's slaves practically as their own and do the same with horses and dogs and with the fields around the countryside, if they need food for a journey.

Evidently, then, it is better if we own possessions privately, but make them common by our use of them. And it is the legislator's proper task to see that the right sort of people develop.

Further, it is unbelievably more pleasant to regard something
1263b as one's own. For each person's love of himself[10] is not pointless, but a natural tendency. Certainly, selfishness is quite rightly blamed; but selfishness is not love of oneself, but excessive self-love. The same distinction applies to love of money, since practically everyone loves himself and loves money. Moreover, the pleasantest thing is to please or to help our friends or guests or companions, and we can do this when ownership is private.

These, then, are the results for those who unify the city excessively. Moreover, they evidently remove any function for two virtues—temperance toward women (since it is a fine action to refrain because of temperance from a woman who is someone else's wife) and generosity with our possessions (since no one's generosity will be evident, and no one will do any generous action—for generosity has its function in the use of possessions).

* * * * * * *

10. **love of himself**: See *EN* 1168a22–b10.

Book III

[*CITIZENSHIP AND THE CITY*][1]

1

In investigating a political system and asking what, and of what sort, each system is, our first question should be to ask what the city is. For as things are, this is disputed; some assert that the city has done some action, while others assert that it was not the city, but the oligarchy or the tyrant that did it. Moreover, we see that the politician's and the legislator's whole concern is with the city, and that the political system is a particular sort of ordering of those who live in the city.

Since the city is a composite, and we must proceed as we do with other wholes that are constituted of many parts, it is clear that we must first of all inquire into the citizen, since a city is a particular sort of mass of citizens. And so we should examine who ought to be called a citizen and who the citizen is. For in fact there is often dispute about the citizen as well <as about the city>, since not everyone agrees that the same person is a citizen; someone who is a citizen in a democracy is often not a citizen in an oligarchy.

We should omit those who acquire the title of citizen in some other way <than by birth>—those who are created citizens, for instance. Someone is not a citizen if he simply lives in a particular place; for resident aliens and slaves live in the same place <as the citizens, but are not citizens>. Nor is someone a citizen if he simply shares in the judicial system to the extent of claiming justice and submitting to it; for this is also true of those who share judicial arrangements by treaty. (In many cities, indeed, resident aliens do not share fully in the judicial system, but must find a representative <to take up their case>, so that their share in this sort of community is in a way incomplete.)

1. In Bk iii Aristotle turns to his own constructive theory, beginning with questions about who is appropriately a member of the political association.

What we say about these cases is similar to what we say about boys who are not yet of an age to be enrolled and about old men who have been released <from active participation>. For we say that these are citizens in a way, but not without qualification; we add the qualification that boys are incomplete citizens and that the old men are citizens past the proper age, or something like that (it does not matter exactly what we say, since what we mean is clear). For we are inquiring about those who are citizens without qualification, in such a way that their claim admits of no ground for objection needing to be rectified. Similar puzzles and solutions apply to the dishonored and to exiles.

A citizen without qualification is defined, above all, as one who shares in judging and ruling. Some types of rule are limited in time, so that some ruling offices can never be held by the same person twice or can be held again only after a specified interval. Another type of ruler, however, is indefinite <in time>—for instance, the juryman or the assemblyman. Now, perhaps someone might say that these people are not rulers at all and that these functions do not count as sharing in ruling. Surely, however, it is ridiculous to deny that those with the most complete control are rulers. Still, we need not suppose that this matters; it is simply an argument about a name, since the common feature applying to the juryman and the assemblyman has no name. And so, to make clear the distinction, let us call it indefinite rule. We take it, then, that those who share in ruling on these terms are citizens.

This, then, is more or less the definition of citizen that best fits all those called citizens. We must notice, however, that in cases where the subjects <of a property F> differ in species, and one is the primary F, another secondary, and so on in order, their common feature, insofar as they are F, is nothing, or only slight. Now, we see that political systems differ in species and that some

1275b are prior and some posterior, since the erroneous and deviant systems must be posterior to the correct ones (the meaning of 'deviant systems' will be clarified later); and so a different type of citizen must also correspond to each political system.

That is why the citizen fitting our definition is a citizen in a democracy more than in the other systems, and in the other systems the citizen may <have these functions>, but need not have them. For some systems have no popular body, or recognized assembly <of all the people>, but only convocations <of selected members>, and different judicial cases are decided by different select bodies. (In Sparta, for instance, different types of cases arising from treaties are decided by a different Overseer, cases of homicide by the Elders, and other cases presumably by some other ruling official. The same is true in Carthage, where ruling officials judge all the cases.[2])

Our way of distinguishing a citizen can still be corrected.[3] In the nondemocratic political systems the assemblyman or juryman exercises a definite, not an indefinite, rule; for either all or some of these are assigned the task of deliberating and sitting on juries, either on all questions or on some. From this, then, it is clear who the citizen is; if it is open to someone to share in deliberative and judicial rule, we say he is thereby a citizen of this sort of city; and a city (to speak without qualification) is the collection of such people that is adequate for self-sufficient life.

* * * * * * *

4

The next question to be examined among those we have just mentioned is whether or not we must take the virtue of a good man and of an excellent citizen to be the same or different. And if we must search for this, we must first grasp in some rough outline the virtue of a citizen.

Well, then, we say that a citizen, like a sailor, is one of a number of associates. Now, sailors are dissimilar in their capacities—for one is an oarsman, one a pilot, one a lookout, and another has some other name—and clearly the most exact account of each one's virtue will be special to him, but similarly some common account will also fit them all, since the function of them all is to secure a safe voyage, and that is what each sailor aims at. Similarly, then, the function of citizens, despite their dissimilarity, is to secure the safety of the community; the political system is the community; hence the virtue of the citizen must be relative to the political system.

If, then, there are several species of political system, there

2. **In Sparta . . . judge all the cases**: Aristotle contrasts these cases with the practice in Athens, where nearly all legal cases came before popular jury-courts.

3. **corrected**: to fit the cases mentioned in the previous paragraph.

clearly cannot be one virtue—complete virtue—of the excellent citizen. The good man, by contrast, is good precisely insofar as he has one virtue—complete virtue. Evidently, then, someone can be an excellent citizen without having the virtue that makes someone an excellent man.

Moreover, we can raise a further puzzle in approaching the same discussion about the best political system. If a city cannot be composed entirely of excellent men, still each must perform his own function well, and this requires virtue; and since the citizens cannot all be similar, the virtue of a citizen cannot be the same as that of a good man. For all must have the virtue of the excellent citizen, since that is needed if the city is to be best; but they cannot all have the virtue of the good man, if the citizens in the excellent city cannot all be good men.

Further, a city is constituted of dissimilar people, just as an animal is necessarily constituted of soul and body, a soul is constituted of reason and desire, a household is constituted of husband and wife, and possession is constituted of master and slave. A city is constituted of all of these, and moreover of different kinds of people; and so the citizens cannot all have the same virtue, any more than the chorus-leader and an ordinary member of the chorus can have the same virtue.

This makes it evident why <the virtue of an excellent man and of an excellent citizen> are not the same without qualification. But will the virtue of one type of excellent citizen be the same as the virtue of an excellent man? We say that an excellent ruler is good and intelligent, but that a citizen need not be intelligent, so that (in some people's view) a ruler should have a different type of education (just as we see the sons of kings educated in horsemanship and warfare, and Euripides[4] says, 'For me none of these subtleties . . . but what the city needs', on the assumption that there is a type of education proper to a ruler).

Now, if the virtue of a good ruler and of a good man are the same, and both the ruler and the ruled are citizens, it follows that the virtue of a man is not the same without qualification as the virtue of a citizen but is the same as the virtue of a certain kind of citizen <—a ruler>; for the virtue of a ruler is not the same as the virtue of a citizen, and presumably that is why Jason said he

4. **Euripides**: in a lost tragedy. Cf. Plato, *Gorg*. 485e–486a.

was starving when he was not tyrant, suggesting that he did not know how to be a private citizen.

And yet someone is praised for being able both to rule and to be ruled, and the virtue of an estimable citizen seems to be the ability both to rule and to be ruled finely. If, then, we take the good man's virtue to be a virtue in ruling, and the citizen's virtue to be both <in ruling and being ruled>, the two abilities cannot be praiseworthy in the same way. Since, then, they seem to be different in some cases, and it seems that the ruler and the ruled must learn different things, while the citizen must know and share in both ruling and being ruled, we may see what follows from that.

One type of rule is a master's rule over slaves. We say that this is concerned with necessities; the ruler needs the knowledge of how to use these, not the knowledge of how to produce them, which would actually be slavish—I mean the ability to perform the actions of a servant. We speak of several types of slaves, since there are several types of work. One type of work belongs to manual workers; as the name itself indicates, these are the ones who live by the work of their hands, and they include the menial 1277b
craftsmen. That is why some cities gave the manual workers no share in ruling offices, before the extreme type of democracy arose. Hence neither the good politician nor the good citizen must learn the functions of people who are ruled in this way, unless he needs them for himself (for then it no longer involves a master and a slave).

However, there is a type of rule that is exercised over people who are free and similar in kind <to the ruler>; this is called political rule. A ruler must learn this type of rule by being ruled himself—for instance, he must be ruled by a cavalry officer to learn to rule as a cavalry officer, and ruled by a general or troop-leader or squadron-leader to learn to rule in these positions. Hence this is also a sound maxim, that you cannot rule well until you have been ruled. These virtues of ruler and ruled are different, but the good citizen must have the knowledge and ability both to be ruled and to rule; and the virtue of a citizen is this knowledge of rule over free people, from both points of view.

Hence the good man has both virtues, even if the ruler has a different kind of temperance and justice. For, clearly, if a good person is ruled, but is a free citizen, his virtue—justice, for instance—is not of only one kind, but includes one kind for ruling and another for being ruled. Similarly, a man and a woman have different kinds of temperance and bravery—for a man would seem cowardly if he were <only> as brave as a brave woman, and a woman would seem talkative if she were <only> as restrained as the good man is; and similarly household management is different for a man and a woman, since it is the man's task to acquire the goods and the woman's task to preserve them. Intelligence is the only virtue that is distinctive of the ruler; for all the others, it would seem, must be common to rulers and ruled, but true belief, not intelligence, is the virtue of the ruled, since they correspond to flute-makers, whereas the rulers correspond to flute-players who use the flutes.[5]

From this, then, it is evident whether the virtue of the good man and of the excellent citizen are the same or different, and in what ways they are the same, and in what ways different.

* * * * * * *

9

1280a7 First, we must understand the received formulae of oligarchy and democracy, and the oligarchic and democratic <views of> justice; for everyone touches on some sort of justice, but they make only limited progress and do not describe the whole of what is fully just. Justice seems to be equality, for instance, and indeed it is—but for equals, not for everyone. Again, inequality seems to be just; and so it is—but for unequals, not for everyone. But these <partisans of each view> omit this part—equality or inequality for whom—and so make the wrong judgment. The reason is that they are giving judgment in their own case, and most people are practically always bad judges in their own cases.

Justice is justice *for* certain people, and the division in the things <to be distributed> corresponds to the division in those to whom <they are distributed>, as we have said before in the *Ethics*.[6] Hence all sides agree about the equal amount of the thing <to be distributed> but dispute about who should receive it. They do this mainly for the reason we have just given, that people are bad

5. **use the flutes**: The user knows what the flute should be like. Cf. Plato, *Rep*. 601de.

6. ***Ethics***: 1131a14–24.

judges in their own cases, but also because each side makes some progress in describing a sort of justice and so thinks it describes unqualified justice. For <supporters of oligarchy> think that if they are unequal in some aspects—wealth, for instance—they are altogether unequal, whereas <supporters of democracy> think that if they are equal in some aspect—free status, for instance—they are altogether equal.

But they fail to mention the most important aspect. For if people combined and formed a <political> community in order to acquire possessions, then someone's share in the city would correspond to his possessions, and the supporters of oligarchy would seem to have a strong argument; for, they say, if A has contributed one out of 100 minas and B has contributed the other 99, it is not just for A to get the same return as B, either of the original sum or of any later profits.

In fact, however, the <political> community does not aim simply at staying alive, but aims predominantly at a good life. For if it aimed simply at staying alive, then slaves and nonhuman animals would be members of a city, whereas in fact they are not, since they do not participate in happiness or in a life guided by decision.

Nor does the city aim at an alliance, to prevent anyone from doing injustice to anyone; or at exchange and dealings between its members. For if this were the aim, then the Etruscans and the Carthaginians—and any other peoples related by treaty—would all count as citizens of a single city; at any rate, these have made conventions about imports, treaties to prohibit doing injustice, and written articles of alliance. These peoples, however, have no common government, but each has its own government. 1280b Moreover, neither people is concerned about the right character to form in the citizens of the other city, or about how to remove injustice or any other vice from the other city that is bound by the agreements; each is concerned only to prevent the other city from doing injustice to it. By contrast, those who are concerned with good government consider the virtues and vices of citizens.

Hence it is evident that whatever is correctly called a city, not just for the sake of argument, must be concerned with virtue. For <otherwise> the community turns out to be <merely> an alliance, differing only in the proximity of its members from the other alliances with more distant members. In that case law turns out to be an agreement and, as Lycophron the sophist said, a mutual guarantor of just treatment, but unable to make the citizens good and just.

To make it evident that we are right, suppose that we actually joined the territories <of two allied states>, so that the cities of the Megarians and the Corinthians had their walls adjacent; even so, they would not be one single city, even if their citizens intermarried—though that is one sort of community that is distinctive of a city. Similarly, suppose people lived apart, though not too far to prevent community, but had laws prohibiting unjust treatment in exchanges (if, for instance, one was a carpenter, another a farmer, another a cobbler, and so on), and there were ten thousand of them, but their community extended no further than such matters as commerce and alliance; that would still not be enough to make a city.

Why is this? Surely it is not because their community is scattered. For if they even lived closer together but in the same sort of community, each treating his own household as a city, and they formed a purely defensive alliance against unjust actions—even so, an exact study would not count this as a city, if their intercourse when they live closer together is no different from what it was when they lived apart.

Evidently, then, a city is not a community for living in the same place, for preventing the unjust treatment of one member by another, and for exchange. All these are necessary conditions for a city, but their presence does not make a city. Rather, the city is a community for living well for both households and families, aiming at a complete and self-sufficient life (but this requires them to live in the same place and to intermarry). That is why kinship-groups, brotherhoods, religious societies, and pursuits that involve living together have developed in cities; these are the product of friendship, since the decision to live together is friendship.

The end of a city, then, is living well, and these <pursuits> are for the sake of the end. A city is the community of families and villages in a complete and self-sufficient life. This sort of life, as we say, is a happy and fine life; hence we should suppose that a city aims at fine actions, not <merely> at living together.[7]

That is why someone who contributes most to this sort of community has a greater share in the city than that of someone who is

7. **living together**: This is used in a narrower sense (excluding the pursuit of fine actions and living well) than in the previous paragraph referring to friendship (where it included these pursuits).

equal or superior in free status or in family, but unequal in a citizen's virtue, and a greater share than that of someone who excels in wealth but is excelled in virtue.

It is evident, then, from what we have said that each of the parties disputing about political systems is describing a part of justice.

* * * * * * *

11

Most of these puzzles must be postponed to another discussion. 1281a39
But it seems that the claim that the masses rather than the few best people must be in control is generally accepted, and it seems that, though it raises a puzzle, it perhaps contains some truth.

For even though each one among the many is not an excellent 1281b
man, still it is possible that when they combine they are collectively, though not individually,[8] better than the few best people, just as a dinner provided by many people's contributions is better than one provided at an individual's expense; for (on this view) they are many, and each has some part of virtue and intelligence, so that when they combine, the masses become like one human being, with many feet, many hands, and many senses, and similarly for characters and for intellect. That is why the many are also better judges of the products of music and of poets; different individuals are better judges of different parts, and all of them together are better judges of the whole.[9]

Indeed it is this <combination of qualities> that makes an excellent man better than an ordinary individual among the many, just as it (supposedly) makes handsome people more handsome than plain people and makes a statue more handsome than the real things; for <in the statue> the dispersed features are gathered together in one figure, even though, taken separately, this person's eye and some other part of someone else might be more handsome than <the corresponding parts of> the statue.

Now, it is not clear whether this claim about the superiority

8. **collectively . . . individually**: Cf. 1261b27.

9. **That is why . . . the whole**: In Athens the prizes for the three best tragedies and comedies in the annual festivals were awarded by a panel chosen by lot.

of the many over the few excellent ones could be true of every sort of common people and every sort of mass of people. Indeed, presumably, there are some of which it cannot be true; for if it were true of them, it would also be true of beasts; and indeed there are some who are practically no better than beasts. But the claim may still be true for masses of a certain sort.

Hence we can use this argument to solve the previous puzzle, and the next one—which things should be controlled by the free citizens and the mass of the citizens, those who have neither wealth nor any other claim to reputation for virtue? For it is not safe for them to share in the highest ruling offices, since an unjust character is bound to cause unjust actions, and lack of intelligence is bound to cause errors. On the other hand, if they are given nothing and have no share, that is dangerous; for any city that holds many poor people in dishonor is bound to be full of enemies.

The remaining option, then, is for them to share in deliberating and judging. That is why both Solon and some other legislators assign them the election of ruling officials and the scrutinizing of officials,[10] but do not allow them to hold office individually. For all combined have adequate sense, and when they are mixed with the better people, they benefit cities (just as impure food mixed with pure makes the whole more useful than the smaller amount <of pure food>), but each taken separately is incompletely equipped for judging.

The first puzzle raised by this organization of the political system is this: The task of judging who has applied medicine correctly seems to belong to the person who also has the task of applying the medicine and curing the patient from his present illness; and this is the medical expert. And the same is true for the other empirical techniques and for the crafts. And so just as a medical expert should submit his conduct to scrutiny by medical experts, other experts should also be scrutinized by their peers.

Medical experts, however, include not only the practitioners and the supervising experts, but also those who are educated about the craft—for in practically every craft there are people educated about it. And we assign the task of judging to the educated people no less than to those who know$_{o}$ the craft.

10. **scrutinizing of officials**: At Athens their conduct during their year of office was subject to a scrutiny by a jury-court (chosen by lot from the citizens) after they had held office.

The same puzzle seems to arise about selection <as about judging>. For selection is also properly a task for those who know$_o$ the craft; it is the task of geometers, for instance, to select a geometer, and of pilots to select a pilot.[11] For even if laymen have some share in selection for some types of production and craft, their share is no greater than that of people who know the craft. Hence, on this argument, the masses should not be given control either of selecting rulers or of scrutinizing them.

Presumably, however, this argument is not completely correct. First, it is refuted by our earlier argument, as long as the masses are not too slavish; for though each one individually is a worse judge than one who knows the craft, all combined are better, or no worse. Second, the argument is mistaken because in some cases the producer is neither the only judge nor the best judge; this is so whenever laymen also know$_g$ the products of a craft. It is not only the builder of the house, for instance, who knows$_g$ it; its user—the householder—is an even better judge. Similarly, a pilot is a better judge of a rudder than a carpenter is, and the diner, not the cook, is the judge of a feast. This, then, might seem to be an adequate solution of the puzzle.

There is another puzzle, however, following this one. For it seems absurd for base people to control issues that are more important than the ones controlled by decent people; but scrutinies and elections to ruling offices are the most important thing, and in some political systems, as we have said, these functions are assigned to the common people, since the assembly[12] controls all of these. And yet participation in the assembly, deliberative council, and jury-court[13] requires only a small property-qualification and no minimum age, whereas a large qualification is needed to be a financial officer or general or to hold the highest ruling offices.

Well, the same solution applies to this puzzle also. For presumably this <policy that raises the puzzle> is also correct. For the ruler is not the individual juryman or councilman or assemblyman, but the jury-court, the council, and the assembly; each indi-

11. **it is the task . . . a pilot**: Cf. Plato, *Prot*. 318bc.

12. **assembly**: All citizens were eligible to attend and vote in the assembly (at Athens and in other democracies).

13. **deliberative council and jury-court**: In Athens, the members of these were chosen by lot from the citizens.

vidual councilman, assemblyman, or juryman is a part of the <collectives> we have mentioned. Hence it is just for the masses to control the most important things, since the common people, the council, and the jury-court are all composed of many members. Moreover, the property of all these <collectively> is greater than the property of those who, one at a time or a few at a time, hold
1282b the high ruling offices. This, then, is how we settle these questions.

The puzzle that was raised first makes it especially evident that the laws, when they are correctly framed, must be in control, and that the ruler, either one or many, must be in control where the laws are incapable of giving the exactly correct guidance, since it is not easy to determine these cases in a universal rule. But what sorts of laws are the correctly framed ones? This is not yet clear, and the previous puzzle remains unsolved. For the baseness or excellence, and justice or injustice, of laws depends on, and matches, the character of political systems. It is evident, however, that the laws must at any rate be framed to fit the political system. And if this is so, then, clearly, the laws corresponding to correct systems will necessarily be just, and those corresponding to deviant systems not just.

12

In all types of science and craft the end is a good, and the greatest and best good is the end of the science that most controls all the others, and this is the political capacity. The political good is justice, and justice is the common benefit. Everyone thinks justice is some sort of equality, and hence to some extent they all agree with the philosophical discussions in which we have determined ethical questions; for they say that what is just is relative to the people involved and that it must be equality for equals. But we must find the relevant respect of equality or inequality; for this question raises a puzzle that concerns political philosophy.

For presumably someone might say that ruling offices ought to be unequally distributed in accordance with superiority in any good at all, if people are alike and not at all different in all of the other goods; for, it will be argued, superior people justly deserve to get more than other people get. In that case, however, anyone who excels in complexion, size, or any other good at all, will have a politically just <claim> to get more <goods>.

Surely the falsity in this view is easy to spot, and is evident in the other sciences and capacities. If two flute-players are at the same level in their craft, we ought not to assign more flutes to the better-born one, since his birth does not make him a better flute-player; rather, the one who excels in the relevant function must be assigned the extra instruments.

If our point is not yet clear, it will become still more evident if we develop it further. Suppose that A is superior to B in the flute playing craft, but far inferior to B in birth or beauty. Suppose even that each of these other goods—i.e., good birth and beauty—is a greater good than the flute playing craft, and that B's superiority <in these respects> over A's flute playing is proportionately greater than A's superiority over B in the flute playing craft. Even in this case A should be given the better flutes. For if superiority in birth and wealth is relevant <to a distribution>, it ought to contribute to the relevant function, but in this case it contributes nothing to it.

Moreover, the argument we are opposing implies that every good is comparable with every other; for if some particular size competes <with some other good>, then size in general will also compete with wealth and free status. And so if A's superiority over B in size is greater than B's superiority over A in virtue, even though virtue in general is a greater good than size, then all goods will be comparable; for if some amount is greater than some other, clearly some amount is equal to it.

But since this is impossible, clearly it is also reasonable that in politics not every sort of inequality is a ground for dispute about ruling offices. For if A is quick and B is slow, it does not follow that A should have more and B less; this sort of superiority receives its honor in gymnastic contests. The goods that are grounds for dispute must be those that constitute the city.

Hence it is reasonable that the well-born and the free citizens and the rich lay claims to honor. For <citizens> must be freemen, with some property-qualification, since a city could not be composed entirely of disadvantaged people, any more than it could be composed of slaves. And yet, if the city needs these, clearly it also needs justice and political virtue, since these are also necessary conditions of living in a city. The difference is that birth, free status, and wealth are <simply> necessary for a city to exist, whereas justice and political virtue are necessary for living finely in a city.

* * * * * * *

Book VII

[*THE BEST STATE AND THE BEST SYSTEM*]

1

Anyone who is inquiring along the appropriate lines into the best political system must first determine what the most choiceworthy life is. If it is left unclear what this is, it must also be unclear what the best political system is; for those who have the best political system in their circumstances will characteristically be best-off, if nothing unexpected happens. That is why we must first agree on what sort of life is most choiceworthy for (we may say) everyone, and then agree on whether such a life is or is not the same for an individual as for a community. We may take it then, that the best life is discussed at sufficient length even in <our> popular discussions; and so we should use those now.

For certainly no one would dispute one classification <of goods>, at least, into external goods, goods in the body, and goods in the soul,[1] or would deny that blessedly happy people ought to possess them all. For no one would count a person blessedly happy if he had no part of bravery, temperance, justice, or wisdom, but was afraid of every passing fly, sank to any depth to satisfy his appetite for food or drink, ruined his closest friends for some trivial gain, and had his mind as full of senseless illusion as a child's or a madman's.

Everyone would agree with these statements, but people disagree about how much <of each good is needed> and about large amounts of them. For whereas they think any slight degree of virtue is quite enough, they seek extreme abundance of wealth, valuables, power, reputation, and all such things, without limit. We will tell them, on the contrary, that it is easy to reach a confident belief about these questions, by simply attending to the facts.

For we see that people possess and keep external goods by having the virtues, not the other way round. Further, as we see,

1. **one classification . . . the soul**: Cf. *EN* 1099a12–20.

a happy life—whether such a life for human beings consists in enjoyment or in virtue or in both—belongs to those who go to extremes in well-ordered character and intellect, but possess a moderate level of external goods, rather than to those who have more external goods than they can use, but are deficient in character and intellect.

Moreover, the same point is easy to notice if we approach the question by argument. For externals, like instruments, and everything useful for some purpose, have a limit, and excess of them is bound to harm, not to benefit, the possessor;[2] but each good of the soul becomes more useful as it exceeds (if we are to attribute usefulness as well as fineness even to these goods).

And in general, clearly we will say that the best condition of one thing surpasses the best condition of another in proportion to the superiority of the first thing over the second. And so, if the soul is more honorable, both without qualification and in relation to us, than possessions and the body, it follows that its best condition must be proportionately better than theirs. Further, these other things are naturally choiceworthy for the sake of the soul, and every intelligent person must choose them for its sake, not the soul for their sake.

Let us, then, take it as agreed that each person achieves happiness to the extent that he achieves virtue and intelligence, and acts in accordance with them. We appeal to the god as evidence; for he is happy and blessed, because of himself and the character that is naturally his, not through any external good. Indeed this is also why good fortune cannot be the same as happiness; for chance and fortune produce goods external to the soul, whereas no one is just or temperate from fortune or because of fortune.

The next point, relying on the same arguments, is that the happy city is also the best one, the one that acts finely. But no one can act finely without doing fine actions, and neither a man nor a city does any fine actions without virtue and intelligence. Moreover, the bravery, justice, intelligence, and temperance of a city have the same capacity and form$_{m}$ that belongs to a human being who is called brave, just, intelligent, and temperate.

So much, then, for a preface to our argument; for we can neither leave these questions untouched nor go through all the appropriate arguments, since this is a task for another discipline.

2. **For externals . . . possessor**: Cf. *EN* 1129b1–6.

For now, let us simply assume that the best life for an individual 1324a by himself, and the best common life for cities, is the life involving virtue that has sufficient <external> resources to share in actions expressing virtue. In our present line of inquiry we must leave aside objections, and consider them later, if someone turns out to be unpersuaded by what we have said.

2

It remains to be said, however, whether we should or should not take happiness to be the same for an individual human being and for a city. But the answer to this is also evident; for everyone would agree that it is the same. For those who think an individual lives well in being rich also count a whole city blessed if it is rich, whereas those who honor the tyrant's way of life above all others would say that the happiest city is the one that rules over the most people; and if anyone thinks that virtue makes an individual happy, he will also say that the more excellent city is happier.

But now there are two questions to be investigated. First, which of these two lives is more choiceworthy—the one that involves taking part in political activities and sharing in the city, or the life of an alien, released from the political community? Second, what political system and what condition of the city should we regard as best (no matter whether we decide that participation in the city is choiceworthy for everyone, or only for most people, not for everyone)? This second question—not the question about what is choiceworthy for the individual—is the task of political thought and study; and since we have decided to undertake a political investigation now, that first question will be a side-issue, and the second will be the main issue for this line of inquiry.

First, then, it is evident that the best political system must be the order that guides the life of anyone at all who does best and lives blessedly. But even those who agree that the life involving virtue is the most choiceworthy disagree about whether the active life of the citizen is choiceworthy, or the life of someone released from all externals—some life of study, which some people think is the only life for a philosopher—is more choiceworthy. For practically all those, both in the past and now, who have most eagerly pursued virtue have evidently decided on one or other of these two lives, the political and the philosophical; and it is quite important to decide which view is correct, since the intelligent individual, and the intelligent political system no less, will necessarily order life to aim at the best goal.

Some people, however, think that ruling over one's neighbors as a master over slaves involves one of the worst injustices, and that even rule as a citizen over citizens, though it has nothing unjust about it, still interferes with the ruler's well-being. Others take just about the contrary view, supposing that the only life for a man is the life of political activity, since, in their view, the actions resulting from each virtue are open to those who undertake political action for the community, no less than to a private individual.

Some, then, hold this view. But still others say that only the form of political system that rules as a master and a tyrant is happy. And so in some cities the very aim of the political system and laws is to rule over neighboring peoples as slaves.

And so, while most laws in most cities are pretty haphazard, still any city that has laws aiming to any extent at some end has them all aiming at domination, as in Sparta and Crete both the education and most of the laws are organized for war. Moreover, all the <non-Greek> nations that have the power to get more <at the expense of others> honor this sort of power. For in some places there are even laws that incite them to this sort of virtue. The Carthaginians, for example, so it is said, decorate soldiers with bracelets for the number of campaigns they have served in. Once the Macedonians had a law that someone who had not killed an enemy should wear a rope around his waist instead of a belt. The Scythians used to pass around a cup at feasts and forbade it to anyone who had not killed an enemy. And the warlike Iberian nation place around someone's grave a number of stakes to mark the number of enemies he has killed. Many peoples have many similar practices established by laws or customs.

If we are willing to examine this question, however, we will find it utterly absurd to suppose that the politician's task is the ability to study ways of ruling over neighboring peoples as willing or unwilling slaves. For how could this be a politician's or lawgiver's task, since it is not even lawful?[3] It is unlawful to rule without regard to justice or injustice, and domination may quite possibly be unjust. Moreover, we never see this in the other sciences; it is

3. **not even lawful**: Aristotle does not mean that there is any positive law against it, but that it is contrary to the rule (*nomos*) of JUSTICE.

not the doctor's or pilot's task to force his patients or passengers if he fails to persuade them.

Most people, however, would seem to think the science of mastery over slaves is political science; and they are not ashamed to treat other peoples in ways that they reject as unjust and harmful among individuals. For among themselves they seek to rule justly, but in relations with other peoples they are indifferent to justice.

It is absurd, however, to deny that some creatures are, and some are not, naturally suited to be ruled by masters. And so, if this is true, we must try to rule as masters only over those suited to be ruled, not over everyone, just as we must not try to hunt human beings for a feast or sacrifice, but only animals that are suitable to be hunted; these are the wild animals that are suitable to eat.

Besides, a single city even by itself—if it has a fine political system, of course—can be happy, if it is possible for a city to live in isolation somewhere, governed by excellent laws. The organization of this political system will not aim at war or at domination over enemy states, since it is assumed to have no enemies or wars.

Clearly, then, all the ways of training for war should be regarded as fine—not, however, as the ultimate end of everything, but as promoting that end. The excellent legislator's task is to consider how a city, or people, or any other community, is to participate in a good life and in the happiness available to it. However, some prescriptions of law will vary; and it is the task of legislative science, if a city has neighbors, to see what practices should be cultivated in relations with different sorts of neighbors and how to apply the suitable ones to dealings with each neighboring city.

This question, however, about the right aim for the best political system, will receive the proper discussion later.

* * * * * * *

13

We should now discuss the political system itself and say which people, and of what character, must constitute a city if it is to be blessedly happy and to have a fine political system.

Everyone's welfare depends on two conditions; the goal and end of actions must be correctly laid down, and the actions promoting the end must be found. For these may either conflict or harmonize with each other. Sometimes the goal has been finely laid down, but we fail to obtain it in our actions; sometimes we attain everything that promotes our end, but have laid down a bad end; and sometimes we fail on both counts (as in medicine, for instance, when sometimes they neither make a correct judgment about the character of a healthy body nor manage to find the right productive process relative to the standard that has been laid down). In crafts and sciences we must master both the end and the actions advancing toward it.

It is evident, then, that everyone aims at living well and at happiness. In fact, however, these are open to some and not to others, because of something in fortune or nature—for living finely also needs resources, fewer if our condition is better, and more if it is worse. Others again, though happiness is open to them, seek it in the wrong way from the start. Our task is to see the best political system, the one that will result in the best political life in the city; this will be the one that most of all results in happiness for the city. Hence we must not be ignorant of what happiness is.

We say, then—as we define it in the Ethics,[4] if those discussions are of any benefit—that happiness is complete activity and exercise of virtue, complete without qualification, not conditionally. By 'conditionally' I mean what is necessary, and by 'without qualification' I mean what is done finely. For in the case of just actions, for instance, penalties and corrective treatments result from virtue, but are necessary, and are done finely only to the extent that is possible for necessary actions, since it is more choiceworthy if neither a man nor a city needs any such thing. By contrast, actions leading to honors and prosperity are the finest actions without qualification; for while the other type of action involves merely the removal of some evil, these, on the contrary, construct and generate goods.

Now, certainly the excellent man will act finely in response to poverty or disease or any other ill fortune. Still, blessedness consists in the contrary of these. For we have determined this also in our ethical discussions, that the excellent person is the sort

4. **Ethics**: Cf. *EN* 1098a16, *EE* 1219a38.

whose virtue makes unqualified goods good for him;[5] and clearly the ways in which he uses them must also be excellent and fine without qualification. Indeed this is why human beings think external goods cause happiness; it is as though they took the lyre rather than the performer's craft to be the cause of a splendidly fine performance.

It follows, then, from what has been said, that some conditions must be presupposed, but some must be provided by the legislator. That is why, in establishing the city, we assume that the goods we want that are controlled by fortune (since we take fortune to control <externals>) are provided at the level we aspire to, but when we come to making the city excellent, it is a task not for fortune, but for science and decision.

Moreover, a city is excellent because the citizens who participate in the political system are excellent; and in our city all the citizens participate in the political system. Hence we must consider how an excellent man comes to be; for even if it is possible for the citizens to be excellent all together without being so individually, still it is more choiceworthy for each to be excellent individually, since being excellent individually also implies being excellent all together <but the converse is not true>.

Now, people come to be good and excellent through three means—nature, habit, and reason. For, first of all, we must be born with the nature of a human being, not of some other animal; and then we must have the appropriate sort of body and soul. But in some cases being born with a given quality is no help, since habits alter it; for nature makes some things able to go either way, and habits change them for the worse or the better.[6]

Now, whereas the other animals live mostly by nature, while some live to some slight extent by habit, a human being also lives by reason, since he is the only animal who has it. And so these three ought to be in accord; for people do many actions contrary to habituation and nature because of reason, if they are persuaded that another way is better.

We have previously defined, then, the sort of nature that is needed if people are to be easily handled by the legislator. Thereaf-

5. **makes . . . for him**: Cf. *EN* 1129b1–6, *EE* 1248b26.

6. **for nature . . . the better**: On the contributions of nature and of habituation see *EN* 1103a28, 1179b21.

ter the task falls to education, since some things are learned by habituation, others by instruction.

* * * * * * *

15

The goal appears to be the same for a community of human beings 1334a11 as for an individual, and the best political system must conform to the same standard that the best man conforms to. Evidently, then, it must possess the virtues applying to leisure; for, as we have often said, the goal of war is peace, and the goal of labor is leisure.

The virtues that are useful for leisure and for spending one's leisure time are those whose function applies to leisure and those whose function applies to labor; for many necessary <goods> must be presupposed if leisure is to be open to us. Hence it is fitting for the city to be temperate, brave, and resistant; for, as the proverb says, slaves have no leisure, and those who cannot face dangers bravely are slaves of their attackers.

Now, bravery and resistance are needed for labor, philosophy for leisure, and temperance and justice in both circumstances—indeed, even more in peace and leisure. For war compels us to be just and temperate, but enjoyment of good fortune and of peacetime makes people wantonly aggressive instead. Much justice and temperance, then, are needed by those who seem to do best and to enjoy the <external> goods that bring congratulation for blessedness. This will be true, for instance, of the people in the Isles of the Blessed, if there are any, as the poets say there are; for these will have most need of philosophy, temperance, and justice, to the extent that they more than anyone else are at leisure, with abundance of all those <external> goods.

It is evident, then, why the city that is to be happy and excellent needs to share in the virtues. For it is shameful to be incapable of using goods <properly>; it is even more shameful to be incapable of using them in leisure, so that we appear good when we are laboring and fighting wars, but slavish when we are at leisure in time of peace.

That is why we must not cultivate virtue as Sparta does. For the Spartans are superior to other people not by rejecting other people's 1334b view that the <externals> are the greatest goods, but by believing that a particular virtue is the best way to secure these goods. But since they esteem these goods and the enjoyment of them more highly than the enjoyment of the virtues[7] . . . and that <virtue is to be cultivated> for itself, is evident from this. The next thing to attend to, then, is the means and method of acquiring virtue.

We have previously determined, then, that the acquisition of virtue depends on nature, habit, and reason; and among these we have previously determined the sort of natural characteristics people should have. The remaining question to study is whether education by reason or by habit should come first.

For reason and habit must achieve the best sort of harmony, since it is possible both for reason to fall short of the best basic assumption and for upbringing by habits to fail similarly. This at least, then, is evident first of all, as in other cases, that coming to be has some starting point, and the end resulting from one starting point is itself the starting point of another end. Now, the goal of nature for us is reason and understanding; hence the coming to be and the practice of habits must be arranged to aim at these.

Further, just as soul and body are two, so also we see that the soul has two parts, the nonrational and the rational, and these have two <characteristic> states, desire and understanding <respectively>. And just as the body comes to be before the soul, so also the nonrational part of the soul comes to be before the rational. This also is evident from the fact that emotion, wish, and also appetite are present in children as soon as they are born, whereas reasoning and understanding naturally arise in the course of growth.

First of all, then, attention to the body must precede attention to the soul, and, next, attention to desire must precede attention to understanding. Nonetheless, attention to desire must be for the sake of understanding, just as attention to the body must be for the sake of the soul.

* * * * * * *

7. **virtues . . .**: There seems to be a passage missing from the manuscripts at this point.

POETICS

* * * * * * *

[*THE ELEMENTS OF TRAGEDY*]

6

We will discuss imitative hexameter poetry and comedy later. *1449b21* Let us now discuss tragedy, after recapitulating the definition of its essence$_{o}$ that emerges from what we have said.

Tragedy, then, is an imitation of an action that is serious and complete, one that has some greatness. It imitates in words with pleasant accompaniments, each type belonging separately to the different parts <of the work>. It imitates people performing actions and does not rely on narration. Through pity and fear it achieves purification[1] from[2] such feelings.

By 'words with pleasant accompaniments' I mean words with rhythm, harmony, and song. By 'the type belonging separately' I mean that some parts are executed in verse alone, and other parts in song.

Since the imitation is produced by action, the parts of the tragedy must include, first of all, the visual display, and second, song and speech; for in these the imitation is produced. By 'speech' I mean the composition of the verses, and what I mean by 'song' is clear to everyone.

It is an imitation of action, and action is done by agents. These must have some qualities of character and thought, since it is through these that we attribute qualities to the action also. Hence *1450a* there are by nature two causes of actions—intellect and thought—and actions are what make every agent succeed or fail.

1. **purification**: *katharsis*. Or 'purgation'.
2. **from**: Or 'of'. Aristotle might have in mind: (a) A purification that consists in or works through pity and fear. (b) A purgation, i.e., removal, of pity and fear. (c) A purification from excessive pity and fear, i.e., their replacement with feelings closer to the MEAN. (d) A purification, i.e., making purer, of pity and fear.

The story is the imitation of the action; for by 'story' I mean the combination of actions;[3] By 'characters' I mean whatever makes us attribute some quality to an agent. By 'thought' I mean the ways in which the agent demonstrates a view.

Every tragedy, then, must have six parts, which give the tragedy its quality. These are story, characters, speech, thought, visual display, and song. For two of these are the means by which we imitate, one is the way we imitate, three are the things we imitate, and there is nothing besides these six. Quite a few dramatists, we may say, have used these different kinds of parts. For every drama has visual displays, character, story, speech, song, and thought likewise.

The most important of these is the combination of actions. For tragedy is an imitation, not of human beings, but of an action and a way of life and of happiness and unhappiness. Happiness and unhappiness are found in action, and the end <we aim at> is a type of action, not a quality <of character>; people's characters make them people of a certain sort, but it is their actions that make them happy or unhappy. Hence they do not perform the actions <in a drama> to imitate characters, but rather include the characters in order to imitate the actions. And so it is the actions and <hence> the story that are the end of a tragedy, and the end is most important of all.

Further, there can be no tragedy without action, but there can be one without <presentation of> characters. For the ones by most of the recent authors are without character; and in general this is true of many poets. It is similar to the difference between Zeuxis and Polygnotus among painters; for Polygnotus is a good painter of character, whereas Zeuxis's painting contains no presentation of character. Moreover, a poet will not achieve what we have seen to be the function of a tragedy simply by arranging in order discourses that present character, well composed in their speech and thought. He will achieve it much better in a tragedy that is inferior in these points but has a story and a combination of actions.

Besides, the main aspects by which a tragedy appeals to our feelings are parts of the story—the reversals and the recognition.

3. **actions**: *pragmata*. The unifying action of a play is the *praxis* (singular). The *pragmata* are the actions (plural) done in the course of this single action.

Further evidence is the fact that beginners in composition are able to get the speech and characters exactly right before they can correctly combine the actions; this was true, for instance, of practically all the earliest poets.

The story, then, is the principle and, we might say, the soul of
the tragedy, and the characters are secondary. For it is similar in 1450b
the case of painting also; for if a painter covered the canvas with the most beautiful colors in no order, he would please us less than if he produced a black and white sketch. Similarly, the story is an imitation of action; it imitates agents primarily in order to imitate the action.

The third part is thought. This is the capacity to say what is involved in the situation and suitable to it, which, in the case of speeches, is the task of political science and rhetoric. For the early poets presented people speaking in a politician's manner, whereas contemporary poets present them speaking them in a rhetorician's manner.

Character is the sort of thing that makes clear what sort of decision is made when it is not clear whether someone is deciding for or against an action; that is why the speeches that do not present anything to be decided for or against do not present any character. Thought, by contrast, is that in which someone demonstrates that something is so or is not so, or makes some general pronouncement.

The fourth of the elements found in discourse is speech. By 'speech' I mean, as I said before, the expression <of thought> through the use of words, which has the same force in meter and <prose> discourses.

Among the remaining parts, the song is the most important of the pleasant accompaniments. The visual display appeals most to our feelings, but involves the least craft and is the least proper to poetry. For the power of tragedy can be achieved without a performance and actors; moreover the equipment-maker's craft, more than the poet's, is properly in control of the production of visual display.

* * * * * * *

9

1451a36 It is also evident from what we have said that it is the poet's function to describe not what has happened, but the sorts of things that would happen and are possible, in a necessary or
1451b likely sequence. For the difference between a historian and a poet is not that one writes in verse and the other in prose; for you could put Herodotus' work into verse, and it would be a history in verse no less than it would be in prose. The difference is that the historian describes what has happened, whereas the poet describes the sorts of things that would happen.

This is why poetry is more philosophical and more serious[4] than history; for it speaks more of what is universal, whereas history speaks of what is particular. What is universal is, for instance, that in a necessary or likely sequence the result is that this sort of person says or does things of this sort; this is what poetry aims at, attaching names to it. What is particular is, for instance, what actions Alcibiades did or what things happened to him.

The case of comedy makes this difference clear at once. For there the poet first composes his story, relying on likely sequences, and then supplies any old names; his work is not about a particular person, as a lampoon is. In the case of tragedy, however, the poet retains names of actual people of the past. The reason for this is that what persuades us is <what we find> convincing, and if something has not happened, we are not yet convinced that it is possible, whereas if it has happened, then evidently it is possible (since it would not have happened if it had been impossible).[5]

Still, some tragedies have one or two names of known$_g$ people, while the other names are fictitious. And some tragedies even have no <names of actual people>, as is true in the *Antheus* of Agathon; for in this both the actions and the names are alike fictitious, and nonetheless pleasing for that.

We must not seek, then, to retain at all costs the traditional stories that tragedies are about. Indeed, it would be ridiculous to

4. **more serious**: since SCIENCE is concerned with UNIVERSALS.

5. **whereas . . . impossible)**: Aristotle assumes that a contemporary audience would take the traditional myths to be historically accurate (at least in outline).

seek to do this, since even the <incidents> that are known are known to few people, but still are pleasing to everyone.

Hence it is clear that the poet must be a composer[6] of stories rather than verses, insofar as it is his imitating that makes him a poet, and the things he imitates are actions. And so even if it happens that the incidents in his composition have actually happened, it does not follow that he is any less a composer. For it is quite possible for some things that have happened to be the sorts of things that are likely to happen, and capable of happening; and insofar as they are <likely and capable of happening>, he is the composer of them.

Among simple stories and actions the episodic ones are the worst. By 'episodic story' I mean one in which the episodes follow in neither a necessary nor a likely sequence. Bad poets compose such stories because of their own incompetence. But good poets also compose such stories, for the sake of the actors; for since they are composing plays for a competition and stretching the story beyond its capacity, they are often compelled to distort the 1452a sequence.

Now, a tragedy imitates not only a complete action, but also incidents arousing fear and pity. And incidents have this effect most of all when they happen unexpectedly because of each other. For this <causal connection> will make them more amazing than if they happened by chance and luck. For even among things happening by luck the ones that seem most amazing are those that appear to have happened as though on purpose. That is true, for instance, of the statue of Mitys in Argos that killed the man responsible for Mitys' death, by falling on him when he was looking at it; for such things look as though they do not happen at random. Hence stories of the same sort are bound to be better.

* * * * * * *

13

After what we have said, our next task is to say what the poet 1452b28 should aim at and what he should avoid in constructing his stories, and how to achieve the function of a tragedy.

6. **poet . . . composer**: Both words translate *poiētēs* (lit. 'producer').

Now, the construction of the finest tragedy must be complex, not simple, and must imitate things that arouse fear and pity; for this is distinctive of this type of imitation. First of all, then, it is clear that decent men must not be shown passing from good to bad fortune. For this is not an object of fear or pity, but of abhorrence. Nor must vicious people be shown passing from bad fortune to good. For this process is the most untragic of all; it has none of the features needed <in a tragedy>, since it arouses neither our feeling for humanity nor our pity nor our fear. Nor must an extremely base person be shown falling from good fortune to bad. For though this construction appeals to our feeling for humanity,[7] it arouses neither pity nor fear. For pity is felt for someone suffering ill fortune who does not deserve it, and fear for someone like <ourselves>. Hence the result <of this sort of story> arouses neither pity nor fear.

The remaining case is the person between these. He is a person who is not superior in virtue and justice who passes into ill fortune, not because he is bad and vicious, but because he makes some error[8]—someone in high esteem and good fortune, such as Oedipus, Thyestes, and the <other> illustrious men of such <noble> families.

And so a story that is well constructed must be single, not, as some say, double. It must involve passing from good fortune to bad, not the other way round, and this must happen because of some great error by an agent who is either the sort of person we have described or better than that rather than worse. What actually happens is evidence for our claim. For in the earliest times poets used just any old story, but at present the finest tragedies are composed about a few families—for example, about Alcmaeon, Oedipus, Orestes, Meleager, Thyestes, Telephus, and all the others for whom it turned out that they did terrible things or had terrible things happen to them.

And so the tragedy that counts as finest on the principles prescribed by the craft has this structure. That is also why Euripi-

7. **feeling for humanity**: This might refer either to (1) our sympathy for the victims (good or bad) of ill fortune, or (2) our feeling that people have got what they deserved.

8. **error**: *hamartia*. Different interpretations: (1) A fault of character (the 'tragic flaw'). (2) A mistake of fact that is not blameworthy. (3) A blameworthy mistake.

des' critics are in error when they make it a ground of accusation against him that he does this in his tragedies, so that many of them end with ill fortune. For, as we have said, this is the correct sort of ending. The best evidence of this is the fact that on the stage and in performance these sorts of plays appear the most tragic, if they are successfully executed, and even if Euripides does not arrange the other things well, still he appears the most tragic of the poets.

The second-best type of structure is the one that some people say is best, the one that has a double structure, such as the *Odyssey* has, that ends with contrary results for the better and the worse people. This is regarded as best because of the weakness of the audiences; for the poets follow them and compose what will please the audience. But the pleasure <resulting from this structure> is not the pleasure from tragedy, but is more proper to comedy. For there the bitterest enemies in the story—Orestes and Aegisthus, for instance—become friends at the end and walk off <together>, and no one kills anyone.

* * * * * * *

GLOSSARY

ABSTRACTION, *aphairesis*

If x is F, G, and H, but I want to examine what is true of x INSOFAR AS it is F (x qua F), then I 'abstract' or 'remove' G and H from x in thought; my claims and arguments about x do not rely on the assumption that x is G and H. See *APo* 74a32–b4, *DA* 429b18–20. Abstraction in mathematics: see *Phys*. 193b31–194a12, *DA* 403b15. Abstraction in metaphysics: see *PA* 641b10–12, *Met*. 1004b10–17, 1029a16, 1036b21–30.

ACCOUNT: see REASON

ACHIEVEMENT: see FUNCTION

ACT, ACT ON: see PRODUCE

ACTED ON: see ATTRIBUTE

ACTION, *praxis*

Aristotle uses *praxis* and the verb *prattein* (1) in a broad sense parallel to 'do'; (2) to distinguish VOLUNTARY actions from things that happen to us or things over which we have no control (e.g., *DI* 19a8, *EN* 1096b34); (3) for rational action on a DECISION, which is not open to non-rational animals or to children (*Phys*. 197b1–8, *EN* 1139a18–20); (4) for rational action in which the action itself is the end, as opposed to PRODUCTION, in which the end is some product distinct from the action (*Met*. 1048b22, *EN* 1139a35–b4, 1140b6–7, *Pol*. 1254a2).

ACTUALITY, ACTUALIZATION, ACTIVITY, REALIZATION, *energeia, entelecheia*

Energeia (or *entelecheia*) is contrasted with POTENTIALITY, as actually walking, e.g., is contrasted with merely having the potentiality to walk, *DI* 19a9, *Phys*. 201a9–15, *Met*. 1048a25–b9. Aristotle sometimes distinguishes (a) first actuality (sometimes equivalent to STATE, *hexis*) from (b) second actuality, as in (a) knowing French, but not thinking or speaking in French now, in contrast to (b) speaking or thinking in French now. See *DA* 412a22–7, 417a21–b9, *EN* 1098a5–7.

ADMIT OF, *endechesthai*: see POTENTIALITY

AFFECT, AFFECTION: see ATTRIBUTE

aisthēsis: see PERCEPTION

aition, aitia: see CAUSE

akrasia: see INCONTINENCE

.vAYS, *aiei*; EVERLASTING, *aidion*

What is always the case is sometimes identified with what is NECESSARY; see *APo* 73a28–b28, *Phys*. 196b10–13, 198b25, *GC* 337b35–338a5.

ANALYTICS: see LOGICAL

ANAXAGORAS

One of the later Presocratic NATURALISTS (500–428?; cf. *Met*. 984a11–16). See *Met*. 985a18–21 (cf. Plato, *Phaedo* 98b7–c2).

ANAXIMENES

An early Presocratic NATURALIST (fl. 546), probably a younger contemporary of ANAXIMANDER.

ANIMATE, *empsuchos*: see SOUL

ANTIPHON

A sophist, rhetorician, and natural philosopher (?480–411?). See *Phys*. 193a12.

ANTISTHENES

A follower of Socrates (c. 445–c. 360), and a reputed founder of Cynic philosophy. See *Top*. 104b20, *Met*. 1043b24.

ANY OLD THING: see LUCK #2.

aporia: see DIALECTIC

APPEARANCE, *phantasia*

In its most general sense '*phantasia*' is simply the abstract noun corresponding to *phainesthai*, 'appear', *DA* 402b23. In its more specific sense *phantasia* is more closely connected to the senses, as opposed to the intellect, *DA* 428b10–17. On PERCEPTION and appearance see *DA* 428a11–12, *Met*. 1010b1–3. On appearance and UNDERSTANDING: *DA* 403a8–10, 428a16–24, 431a14–17, 432a9–13.

APPEARANCES, *phainomena*

Both empirical inquiry and dialectic begin from the appearances, *PA* 639b5–10, *EN* 1145b2–7. In a dialectical inquiry the appearances are COMMON BELIEFS, *endoxa*. Aristotle does not assume that all appearances are true; but a theory must respect and account for the most reasonable ones, *Phys*. 189a16, *EN* 1145b2–7, 28.

APPETITE, *epithumia*: see DESIRE

archē: see PRINCIPLE

ARCHYTAS

A writer (1st half 4th cent.) on mathematics and harmonics. See *Met.* 1043a21.

aretē: see VIRTUE

ARGUMENT: see REASON

ASSUMPTION, *hupothesis*

Sometimes 'x is F on an assumption' is contrasted with 'x is F WITHOUT QUALIFICATION (*APo* 72b15, *Pol.* 1278a5). In a SCIENCE, the assumptions are PRINCIPLES from which all the other propositions are DEMONSTRATED. See *APo* 72a18–20, 76b23–34, *Met.* 1005b14–16. See also CONDITIONAL.

ATTEND TO: see STUDY

ATTRIBUTE, AFFECTION, FEELING, *pathos*; BE ACTED ON, BE AFFECTED, UNDERGO, *paschein*

The verb *paschein* is correlative to *poiein* ('act on', 'PRODUCE'), *Catg.* 2a3–4, *Met.* 1048a6–8, *Poet.* 1451b11. In a wide sense (rendered by 'attribute', e.g., *GC* 317b11) a *pathos* of x is something that 'happens to' x quite generally, i.e., something that is true of x. In a narrower sense (rendered by 'affection' or 'feeling') a *pathos* is an 'affection' or 'passion', a mental state involving pleasure or pain, *EN* 1105b21, 1151a20–4.

AXIOM, *axioma*

Axioms include the Principles of Noncontradiction and Excluded Middle discussed in *Met.* iv, and the Axiom of Equals; see *APo* 72a17, 75a41, *Met.* 1005a20, 1008a3. They are contrasted with the proper PRINCIPLES of a specific SCIENCE, since every science relies on them.

BE, EXIST, *einai*

1. Aristotle uses the same word to indicate predication ('x is F') and existence ('x is', i.e., x exists). It is sometimes difficult to know which rendering suits a given context better. See *Catg.* 14b12, *DI* 16b15, *APo* 71a12n, 93a4, *Met.* 985b6.

2. Aristotle claims that being (*to on*, present participle) and beings (or things that are; *ta onta*) are spoken of in many ways (see HOMONYMY), corresponding to the categories (see PREDICATIONS). See *Top.* 103b27–39, *Met.* 1003a31–b10, 1017a22–30, 1028a10–20, *EN* 1096a23–9.

3. 'Being F' (e.g., 'being a man') is used to translate *to anthrōpō(i) einai* (etc.). See ESSENCE #2.

BEAUTIFUL: see FINE

BEING$_o$: see SUBSTANCE #1

BETTER KNOWN: see KNOWN

CAPABLE, CAPACITY: see POTENTIALITY

CATEGORIES: see PREDICATIONS

CAUSE, REASON, EXPLANATION, *aition, aitia*

In *Phys*. ii 3, *PA* 639b12, *Met*. 983a24–b6, Aristotle distinguishes the four types of *aition*: MATTER, FORM, the PRINCIPLE of MOTION (see *Phys*. 194b29), and the FOR SOMETHING. These are standardly known as the 'four causes'—material, formal, efficient, and final. (Aristotle himself does not use the last two labels.) An *aition* answers the question 'Why?', *Phys*. 194b19. Some examples (e.g., the mathematical one, *Phys*. 194b27) show that an *aition* need not be a causal explanation, but 'cause' is appropriate in most instances, and has been used in the translation.

Aristotle counts different kinds of things as *aitia*: substances, *Phys*. 194b20; events, *APo* 93b36–94a2; states, *Phys*. 194b33; substances performing or failing to perform actions, *Phys*. 195a13, 195b5–6.

CHANCE: see LUCK

CHANGE: see MOTION

CHARACTER, *ēthos*

Character is a STATE formed by habituation, *ethismos*, *EN* 1103a14–26, of DESIRES, feelings (see ATTRIBUTE), pleasures, and pains, so that they are rightly guided by the rational part of the SOUL. A well formed state of character is a VIRTUE, 1105b25–8.

CHARONDAS

A Sicilian lawgiver (6th cent. B.C.?); *Pol*. 1252b14.

CITY, STATE, *polis*

A typical Greek *polis* of the sort that Aristotle was familiar with had the area and population of a modern city (cf. *EN* 1170a3), but a degree of political independence more characteristic of a modern state. Hence 'city' and 'state' are appropriate in different contexts. For Aristotle the city is the complete COMMUNITY, the association of citizens, *politikē koinōnia*, *Pol*. 1252a1–7, 1252a37–1253a7, 1280a25–1281a4. Aristotle often relies on the verbal connections between *polis*, *politikē* (political science), and *politēs* (citizen).

CLOAK, *himation*

Aristotle uses this term simply as a dummy (where we might use 'x'), e.g., *Met*. 1029b27, 1045a26. Contrast the example at *DI* 19a12 and elsewhere.

COINCIDENT, *sumbebēkos*

Sumbebēkos is derived from *sumbainein*, 'come about together', which often just means 'happen' or 'turn out'. Aristotle recognizes two sorts of coincidents: (1) G is a coincident of F if (a) G belongs to F IN ITS OWN RIGHT, but (b) G is not the ESSENCE of F; e.g., a triangle has two right angles in its own right, but this is not the essence of a triangle (since a triangle is essentially a three-sided plane figure, from which it follows that a triangle has two right angles). See *APo* 75a42–b2, *DA* 402b16–28, *Met*. 995b20, 1025a30–4. (2) G is a coincident of F if (a) G belongs to F, but (b) F is not essentially G (or: if F is not necessarily G; for different statements of clause (b) see *Met*. 1025a14–16, *Top*. 102b4–9). In this case F's being G does not follow from the essence of F. See *APo* 83a10, *Phys*. 188a34, *Met*. 1017a7–13, 1031b22–8.

COLUMN, *sustoichia*

Columns of opposites: see *GC* 319a15, *Met*. 986a23–7, 1004b27, 1046b14, 1072a31.

COME TO BE, *gignesthai*; COMING TO BE, *genesis*

In unqualified (see WITHOUT QUALIFICATION) coming to be, a SUBSTANCE did not exist at time t1, but exists at t2; hence we can say 'the tree came to be (= came into being)'. In qualified coming to be, one and the same substance remains in existence and changes in one of its nonessential properties; hence from 'The tree came to be taller (= became taller)' we cannot infer 'The tree came to be (= came into being)'. See *Catg*. 4a10–13, *Phys*. 190a31–3, *GC* 318a25–319a22. Analogous distinctions apply to perishing, *phthora*.

COMMON BELIEFS, *endoxa*

These are the starting point of DIALECTIC, *Top*. 100a29–30, 104a8–20, 105b30–1. They are one type of APPEARANCES, *EN* 1145b3, 20, 28. Aristotle often reports the *endoxa* by using 'seems' (*dokei*, cognate with *doxa*, 'belief'), e.g., *Phys*. 189a31–2, *EN* 1097b8.

COMMUNITY, *koinōnia*

Koinōnia is cognate with *koinon*, 'common'. Aristotle believes that a *koinōnia* is created by every type of FRIENDSHIP. Hence the term includes both loose alliances and relatively casual relationships, close-knit communities and societies. See *EN* 1170b11, *Pol*. 1252b12–34, 1280b15 ff.

COMPLETE, *teleion*

Teleion is cognate with *telos*, 'end' (see FOR SOMETHING). It applies to something that has reached its *telos*, and hence to a mature, adult organism, *Met*. 1072b24. 'Final' and 'perfect' are other possible translations. Aristotle explains completeness in *Met*. v 16. He attributes it to HAPPINESS, *EN* 1097a25–b21, 1098a18, 1101a13, and to the CITY, *Pol*. 1252b27–30 (cf. 1281a1).

COMPOUND: see FORM

CONDITIONAL, *ex hupotheseōs*

Lit. 'on an assumption'. See NECESSITY #2.

CONTINENT: see INCONTINENT

CONTRARY, *enantion*: see OPPOSITE

CONTROLLING, FULL, STRICT, AUTHORITATIVE, OVERRIDING, IMPORTANT, *kurion*

1. To be *kurion* of x is to be in control of x, or to have authority over x, or both. See *PA* 640b28, *Met*. 981b11, 1003b16, 1010b13, 1048a12. *EN* 1113b32, 1114a32, *Pol*. 1252a5, 1275a28, 1281a11, 40, 1281b23, 1282a25.

2. The *kurion* use or application of a word controls its other uses, which are derived from it; here 'fully', or 'strictly', or 'full sense' is used. See *Catg*. 2a11, *Phys*. 191b7, *GC* 317a33, *DA* 412b9, 418a3, 24, *EN* 1144b4.

CONVENTION: see LAW

CRAFT, CRAFT-KNOWLEDGE, *technē*

1. A craft is a rational discipline, distinct from a theoretical science (see KNOW) insofar as (1) it aims at PRODUCTION, and (2) it does not provide DEMONSTRATIONS. See *APo* 100a9, *Met*. 980b25–981a30, *EN* 1140b2, 34.

2. Craft imitates NATURE, *Phys*. 194a21, 199a8–20, especially in being FOR SOMETHING. Aristotle often uses examples of crafts to explain points about matter and form in natural organisms; but he is careful to distinguish the two cases. See *DA* 412b10–17, *Met*. 1032a27–b14.

3. Craft v. INTELLIGENCE: *EN* 1104a5–11, 1112a34–b31, 1141b14–22.

4. Craft v. VIRTUE; *Top*. 101b6, *Met*. 1046b4–22, 1048a8–11, *EN* 1106a4–10, 1140b21–5.

CRATYLUS

A contemporary of Socrates, and an extreme Heracleitean. See Plato, *Cratylus* 402a, 439b–440a, *Met*. 987a32, 1010a12.

DECISION, *prohairesis*

A decision results from wish (i.e., rational desire) for some end, focussed by deliberation about what promotes the end; the result is a rational choice about what to do here and now to achieve the end. See *Phys*. 196b18, 197b8, *EN* iii 2–3, 1139a22–6.

DEDUCTION, INFERENCE, *sullogismos*

'*Sullogismos*' applies to inference generally, and specifically to valid deductive inference proceeding from more general principles rather than from particular cases (in contrast to INDUCTION). See *APr* 24b18–20, *APo* 71b23, *Top*. 100a25–7, 105a12–19, *EN* 1144a31, 1149a33. A 'syllogism' in the technical sense is a valid deductive argument with one of the formal structures that Aristotle describes in the *APr*.

DEFINE, *horizein*; DEFINITION, *horismos*; see also FORMULA

1. The definition of F can replace the name 'F' while preserving truth, by saying what F is, and thereby stating the ESSENCE of F, *Top*. 101b38–102a5, 141a35.

2. A 'nominal definition' (not an Aristotelian term) says what we take a name to SIGNIFY (e.g., 'thunder is a noise in the clouds') when we begin an inquiry. A 'real definition' states the essence. See *APo* ii 10, *DA* 413a13–20.

3. DEMONSTRATIONS begin with a definition of the subject whose intrinsic COINCIDENTS are demonstrated, *APo* 72a18–24, 74b5–12, 75a28–b2.

4. PARTICULARS do not have definitions (or at least do not have definitions of the primary sort), *Met*. 1039b27–1040a7.

5. Aristotle also speaks of the *horismos* when he refers to what the definition is of, i.e., the essence. He speaks of the *logos* in the same way; see *Phys*. 200a35, REASON.

6. Aristotle denies that one definition invariably corresponds to one name. See HOMONYMY.

DEMOCRITUS

Democritus (c. 460–c. 360?) and Leucippus are the founders of Atomism. See *Phys*. 184b21, *Met*. 985b4–20, 1039a7–11.

DEMONSTRATION, *apodeixis*

Scientific KNOWLEDGE has to be expressed in a demonstration—the particular sort of DEDUCTION from ASSUMPTIONS, with appropriately NECESSARY, explanatory, and better known premisses, that is described in *APo* 71b16–25. See also *APo* 72b5–73a6, 93a1–15, b15–20, 100b9–14, *DA* 402b25, *Met*. 1006a6–18, 1039b27–1040a5.

DESIRE, *orexis*

Aristotle recognizes three types of desire (cf. Plato, *Rep*. 435ff): (1) Rational desire or wish, *boulēsis*, directed at some end regarded as GOOD, *Met*. 1072a28, *EN* 1111b26, 1113a15. (2) Appetite, *epithumia*, non-rational desire directed at an object regarded as pleasant, 1103b18, 1111a31. (3) Emotion, *thumos* (which might also be rendered by 'spirit'), connected especially with shame, honor, and anger, 1111b18, 1116b23, 1149a25. See *DA* 414b2, 432b4–7, *EN* 1111a27, b10–30, *Pol*. 1334b22–8.

DETERMINE: see DEFINE

DIALECTIC, *dialektikē*

Dialektikē is the method Aristotle ascribes to SOCRATES in Plato's dialogues, *Met*. 1078b17–25. The *Topics* is devoted to a description of dialectical methods and arguments; see 100a18–30, 101a25–b4, 159a25–37, 165a38–b11. Aristotle practises dialectic constructively in his major philosophical works; see *Phys*. 184a16–b14, *Met*. 1004b17–26, *EN* 1145b2–7.

DIFFERENTIA, *diaphora*

A differentia divides a GENUS into its SPECIES, *Catg.* 3a21–8, *Top.* 122b12–24, *Met.* 1020a33–b1, 1038a18–21.

DISTINCTIVE, PROPER, PRIVATE, *idion*

Aristotle uses *idion* as a technical term (Latin 'proprium') for a non-ESSENTIAL but necessary property of F, belonging to all and only Fs, *Catg.* 3a21, 4a10, *Top.* 102a18–30. He also uses the term less strictly, so that it includes essential properties, *APo* 73a7, *DA* 402a9, *Met.* 1004b11, *EN* 1097b34. *Idion* is rendered by 'proper' where Aristotle uses it for the object that is peculiar to each sense (e.g., color for sight, sound for hearing and so on), *DA* 418a10.

dunamis, dunaton: see POTENTIALITY

eidos: see FORM

ELEMENT, LETTER, *stoicheion*

The term refers originally to a letter of the alphabet (an element of a syllable). Aristotle also uses it to refer to elements (e.g., the four primary BODIES) of other sorts of compound; *Met.* 985b15, 1034b26, 1035a14, 1041b11–33, 1086b20.

EMOTION, *thumos*: see DESIRE

EMPEDOCLES

A natural philosopher and poet (c. 495–35). See, e.g., *Phys.* 194a20, 198b31–2, *DA* 415b28–416a9, *PA* 640a19–25, 642a18–24, *Met.* 984a8–11, 985a21–b3, 1072a6, 1075b1–7.

END, *telos*: see FOR SOMETHING

energeia: see ACTUALITY

entelecheia: see ACTUALITY

EPIMENIDES

A Cretan religious teacher (6th cent. B.C.?); *Pol.* 1252b14.

epistēmē, epistasthai: see KNOW

epithumia: see DESIRE

EQUAL, FAIR, *isos*

The term may be used to mean either (a) neither more nor less than a given quantity, or (b) neither more nor less than the right quantity. When Aristotle describes JUSTICE as a sort of equality (*EN* 1129a33, 1131b31, *Pol.* 1280a11–25), he normally has (b) in mind, and in these cases 'fair' is often the better rendering.

ergon: see FUNCTION

ESSENCE

To state the essence of F is to answer the question 'What is F?', and to state the (real) DEFINITION of F. Aristotle uses different phrases to refer to the essence: (a) 'Being F' (*to einai F*, also referring more generally to the definition or concept of F). (b) 'What F is' (*ti esti F*) or in general 'the what-it-is' (*to ti esti*). (c) 'What it is to be F' (*to ti ēn F einai*). See *Top.* 101b38, *Met.* 1029b14, 1030a30–1. (d) 'F is essentially G' renders 'F is *hoper* G' (i.e., 'F is precisely what is G', especially where G is the GENUS of F), *Met.* 1006b13, 1030a3, 5.

ESSENCE$_0$: see SUBSTANCE #2

eudaimonia: see HAPPINESS

EURIPIDES

Athenian tragic dramatist (c. 485–c. 406), a younger contemporary of SOPHOCLES.

EVERLASTING: see ALWAYS

EXIST: see BE

EXPERIENCE, EMPIRICAL TECHNIQUE, *empeiria*

Empeiria is the product of PERCEPTION and memory, and a necessary, though insufficient, condition for the KNOWLEDGE that is characteristic of both CRAFTS and theoretical sciences, *APo* 100a5, *Met.* 980b25–981a30, *EN* 1143b14, *Pol.* 1282a1.

EXPLANATION: see CAUSE

FAIR: see EQUAL

FEELING: see ATTRIBUTE

FIGURE, *schēma*

'*Schēma*' often refers to something's geometrical shape, but sometimes to the FORM. See *DA* 414b21, *PA* 640b27–34, 641a8, 20, *Met.* 985b16, 1029a4, 1042b15.

FINAL CAUSE: see FOR SOMETHING

FINE, BEAUTIFUL, *kalos*

The term is applied generally to whatever deserves admiration, and so includes aesthetic beauty (e.g., *EN* 1099b3). In moral contexts it is used for what is praiseworthy and admirable, 1104b31, 1162b35; hence the virtuous person is expected to choose fine action for its own sake, 1115b12, 1116a28, 1120a12, 23. Its opposite is *aischros* (ugly, shameful, disgraceful).

FIRST PHILOSOPHY: see PHILOSOPHY

FOR SOMETHING, WHAT SOMETHING IS FOR, FINAL CAUSE, *heneka tou, hou heneka*

Aristotle uses 'for something' (*heneka tou*) for a goal-directed process. He uses 'what something is for' (or 'that for the sake of which' (*to hou heneka*)) for the goal or end (*telos*) to which the process is directed, *Phys*. 194a35, *Met*. 1072b2. 'Final cause' (from Latin 'finis', 'end') is a convenient technical term. Aristotle believes that the final cause is found in natural processes as well as in the products of CRAFT, *Phys*. ii 8, *DA* 415b28–416a18, *PA* 639b12–21, 640a12–b5. In production by crafts (and non-productive intentional ACTION), the end that plays a causal role is the result aimed at by a designer or producer. In natural processes there is (in Aristotle's view) no intention or design (*Phys*. 199a20–30). Nonetheless some processes in natural organisms happen for the sake of a beneficial result to the organisms. This is true in cases where the fact that the process benefits the organism contributes to the causal explanation of why the process happens; see *Phys*. 198b23–199a8.

FORM, SPECIES, SORT, *eidos*

1. In the most general sense, something's *eidos* is its character, sort, or type. Aristotle sometimes uses the term more narrowly, so that the *eidos* is what the MATTER acquires in COMING TO BE, (when, e.g., the bronze is made into a statue, or the wood composes a tree); see *Phys*. i 7. Here the form is PREDICATED of the matter, and is the formal CAUSE.

2. Aristotle argues that the form, rather than the matter or the compound of form and matter, is the primary sort of SUBSTANCE, *Met*. 1029a5–7. Form is a THIS, (*Met*. 1042a29, 1049a35), the ACTUALITY that realizes the POTENTIALITY of the matter (*DA* 412a10, *Met*. 1038b6, 1042b10), and the primary subject of growth (*GC* 321b22–322a4, 322a28).

3. The form of F is what is defined in the DEFINITION or account of F, stating the ESSENCE of F, *Met*. 1032b1–2, 1035a7–9, 1035b33–1036a2, 1037a21–5. Hence 'account', *logos*, is often used interchangeably with 'form'. In such cases 'form_l' is sometimes used to translate *logos*, where 'account' would be misleading (see also REASON #5).

4. '*Morphē*' (lit. 'shape') sometimes refers to the form, (translated by 'form_m', e.g., at *PA* 640b30). See also FIGURE.

5. Aristotle uses '*eidos*' for the species (e.g., man, horse), in contrast to both the PARTICULARS (e.g., this man) and the GENUS (e.g., animal). In these contexts it is translated 'species', e.g., *Catg*. 2a14. When the contrast between *eidos* and matter is involved, 'form' is used. Sometimes, however, it is difficult to choose between the two renderings, e.g., at *Met*. 1034a5–8.

6. Sense-PERCEPTION involves the reception of the perceptible form (not the form that is identified with the substance) without the matter it is embodied in, *DA* 424a18 (cf. *Met*. 1032b1).

7. For similar reasons, UNDERSTANDING is the reception of intelligible forms without matter, *DA* 429a15–18, *Met*. 1072b18–21.

FORM$_l$: see REASON #5.

FORM$_m$: see FORM #4.

FORM, IDEA (PLATONIC), ***eidos, idea***

As well as using *eidos* for the substantial forms and species that he believes in, Aristotle uses the term (interchangeably with *idea*, following Plato's practice; for the more general use of *idea* as 'character' see *Met*. 1029a4) for the Forms or Ideas recognized by Plato.

FORMULA, TERM, STANDARD, ***horos***

Sometimes *horos* (lit. 'boundary', 'limit', cognate with *horizein*, 'define') is used for a linguistic term, or for what it refers to. Sometimes, however, it is equivalent to *horismos*, 'DEFINITION', e.g., *Top*. 101b22, *Phys*. 194a2, *DA* 413a11, *Met*. 987b6, 1030a8, 1038a21, 1039a20, 1040a6, *Pol*. 1280a7.

FORTUNE: see LUCK

FRIENDSHIP, ***philia*****; LOVE,** ***philein***

'Friendship' does not sound equally natural for all the different types of cooperative relations that Aristotle classifies as types of *philia* (for the cognate verb *philein*, 'love' has to be used); see *EN* viii–ix. *Philiai* include business partnerships and family relations that we might not readily recognize as constituting friendships in their own right. While Aristotle sees some common or overlapping features (e.g., 1155b32–1156a10), he is mainly concerned to show the ethical differences between types of *philia* in individual and political relations (cf. viii 10–11).

FULL, FULLY: see CONTROLLING

FUNCTION, TASK, ACTIVITY, ACHIEVEMENT, ***ergon***

Ergon has the range of uses of the English 'work'. It is applied to an activity ('this is hard work') as well as to the result ('a great work of art'; see *Poet*. 1452b30). Often 'function' is suitable. See *Met*. 1029b5, 1045b35, *EN* 1097b25, *Pol*. 1253a23.

genesis: see COME TO BE

GENUS, ***genos***

The term is cognate with *gignesthai*, 'COME TO BE', and originally means 'family' or 'race', *Met*. 1024a29–36. Aristotle uses it in a broader sense for a sort or kind (not always sharply distinguished from *eidos*, e.g., at *PA* 645a30; see FORM), and in a narrower, technical sense. In the technical sense a genus is a secondary SUBSTANCE (e.g., animal) and a UNIVERSAL, divided by DIFFERENTIAE (e.g., biped, quadruped) into species (e.g., man, horse; see FORM #9), *Catg*. 2a17–19, *Top*. 102a31–5.

gignōskō: see KNOW

GOD, *theos*
Aristotle mentions the traditional Olympian gods, without committing himself to the traditional conception of them, *Pol*. 1252b24, 1254b35; he rejects anthropomorphizing views of the nature of the gods, *EN* 1178b9. He refers generally to 'the god' when he has no particular god in mind, *Met*. 983a8, 1072b35, *Pol*. 1323b23. He believes that there is something divine about the order and workings of nature, *Phys*. 192a16, *DA* 415a29, and still more divine in the heavenly substances, *PA* 644b22–645a7, *Met*. xii 7–10.

GOOD, *agathos*
Aristotle connects 'good' (and the corresponding adverb *eu*, 'well') closely with ends (see FINAL CAUSE). A good F (e.g., knife, horse, person) has a VIRTUE that is defined by reference to the FUNCTION of F, and therefore to the ESSENCE of F, *EN* 1098a8, 1106a15. Something is good for a substance F insofar as it promotes F's good or welfare, *Pol*. 1261b9; F's good is determined by F's function and essence, *EN* 1094a18–22, 1097a15–24, 1097b22–1098a5. The good for human beings is their HAPPINESS, which is their ultimate end.

GROWTH: see FORM #2.

HABITUATION, *ethismos*: see CHARACTER

haplōs: see WITHOUT QUALIFICATION

HAPPINESS, *eudaimonia*
The term is derived from *eu*, 'well' (see GOOD), and *daimōn*, 'divine being', and so suggests a life favored by the gods. Following common beliefs, Aristotle identifies happiness with the highest good, also described as 'living well', 1095a18, 1097a15–b21. Happiness is the COMPLETE end fully satisfying a person's correct rational DESIRE. The English 'happiness' may mislead, if it suggests that Aristotle thinks pleasure or contentment or 'feeling happy' is the highest good. In fact he denies (*EN* x 1–5) that pleasure is the same as *eudaimonia*; he thinks *eudaimonia* consists in living and acting (in accordance with VIRTUE), not simply in having a certain kind of pleasure.

HEAVEN, *ouranos*
Aristotle uses *ouranos* both for the upper universe in contrast to the earth and for the universe including the earth. See *Phys*. 196a25, 251b18, 338a19, *PA* 641b16, *Met*. 1042a10, 1072b14.

HERACLEITUS
Heracleitus (fl. 500?) was, in Aristotle's view, one of the early materialist

NATURALISTS. See *Phys.* 185a5–7, *Met.* 984a7–8, 987a32–b1, 1005b23–5, 1010a10–15.

HERODOTUS

Historian (c. 484–c. 427). See *Poet.* 1451b2.

HESIOD

Didactic poet (8th cent.) See *Met.* 984b23, 1000a9, 1071b27, *EN* 1095b10, *Pol.* 1252b10.

HOMER

Aristotle often quotes Homer (8th cent.), sometimes to illustrate the mythological as opposed to the NATURALIST worldview, sometimes as a source of familiar and respectable ethical or political views. See *Met.* 1009b28, *EN* 1109b8, 1113a8, 1116a21, *Pol.* 1253a5.

HOMONYMOUS, *homōnumon*; SPOKEN OF IN MANY WAYS, *pollachōs legomenon*

Homonymy and being spoken of in many ways are primarily (but cf. *GC* 322b29–30) relations between the things that have names, not between names themselves. *Homōnuma* are, literally, 'things that have the same NAME (*onoma*)'. In Aristotle's technical sense (contrast *Met.* 987b10, 990b6, 1034a22), two or more F things are F homonymously if and only if they share the name 'F', but they do not share the DEFINITION or ACCOUNT corresponding to 'F', *Catg.* 1a1–6, *Top.* 106a1–8. 'Homonymy' is often used equivalently to 'spoken of in many ways'. Sometimes, however, Aristotle says that certain things are spoken of in many ways (since they have no single definition), but are non-homonymous (since their definitions all refer to one thing); see *Met.* 1003a3–b10, 1004a23–5, 1028a10–13, 1030a32–b3, *EN* 1096b26–9.

idea: see FORM, IDEA

IN GENERAL, ALTOGETHER, *holōs*

Holōs normally means 'in general' in the sense of 'speaking quite generally, and without exception'; and so its sense (in, e.g., *Met.* 1029b6, *Pol.* 1280a23) is often close to that of WITHOUT QUALIFICATION. See *DA* 403a7, 412b7, *Met.* 1033b11, *EN* 1140a25–31, *Pol.* 1254a10, 1263a26.

IN ITS OWN RIGHT, IN ITSELF, INTRINSIC, *kath'hauto*

G may belong to F in its own right (per se; lit. 'in accordance with itself') in either of two ways: (a) G is part of, or derivable from, the ESSENCE and DEFINITION of F, and G belongs to F INSOFAR AS it is F (belongs to F qua F), *APo* 73a34–b24, *Met.* 1029b13–19; or (b) G contains F in its definition (as odd belongs to number in its own right, though not every number is odd), *APo* 73a37–b5, *Met.* 1030b16–26. Because of its connection with the essence, what belongs to F in F's own right is often contrasted with what belongs to F coincidentally, *Met*. 1017a7–8. Aristotle, however, also recognizes coincidents of F in its own right; see COINCIDENT.

INCONTINENCE, *akrasia*

Incontinent or 'uncontrolled' people lack control (*kratein*) over their nonrational DESIRES; hence they act on appetite in opposition to their correct DECISION, and choose what they know (in some way that Aristotle tries to describe more precisely) what is worse for them. See *DA* 434a10–21, *EN* 1102b14–28, 1111b13–15, vii 3.

INDEFINITE: see INFINITE

INDETERMINATE: see INFINITE #3

INDIVIDUAL, INDIVISIBLE, *atomon*

What is *atomon* is in some way indivisible (lit. 'uncuttable'). Aristotle applies the term to mathematical points, *Phys*. 232a24, and to the 'atoms' recognized by DEMOCRITUS, *Phys*. 265b29, *DA* 404a2, *Met*. 1039a19. (Aristotle himself rejects indivisible magnitudes, *GC* 315b26 ff.) Aristotle says that x is an *atomon* F when he means that x is not divisible into further Fs. Hence '*atomon*' may refer to a PARTICULAR man (not divisible into further men, *Catg*. 1b6, 3a38, b12, *Met*. 995b30) or to the species (see FORM) man (not divisible into further species, *DA* 414b27, *Met*. 1034a8). 'The individual man' etc. is used to translate *ho tis anthropōs*, lit. 'the some man', *Catg*. 1a22 etc. The indefinite *tis* ('some') is the nearest thing in Greek to an indefinite article; cf. *APo* 93a23.

INDUCTION, *epagōgē*

Induction and DEDUCTION are the two ways of reaching rational CONVICTION, *APo* 71a5, *EN* 1139b26–31. In contrast to deduction, induction proceeds from PARTICULAR to UNIVERSAL, *APo* 72b29, 100b4, *Top*. 105a11–19. Aristotle speaks of induction not only where we form some general conclusion on the basis of EXPERIENCE of particular instances, but also where we come to understand some general principle or concept on the basis of some particular illustrations, *Met*. 1048a36 (cf. *Phys*. 191a8).

INFERENCE, *sullogismos*: see DEDUCTION.

INFINITE, UNLIMITED, INDEFINITE, *apeiron*; INDEFINITE, INDETERMINATE, *ahoriston*

1. Aristotle uses *apeiron* for an infinite series, one in which there is always another member besides those previously counted. See *Phys*. 206a27–9, 207a7–8, 218a21, 263a28, *GC* 318a19, *Met*. 1048b9–17.

2. Aristotle rejects the possibility of some types of infinite series. See *APo* 72b7–11, *Phys*. 256a17–19, *EN* 1094a20–1. But he believes, against ZENO, that an infinite series of the sort required by MOTION is acceptable, *Phys*. vi 9, 263a15–b9.

3. '*Apeiron*' is translated by 'unlimited' where it seems to indicate not that a series can never be completed, but that there is no reason to suppose that it stops at any definite place. See *DI* 16a28, b14, *Phys.* 196b27–9, *DA* 416a15, *Met.* 987b25, 1006a34–b11, 1007a13–15, b1, b26–9.

INSOFAR AS, *hē(i)*

This is the dative of the relative pronoun, and means literally 'by which' or 'in the respect in which', often Latinized as 'qua'. When Aristotle says that x is G insofar as x is F, he means that x is G because x is F; x's being F is the basis for correctly predicating G of x. Socrates, e.g., is both a man and a musician; but it is qua man that he is an animal, and qua musician that he is incompetent. See *APo* 73b27, *Phys.* 191b4, 193b32, *Met.* 1003a21, 1004b10–17, 1035a8, *EN* 1096b24, 1130a12–13.

INTELLECT: see UNDERSTANDING

INTELLIGENCE, UNDERSTANDING, *phronēsis*

Aristotle uses '*phronēsis*' (1) in a wider sense, referring to intelligent consciousness or understanding in general, *DA* 417b8, *Met.* 980b1, 982b24, 1009b30; (2) in his own specialized sense, for the deliberative VIRTUE of practical intellect, discussed in *EN* vi, esp. vi 5, 7–8, 12–13.

JUSTICE, *dikaiosunē*

Justice is the other-regarding virtue especially associated with the CITY, or political COMMUNITY. Aristotle distinguishes 'general' justice from the special virtue of 'partial' justice, in *EN* v 1–2, and analyzes the types of partial justice in v 3–5. On political justice see *Pol.* iii 9, 12. On LAW and justice see *EN* 1134b18–1135a5.

kalos; see FINE

katēgorein: PREDICATE

kath'hauto: IN ITS OWN RIGHT

kath'hekaston: PARTICULAR

katholou: UNIVERSAL

kinein, kinēsis: see MOTION

KNOW, *epistasthai, gignōskein, eidenai*; KNOW SCIENTIFICALLY, *epistasthai*; KNOWLEDGE, *gnōsis, epistēmē*; SCIENCE, SCIENTIFIC KNOWLEDGE, *epistēmē*; KNOWN, *gnōrimon, epistēton*

1. The occurrences of Aristotle's different epistemic verbs are marked by subscript initial letters (the same verb is used until a different subscript letter appears). 'Know_e' is used for *epistasthai*; 'know_g' for *gignōskein*; and 'know_o' for *eidenai* (since the first person singular is *oida*). In general: (1) *epistasthai* is most frequently associated with demonstrative science, or

at any rate with a systematic discipline. (2) *gignōskein* and its cognates often seem rather weaker. It is appropriate to apply *gignōskein* to knowing or recognizing people and ordinary perceptible objects, but it would be odder to use *epistasthai* in such a context. (3) *eidenai* seems less specialized than either of the other two terms. (4) In English 'S knows that p' implies that (i) p is true and (roughly) (ii) S is justified in believing that p. While (i) holds for *epistasthai* and *eidenai*, it may not hold for *gignōskein* (and certainly does not hold in the phrase translated 'known to us'; see below). Something like (ii) holds (see *APo* i 2) for *epistasthai* and probably for *eidenai*, but it is less clear that it holds for *gignōskein*.

2. Aristotle often contrasts what is better known (*gnōrimon*) 'to us' (i.e., better known as far as we are concerned') with what is better known 'by nature' or 'WITHOUT QUALIFICATION' (i.e., the sort of thing that is an appropriate object of knowledge), *APo* 71b33–72a5, *Phys*. 184a16–23, *Met*. 1029b3–12, *EN* 1095b2–4 (cf. *Top*. 105a16–19).

3. Sometimes (e.g., *APo* 71b9–25) Aristotle takes DEMONSTRATION to be necessary for *epistēmē*. But he does not always use '*epistēmē*' so narrowly; sometimes 'sciences' seem to include CRAFTS as well as strictly demonstrative sciences, *EN* 1094a28, 1180b13–16.

LAW, CONVENTION, *nomos*

Nomos is the product of human enactment or belief, or a norm for guiding behavior; it is not confined to positive law enacted by some legislature (see esp. *Pol*. 1324b27). It is sometimes contrasted with NATURE. See *Phys*. 193a15, *EN* 1094b16, 1129b12, 1134b19, *Pol*. 1282b1–13.

LETTER: see ELEMENT

LEUCIPPUS: see DEMOCRITUS

LOGICAL, *logikos*

'Logical' problems are a subset of DIALECTICAL problems. They have no specific subject matter, but may be expected to apply generally to inquiries in different specific areas, *Top*. 105b19–29. 'Logical' arguments are contrasted with arguments specific to the subject matter at hand, *APo* 93a15, *Met*. 1005b22, 1029b13, 1030a27–8, 1041a27–8, *EN* 1147a24. 'Logical' argument is not confined to formal 'logic' in the modern sense. Aristotle refers to his formal logic as 'analytics'; *Met*. 1005b4, 1037b8 (since it analyzes arguments to reveal the basic patterns of deductive argument, *APr* 47a2–5, 49a11–18).

logos: see REASON

LOVE: see FRIENDSHIP

LUCK, CHANCE, FORTUNE, *tuchē*; CHANCE, ***to automaton***

In Aristotle's strictest use, *to automaton* refers to an event that is of the right sort to have a FINAL CAUSE, but does not actually have one. The subset of these events that come about from a DECISION are matters of *tuchē*, *Phys.* 196b21–9, 197b18–22, *Poet.* 1452a5. In these cases *tuchē* is rendered by 'luck', and *to automaton* by 'chance'. When Aristotle does not have this contrast between luck and chance in mind, he tends to use *tuchē* (and cognates) to include *to automaton*, and even to include COINCIDENTAL results more generally, *DI* 18b7, 19a19, 38.

'Any old thing' translates *to tuchon* (lit. 'what happens' or 'what happens by chance'), which Aristotle uses (e.g., *Phys.* 188a33, *Met.* 1075a20) to refer to what happens on no definite principle or rule. The phrase is also used to mean 'anything picked out at random' and so 'nondescript', 'undistinguished'.

LYCOPHRON

A SOPHIST of unknown date. See *Met.* 1045b10, *Pol.* 1280b10.

MAN, HUMAN BEING, *anthrōpos*

Anthrōpos corresponds to the Latin 'homo' (referring to the human species), as opposed to *anēr*, 'vir' (adult male). In contexts where *anthrōpos* is used as a species term coordinate with 'horse', 'tree' etc., 'man' is the best rendering (since the grammatical form of 'human being' makes it unsuitable for understanding some of Aristotle's linguistic points). In other contexts (e.g., ethical) 'human being' is a better rendering, and 'man' is used for *anēr*. On human beings and other animals see REASON #1.

MATTER, *hulē*

1. In ordinary Greek *hulē* means 'wood'. Aristotle extends this use to raw material in general, *Phys.* 191a8–12, 195a16 (cf. Plato, *Philebus* 54c2). Matter is the SUBJECT of COMING TO BE and perishing, and so it is the subject from which a substance comes to be; the bronze from which a statue is made, and the material elements of which an organism is composed, are the matter, *Phys.* 190b3–10. Since matter explains some features of artifacts and organisms by reference to their composition, it is a CAUSE.

2. Different types of matter are relative to different levels of organization, *Phys.* 193a10, 29, 194b8–9. Wood is the 'proximate' (or 'closest'; cf. *Met.* 1044b1–3) matter of the box, but earth is the matter of the wood, and only indirectly the matter of the box, *Met.* 1023a26–9, 1044a15–20, 1049a18–24.

3. It is usually (though not always) believed that at the lowest level of organization Aristotle recognizes 'prime' (i.e., first) matter. This is the subject of the most basic qualities, and it remains throughout changes of one element into another. See *Phys.* 193a17–21, *GC* 332a17–20, 35.

4. Matter is a kind of SUBSTANCE, but neither the only nor the primary kind, *Phys.* 191a12–14, 193a9–12, *DA* 412a9, *Met.* 1029a10–33, 1035a1–4, 1040b5–10, 1042a25–b8, 1049a34–6.

5. A living organism has two types of matter: (a) The living BODY and its organic PARTS are matter (*DA* 412a17–19); they do not exist—except HOMONYMOUSLY—after the death of the organism, *DA* 412b13–15, 20–2, *PA* 640b35–641a6, 645a35, *Met.* 1035b23–5, 1036b30–2, *Pol.* 1253a18–25. (b) The material constituents of the living body and of its parts still exist after the death of the organism, *DA* 412b25–6, *Met.* 1035a18–19, 31–3.

MEAN, *mesotēs*; INTERMEDIATE, *meson*

Aristotle identifies VIRTUE of character with a mean, i.e., an intermediate state between excess and deficiency. The limited application of the quantitative analogy is explained in *EN* 1106a26–b27. The appeal to a mean does not imply advocacy of moderation in behavior or feelings.

MIND: see UNDERSTANDING

MORE, RATHER, *mallon*

To say that x is *mallon* F than y can mean (a) 'x rather than y is F' (i.e., x is F and y is not F), or (b) 'x is F more than y' (i.e., x is F to a higher degree than y is—without implying that either x or y either is or is not F). In some cases it is not obvious whether Aristotle has (a) or (b) in mind, e.g., *DI* 19a20, 38, *Phys.* 193b6, *Met.* 1029a29, *Poet.* 1451b7.

morphē: see FORM #4

MOTION, PROCESS, CHANGE, *kinēsis*; MOVE, *kinein*

Kinēsis extends more widely than motion, as we normally conceive it; see *Phys.* 225a5–9, 226a23–b8. On 'change', *metabolē*, and *kinēsis* see *Phys.* 218b20, 225a34–b3, 226a35, 229a30–2, *Met.* 991a11). Motion is defined as the ACTUALITY of what is potentially F, insofar as it is potentially F (*Phys.* 201b5).

NAME, *onoma*

At *DI* 16a19–21 Aristotle uses *onoma* for nouns in contrast to verbs and other parts of speech. Sometimes, however, he uses it to include other parts of speech.

NATURALIST, *phusiologos*

Aristotle uses this term (as opposed to the broader term *phusikos*, 'student of NATURE') to refer to those who concentrate on the material side of the study of nature. They include the 'Presocratics', the natural philosophers before and during the lifetime of Socrates. See *PA* 641a7, *EN* 1147b8 (translated 'natural scientists').

NATURE, *phusis*

1. A subject has a nature if and only if it has an internal PRINCIPLE initiating the subject's own MOTION and rest, *Phys.* 192b13–15. This definition includes (a) the four ELEMENTS, which, in Aristotle's view, have

their own natural local motion, *Phys.* 255a1–5, *DC* 301b16–30; (b) living organisms, i.e., those natural objects whose internally caused motions include self-nourishment and reproduction, *DA* 412a11–15.

2. Aristotle also uses 'nature' to refer to nature in general—the natural world of material SUBSTANCES that have natures.

3. The USUAL as well as the necessary is characteristic of nature, *GA* 727b29–30.

4. Nature does nothing 'pointlessly', *matēn*, *DA* 415b16–17, 434a30–b8, *PA* 641b12–15, *Pol.* 1252b1–3, 1253a9–18, 1263a41.

NECESSITY, *anankē*; NECESSARY, *anankaion*

1. Aristotle often suggests that it is necessary that p if and only if it is not possible that not-p, *DI* 22b3–10, *APo* 71b15, 73a22, *Met.* 1015a33–6. Sometimes, however, he seems to imply that this is not sufficient for necessity, *APo* 73b25–32.

2. Aristotle contrasts unqualified (see WITHOUT QUALIFICATION) with conditional (lit. 'on an ASSUMPTION') necessity. He has different sorts of conditions or 'assumptions' in mind in different contexts. See *DI* 19a26, *Phys.* 199b34–200a30, *DA* 415b28–416a18, *PA* 639b21–640a8, 642a3–13, 642a31–b4, *Met.* 1072b11.

3. The necessary is contrasted both with the USUAL and with matters of chance (see LUCK) and COINCIDENCE, *APo* 87b19–27, *Met.* 1026b27–1027a5.

nous: see UNDERSTANDING

ONE

Different kinds of sameness and oneness are distinguished in *Top.* i 7; see also *DA* 412b8–9, *Met.* 1003b22–34, v 6, 1040b16–19, 1072a32. On numerical (v. specific) unity, attributed especially to PARTICULARS, see *Catg.* 1b6, 3b12–18, *Phys.* 190a15, *DA* 415b4, *Met.* 1040b8–10, 25–6, 1086b26.

OPPOSITE, *antikeimenon*

Opposites include contradictories (e.g., pale and not pale) as well as contraries, *enantia* (e.g., pale and dark). Contraries must be in the same GENUS, but contradictories need not be; see *Catg.* 11b7, 14a19, *DI* 19b1, *Phys.* 188a35–b3, *Met.* 1004a9.

ORIGIN: see PRINCIPLE

ousia: SUBSTANCE

PARMENIDES

A Presocratic (c. 515–after 450; see HERACLEITUS). He wrote a poem in two parts, the 'Way of Truth', and the 'Way of Opinion'. See *Phys.* i 2–3, 191b36–192a2, *GC* 318b2–7, *Met.* 984b1–5, 25, 1009b20–5.

PART, ***meros, morion***

Aristotle distinguishes uniform (*homoiomerēs*, 'having parts similar to the whole') from non-uniform parts. Flesh or water is divisible into more flesh or water; but arms are not divisible into more arms. Hence Aristotle calls flesh etc. uniform parts, and arms etc. non-uniform parts, *GC* 314a20, *Metr*. 389b23–9, *PA* 640b20. The non-uniform parts of organisms depend on the whole, *Met*. 1035b18–27, 1036b30–2 (see MATTER #5 and HOMONYMY), *Pol*. 1253a10–29.

PARTICULAR, ***kath'hekaston***

'Taking Fs *kath'hekaston*' means 'taking Fs each one at a time', or 'taking Fs in turn' (*Phys*. 233a23), and so Aristotle uses the phrase *kath'hekaston* as a noun for each of the particular Fs. A particular is defined, in contrast to a UNIVERSAL, as what is not predicated of many things, *DI* 17a39–40. It is characteristic of a particular to be INDIVIDUAL and numerically ONE, *Catg*. 1b6–7, 2b3. See also THIS. Aristotle also uses 'particular' and 'universal' to mark a contrast between the more and less specific or determinate; hence the 'particulars' are sometimes, e.g., the species (and hence universals) of a genus, rather than particulars such as Callias; *Phys*. 189b30, 195a32, *PA* 639b6. Particulars (in the sense in which no universal is a particular) are not—as such—the objects of DEFINITION or scientific KNOWLEDGE, *Met*. 1035b34–1036a9, 1039b27–1040a7, *Poet*. 1451b7. Contrast *Met* xiii 10.

pathos: see ATTRIBUTE

PERCEPTION, SENSE, SENSE-PERCEPTION, ***aisthēsis***

Aisthēsis includes the five senses and the cognitive activity we perform with them, *DA* ii 6. Each sense has its own proper (see DISTINCTIVE) object (e.g., color for sight), *DA* 418a11–16, and the senses taken together have common objects, *DA* 425a14–b11. When we see an ordinary physical object (e.g., a chair, the son of Cleon), that is COINCIDENTAL perception, resulting from perceiving the perceptible qualities of the object, *DA* 418a20–5, 425a24–7. Perception primarily makes us aware of PARTICULARS, as opposed to UNIVERSALS, *APo* 87b28–88a2, 100a16–b1, *Met*. 1036a2–8, 1039b28–31, 1087a19–20.

phainomena: see APPEARANCES

phantasia: see APPEARANCE

PHILOSOPHY, ***philosophia***

1. Aristotle uses '*philosophia*' in a general sense (in keeping with its etymology, 'love of WISDOM') for studies concerned with the truth, apart from any immediate practical application, *Top*. 101a17, *PA* 640b5, 642a30, 645a10, *Met*. 982b13, 983b20, 1009b33–1010a1. Hence he takes DEMONSTRATIVE sciences to belong to philosophy, *Poet*. 1451b5.

2. He also uses the term in a narrower sense for the discipline—also called 'the science of being' or 'first philosophy'—that is introduced in the *Met*. See 1003a21, b19, 1004a6, 34, b9, b25–6. The traditional title of Aristotle's treatise on first philosophy is *ta meta ta phusika*, 'the things beyond natural things'. First philosophy goes 'beyond' the study of nature because (1) it studies entities outside the natural order; (2) it starts from the study of nature (treating it as better KNOWN to us) and goes beyond it to its foundations and presuppositions.

phusis, phusikos: see NATURE

PLATO

Plato (428–347) deeply influenced many aspects of Aristotle's philosophy, through his dialogues, through his oral teaching, and through discussions in Plato's philosophical school, the Academy (of which Aristotle was a member from 367–347). Aristotle often refers to Plato's dialogues (e.g., *GC* 335b10, *Met*. 1025a6, *Pol*. 1261a6), sometimes without naming them (e.g., *Met*. 1039a2, *EN* 1145b33). Sometimes he also cites Plato's 'unwritten teachings' (*Phys*. 209b11–16; cf. 192a6, *Met*. 987b18–29).

POETRY: see PRODUCE

POINTLESS, *matēn*: see NATURE #4

poion: see QUALITY

polis: CITY

POLUS

A rhetorical theorist of the mid-fifth century, and a pupil of Gorgias. He is a character in Plato's *Gorgias*.

POPULAR

When Aristotle refers to 'popular' (*exōterika*) works he probably refers to his own works written for more general circulation than he intended for the lectures that have been preserved. See *EN* 1096a13, 1102a26, 1140a3, *Pol*. 1254a33, 1278b31, 1323a22.

POSSIBILITY: see POTENTIALITY

POTENTIALITY, CAPACITY, *dunamis*; POSSIBILITY, POSSIBLE, CAPABLE, POTENTIALLY, *dunaton*

1. 'Possible' translates *dunaton* applied to a state of affairs ('it is possible that it will rain tomorrow'). 'Can' or 'capable' translates *dunaton* and the cognate verb *dunasthai* applied to substances. 'Potentiality' (or 'potentially') or 'capacity' translates the cognate noun *dunamis* applied to substances (see #3). This broad application of *dunaton* and its cognates sometimes creates some ambiguity in Aristotle's claims (e.g., *Met*. ix 3–4). 'Admit of', *endechesthai*, normally applies only to states of affairs.

2. What is possible is defined as (i) what is not impossible ('one-sided' possibility) or as (ii) what is neither NECESSARY nor impossible ('two-sided' possibility), *DI* 21b13–14, *APr* 25a37, 32a18–20, *Met.* 1047a24–5.

3. x has a potentiality for F (in the primary way) by having an internal PRINCIPLE of F, *Phys.* 251a11, *Met.* 1046a9–11; in that case F is the ACTUALITY of the potentiality. Every such potentiality is a potentiality for F not in all circumstances, but in the appropriate circumstances, *Phys.* 251b1–5, *DA* 417a28, *Met.* 1048a13–16.

PREDICATE, *katēgorein,* THING PREDICATED, PREDICATION, *katēgoria*

Normally, F is predicated of x if x is F; in this case x (e.g., this man) is the SUBJECT and F (e.g., man) is the thing predicated, *Catg.* 1b10–15. Hence predication is normally a relation between non-linguistic items, not between words (though cf. *Catg.* 2a19–34). In most cases the thing predicated is a universal, *Catg.* 1b10, 2a12–13, *DI* 17a39–40, *Met.* 1038b16–17. Contrast, however, *Met.* 1049a34–6.

PREDICATIONS, *katēgoriai*

Aristotle usually refers to substance, quality, etc. (listed in, e.g., *Catg.* 4, *Top.* 103b20–7, *GC* 317b5–11, 319a11–12, *Met.* 1017a22–7, 1028a10–13, *EN* 1096a19–29) as 'the figures (i.e., types) of predication', or 'the GENERA of predications', *genē tōn kategoriōn*, *APo* 83b16, *Top.* 103b20. Sometimes he speaks of 'the predications', *katēgoriai*, *GC* 317b6, 9, 319a11, *DA* 402a25, *Met.* 1032a15; this is the basis for the traditional label 'categories'. The categories exemplify the fact that being is spoken of in many ways (see BE, HOMONYMOUS).

PRINCIPLE, ORIGIN, BEGINNING, SOURCE, STARTING POINT, RULE, RULING OFFICE, *archē*

Archē (Latin 'principium') is cognate with *archein* ('begin, rule'), and the *archē* of x is in some way or other first in relation to x. Hence it is the beginning or origin, *Met.* 1072b33, *EN* 1098b7, *Pol.* 1252a24. Each of the four CAUSES is an *archē*, *Met.* 1013a16–17. In these cases the *archē* is something non-linguistic and non-propositional. In an argument, description, or theory, the *archē* is 'that from which primarily a thing is known', *Met.* 1013a14–15.

PRIOR

On different types of priority see *Catg.* 13, *Met.* v 11, 1028a32–b2, 1038b27, 1049b4–12, 1071b5, *Pol.* 1253a19. Aristotle usually mentions (a) priority by nature (x can exist without y (and so is SEPARABLE from y), but y cannot exist without x); (b) priority in knowledge (x can be known without y, but knowledge of y requires knowledge of x); (c) priority in definition (the definition of x does not include mention of y, but the definition of y includes mention of x).

PRODUCE, *poiein*; PRODUCTION, *poiēsis*

Poiēsis is production, action that has some end (e.g., a house) external to the productive action itself, in contrast to *praxis* (see ACTION) that is its own end, *EN* 1140b6–7. Production is characteristic of CRAFT, whereas action is characteristic of VIRTUE. Aristotle also uses *poiētikē* (lit. 'productive (sc. craft)') for what we call poetry. See esp. *Poet*. 1447b13–25.

PROPERTY

This usually corresponds either to nothing in the Greek (Aristotle uses fewer abstract nouns than it is natural to use in English) or to some term of general scope, such as *pragma*, 'thing'.

PROTAGORAS

Protagoras (?485–415?) was a leading SOPHIST. See *Met*. 1007b22, 1009a5, *EN* 1113a29, 1164a20, 1166a12, 1170a21, 1176a16.

PROTARCHUS

An orator and pupil of Gorgias. See Plato, *Philebus* 58a.

PYTHAGORAS

The Presocratic Pythagoras (fl. 530?) became a subject of legend and fable. Aristotle ascribes specific doctrines not to Pythagoras himself, but to 'the Pythagoreans'. See *DA* 407b20–4, *Met*. 985b22–986b8, 987a9–28, b10–13, 23, 31, 996a6, 1036b18, 1072b30–4, *EN* 1096b5–7, 1106b29–30.

QUA: see INSOFAR AS

QUALITY, SORT OF THING, *poion*

The question '*poion estin x*?' may be translated 'What sort of thing is x?'. Aristotle uses *poion* in two different cases: (a) It sometimes refers to the category (see PREDICATIONS) of quality. (Cf. 'What sort of meal was it?' 'Terrible.') (b) It sometimes refers to the species in any category, including the category of substance. (Cf. 'What sort of animal is it?' 'A horse.') See *Catg*. 3b15–21, *GC* 319a12, *DA* 415b7, *Met*. 1010a25, 1020a33–b18, 1038b23–1039a2. The cognate term *toionde* is translated by 'this sort of thing'; see *Top*. 179a2, *GC* 319a12, *Met*. 1033b22, 1039a2.

RATHER: see MORE

RATIO: see REASON #6

REALIZATION: see ACTUALITY

REASON, ACCOUNT, ARGUMENT, RATIONAL DISCOURSE, SENTENCE, STATEMENT, RATIO, *logos*

1. *Logos* refers to reason, as distinct from non-rational affection, *pathos* (see ATTRIBUTE), *EN* 1147b16. It is characteristic of human beings, in contrast to non-rational animals, who cannot grasp UNIVERSALS, *DA* 415a7–11,

428a22–4, *EN* 1147b3–5. *Logos* belongs to one part of the SOUL, *EN* 1098a3–5.

2. One characteristic expression of *logos* is significant rational discourse, formed by the combination of thoughts. The smallest such combination is a sentence. See *Catg*. 2a4–7, *DI* 16b26–32, *Met*. 1006a13–15, 22–4, 1008b10–12 *Pol*. 1253a9–18, 1332b3–6.

3. The combination of thoughts and sentences produces a *logos*, i.e., argument, *Top*. 100a25–7, *Pol*. 1254a21.

4. The *logos* of F is a verbal formula corresponding to the name 'F', *Catg*. 1a2, *Phys*. 191a33, *Met*. 983a28, 1006b1. (Hence 'a horse is a quadruped' can be replaced by 'a horse has four legs'.) It is often equivalent to a DEFINITION.

5. *Logos* is sometimes used for the thing or property defined rather than for the defining formula itself, e.g., *Phys*. 193a31, *Met*. 1035a4, 1042a28; in Aristotle's view, the thing defined by a definition of x is the FORM of x rather than the MATTER of x. Hence 'the *logos* of x' is often equivalent to 'the form of x'. In these cases 'form$_1$' is used to indicate an occurrence of *logos*; see *Phys*. 194b27, 200a35, *DA* 412b16, 414a27 (cf. 414a13), 424a24, 27, 31, *PA* 639b15, 642a20.

6. In mathematical contexts the *logos* is the ratio or proportion, *Phys*. 194b27, *DA* 416a7.

REASON: see CAUSE

RULE, RULING OFFICE: see PRINCIPLE

SAME: see ONE

SCIENCE: see KNOW

SENSE: see PERCEPTION

SENTENCE: see REASON

SEPARABLE, *chōriston*

Chōriston is formed from *chōrizein*, 'to separate'; it is hard to know whether in a given context it means 'separate' (i.e., is actually separated from something) or 'separable' (i.e., can be separated from something). Separability includes: (a) separability WITHOUT QUALIFICATION, i.e., x is separable from y if and only if it is possible for x to exist without y, *GC* 317b10, *DA* 403b9–19, 413a4, 31; (b) separability in account, *logos* (see REASON), i.e., definitional independence, *Phys*. 193b34, *DA* 413b13–16, 429a11, 432a20, 433b24, *Met*. 1042a29, *EN* 1102a28–32.

SHAPE: see FORM #5

SIGNIFY, *sēmainein*

Sēmainein is cognate with *sēmeion* ('sign', 'indication'), and so means 'indicate'. Aristotle standardly uses *sēmainein* where we would be inclined to speak of the meaning of a word. See, e.g., *DI* 16a17, 19, *APo* 71a15, 93b30. However, not only words (e.g., 'man'), but also the corresponding things (e.g., man) are said to signify (as we say that spots signify measles), *Catg*. 3b12, *APo* 73b8.

SIMONIDES

Poet (556?–468). A source of familiar tags and proverbs. See *Met*. 982b30, *EN* 1100b21.

SIMPLE: see WITHOUT QUALIFICATION

SOCRATES

Aristotle sharply distinguishes the doctrines and concerns of the historical Socrates (469–399) from those of Plato; see *Top*. 183b7, *PA* 642a28–31, *Met*. 987b1, 1078b17–31, 1086b3.

SOCRATES THE YOUNGER

An associate of Socrates. See *Met*. 1036b25, Plato, *Theaetetus* 147d1, *Sophist* 218b2.

SOLON

An Athenian legislator and poet (fl. 594). See *EN* 1100a11, 1179a9, *Pol*. 1281b32.

SOPHIST, *sophistēs*

Sophistēs is cognate with *sophos*, 'wise'. Usually, Aristotle uses 'sophist' to refer to those who use fallacious arguments that seem convincing when they are not. See *APo* 71b10, 74a28, 74b23, *Top*. 183b2, *Met*. 1004b22, 1032a6, *EN* 1146a21, *Pol*. 1260b34.

SOPHOCLES

An Athenian tragic dramatist (c. 496–406). His plays strongly influenced Aristotle's conception of tragedy.

SORT: see QUALITY

SOUL, *psuchē*

To attribute soul to something is not, in the view of Aristotle and his contemporaries, to make a disputable metaphysical claim about it. Aristotle assumes general agreement that animals (on plants see *DA* 402a6, 409a9–10, 410b22–4, 411b27) have souls; he takes the dispute to be about the nature of soul. On the connection between life, MOTION, and soul see *DA* 403a3–8, b25–7, 412a13–15, *EN* 1098a3–8. The adjective *empsuchos*, lit. 'ensouled', is translated by 'animate' or by 'having a soul' (in contexts where Aristotle clearly relies on the connection between *empsuchos* and *psuchē*).

SOURCE: see PRINCIPLE

SPECIAL: see DISTINCTIVE

SPECIES: see FORM

SPEUSIPPUS

Speusippus (?407–339) succeeded Plato as head of the Academy. See *Met*. 1028b21–4, 1072b31, *EN* 1096b7, 1153b5.

SPOKEN OF IN MANY WAYS: see HOMONYMOUS

STANDARD: see FORMULA

STARTING POINT: see PRINCIPLE

STATE, *hexis*

Hexis is the abstract noun from *echein* 'have', which together with an adverb means 'be disposed in some way' (*echein pōs*); and so a *hexis* is a relatively fixed and permanent way a subject is disposed, *Catg*. 8b25–9a13, *EN* 1105b25–8 (it is a first, as opposed to a second, ACTUALITY, *DA* 412a21–8, 417a21–b16). Hence Aristotle identifies the VIRTUES of CHARACTER with states.

STATE: see CITY

STUDY, ATTEND TO, OBSERVE, *theōrein*

Theōrein (lit. 'view', 'gaze on') is the second ACTUALITY of knowing, i.e., actually attending to an item of one's knowledge, *DA* 412a23, 417a28, *Met*. 1048a34, 1072b24, 1087a20, *EN* 1146b33. *Theōria* is the life of intellectual activity that Aristotle recognizes as the highest element of HAPPINESS for a human being, *EN* 1177a18. The adjective *theōrētikos* sometimes refers to theoretical pursuits, as opposed to practical (concerned with *praxis*) or productive (concerned with *poiēsis*) pursuits, *PA* 640a2, *Met*. 1075a2. Hence 'theoretical' is used at *Met*. 982a1.

SUBJECT, *hupokeimenon*

A subject (lit. 'underlying thing') is what has things PREDICATED of it, *Catg*. 2b15–16, *Met*. 1028a36–7. Predication need not be a grammatical relation, and the subject referred to in a predication need not be what is named by the grammatical subject of a sentence; see *APo* 83a6–7. A subject underlies every change (see MOTION), both in non-substance categories and in the category of SUBSTANCE. See *Catg*. 4a10–12, *Phys*. 190a13–15, 190a31–b5, 191a7–20, *DA* 412a19, *Met*. 983b16–18.

SUBSTANCE, ESSENCE$_o$, ousia

1. *Ousia* is the abstract noun formed from the verb 'to BE', and sometimes 'being' is the right translation (hence 'being$_o$' at e.g., *PA* 640a18, *Met.* 983a27). But 'being' is normally reserved for *to on*, the participle (= something that is) or for *einai* (the infinitive 'to be'). Aristotle sometimes (e.g., *Pol.* 1279b18) uses *ousia* with its ordinary Greek sense of 'property' (as in 'private property').

2. Aristotle seems to pick out *ousia* in two ways: (a) It is the SUBJECT of the other categories (see PREDICATIONS). It is either a primary substance, which is a THIS and a PARTICULAR, and so a basic subject, or a secondary substance, which is a species (see FORM #5) or GENUS of primary substances. (b) *Ousia* is what something is; the answer to the question 'What is F?' tells us the *ousia* of F. In these cases it is rendered by 'essence$_o$'.

sullogismos: DEDUCTION

sumbebēkos: COINCIDENT

SYNONYMOUS, *sunōnumon*

In non-technical usage, *sunonumon* often means 'being named together', i.e., having the same NAME. In Aristotle's technical sense, x and y are synonymously F if and only if they have both the same name 'F' and the same DEFINITION of F. See *Catg.* 1a6–12, *Met.* 1003b12–15, 1006b18. The term is applied primarily to things, not to words.

technē: CRAFT

TERM: see FORMULA

THALES

Aristotle regards Thales (fl. 585) as the first of the Presocratic NATURALISTS. See *Met.* 983b6, 984a5.

theōria: STUDY

THIRD MAN

An argument against Plato's Theory of FORMS, derived from Plato, *Parmenides* 132a–c, and mentioned in *Top.* 178b36, *Met.* 990b17, 1039a2.

THIS, *tode ti*

1. The Greek might be rendered: (1) 'this something' (e.g., this dog); (2) 'some this', i.e., either (2a) some particular thing or (2b) something of some kind (e.g., some dog).

2. 'This' is a standard way of referring to the category of substance, and being a this is especially characteristic of substance (though perhaps not confined to substance; cf. *Catg.* 1b6, 3b10, *GC* 318b15). See *APo* 73b7, *GC* 317b9, 21, 319a12, *DA* 402a24, *Met.* 1017b24–6, 1029a28.

3. A this is numerically ONE, in contrast to a 'such' (see QUALITY), *Catg.* 3b10–13, *Top.* 178b38, *Phys.* 190b25, *Met.* 1039a1.

THIS SORT OF THING, *toionde*: see QUALITY

THOUGHT: see UNDERSTANDING

UNDERSTANDING, MIND, THOUGHT, INTELLECT, *nous*; INTELLIGIBLE, *noēton*

1. Aristotle applies *nous* to the faculty or capacity (see POTENTIALITY) of rational thought (e.g., *Met.* 985a19; see also REASON) and to its exercise in acts of rational thinking. Hence the term is applied to both the first and the second ACTUALITY. See *DA* iii 4. Often (e.g., at *Met.* 1074b15) 'thought' would be a suitable rendering.

2. Often, however, when Aristotle says I have *nous* that p, he means that I believe (and indeed KNOW) that p. For these contexts 'understanding' is more suitable. In *DA* iii 4, e.g., Aristotle seems to treat *noein* as a form of knowledge.

3. In its narrowest use, *nous* applies to the non-demonstrative grasp of the PRINCIPLES that are premisses for a DEMONSTRATION; in this case it is superior to *epistēmē* (see KNOW). See *APo* 72b13–15, 100b5–17, *DA* 429a13.

UNIFORM, *homoiomerēs*; see PART

UNIVERSAL, *katholou*

1. Aristotle's term is derived from the prepositional phrase *kata holou*, meaning 'taken as a whole' (cf. Plato, *Meno* 77a6), as opposed to 'taking each in turn' (*kath'hekaston*; see PARTICULAR). Sometimes it is appropriately rendered by 'generally' (equivalent to *holōs*; see GENERAL), *DA* 417a1, 424a17, *Met.* 1032a22.

2. A universal is contrasted with a particular: 'By "universal" I mean what is naturally predicated of more than one thing; by "particular", what is not', *DI* 17a39; cf. *APo* 100a7, *Met.* 1038b16, 1040b25–7, 29–30.

3. Universals are the primary objects of DEFINITION and scientific KNOWLEDGE, *Met.* 1035b34–1036a9, 1039b27–1040a27 (but cf. *Met.* xiii 10), *Poet.* 1451b7.

UNQUALIFIED: see WITHOUT QUALIFICATION

USUAL, *hōs epi to polu*

The phrase means 'for the most part' or 'as a general rule'. It is applied to what happens in most but not all cases of a given sort, *APr* 32b4–10. Sometimes Aristotle seems to identify a usual regularity with a mere statistical frequency. Sometimes, however, the usual is contrasted with both NECESSITY and chance (see LUCK), *DI* 19a18–22, 37–9, *Phys.* 196b12–17, 196b36–197a1, 197a18–20 (but cf. 198b6), 198b35. The usual is even a legitimate object of SCIENCE, *Met.* 1026b27–1027a15, and is open to scientific DEMONSTRATION, *APo* i 30 (but cf. *EN* 1094b19–27, 1139b14–19).

VIRTUE, *aretē*

Something has an *aretē* insofar as it is GOOD at or for something; hence *aretē* is closely related to FUNCTION, and the term may refer to all sorts of excellences (see *EN* 1098a8–12). More narrowly understood, the virtues are the praiseworthy STATES of CHARACTER and intellect that are discussed in the *EN*; these order the different parts of the SOUL so that they are properly suited to fulfill the human function in achieving the human good; see 1103a3–10, 1106a14–24, 1139a15–17, 1144a6–9.

VOLUNTARY, *hekousion*; WILLING, *hekōn*

In ordinary Greek these terms (used interchangeably by Aristotle) have the range of uses suggested by 'volunteer', 'voluntary' (as opposed to 'compulsory'), 'willing' (as opposed to 'against my will'). Aristotle, however, applies them to all actions that an agent can be praised or blamed for (including those that are done 'unwillingly' or 'reluctantly' or 'against one's will' in the ordinary sense; see esp. *EN* 1110a4–b9). In his view, agents are fairly held 'responsible' (*aitios*; see CAUSE #3) for their voluntary actions.

WHAT-IT-IS: see ESSENCE

WHAT SOMETHING IS FOR: see FOR SOMETHING

WISDOM, *sophia*

In ordinary Greek *sophia* is applied to all sorts of CRAFT and other types of KNOWLEDGE (cf. *Met.* 981a25, 27, b1, *EN* 1141a9). Aristotle, however, confines it to theoretical wisdom, contrasted with practical INTELLIGENCE, *EN* vi 7. It is the general understanding of reality that Aristotle seeks in the *Met.*; see 981b10–982a3.

WISH, *boulēsis*: see DECISION, DESIRE

WITHOUT QUALIFICATION, UNQUALIFIED, SIMPLY, UNCONDITIONALLY, WITHOUT EXCEPTION, *haplōs*

1. The adjective *haplous* is translated 'simple' (in contrast to compound), *Phys.* 189b33, *DA* 429b23, *Met.* 1072a31–4.

2. To say that x is F without qualification ('simpliciter') is to say that x is F without some addition; see *Top.* 115b29–35 (cf. *Met.* 1039b22). Hence being F without qualification is contrasted with being a sort of F, or being F only in a particular way, or in a particular respect, or on an ASSUMPTION.

3. In different contexts 'x is F without qualification' may imply (a) that 'x is F' is true entirely without exception, so that no qualification is needed (see *Catg.* 1b6, 4b10, *Phys.* 197a34–5, 198b6) or (b) that 'x is F' is

true in standard, or appropriately understood, conditions, so that the relevant qualification is taken for granted (*Met*. 1030a16, *EN* 1129b1–6).

WORK: see FUNCTION

XENOPHANES

Aristotle regards Xenophanes (c. 570–c. 475) as the originator of the monism of Parmenides and Melissus. See *Met*. 986b18, 1010a6, *Poet*. 1460b35–1461a1.

ZENO

Plato regards Zeno (c. 490–?) as a follower of Parmenides, seeking to show that COMMON BELIEFS in plurality are self-contradictory. See *Phys*. 209a23–5, 210b22–7, 233a21–b15, 250a19–26.

FURTHER READING

Abbreviations used below:

[T] = translation with explanatory notes, or glossary, or both.
[E] = collection of essays (usually including bibliography).
[B] = especially useful for beginners.

Texts

The first modern text of Aristotle (which is the source of the page and line references standardly used) is

Aristotelis Opera, ed. I. Bekker (Berlin, 1831-70).

Many of Aristotle's works are most conveniently available in

Oxford Classical Texts (Oxford, various editors and dates).

The Greek text with a facing English translation is included in:

The Loeb Classical Library (Cambridge, Mass., various editors and dates).

For the biological works, the Loeb translations are generally good; for the *Ethics* and *Politics*, adequate; for other works, often to be avoided.

Translations

The standard English translation is

Barnes, J., ed., *The Complete Works of Aristotle*. 2 vols. (Princeton, 1984). Volume 2 contains an index.

This is mostly a revision of the Oxford Translation:

Ross, W. D., and Smith, J. A., eds., *The Works of Aristotle* (12 vols., Oxford, 1908-54).

A convenient selection from the unrevised Oxford Translation is

McKeon, R., ed., *The Basic Works of Aristotle* (New York, 1941).

Introductory and General

Good short introductory books on Aristotle:

[B] Ackrill, J. L., *Aristotle the Philosopher* (Oxford, 1981).
[B] Barnes, J., *Aristotle* (Oxford, 1982).

A useful description and summary of Aristotle's works:

Ross, W. D., *Aristotle* (London, 1923).

Essays on Aristotle, with useful bibilographies, are included in the different volumes of

[E] Everson, S., ed., *Companions to Ancient Thought* (Cambridge, 1990 onward).

A large and well-arranged bibliography is included in

Barnes, J., ed., *The Cambridge Companion to Aristotle* (Cambridge, 1994).

Background to Aristotle

A short account of ancient philosophy:

Irwin, T.H., *Classical Thought* (Oxford, 1988).

Fragments of the Presocratics are collected in:

McKirahan, R., *Philosophy Before Socrates* (Indianapolis, 1994).

Translations (not always the best) of most of Plato's dialogues are collected in:

Hamilton, E., and Cairns, H., eds., *Plato: The Collected Dialogues* (Princeton, 1961).

Natural Philosophy (*Phys., GC, PA, MA*).

[T] Charlton, W., tr., *Physics I and II* (Oxford, 1970).
[T] Williams, C.J.F., tr., *De Generatione et Corruptione* (Oxford, 1982).
[T] Balme, D. M., tr., *De Partibus Animalium* (Oxford, 1972).
[E] Judson, L., ed., *Aristotle's Physics* (Oxford, 1991).
[E] Gotthelf, A., and Lennox, J., eds., *Philosophical Essays on Aristotle's Biology* (Cambridge, 1987).
[B] Sorabji, R., *Necessity, Cause, and Blame* (London, 1980).

Metaphysics, Substance, Matter, and Form (*Catg., Met.*).

[B] [T] Ackrill, J. L., tr., *Categories and De Interpretatione* (Oxford, 1963).
[T] Kirwan, C. A., tr., *Metaphysics IV, V, VI* (Oxford, 1971, 2nd ed., 1993).
[T] Bostock, D., tr., *Metaphysics VII-VIII* (Oxford, 1994).
[B] Witt, C. *Substance and Essence in Aristotle* (Ithaca, 1989).
Loux, M. J., *Primary Ousia* (Ithaca, 1991).

FURTHER READING

Knowledge (*Posterior Analytics*)

[T] Barnes, J., tr., *Posterior Analytics*, 2nd ed. (Oxford, 1993).

Soul (*De Anima*)

[T] Hamlyn, D. W., tr., *De Anima II-III* (Oxford, 1968).
[E] Nussbaum, M. C., and Rorty, A. O., eds., *Essays on Aristotle's De Anima* (Oxford, 1992).
Hartman, E. M. *Substance, Body, and Soul* (Princeton, 1977).

Ethics

[T] Irwin, T. H., tr. *Aristotle: Nicomachean Ethics* (Indianapolis, 1985).
[B] Urmson, J. O., *Aristotle's Ethics* (Oxford, 1988).
[E] Rorty, A. O., ed., *Essays on Aristotle's Ethics* (Berkeley, 1980).
Hardie, W.F.R., *Aristotle's Ethical Theory*, 2nd ed. (Oxford, 1980).

Politics

[T] Saunders, T. J., tr., *Politics I and II* (Oxford, 1995).
[E] Keyt, D., and Miller, F. D., eds., *A Companion to Aristotle's Politics* (Oxford, 1991).

Poetics

[T] Janko, R., tr., *Aristotle's Poetics* (Indianapolis, 1987).
[E] Rorty, A. O., ed., *Essays on Aristotle's Poetics* (Princeton, 1992).